LONELY PLANET PUBLICATIONS

D0009650

MARA VORHEES

MOSCOW
CITY GUIDE

Ivan the Great Bell Tower (p69)

Moscow is a city of superlatives. It boasts the most billionaires, the most expensive cups of coffee and – coming soon – the most colossal building in the world.

It is also the most expensive and, according to one poll, the most unfriendly city in the world. It is no wonder that a popular nightclub is called simply The Most (p184).

Moscow may occupy the number one spot, but these lists hardly capture the reality – the vitality – of the capital. Free (relatively) from the strictures of censorship and hardship, Russia's capital city is experiencing a burst of creative energy, evident in all aspects of contemporary culture. Former factories and deserted warehouses have been converted into edgy art galleries and intriguing underground clubs. World-class venues such as the Pushkin Fine Arts Museum (p115) are experimenting and expanding. Tchaikovsky and Chekhov are well represented at Moscow theatres but you can also see world premieres by up-and-coming composers, choreographers and playwrights.

The ancient city has always been a haven for history buffs. Now history is being examined in innovative ways, as institutions such as the ZKP Tagansky Cold War Museum (p126) and the Gulag History Museum (p87) broach subjects that were long brushed under the carpet.

The capital is even experiencing an unprecedented growth in birth rates (Muscovites are really getting busy). From artistry and history to recreation and procreation, Moscow is a cauldron of creativity. Dare we say that it is so much *more* than The Most?

MOSCOW LIFE

Moscow's word of the day is 'exclusive'. The hottest clubs have the most expensive drinks and tightest 'face control'. Travelling by big, black car is way cooler than going metro, and designer labels fly off the racks at pricey boutiques. Muscovites eat sushi instead of herring, drink French champagne instead of *Sovietskoe shampanskoe*.

'As Muscovites embrace the ecstasies of capitalism, they also grapple with its challenges.'

Yet for all Moscow's status consciousness, driving Hummers and dressing in Armani are privileges reserved for a small – albeit visible – elite. Nevertheless, most Muscovites are now enjoying disposable income like never before.

Over three million cars clog Moscow's streets: plenty of Mercedes, but also old-fashioned Ladas. Restaurants include bohemian bars, not just upscale eateries. Many nightclubs are branded 'exclusive' but others are 'democratic'. Even eating raw fish has become a populist experience.

As Muscovites embrace the ecstasies of capitalism, they also grapple with its challenges. Moscow ranks amongst the world's most expensive cities, and the vast divide between rich and poor is only getting wider. Thirteen per cent of the population lives below the poverty level. And Moscow's ancient avenues can hardly handle the proliferation of automobiles, their emissions compounding a pollution problem.

Corruption continues to be endemic. In 2008, Transparency International reported that the problem is worsening, as people pay bribes to receive health care, to school their children and to obtain business and driving licences. In Moscow, 42% of residents reported they'd paid bribes. Recognising that this lawlessness undermines economic productivity and government authority, President Medvedev declared war on corruption. But few individuals recognise any concrete results.

Nonetheless, the capital remains upbeat. The optimism is pervasive. It's evident in the construction of skyscrapers, shopping malls, theme parks and theatres; in the 'world premieres' and 'grand openings', and on the faces of shoppers, strollers, diners and drinkers in the crowded streets. Indeed (to borrow a communist slogan), 'the future is bright!'.

Glazunov's Market of Our Democracy in Glazunov Gallery (p116)

HIGHLIGHTS

KREMLIN

The ancient fortress is the founding site of Moscow and the ultimate symbol of political power in Russia.

❶ Annunciation Cathedral
Admire the amazing artistry of Russia's greatest icon painters (p71)

❷ Assumption Cathedral
Examine the iconostasis, parts of which date to the 14th century (p67)

❸ Tomb of the Unknown Soldier
Scrutinise the perfect synchronicity of the changing of the guard and admire the bouquets left by newlyweds (p72)

❹ Armoury
Gawk at the treasure trove that fuelled a revolution (p72)

❺ Archangel Cathedral
Shed a tear for Ivan the Great, Ivan the Terrible and Tsarevitch Dmitry (p70)

RED SQUARE

Stepping onto Red Square never ceases to inspire, with Moscow's most iconic buildings encircling a vast stretch of cobblestones. Individually they are impressive, but the ensemble is electrifying.

1 **Lenin's Tomb**
Pay your respects to the founder of the Soviet state (p74)

2 **State History Museum**
Explore the history of Russia in an artistic setting (p75)

3 **St Basil's Cathedral**
Be awestruck by the chaotic, kaleidoscopic icon of Russian architecture (p73)

4 **GUM**
Shop till you drop in Moscow's historic shopping centre (p75)

5 **Kazan Cathedral**
Listen to angelic voices drifting down from the choir loft (p75)

① **Church of St Nicholas in Khamovniki**
Admire the artistry on one of Moscow's ancient merchant churches (p117)

② **Kitay Gorod**
Wander the age-old streets where Moscow grew up (p134)

③ **Starye Polya**
Imagine the stone wall that surrounded Kitay Gorod so many years ago (p76)

④ **Ascension Church**
See the precursor to St Basil's Cathedral at the Kolomenskoe Museum-Reserve (p133)

MEDIEVAL MOSCOW

The capital is rich with history dating back to the earliest days of Muscovy, from the ancient 'suburb' where the merchants traded to the elaborate churches that they funded.

1 Art Muzeon Sculpture Park
Pay a visit to Lenin and Stalin now that they're off their pedestals (p119)

2 All-Russia Exhibition Centre
Witness the kitschiest of socialist realism and the tackiest of capitalist consumerism (p130)

3 Contemporary History Museum
Celebrate the glorious socialist revolution (p92)

4 Gulag History Museum
Remember the millions who suffered in the Soviet labour camps (p87)

5 ZKP Tagansky Cold War Museum
Go underground to explore a Cold War communications command centre (p126)

6 Petrovich
Relive the Soviet experience at a retro club (p180)

RED MOSCOW

The remains of the Soviet state are scattered all around the city. Monuments remember fallen heroes and victorious battles, while museums attempt to analyse and synthesise the past.

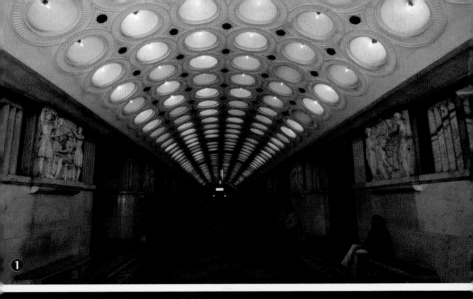

MOSCOW BY DAY

Moscow is the epicentre of New Russia and everything that it represents. By day, it boasts commerce and culture to compete with the most cosmopolitan of cities.

❶ Moscow Metro
Admire the marble, mouldings and mosaics in this underground museum (p143)

❷ Kamergersky Pereulok
Pick a café that offers prime seating for Moscow's best people-watching (p165)

❸ The Morning After
Watch the sunrise over the Moscow skyline from Universitetskaya ploshchad (p132)

❹ Moskva-City
Strain your neck to see the capital's new business district (p95)

❶ Red Square After Hours
Stroll across the spectacular square after sundown (p73)

❷ Club-Café
Admire the art, groove to the music, munch on lunch (p183)

❸ Clubbing
Get gussied up for a night at Moscow's hottest clubs (p183)

MOSCOW BY NIGHT

Night owls enjoy a dynamic and diverse scene out on the town – not only exclusive clubs, but also bohemian art cafés, underground blues bars, get-down discos and drink-up dives.

ART

Moscow's museums are famed for their collections of ancient icons and Peredvizhniki paintings. Today these museums are joined by cutting-edge contemporary galleries and head-scratching avant-garde exhibits.

❶ Tretyakov Gallery
Peruse the paintings of the Peredvizhniki (p118)

❷ Tsereteli Gallery
Visit Zurab Tsereteli's personal gallery, for an insight into contemporary Russian art (p117)

❸ Moscow Museum of Modern Art
Focus on futurism, explore the avant-garde, ponder primitivism (p90)

❹ Rerikh Museum
Marvel at the majestic paintings of this artist, archaeologist and explorer (p116)

1 Rock Out
Catch a band at an edgy indie club, such as Ikra (p185)

2 Bolshoi Theatre
Hear the high notes and see the high kicks at the glittering historic theatre (p189)

3 Roadhouse
Get the blues at this down-and-out blues bar (p186)

4 Moscow International House of Music
Get tuned in to the National Philharmonic of Russia (p188)

MUSIC

The classical performing arts in Moscow are still among the best and cheapest in the world. But New Russia comes with new forms of entertainment. Experience the bohemian side of Moscow – be it a classical concert or a beatnik band.

FOOD

It's not an obvious choice for a culinary holiday, but visitors to the capital will be amazed by the options – foodies are flocking to wine bars, coffee bars, sushi bars and beer bars.

❶ Refuel at a Coffee Hotspot
Relax under the high ceilings at Coffee Bean's flagship outlet (p169) or celebrity-spot at Coffee Mania (p172)

❷ Skazka Vostoka
Flavours of Central Asia and the Caucasus, including great shashlyk (p174)

❸ Café Pushkin
Indulge in a spread of *zakuski* (appetisers) and a bottle of vodka (p167)

❹ Varvary
Sample molecular cuisine at this Anatoly Komm venue (p165)

❺ GQ Bar
Start your night at Arkady Novikov's latest hot spot (p182)

❶ Tretyakovsky Proezd
Cruise across the cobblestones of Moscow's most exclusive shopping address (p149)

❷ Valentin Yudashkin
Admire the class and quality of Moscow's most prestigious designer (p154)

❸ Simachyov Boutique & Bar
Find some funky fashions or some funky friends (p152)

❹ Chapurinbar
Combine fashion and food at Igor Chapurin's superhip café (p152)

FASHION

Muscovites – especially the females of the species – are famed for always looking fabulous. The capital is now home to a burgeoning fashion industry, to make sure these devki strut their stuff in style.

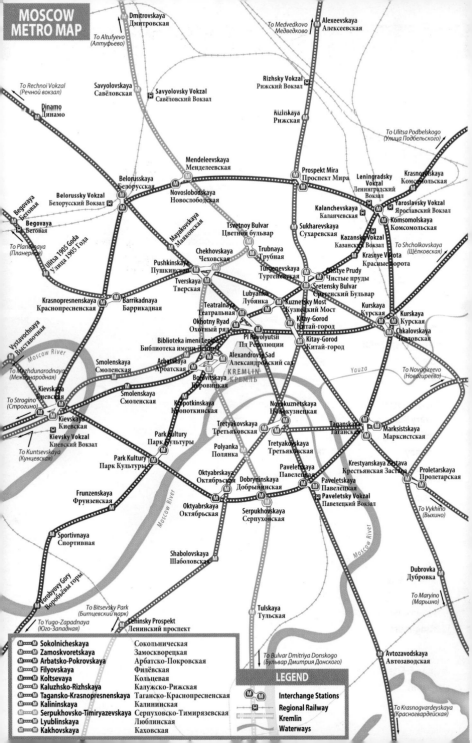

CONTENTS

THE AUTHORS

Mara Vorhees

Mara's first visit to Moscow was in 1990, when the lines inside GUM were dwarfed only by the lines outside Lenin's tomb. She witnessed the postcommunist transition from her vantage point in the Urals, where she spent time working on a foreign-aid project and fighting with the tax police (and losing). During those years in the Wild East, the capital was a frequent destination for 'recovery trips', which usually required recovering from.

The pen-wielding traveller has worked on Lonely Planet's *Russia*, *Trans-Siberian Railway* and *St Petersburg City Guide*. Her stories about Russia have appeared in *National Geographic Traveler* and *Lifestyle & Travel*. When not roaming around Russia, Mara lives in a pink house in Somerville, Massachusetts with her husband and her cat. Follow her adventures at www.maravorhees.com.

MARA'S TOP MOSCOW DAY

The sun is streaming through the window of my flat in the Tverskoy (p87) district, so I drag my body out of bed and down the street to Volkonsky Keyser (p169) for a delectable almond pastry and a steaming cup o' joe. Properly revived, I hop on the metro (p243) and ride to Khamovniki (p109). I spend the morning at the Pushkin Fine Arts Museum (p115), or at one of myriad smaller museums in this art district – my favourites being the Rerikh Museum (p116) and the Museum of Private Collections (p115).

Admiring all that artistry has worked up an appetite, so I stop for a little lunch at Gogol-Mogol (p175) before strolling across the pedestrian bridge behind the Cathedral of Christ the Saviour (p109), admiring the expansive views of the Kremlin towers and cathedral dome.

Now in Zamoskvorechie (p118) I make my way past the iconic Krasny Oktyabr chocolate factory (p122). If the studios at Art Strelka (p155) are open, I pop in to see what creative masterpieces are on display. Otherwise, I continue along the embankment, past the massive statue of Peter the Great (see the boxed text, p113) and into the whimsical Art Muzeon Sculpture Park (p119). I wander among the stone figures from past and present, and perhaps duck into TsDKh (p155) to graze in the galleries.

As the sun starts to sink lower in the sky, I head across the street to Gorky Park (p119), where the kids are frolicking on the carousel. My feet are beat, so I flag down a pedicab and catch a lift across the park to Chaikhona No 1 (see the boxed text, p180) for a cool cocktail.

Perked up by the aperitif, I walk across the pedestrian bridge back to Khamovniki. I might stop for dinner at Skazka Vostoka (p174) or make my way to Roadhouse (p186) for an evening of down-and-out blues music.

So you are planning a trip to Moscow? You are in for a treat and a challenge. Russia's capital is an intriguing, intoxicating and sometimes incomprehensible destination.

Moscow is a far easier place to travel than it was a decade ago. Thanks to the proliferation of privately owned hostels and Western-operated luxury hotels, travellers at either end of the budget spectrum should have no problem finding an excellent place to stay; midrange travellers will face more of a challenge. In any case, you'll probably want to reserve in advance, especially if you will be in Moscow midweek.

Upon arrival, you may not think that things are geared to tourists: immigration lines at the airport are sometimes endless and signs around town are not necessarily in English. But this is like Disneyland compared with the 'olden days'. Appreciate the advancements that have been made, and accept the rest as part of the adventure.

One word of warning: the single most annoying thing you will have to do is take care of your visa. Apply early and apply often.

WHEN TO GO

Standout seasons to visit Moscow are late spring (May or June) and early autumn (September or October), when the city's parks are filled with flowering trees or colourful leaves. The city is spruced up for the May holidays and September's City Day, both festive times in the capital. Summer is also pleasant – though hot – and long hours of sunlight bring out the revellers.

The deepest, darkest part of winter is undeniably cold but if you are prepared it can be an adventure. Furs and vodka keep people warm and snow-covered landscapes are picturesque. A solid snowpack covers the ground from November to March. The city gets fired up to ring in the New Year, when Muscovites emerge from their warm homes into the winter night for free concerts and fireworks.

FESTIVALS

Cultural festivals and special exhibits occur throughout the year for lovers of art, music, theatre and film. For additional information on events in Moscow, refer to the *Moscow Times* or *element* (p252). For details on public holidays, see p250.

January

Though January represents the deepest, darkest days of winter, it is a festive month, kicked off by New Year's celebrations in the grandest tradition. Orthodox Christmas, or Rozhdestvo, is celebrated on 6 January. Many offices and services are closed for the first week of January.

WINTER FESTIVAL

An outdoor fun-fest during the first two weeks in January, for those with anti-freeze in their veins (though plenty of people use vodka for this purpose). Teams compete to build elaborate ice sculptures in front of the Pushkin Museum (p115) and on Red Square (p73). In 2007, Pushkinskaya pl was the site of the first-ever international ice-chess tournament, which took place simultaneously on Trafalgar Sq in London.

February

Maslenitsa marks the end of winter, but it does seem premature. Temperatures continue to be cold, hovering around -10°C for weeks. Occasional southerly winds can raise temperatures briefly to a balmy 0°C. The city continues to sparkle with snow, and sledders and skiers are in heaven.

DEFENDER OF THE
MOTHERLAND DAY   23 February

This unofficial holiday traditionally honours veterans and soldiers. It has become a sort of counterpart to International Women's Day and is now better known as 'Men's Day'. Women are supposed to do nice things for the men in their lives, but the extent of the celebration is limited.

MASLENITSA
www.maslenitsa.com
Akin to Mardi Gras, this fete celebrates the end of winter and kicks off Orthodox Lent. 'Maslenitsa' comes from the Russian

top picks

CULTURAL EVENTS

- December Nights Festival (p23)
- Golden Mask Festival (below)
- Moscow International Film Festival (p22)
- Moscow Biennale of Contemporary Art (right)
- Moscow Forum (p23)

word for butter, which is a key ingredient in the festive treat, bliny (crêpes). Besides bingeing on Russian crêpes, the week-long festival features horse-drawn sledges, story-telling clowns and beer-drinking bears. The festival culminates with the burning of a scarecrow to welcome spring. Exact timing depend on the dates of Orthodox Easter, but it is usually in February or early March. Look out for events around town and special bliny menus at local restaurants.

March & April

During the spring thaw – in late March and early April – everything turns to mud and slush.

INTERNATIONAL WOMEN'S DAY 8 March

Russia's favourite holiday was founded to honour the women's movement. On this day men buy champagne, flowers and chocolates for their better halves – and for all the women in their lives.

GOLDEN MASK FESTIVAL

www.goldenmask.ru

This festival involves two weeks of performances by Russia's premier drama, opera,

dance and musical performers, culminating in a prestigious awards ceremony. The festival brightens up otherwise-dreary March and April.

MOSCOW BIENNALE OF CONTEMPORARY ART

www.moscowbiennale.ru

This month-long festival, held in odd-numbered years, is organised and partly funded by Russia's Ministry of Culture, with the aim of establishing the capital as an international centre for contemporary art. Venues around the city exhibit works by artists from around the world.

EASTER

19 April 2009; 4 April 2010; 24 April 2011; 15 April 2012; 5 May 2013

The main holiday of the Orthodox Church is Easter, or Paskha. The date varies, but it is usually in April or early May – often a different date from its Gregorian counterpart celebrated by non-Orthodox churches. Forty days of fasting, known as Veliky Post, lead up to the religious holiday. Easter Sunday kicks off with celebratory midnight services, after which people eat kulichy (special dome-shaped cakes) and paskha (curd cakes), and they may exchange painted wooden Easter eggs. Many banks, offices and museums are closed on Easter Monday.

FASHION WEEK IN MOSCOW

www.fashionweekinmoscow.com

They have Fashion Week in London, Paris, New York and Milan, so why not in Moscow? This is the chance for Russia's top designers to show the world their sexiest stuff in the age-old halls of Gostiny Dvor. In recent years, as many as 80,000 people

A TOAST TO THE LADIES

Ask any Russian woman her favourite holiday, and she is sure to answer International Women's Day, celebrated every year on 8 March. Men buy flowers and chocolate for the females in their lives – wives, girlfriends, mothers and colleagues. Some cynics say it is the one day a year that Russian men are nice to their mates.

International Women's Day has been recognised in various countries since the late 19th century, but in Russia, the festive day has revolutionary roots. On 8 March 1917, textile workers in St Petersburg protested against the food shortages, which were directly related to Russia's involvement in WWI. The women's strike 'for bread and peace' merged with riots that were spreading throughout the city. The uprising, which would become known as the February Revolution, forced the abdication of Tsar Nicholas II. Later, the celebrated Soviet feminist and communist Alexandra Kollontai convinced Lenin to make 8 March an official holiday.

These days, most Russians have forgotten about the political implications of the day. But nobody misses the opportunity to drink champagne and toast the ladies.

have attended events at Moscow show-rooms during this week in March. The autumn show takes place at the same location in October.

RUSSIAN FASHION WEEK

http://russianfashionweek.com

This fashion event is only four years old, but still manages to attract top-name Russian and international fashion designers to unveil their new collections on Moscow runways. The event takes place at the World Trade Centre in April and again in October or November.

May

Spring arrives in the capital! Many services, offices and museums have limited hours during the first half of May, due to the run of public holidays. Nonetheless, it is a festive time, as the parks are finally green and blooming with flowers, and the streets are filled with people celebrating.

VICTORY DAY
9 May

Parades on Tverskaya ul and other events at Victory Park (p106).

June

June is Moscow's most welcoming month. Temperatures become mild and the days are long and sunny. Little girls wear giant white bows in their hair to celebrate the end of the school year.

MOSCOW INTERNATIONAL FILM FESTIVAL

www.moscowfilmfestival.ru

This week-long event attracts filmmakers from the US and Europe, as well as the most promising Russian artists. Films are shown at theatres around the city. See also p48.

July & August

Many Muscovites retreat to their dachas (see the boxed text, p220) to escape summer in the city, and the cultural calendar is quiet. Maximum temperatures are usually between 25°C and 35°C, although the humidity makes it seem hotter. July and August are also the rainiest months, although showers tend to be brief. While residents make themselves scarce, tourists flood the capital during this season. Train tickets and accommodation can be more difficult to secure, and attractions around Moscow tend to be overrun with visitors.

Summer is the time for outdoor music festivals, including huge rock events such as Krylya and Nashestviye, which take place out of the city. For more information, see the boxed text, below.

RUSSKY ROCK *Kathleen Pullum*

Huge stadium shows and colossal festivals have become pillars of Russian rock culture, with the largest rock events of the year enticing fans to relax with a few beers, wreak some havoc and rock out with 50,000 of their closest friends. The most prominent festivals take place in summer, mostly due to weather constraints.

Krylya (www.krylya.ru), or 'Wings', is generally held the last weekend of July. This festival gained notoriety when it was targeted by two Chechen female suicide bombers in 2003. (The women were stopped by security but ended up killing a score of people.) After a brief relocation to Luzhniki Stadium, where security could be better monitored, the festival returned to the Tushino airfield outside of Moscow in 2005. The two-day event draws tens of thousands of visitors and several dozen bands from Russia and the Commonwealth of Independent States (CIS). Performers in 2007 included veterans Spleen and current stars such as Nogu Svelo.

The granddaddy of Russian rock festivals, however, is Nashestviye (www.emmausfest.ru), which is hosted by Russian rock radio station Nashe (meaning 'Ours') in the first or second week of August. Nashe broadcasts all over Russia, and is widely considered *the* forum where emerging Russian musicians get their start. Nashestviye is a three-day festival that expands every year. In 2005 the event added more performers and three stages, allowing different subcategories in Russian rock to emerge. Alternative rock, Russian reggae, 'wild music' and others are all grouped together in the concert schedule. Among a list of nearly 100 performers, from old legends to new faces, 2008 highlights included Russian punk-styled, notoriously naughty Leningrad – barred by Moscow's mayor from performing in the capital city – along with B-2, Agatha Christie, Pelageya and many more well-known acts. Nashestviye is held at Emmaus, near Tver, accessible by *elektrichka* (suburban train) from Leningradsky vokzal.

Kathleen Pullum is the former editor-in-chief of the magazine, element

---

MOSCOW INTERNATIONAL BEER FESTIVAL

www.beer-festival.ru

This weeklong beer-drinking fest gives participants a chance to sample local brews and vote for their favourites. The price of admission also includes live music and other entertainment.

September & October

Early autumn is another standout time to be in the capital. The heat subsides and the foliage turns the city splendid oranges, reds and yellows. October usually sees the first snow of the season.

CITY DAY

City Day, or *den goroda* in Russian, celebrates Moscow's birthday every year on the first weekend in September. The day kicks off with a festive parade, followed by live music on Red Square (p73) and plenty of food, fireworks and fun.

KREMLIN CUP

www.kremlincup.ru

This international tennis tournament is held every October at the Olympic Stadium, near the Renaissance Moscow Hotel. Not surprisingly, Russian players have dominated this tournament in recent years. See also p201.

MOSCOW FORUM

www.ccmm.ru

This is a contemporary music festival held every year since 1994. It features avant-garde musicians from Russia and Europe performing at the Moscow Conservatory (p188).

November

Winter sets in. The days are noticeably short and temperatures are low. By now, the city is covered in a blanket of snow, which reflects the city lights and lends a magical air.

DAY OF RECONCILIATION & ACCORD

7 November

The former October Revolution day is still an official holiday, though it is hardly acknowledged. It still is, however, a big day for flag waving and protesting by old-school Communist Party members, especially in front of the former Central Lenin

Museum (p76) and on Tverskaya ul. It makes for a great photo op.

December

Short days and long nights keep most people inside for most of the month. On 12 December, Constitution Day marks the adoption of the new constitution in 1993. But political holidays are not what they used to be, and no one pays much attention.

DECEMBER NIGHTS FESTIVAL

www.museum.ru/gmii

Perhaps Moscow's most prestigious music event, this annual festival is hosted at the Pushkin Fine Arts Museum (p115), with a month of performances by high-profile musicians and an art exhibit to accompany it.

COSTS & MONEY

Experts estimate that the average Muscovite earns about R30,500 a month, far in excess of the average of R13,800 earned elsewhere in the country. However, this figure is misleading, as about 70% of the population earns less than the average. The average pension is only R2700 a month and 13% of the population lives below the poverty level.

Moscow is one of the most expensive cities in the world, up there with London and Tokyo. Expect to pay at least R600 a head for a meal in a restaurant. If you self-cater or dine at cafeterias, you can probably get by on R1000 a day for meals.

Prices for lodging are also high, as the city has a shortage of comfortable, affordable mid-range hotels. Budget accommodation – usually

---

HOW MUCH?

Admission to the Kremlin R350

CCCP T-shirt R600

Souvenir *matryoshka* doll R500

Blin R50

Cappuccino R180

1 hour online R100

1L of petrol R23-29

1L of bottled water R25

Bottle of Baltika beer R70

Metro ticket R20

ADVANCE PLANNING

If you're the organised type, you'll want to take care of a few things before you arrive in Moscow:

- Apply for your visa! This is an absolute must for absolutely everybody. You can do it at the last minute, but it may cost you your first-born child. See p256 for details.
- Reserve a place to stay, especially if you are coming between Monday and Friday. See p204.
- Learn Cyrillic and buy a phrasebook or minidictionary – having a handle on the Russian language will improve your visit immeasurably.
- Log on to the Moscow Times (www.themoscowtimes.ru) to catch up on the latest news and to find out about special events during your visit.
- Check the schedule at the Bolshoi Theatre (p189) and order your tickets ahead of time to ensure great seats and avoid language difficulties.

dorm-style – starts at R700 per person. Expect to pay at least R5000 for a double room in a decent three-star hotel. Prices for top-end hotels start at R10,000 and go all the way up.

Although dual pricing for hotels and transport tickets no longer exists, as a foreigner in Russia you'll still often find yourself paying more than a Russian for museums. The mark-up for foreigners is extreme – often as much as 10 times the price that Russians pay (although you may be able to avoid it if you have student identification). Some major attractions, such as the Kremlin, State History Museum and St Basil's, have ditched foreigner prices. All adults pay whatever the foreigners' price used to be; all students, children and pensioners pay the low price.

INTERNET RESOURCES

www.expat.ru Run by and for English-speaking expats living in Russia. Provides useful information about real estate, restaurants, children in Moscow, social groups and more.

www.maps-moscow.com An energetic group of international journalists raising awareness of architectural preservation issues in Moscow.

www.mbtg.ru The free Moscow Business Telephone Guide is an invaluable, bilingual phonebook.

www.moscowdoesntbelieveintears.blogspot.com An anonymous blog that provides a slightly cynical but totally hilarious look at Moscow's decadent nightlife scene.

www.moscowmaximum.blogspot.com Another anonymous nightlife blog, providing in-depth club reviews and insider info.

www.moscow-taxi.com Viktor the virtual taxi driver provides extensive descriptions of sites inside and outside of Moscow, as well as hotel bookings and other tourist services.

www.readrussia.com There's more to Russia than ballet, Leo Tolstoy and Maria Sharapova, as the website of this groovy quarterly magazine sets out to prove with its hip features on contemporary culture.

www.redtape.ru Like expat.ru but better. Forums offer inside information about any question you might ask.

www.waytorussia.net Written and maintained by Russian backpackers, this site is highly informative and on the ball. Includes an excellent (though not always up-to-date) Moscow guide. Please note that we've received complaints about buying train tickets through third parties associated with the site.

HISTORY
MEDIEVAL MOSCOW
Early Settlement

Moscow began as a trading post, set up by eastern Slav tribes who had migrated eastward from Kyivan Rus. Back in Kyiv, the Grand Prince Vladimir I was anxious to secure his claim of sovereignty over all the eastern Slavs. He made his son Yaroslav the regional vicelord, overseeing the collection of tribute and conversion of pagans.

After Vladimir's death, the descendants of Yaroslav inherited the north-eastern territories of the realm, where they established a series of towns, fortresses and monasteries that is today known as the Golden Ring (p216).

Political power gradually shifted eastward to these new settlements. During the reign of Vladimir Monomakh as Grand Prince, he appointed his youngest son Yury Dolgoruky to look after the region. Legend has it that on his way back to Vladimir from Kyiv, Prince Yury stopped at Moscow. Believing that Moscow's Prince Kuchka had not paid him sufficient homage, Yury put the impudent *boyar* (high-ranking noble) to death and placed the trading post under his direct rule. Moscow's strategic importance prompted Yury to construct a moat-ringed wooden palisade on the hilltop and install his personal vassal on site.

With its convenient access to rivers and roads, Moscow soon blossomed into a regional economic centre, attracting traders and artisans to the merchant rows just outside the Kremlin's walls. In the early 13th century, Moscow became the capital of a small, independent principality, though it remained a contested prize by successive generations of *boyar* princes.

The Rise of Muscovy

In the 13th century, Eastern Europe was overwhelmed by the marauding Golden Horde, a Mongol-led army of nomadic tribespeople, who appeared out of the eastern Eurasian steppes and were led by Chinggis (Genghis) Khaan's grandson, Batu. The ferocity of the Golden Horde raids was unprecedented, and quickly Russia's ruling princes acknowledged the region's new overlord. The Golden Horde's khan would constrain Russian sovereignty for the next two centuries, demanding tribute and allegiance from the Slavs.

The years of Mongol domination coincided with the rise of medieval Muscovy in a marriage of power and money. The Golden Horde was mainly interested in tribute, and Moscow was conveniently situated to monitor the river trade and road traffic. With Mongol backing, Muscovite officials soon emerged as the chief tax collectors in the region.

As Moscow prospered economically, its political fortunes rose as well. Grand Prince Ivan Danilovich earned the moniker of 'Moneybags' (*Kalita*) because of his remarkable revenue-raising abilities. Ivan Kalita used his good relations with the khan to manoeuvre Moscow into

TIMELINE

10th century	1015	1113–1125
Eastern Slav tribes began to migrate from the Kyivan Rus principality further west, eventually assimilating or displacing the Ugro-Fnnic tribes that had previously populated the region.	Upon the death of Vladimir I, his realm is divided among his sons, leading to a protracted and violent period of family feuds. His son Yaroslavl (and descendents) eventually gain control over the eastern territories.	During the reign of Vladimir (Monomakh) II, the Vladimir-Suzdal principality becomes a formidable rival in the medieval Russian realm. As Grand Prince, Vladimir appoints his youngest son, Yury Dolgoruky, to look after the region.

BY GEORGE, IT'S ST GEORGE

Visitors to Moscow are likely to notice the unmistakable likeness of St George around town. Indeed, all city properties display the iconic image of the Holy Helper, riding atop a white steed and sticking it to a scaly dragon below. While George is probably better known as the patron saint of England, he holds the same high status for Moscow.

The real-life George was born in Palestine in the 2nd century AD and rose to high rank in the Roman imperial guard. When Emperor Diocletian ordered all Christian soldiers to convert to paganism, George publicly tore up the edict. Neither the enticement of riches nor the pains of torture could make him renounce his faith, and he died a Christian martyr. Returning crusaders spread the legend of St George across Europe, which somehow came to include the slaying of a villainous serpent.

Moscow's founder prince, Yury Dolgoruky, adopted St George as the city's heavenly protector. Not coincidentally, in the Russian tongue the name George is Yury. Henceforth, St George adorned the coat of arms of the medieval Muscovite principality, featured on coins and stamps. When Catherine the Great ordered all the administrative territories of the empire to design their own heraldic shields, Moscow once again went with the bane of flying reptiles.

But George was eventually knocked off his high horse by the Bolsheviks, who banned old regime regalia. Soviet Moscow was assigned a new city insignia, with proletariat protectors.

When the communist regime fell, Moscow returned St George to his traditional place of prominence. In 1993, Mayor Luzhkov – another Yury – officially restored the prerevolutionary St George image to the capital crest. Perhaps it was a subliminal political message, but Muscovites seemed to like it anyway. A striking St George statue, forged by the mayor's favourite Georgian sculptor (p113), now presides over Manezhnaya pl (p75) next to the Kremlin.

On 23 April 2007, Russia's liberator from red dragons, Boris Yeltsin, died in Moscow. It was the feast day of St George.

a position of dominance in relation to his rival princes. By the middle of the 14th century, Moscow had absorbed its erstwhile patrons, Vladimir and Suzdal.

Soon Moscow became a nemesis rather than a supplicant to the Mongols. In the 1380 Battle of Kulikovo, Moscow's Grand Prince Dmitry, Kalita's grandson, led a coalition of Slav princes to a rare victory over the Golden Horde on the banks of the Don River. He was thereafter immortalised as Dmitry Donskoy. This feat did not break the Mongols, who retaliated by setting Moscow ablaze only two years later. From this time, however, Moscow acted as champion of the Russian cause.

Towards the end of the 15th century, Moscow's ambitions were realised as the once-diminutive duchy evolved into an expanding autocratic state. Under the long reign of Grand Prince Ivan III, the eastern Slav independent principalities were forcibly consolidated into a single territorial entity.

After a seven-year assault, Ivan's army finally subdued the prosperous merchant principality of Novgorod and evicted the Hansa trading league. After Novgorod's fall, the 'gathering of the lands' picked up pace as the young Muscovite state annexed Tver, Vyatka, Ryazan, Smolensk and Pskov.

In 1480 Ivan's army faced down the Mongols at the Ugra River without a fight. Ivan now refused outright to pay tribute or deference to the Golden Horde and the 200-year Mongol yoke was lifted. A triumphant Ivan had himself crowned 'Ruler of all Russia' in a solemn Byzantine-style ceremony, earning him the moniker Ivan the Great.

1147	1237–8	1326–8
Moscow is first mentioned in the historic chronicles, when Yury Dolgoruky invites his allies to a banquet there: 'Come to me, brother, please come to Moscow'.	The Mongols introduce themselves to Moscow by razing the city and killing its governor. Their menacing new presence levels the political playing field in the region, thereby creating an opportunity for a small Muscovite principality.	Moscow emerges as a political stronghold and religious centre. The head of the Russian episcopate departs Vladimir and moves into the Kremlin. Grand Prince Ivan I gains the right to collect taxes from other Russian principalities.

Ivan the Terrible

At the time of the death of Ivan the Great, the borders of Muscovy stretched from the Baltic region in the west to the Ural Mountains in the east and the Barents Sea in the north. The south was still the domain of hostile steppe tribes of the Golden Horde.

In the 16th century, however, the Golden Horde fragmented into four Khanates, which continued to raid Russian settlements. At this time, the grandson of Ivan the Great, Ivan IV (the Terrible), led the further expansion and consolidation of the upstart Muscovy state, defeating three out of four Khanates, securing control over the Volga River and opening up a vast wilderness east of the Urals. Ivan was less successful against the Crimean Tatars, who dominated the southern access routes to the Black Sea.

On the home front, the reign of Ivan IV spelt trouble for Moscow. Ivan came to the throne at age three with his mother as regent. Upon reaching adulthood, 13 years later, he was crowned 'Tsar of all the Russias'. (The Russian word 'tsar' is derived from the Latin term 'caesar'.) Ivan's marriage to Anastasia, a member of the Romanov *boyar* family, was a happy one, unlike the five that followed her early death.

When his beloved Anastasia died, it marked a turning point for Ivan. Believing her to have been poisoned, he started a reign of terror against the ever-intriguing and jealous *boyars,* earning himself the sobriquet *grozny* (literally 'dreadfully serious', but in his case translated as 'terrible'). Later, in a fit of rage, he even killed his eldest son and heir to the throne.

Ivan suffered from a fused spine and took mercury treatments to ease the intense pain. The cure, however, was worse than the ailment; it gradually made him insane.

The last years of Ivan's reign proved ruinous for Moscow. In 1571 Crimean Tatars torched the city, burning most of it to the ground. Ivan's volatile temperament made matters worse by creating political instability. At one point he vacated the throne and concealed himself in a monastery.

Upon his death, power passed to his feeble-minded son, Fyodor. For a short time, Fyodor's brother-in-law and able prime minister, Boris Godunov, succeeded in restoring order to the realm. By the beginning of the 17th century, however, Boris was dead, Polish invaders occupied the Kremlin, and Russia slipped into a 'Time of Troubles'. Finally, Cossack soldiers relieved Moscow of its uninvited Polish guests and political stability was achieved with the coronation of Mikhail as tsar, inaugurating the Romanov dynasty.

IMPERIAL MOSCOW
The Spurned Capital

Peter I, known as 'Peter the Great' for his commanding frame (reaching over 2m) and equally commanding victory over the Swedes, dragged Russia kicking and screaming into modern Europe. Peter spent much of his youth in royal residences in the Moscow countryside, organising his playmates in war games. Energetic and inquisitive, he was eager to learn about the outside world. As a boy, he spent hours in Moscow's European district; as a young man, he spent months travelling in the West. In fact, he was Russia's first ruler to venture abroad. Peter briefly shared the throne with his half-brother, before taking sole possession in 1696.

Peter wilfully imposed modernisation on Moscow. He ordered the *boyars* to shave their beards, imported European advisers and craftspeople and rationalised state administration.

1360	1380	1450s
The Kremlin is refortified and expanded. As the once-small village grew into a prosperous urban centre, Grand Prince Dmitry replaces the wooden walls with a more durable limestone edifice.	Grand Prince Dmitry mounts the first successful Russian challenge to Tatar authority, earning his moniker Donskoy after defeating the Tatars in the Battle of Kulikovo on the Don River.	A separate Russian Orthodox Church is organised, independent of the Greek Church. When Constantinople falls to heathen Turks, the Metropolitan declares Moscow to be the 'Third Rome', the rightful heir of Christendom.

CHECK YOUR CALENDAR

For hundreds of years Russia was out of sync with the West. Until 1700 Russia dated its years from 'creation', which was determined to be approximately 5508 years before the birth of Christ. So at that time, the year 1700 was considered the year 7208 in Russia. Peter the Great – westward-looking as he was – instituted a reform to date the years from the birth of Christ, as they did in the rest of Europe.

Things got complicated again in the 18th century, when most of Europe abandoned the Julian calendar in favour of the Gregorian calendar, and Russia did not follow suit. By 1917, Russian dates were 13 days out of sync with European dates. Which explains how the October Revolution could have taken place on November 7.

Finally, the all-powerful Soviet regime made the necessary leap. The last day of January 1918 was followed by 14 February 1918. All dates since 1918 have been identical to dates in the West.

In this book we use dates corresponding to the current Gregorian calendar that is used worldwide. However, even history is not always straightforward, as other accounts may employ the calendars that were the convention at that time. Tell *that* to your history professor.

He built Moscow's tallest structure, the 90m-high Sukharev Tower, and next to it founded the College of Mathematics and Navigation.

Yet, Peter always despised Moscow for its scheming *boyars* and archaic traditions. In 1712 he startled the country by announcing the relocation of the capital to a swampland, recently acquired from Sweden in the Great Northern War. St Petersburg would be Russia's 'Window on the West' and everything that Moscow was not – modern, scientific and cultured. Alexander Pushkin later wrote that 'Peter I had no love for Moscow, where, with every step he took, he ran into remembrances of mutinies and executions, inveterate antiquity and the obstinate resistance of superstition and prejudice'.

The spurned former capital quickly fell into decline. With the aristocratic elite and administrative staff departing for marshier digs, the population fell by more than a quarter in the first 25 years. The city suffered further from severe fires, a situation exacerbated by Peter's mandate to direct all construction materials to St Petersburg.

In the 1770s, Moscow was devastated by an outbreak of bubonic plague, which claimed more than 50,000 lives. It was decreed that the dead had to be buried outside the city limits. Vast cemeteries, including Danilovskoye and Vagankovskoye, were the result. The situation was so desperate that residents went on a riotous looting spree that was violently put down by the army. Empress Catherine II (the Great) responded to the crisis by ordering a new sanitary code to clean up the urban environment and silencing the Kremlin alarm bell that had set off the riots.

By the turn of the 19th century, Moscow had recovered from its gloom; Peter's exit had not caused a complete rupture. The city retained the title of 'First-Throned Capital' because coronations were held there. When Peter's grandson, Peter III, relieved the nobles of obligatory state service, many returned to Moscow. Moreover, many of the merchants had never left. After the initial shock, their patronage and wealth became visible again throughout the city.

The late 18th century also saw the construction of the first embankments along the Moscow River, which were followed by bridges. Russia's first university and first newspaper were started in Moscow. This new intellectual and literary scene would soon give rise to a nationalist-inspired cultural movement, which would embrace those features of Russia that were distinctly different from the West.

1475–1516	1478–80	1560
Ivan III launches a rebuilding effort to celebrate his military successes, importing Italian artisans and masons to construct the Kremlin's thick brick walls and imposing watchtowers. Traders and artisans set up shop in Kitay Gorod.	Moscow subdues its rival principalities, and the united Russian army defeats the Mongols at the Ugra River. Ivan III is crowned Ruler of all Russia, earning him the moniker 'Ivan the Great'.	Provoked by the death of his wife, the ever-suspicious Ivan IV commences a reign of terror over the *boyars* (high-ranking nobles), thus earning him the moniker 'Ivan the Terrible'.

Moscow Boomtown

Moscow was feverishly rebuilt in just a few years following the Napoleonic War. Monuments were erected to commemorate Russia's hard-fought victory and Alexander's 'proudest moment'. A Triumphal Arch (p106), inspired by their former French hosts, was placed at the top of Tverskaya ul on the road to St Petersburg. The sculpture of Minin and Pozharsky (p74), who had liberated Moscow from a previous foreign foe, adorned Red Square. And the immensely grandiose Cathedral of Christ the Saviour (p109), which took almost 50 years to complete, went up along the river embankment outside the Kremlin.

The building frenzy did not stop with national memorials. In the city centre, engineers diverted the Neglinnaya River to an underground canal and created two new urban spaces: the Alexandrovsky Garden (p72), running alongside the Kremlin's western wall; and Teatralnaya pl (p76), featuring the glittering Bolshoi Theatre and later the opulent Hotel Metropol. The rebuilt Manezh, the 180m-long imperial stables, provided a touch of neoclassical grandeur to the scene.

Meanwhile, the city's two outer defensive rings were replaced with the tree-lined Boulevard Ring and Garden Ring roads. The Garden Ring became an informal social boundary line: on the inside were the abodes and amenities of the merchants, intellectuals, civil servants and foreigners; on the outside were the factories and dosshouses of the toiling, the loitering and the destitute.

A postwar economic boom changed the city forever. The robust recovery was at first led by the big merchants, long the mainstay of the city's economy. In the 1830s, they organised the Moscow Commodity Exchange. By midcentury, industry began to overtake commerce as the city's economic driving force. Moscow became the hub of a network of railroad construction, connecting the raw materials of the east to the manufacturers of the west. With a steady supply of cotton from Central Asia, Moscow became a leader in the textile industry. By 1890, more than 300 of the city's 660 factories were engaged in cloth production and the city was known as 'Calico Moscow'. While St Petersburg's industrial development was financed largely by foreign capital, Moscow drew upon its own resources. The Moscow Merchant Bank, founded in 1866, was the country's second-largest bank by century's end.

The affluent and self-assured business elite extended its influence over the city. The eclectic tastes of the nouveau riche were reflected in the multiform architectural styles of the mansions, salons and hotels. The business elite eventually secured direct control over the city government, removing the remnants of the old *boyar* aristocracy. In 1876, Sergei Tretyakov, artful entrepreneur and art patron, started a political trend when he became the first mayor who could not claim noble lineage.

The increase in economic opportunity in the city occurred simultaneously with a decline in agriculture and the emancipation of the serfs. As a result, the city's population surged, mostly driven by an influx of rural job seekers. In 1890, Moscow claimed over one million inhabitants. The population was growing so rapidly that the number increased by another 50% in less than 20 years. Moscow still ranked second to St Petersburg in population but, unlike the capital, Moscow was a thoroughly Russian city – its population was 95% ethnic Russian.

By 1900, more than 50% of the city's inhabitants were first-generation peasant migrants. They settled in the factory tenements outside the Garden Ring and south of the river in the Zamoskvorechie district. The influx of indigents overwhelmed the city's meagre social services and affordable accommodation. At the beginning of the 20th century, Moscow's teeming

1571	1591–1613	1610–12
Moscow is burned to the ground by Crimean Tatars. As the city rebuilds, a stone wall is erected around the commercial quarters outside the Kremlin.	Ivan IV dies with no capable heir, leaving the country in chaos. His death ushers in the so-called 'Time of Troubles', when Russia is ruled by a string of pretenders to the throne.	The army of the Polish-Lithuanian Commonwealth occupies Moscow, until the arrival of a Cossack army, led by Dmitry Pozharsky and Kuzma Minin, which succeeds at expelling the Poles.

THE BATTLE OF MOSCOW – 1812

In 1807 Tsar Alexander I negotiated the Treaty of Tilsit. It left Napoleon in charge as emperor of the west of Europe and Alexander as emperor of the east, united (in theory) against England. The alliance lasted until 1810, when Russia resumed trade with England. A furious Napoleon decided to crush the tsar with his Grand Army of 700,000 – the largest force the world had ever seen for a single military operation.

The vastly outnumbered Russian forces retreated across their own countryside throughout the summer of 1812, scorching the earth in an attempt to deny the French sustenance, and fighting some successful rearguard actions.

Napoleon set his sights on Moscow. In September, with the lack of provisions beginning to bite the French, Russian general Mikhail Kutuzov finally decided to turn and fight at Borodino (p236), 130km from Moscow. The battle was extremely bloody, but inconclusive, with the Russians withdrawing in good order. More than 100,000 soldiers lay dead at the end of a one-day battle.

Before the month was out, Napoleon entered a deserted Moscow. Defiant Muscovites burned down two-thirds of the city rather than see it occupied by the French invaders. Alexander, meanwhile, ignored Napoleon's overtures to negotiate.

With winter coming and supply lines overextended, Napoleon declared victory and retreated. His badly weakened troops stumbled westward out of the city, falling to starvation, disease, bitter cold and Russian snipers. Only one in 20 made it back to the relative safety of Poland. The tsar's army pursued Napoleon all the way to Paris, which Russian forces briefly occupied in 1814.

slums were a breeding ground for disease and discontent. The disparity of wealth among the population grew to extremes. Lacking a voice, the city's less fortunate turned an ear to the outlawed radicals.

RED MOSCOW
Revolutionary Moscow

The tsarist autocracy staggered into the new century. In 1904 the impressionable and irresolute Tsar Nicholas II was talked into declaring war on Japan over some forested land in the Far East. His imperial forces suffered a decisive and embarrassing defeat, touching off a nationwide wave of unrest.

Taking their cue from St Petersburg, Moscow's workers and students staged a series of demonstrations, culminating in the October 1905 general strike, forcing political concessions from a reluctant Nicholas. In December the attempt by city authorities to arrest leading radicals provoked a new round of confrontation, which ended in a night of bloodshed on hastily erected barricades in the city's Presnya district.

Vladimir Ilych Ulyanov (Lenin) later called the failed 1905 Revolution the 'dress rehearsal for 1917'. He had vowed that next time Russia's rulers would not escape the revolutionary scourge. Exhausted by three years of fighting in WWI, the tsarist autocracy meekly succumbed to a mob of St Petersburg workers in February 1917. Unwilling to end the war and unable to restore order, the provisional government was itself overthrown in a bloodless palace coup, orchestrated by Lenin's Bolshevik Party.

In Moscow, regime change was not so easy, as a week of street fighting left more than 1000 dead. Radical socialism had come to power in Russia.

1613	1712	1755
The *zemsky sobor*, a sort of parliament, elects Mikhail Romanov as tsar. He is rescued from his exile in Kostroma and crowned, inaugurating the Romanov dynasty.	Peter I (the Great) surprises the country by moving the Russian capital from Moscow to St Petersburg. All of the bureaucrats and aristocrats relocate to the north, leaving Moscow to fall into decline.	At the instigation of scientist Mikhail Lomonosov and Minister of Education Ivan Shuvalov, Empress Elizabeth establishes Moscow State University (MGU), the first university in Russia.

Fearing a German assault, Lenin ordered that the capital return to Moscow. In March 1918, he set up shop in the Kremlin and the new Soviet government expropriated the nicer city hotels and townhouses to conduct affairs. The move unleashed a steady stream of favour-seeking sycophants on the city. The new communist-run city government authorised the redistribution of housing space, as scores of thousands of workers upgraded to the dispossessed digs of the bourgeoisie.

The revolution and ensuing civil war, however, took its toll on Moscow. Political turmoil fostered an economic crisis. In 1921 the city's factories were operating at only 10% of their prewar levels of production. Food and fuel were in short supply. Hunger and disease stalked the darkened city. The population dropped precipitously from two million in 1917 to just one million in 1920. Wearied workers returned to their villages in search of respite, while the old elite packed up its belongings and moved beyond the reach of a vengeful new regime.

Stalin's Moscow

In May 1922 Lenin suffered the first of a series of paralysing strokes that removed him from effective control of the Party and government. He died, aged 54, in January 1924. His embalmed remains were put on display in Moscow (p74), St Petersburg was renamed Leningrad in his honour, and a personality cult was built around him – all orchestrated by Josef Stalin.

The most unlikely of successors, Stalin outwitted his rivals and manoeuvred himself into the top post of the Communist Party. Ever-paranoid, Stalin later launched a reign of terror against his former Party rivals, which eventually consumed nearly the entire first generation of Soviet officialdom. Hundreds of thousands of Muscovites were systematically executed and secretly interred on the ancient grounds of the old monasteries.

In the early 1930s, Stalin launched Soviet Russia on a hell-bent industrialisation campaign. The campaign cost millions of lives, but by 1939 only the USA and Germany had higher levels of industrial output. Moscow set the pace for this rapid development. Political prisoners became slave labourers. The building of the Moscow–Volga Canal was overseen by the secret police, who forced several hundred thousand 'class enemies' to dig the 125km-long ditch.

The brutal tactics employed by the state to collectivise the countryside created a new wave of peasant immigrants who flooded to Moscow. Around the city, work camps and bare barracks were erected to shelter the huddling hordes who shouldered Stalin's industrial revolution. At the other end, Moscow also became a centre of a heavily subsidised military industry, whose engineers and technicians enjoyed a larger slice of the proletarian pie. The Party elite, meanwhile, moved into new spacious accommodation such as the Dom na Naberezhnoy (p123), on the embankment opposite the Kremlin.

Under Stalin, a comprehensive urban plan was devised for Moscow. On paper, it appeared as a neatly organised garden city; unfortunately, it was implemented with a sledgehammer. Historic cathedrals and bell towers were demolished in the middle of the night. The Kitay Gorod wall (p76) was dismantled for being 'a relic of medieval times'. Alexander's Triumphal Arch and Peter's Sukharev Tower likewise became victims of unsympathetic city planners, eager to wrench Moscow into a proletarian future.

New monuments marking the epochal transition to socialism went up in place of the old. The first line of the marble-bedecked metro was completed in 1935. The enormous Cathedral of Christ the Saviour was razed with the expectation of erecting the world's tallest building,

1770–80	1810–12	1839–60
The bubonic plague breaks out in Moscow, killing as many as 50,000 people. By the end of the decade, the population of St Petersburg surpasses that of Moscow.	Russia defies its treaty with France, provoking Napoleon and his Grand Army to invade Russia. Muscovites burn down their own city in anticipation of the invasion.	To celebrate the heroic victory over France in the Napoleonic Wars, the Cathedral of Christ the Saviour is built on the banks of the Moscow River.

upon which would stand an exalted 90m statute of Lenin. This scheme was later abandoned and the foundation hole instead became the world's biggest municipal swimming pool. Broad thoroughfares were created and neo-Gothic skyscrapers (p51) girded the city's outer ring.

Post-Stalinist Moscow

When Stalin died, his funeral procession brought out so many gawkers that a riot ensued and scores of mourners were trampled to death. The system he built, however, lived on, with a few changes.

First, Nikita Khrushchev, a former mayor of Moscow, tried a different approach to ruling. He curbed the powers of the secret police, released political prisoners, introduced wide-ranging reforms and promised to improve living conditions. Huge housing estates grew up around the outskirts of Moscow; many of the hastily constructed low-rise projects were nicknamed *khrushchoby*, after *trushchoby* (slums). Khrushchev's populism and unpredictability made the ruling elite a bit too nervous and he was ousted in 1964.

Next came the long, stagnant reign of ageing Leonid Brezhnev. Overlooking Lenin's mausoleum, he presided over the rise of a military superpower and provided long-sought-after political stability and material security.

During these years, the Cold War shaped Moscow's development as the Soviet Union enthusiastically competed with the USA in the arms and space races. The aerospace, radio-electronics and nuclear weapons ministries operated factories, research laboratories and design institutes in and around the capital. By 1980 as much as one-third of the city's industrial production and one-quarter of its labour force was connected to the defence industry. Moscow city officials were not privy to what went on in these secretly managed facilities. As a matter of national security, the KGB discreetly constructed a second subway system, Metro-2, under the city.

Still, the centrally planned economy could not keep pace with rising consumer demands. While the elite lived in privilege, ordinary Muscovites stood in line for goods. For the Communist Party, things became a bit too comfortable. Under Brezhnev the political elite grew elderly and corrupt, while the economic system slid into a slow, irreversible decline. And the goal of turning Moscow into a showcase socialist city was quietly abandoned.

Nonetheless, Moscow enjoyed a postwar economic boom. The city underwent further expansion, accommodating more and more buildings and residents. Brezhnev showed a penchant for brawny displays of modern architecture. Cavernous concrete-and-glass slabs, such as the now defunct Hotel Rossiya, were constructed to show the world the modern face of the Soviet Union. The cement pouring reached a frenzy in the build-up to the 1980 Summer Olympics. However, Russia's invasion of Afghanistan caused many nations to boycott the Games and the facilities mostly stood empty.

Appreciation for Moscow's past began to creep back into city planning. Most notably, Alexander's Triumphal Arch (p106) was reconstructed, though plans to re-erect Peter's tall Sukharev Tower were not realised. Residential life continued to move further away from the city centre, which was increasingly occupied by the governing elite. Shoddy high-rise apartments went up on the periphery and metro lines were extended outward.

The attraction for Russians to relocate to Moscow in these years was, and continues to be, very strong. City officials tried desperately to enforce the residency permit system, but to

1861	1905	1914–17
The 'liberator tsar' Alexander II enacts the Emancipation Reform, which liberates the serfs. Moscow's population surges as thousands of peasants descend on the big city.	The unpopular and unsuccessful Russo-Japanese War provokes general strikes in Moscow and St Petersburg. In Moscow street barricades are set up and fighting takes place in present-day Presnya.	Russia suffers immeasurably from losses in WWI. By 1916, Russia has sustained as many as 1.6 million casualties. High prices and food shortages affect the populace on the homefront.

no avail. In 1960 the population topped six million, and by 1980 it surpassed eight million. The spillover led to the rapid growth of Moscow's suburbs. While industry, especially the military industry, provided the city's economic foundation, many new jobs were created in science, education and public administration. The city became a little more ethnically diverse, particularly with the arrival of petty-market traders from Central Asia and the Caucasus.

TRANSITIONAL MOSCOW
The Communist Collapse

The Soviet leadership showed it was not immune to change when Mikhail Gorbachev came to power in March 1985 with a mandate to revitalise the ailing socialist system. Gorbachev soon launched a multifaceted program of reform under the catchphrase *'perestroika'* (restructuring). Gorbachev recognised that it would take more than bureaucratic reorganisations and stern warnings to reverse economic decline. He believed that the root of the economic crisis was society's alienation from the socialist system. Thus, he sought to break down the barrier between 'us' and 'them'.

His reforms were meant to engage the population and stimulate initiative. *Glasnost* (openness) gave new voice to both a moribund popular culture and a stifled media. Democratisation introduced multicandidate elections and new deliberative legislative bodies. Cooperatives brought the first experiments in market economics in over 50 years. Gorbachev's plan was to lead a gradual transition to reform socialism but, in practice, events ran ahead of him. Moscow set the pace.

In 1985 Gorbachev promoted Boris Yeltsin from his Urals bailiwick into the central leadership as the new head of Moscow. Yeltsin was given the assignment of cleaning up the corrupt Moscow Party machine and responded by sacking hundreds of officials. His populist touch made him an instant success with Muscovites, who were often startled to encounter him riding public transport or berating a shopkeeper for not displaying his sausage. During Gorbachev's ill-advised antialcohol campaign, Yeltsin saved Moscow's largest brewery from having to close its doors.

More importantly, Yeltsin embraced the more open political atmosphere. He allowed 'informal' groups, unsanctioned by the Communist Party, to organise and express themselves in public. Soon Moscow streets, such as those in the Arbat district, were hosting demonstrations by democrats, nationalists, reds and greens. Yeltsin's renegade style alienated the entire Party leadership, one by one. He was summarily dismissed by Gorbachev in 1987, though he would be heard from again.

Gorbachev's political reforms included elections to reformed local assemblies in the spring of 1990. By this time, communism had already fallen in Eastern Europe and events in the Soviet Union were becoming increasingly radical. In their first free election in 88 years, Muscovites turned out in large numbers at the polls and voted a bloc of democratic reformers into office.

The new mayor was economist Gavril Popov, and the vice-mayor was Yury Luzhkov. Popov immediately embarked on the 'decommunisation' of the city, selling off housing and state businesses and restoring prerevolutionary street names. He clashed repeatedly with the Soviet leadership over the management of city affairs. Popov soon acquired a key ally when Yeltsin made a political comeback as the elected head of the new Russian Supreme Soviet.

On 18 August 1991, the city awoke to find a column of tanks in the street and a 'Committee for the State of Emergency' claiming to be in charge. This committee was composed of leaders

1917	1918	1930s
Tsar Nicholas II succumbs to a mob of workers in St Petersburg and abdicates the throne. A provisional government is set up in an attempt to restore order.	The Bolshevik Party seizes power from the ineffective provisional government. In fear of a German attack, Vladimir Ilych Ulyanov (Lenin) moves the capital back to Moscow.	Stalin launches a campaign of modernisation and a reign of terror. Moscow becomes an industrial city, complete with impoverished workers, billowing factories and new construction.

THE BATTLE OF MOSCOW – 1941

In the 1930s Stalin's overtures to enter into an anti-Nazi collective security agreement were rebuffed by England and France. Vowing that the Soviet Union would not be pulling their 'chestnuts out of the fire', Stalin signed a nonaggression pact with Hitler instead.

Thus, when Hitler launched Operation Barbarossa in June 1941, Stalin was caught by surprise and did not emerge from his room for three days.

The ill-prepared Red Army was no match for the Nazi war machine, which advanced on three fronts. History repeated itself with the two armies facing off at Borodino (p236). By December, the Germans were just outside Moscow, within 30km of the Kremlin. Only an early, severe winter halted the advance. A monument now marks the spot, near the entrance road to Sheremetyevo airport, where the Nazis were stopped in their tracks. Staging a brilliant counteroffensive, Soviet war hero General Zhukov staved off the attack and pushed the invaders back.

from the Communist Party, the KGB and the military. They had already detained Gorbachev at his Crimean dacha and issued directives to arrest Yeltsin and the Moscow city leadership.

But the ill-conceived coup quickly went awry and confusion ensued. Yeltsin, Popov and Luzhkov made it to the Russian parliament building, the so-called White House (p98), to rally opposition. Crowds gathered at the White House, persuaded some of the tank crews to switch sides and started to build barricades. Yeltsin climbed on a tank to declare the coup illegal and call for a general strike. He dared the snipers to shoot him, and when they didn't, the coup was over.

The following day, huge crowds opposed to the coup gathered in Moscow. Coup leaders lost their nerve, one committed suicide, some fell ill and the others simply got drunk. On 21 August, the tanks withdrew; the coup was foiled. Gorbachev flew back to Moscow to resume command, but his time was up as well. On 23 August, Yeltsin banned the Communist Party in Russia.

Gorbachev embarked on a last-ditch bid to save the Soviet Union with proposals for a looser union of independent states. Yeltsin, however, was steadily transferring control over everything that mattered from Soviet hands into Russian ones. On 8 December, Yeltsin and the leaders of Ukraine and Belarus, after several rounds of vodka toasts, announced that the USSR no longer existed. They proclaimed a new Commonwealth of Independent States (CIS), a vague alliance of fully independent states with no central authority. Gorbachev, a president without a country or authority, formally resigned on 25 December, the day the white, blue and red Russian flag replaced the Soviet red flag over the Kremlin.

Rebirth of Russian Politics

Buoyed by his success over Gorbachev and coup plotters, Yeltsin (now Russia's president) was granted extraordinary powers by the parliament to find a way out of the Soviet wreckage. Yeltsin used these powers to launch radical economic reforms and rapprochement with the West. In so doing, he polarised the political elite. As Yeltsin's team of economic reformers began to dismantle the protected and subsidised command economy, the parliament finally acted in early 1992 to seize power back from the president. A stalemate ensued that lasted for a year and a half.

The executive-legislative conflict at the national level was played out in Moscow politics as well. After the Soviet fall, the democratic bloc that had brought Popov to power came apart.

1935	1941–44	1953
Members of the Komsomol (Soviet youth organisation) pitch in to construct their namesake Komsomolskaya metro station, earning them the prestigious Order of Lenin. The first line of the Moscow metro, the Sokolniki line, commences operation.	Hitler defies a German-Soviet nonaggression pact and launches an attack on Russia. The Nazi advance on Moscow is halted by a severe Russian winter, allowing the embattled Red Army to fight them back.	Stalin dies and is entombed next to his predecessor on Red Square. After a brief power struggle, Nikita Khrushchev becomes first secretary. His main rival, Lavrenty Beria, is arrested, tried for treason and executed.

In Moscow a property boom began, as buildings and land with no real owners changed hands at a dizzying rate with dubious legality. Increasingly, the mayor's office was at odds with the city council, as well as the new federal government. Popov began feuding with Yeltsin, just as he had previously with Gorbachev.

In June 1992 the impulsive Popov resigned his office in a huff. Without pausing to ask him to reconsider, vice-mayor Yury Luzhkov readily assumed the mayor's seat (see the boxed text, p38). The city council passed a vote of no confidence in Luzhkov and called for new elections, but the new mayor opted simply to ignore the resolution.

Throughout 1993, the conflict between President Yeltsin and the Russian parliament intensified. Eight different constitutional drafts were put forward and rejected. In September 1993 parliament convened with plans to remove many of the president's powers. Before it could act, Yeltsin issued a decree that shut down the parliament and called for new elections.

Events turned violent. Yeltsin sent troops to blockade the White House, ordering the members to leave it by 4 October. Many did, but on 2 and 3 October, a National Salvation Front appeared, in an attempt to stir popular insurrection against the president. They clashed with the troops around the White House and tried to seize Moscow's Ostankino TV tower (p131).

The army, which until this time had sought to remain neutral, intervened on the president's side and blasted the parliament into submission. In all, 145 people were killed and another 700 wounded – the worst such incident of bloodshed in the city since the Bolshevik takeover in 1917. Yeltsin, in conjunction with the newly subjugated parliament, put together the 1993 constitution that created a new political system organised around strong central executive power.

Throughout the 1990s Yeltsin suffered increasingly from heart disease. But come 1996, he was not prepared to step down from his 'throne'. It has been widely reported that in the time surrounding the 1996 presidential election, Russia's newly rich financiers, who backed Yeltsin's campaign, were rewarded with policy-making positions in the government and with state-owned assets in privatisation auctions. In a scene reminiscent of the medieval *boyars,* the power grabs of these 'oligarchs' became more brazen during Yeltsin's prolonged illness.

Economic Prosperity

In the New Russia, wealth was concentrated in Moscow. While the rest of Russia struggled to survive the collapse of the command economy, Moscow emerged quickly as an enclave of affluence and dynamism. By the mid-1990s Moscow was replete with all the things Russians had expected capitalism to bring, but which had yet to trickle down to the provinces: banks, shops, restaurants, casinos, BMWs, bright lights and nightlife.

The city provided nearly 25% of all tax revenues collected by the federal government. Commercial banks, commodity exchanges, big businesses and high-end retailers all set up headquarters in the capital. By the late 1990s, Moscow had become one of the most expensive cities in the world.

When the government defaulted on its debts and devalued the currency in 1998, it appeared that the boom had gone bust. But as the panic subsided, it became clear that it was less a crisis and more a correction for a badly overvalued rouble. In the aftermath Russian firms became more competitive and productive with the new exchange rate. Wages started to be paid again and consumption increased.

1956–61	1964	1979–80
Khrushchev makes a 'secret speech' at the Party Congress, denouncing Stalin's repressive regime and initiating reforms. Stalin is eventually removed from the mausoleum on Red Square and buried in the Kremlin wall.	A coup against Khrushchev brings Leonid Brezhnev to power, ushering in the so-called 'years of stagnation'. Poet and future Nobel laureate Joseph Brodsky is labelled a 'social parasite' and sent into exile.	Russia invades Afghanistan to support its communist regime against US-backed Islamic militants. Relations between the superpowers deteriorate and the USA and 61 other nations boycott the Olympic Games held in Moscow.

MILLENNIUM MOSCOW
Cops in the Kremlin

In December 1999 Boris Yeltsin delivered his customary televised New Year's greeting to the nation. On this occasion the burly president shocked his fellow countryfolk yet again by announcing his resignation from office and retirement from politics. The once-combative Yeltsin had grown weary from a decade full of political adversity and physical infirmity.

Yeltsin turned over the office to his recently appointed prime minister, Vladimir Putin. As an aide to the president, Putin had impressed Yeltsin with his selfless dedication, shrewd mind and principled resolve. It was Yeltsin's plan to spring this holiday surprise on the unprepared political opposition to bolster Putin's chances in the upcoming presidential election. The plan worked. In March 2000 Putin became the second president of the Russian Federation.

Mystery surrounded the cop in the Kremlin: he was a former KGB chief, but an ally of St Petersburg's democratic mayor; well-heeled in European culture, but nostalgic for Soviet patriotism; diminutive in stature, but a black belt in karate.

In his first term, Putin's popular-approval ratings shot through the onion domes. He brought calm and stability to Russian politics after more than a decade of crisis and upheaval. The economy finally bottomed out and began to show positive growth. The improved economic situation led to budget surpluses for the first time since the 1980s and wages and pensions were paid in full and on time.

Putin vowed to restore the authority of the Moscow-based central state, engineering a constitutional reform to reduce the power of regional governors and launching a second war against radical Chechen separatists. His main opponent in the 2000 election, Moscow Mayor Yury Luzhkov, took note and hastily allied his political machine with Putin's new 'Unity' party.

Putin was reelected in 2004. His second term accelerated the disturbing trend toward a more authoritarian approach to politics. Former police officials were named prime minister and speaker of the parliament. Restraints on mass media, civil society and nongovernmental agencies were further tightened. Russia's big business tycoons were cowed into submission after independent-minded oil magnate Mikhail Khodorkovsky was jailed for tax evasion.

Where Russia's young tycoons failed, its senior citizens succeeded. Putin's 2005 attempt to scrap the existing system of subsidised social services was met with unexpected resistance from protesting pensioners. Thousands filled Moscow's streets, denouncing the pension reforms and forcing Putin to back off his plan.

Russia emerged from the 1990s feeling bruised and belligerent toward its supposedly new Western friends. No longer fearful of incurring Western wrath, Russia has antagonised the Brits and Yanks with diplomatic disputes and territorial takings. It is not really a new Cold War but, rather, a continuation of the old one.

Terror in the Capital

Though the origins of the Russian-Chechen conflict date to the 18th century, it is only in recent times that Moscow has felt its consequences so close to home. In September 1999

1982–85	1985	1991
Brezhnev's death ushers in former KGB supremo Yury Andropov as president for 15 months until his death in 1984. His successor, the doddering 72-year-old Konstantin Chernenko, hardly makes an impact before dying 13 months later.	Mikhail Gorbachev is elected general secretary of the Communist Party. Intent on reform he institutes policies of *perestroika* (restructuring) and *glasnost* (openness). Boris Yeltsin is appointed first secretary (mayor) of Moscow.	A failed coup in August against Gorbachev seals the end of the USSR. On Christmas Day, Gorbachev resigns and Yeltsin takes charge as the first popularly elected president of the Russian Federation.

mysterious explosions in the capital left more than 200 people dead. Chechen terrorists were blamed for the bombings, although the evidence was scant. Conspiracy theorists had a field day.

In 2002 Chechen rebels wired with explosives seized a popular Moscow theatre, demanding independence for Chechnya. Nearly 800 theatre employees and patrons were held hostage for three days. Russian troops responded by flooding the theatre with immobilising toxic gas, disabling hostage-takers and hostages alike and preventing the worst-case scenario. The victims' unexpectedly severe reaction to the gas and a lack of available medical facilities resulted in 120 deaths and hundreds of illnesses. The incident refuelled Russia's relentless and ruthless campaign to force the Chechens into capitulation

Chechen terrorists responded in kind, with smaller-scale insurgencies taking place regularly over the next several years. Between 2002 and 2005, suicide bombers in Moscow made strikes on the metro, in airplanes and at rock concerts, leaving hundreds of people dead and injured. The worst incident in Moscow proper was in February 2004, when a bomb exploded in a metro carriage travelling between Avtozavodskaya and Paveletskaya stations, killing 39 and injuring over 100.

Other incidents served as unnerving reminders, including a series of attacks that coincided with the horrific school siege in Beslan, which resulted in 331 deaths. A couple of days before that incident, in late August 2004, two planes that took off from Moscow exploded almost simultaneously in midair, killing all 90 passengers, including the suicide bombers on board. Soon after, a suicide bomber failed to enter Rizhskaya metro station, but still managed to kill 10 and injure 50 people on the street.

Meanwhile, Chechens living in Moscow endured increased harassment, both officially and unofficially. They complained of increasing difficulty in trying to obtain residency permits, and of constant and unwarranted attention from Moscow police. No less damaging was the growing mistrust between Russians and Chechens as the racial tension continued to mount.

Moscow under Medvedev

In 2008 Putin's second term as president came to an end. How would the transition unfold? Some Russian lawmakers volunteered to amend the constitution so that the president could run for a third consecutive term. But Putin said that would not be in the spirit of democracy, and he stepped aside. Or did he?

Putin's hand-picked presidential successor was law professor and Black Sabbath fan, Dmitry Medvedev, whose nomination was ratified in March elections by 70% of voters. Although he hailed from the same St Petersburg cohort as Putin and his police pals, Medvedev worked as a lawyer before jumping into postcommunist politics. In the Russian political system, power is concentrated in the office of the president, so people were curious to see what Medvedev would do with it.

In the first six months there was little evidence that Medvedev was contemplating new policy directions. The 2008 election did not cause a turnover in administration; rather the same dozen guys changed seats around the Kremlin table. Putin may officially be the prime minister, but politicos agree that he acts more like a regent, sitting behind the throne and whispering the answers to the child emperor.

1993	1999	2002
In a clash of wills with the Russian parliament, Yeltsin sends in troops to deal with dissenters at Moscow's White House and Ostankino TV tower. It is Russia's most violent political conflict since 1917.	On New Year's Eve, in a move that catches everyone by surprise, Yeltsin announces his immediate resignation, entrusting the caretaker duties of president to the prime minister Vladimir Putin.	Chechen rebels wired with explosives seize a popular Moscow theatre, holding 800 hostages for three days. Russian troops respond by flooding the theatre with immobilising toxic gas, resulting in hundreds of deaths and illnesses.

MAYOR AGAINST NATURE

One might say that the struggle of humans against the forces of nature is eternal, except that you know that eventually the earth will win. Pompeii is history, New Orleans is drowned and Venice is sinking. Still, it remains the self-appointed mission of modern human to tame Mother Nature. And, in Moscow, this age-old battle is currently being waged by Mayor Yury Luzhkov, armed with his incredible, amazing weather machine.

The communist experiment represented one of humanity's most ambitious campaigns to conquer nature. Party leaders were blinded by Soviet science. Khrushchev issued a decree to convert the semi-arid Central Asian steppe into fertile grain fields and Brezhnev vowed to change the course of mighty Siberian rivers. While these projects came to naught, Soviet science did have its moments. It sent the first rocket to the moon and turned the world's fourth-largest lake, the Aral Sea, into a puddle. As a leading centre for military R&D, Moscow was bequeathed with a rich share of the technological inheritance of Soviet science.

The power of the mayor to alter the weather was first displayed for Moscow's 850th anniversary celebration in 1997. The forecast called for rain that day, but Luzhkov mobilised meteorologists to take to the skies. Eight military jets crisscrossed overhead, shooting silver iodide pellets and dry ice into the clouds, emptying them of moisture. The chemical mix has been refined and the aerial assault against the clouds is now a routine task on the eve of Moscow holidays.

The summer of 2002 was the hottest and driest in Moscow in over a century. A rash of forest fires in the surrounding environs cast stifling smog over the city, endangering the health of residents. Summoned by the mayor once again, Moscow meteorologists revealed their latest creation, a rainmaking machine. The small, cube-shaped metal cage, made of tungsten wires, was brought up to a rooftop in western Moscow, where it emitted a vertical flow of negatively charged oxygen ions. The flow pierced the smog shroud above, stirred the air at a higher level and raised the humidity. Incredibly, a light drizzle began to fall on the city that morning, providing at least temporary relief.

Score one for the humans in the battle between humans and nature. No big surprise to Muscovites, who already know that the city's chief executive usually gets his way. No one will rain on the mayor's parade, although he might rain on yours!

The Party after the Party

Russia's transition to the market economy came at enormous social cost. The formerly subsidised sectors of the economy, such as education, science and healthcare, were devastated. For many dedicated professionals, it became close to impossible to eke out a living in their chosen profession. Sadly, many of the older generation, whose hard-earned pensions were reduced to a pittance, paid the price for this transformation. Many were forced to beg and scrimp on the margins of Moscow's new marketplace.

Since 1999, however, Russia has recorded positive economic growth. After the devaluation of the rouble, domestic producers became more competitive and more profitable. A worldwide shortage of energy resources has heaped benefits on the economy. The Russian oil boom, going strong since 2000, has enabled the government to run budget surpluses, pay off its foreign debt and lower tax rates.

Moscow, in particular, has prospered. The city's congested roadways are replete with luxury vehicles. The new economy has spawned a small group of 'New Russians', who are alternately derided and envied for their garish displays of wealth. According to *Forbes* magazine, the Russian capital boasts the largest contingent of resident billionaires in the world. And in 2005, Yelena Baturina, property magnate and wife of Mayor Luzhkov, became Russia's first female billionaire.

2004	2005	2008
Putin is reelected president. Terrorism continues to rock the capital, as suicide bombers in Moscow make strikes on the metro, in airplanes and at rock concerts, leaving hundreds of people dead and injured.	Mikhail Khodorkovsky is sentenced to nine years in jail for fraud and tax evasion, following a trial seen as a pretext for the government to dismantle his company, Yukos Oil.	A former chairperson of Gazprom, Dmitry Medvedev, succeeds Putin as Russia's third elected president. One of his first acts is to install his predecessor as prime minister.

Following decades of an austere and prudish Soviet regime, Muscovites revelled in their new-found freedom. Liberation, libation, defiance and indulgence were all on open display. Those reared in a simpler time were no doubt shocked by the immodesty of the younger generation.

Finally, the economic rhythms of the city seemed to have steadied. Seven straight years of economic growth mean that wealth is trickling down beyond the 'New Russians'. In Moscow the burgeoning middle class endures a high cost of living, but enjoys unprecedented employment opportunities and a dizzying array of culinary, cultural and consumer choices.

In 2007 Mayor Luzhkov was reappointed for his fifth term in office. Under his oversight, the city continues to undergo a massive physical transformation, with industry emptying out of the historic centre and skyscrapers shooting up along the Moscow River. The population continues to climb, as fortune seekers arrive from the provinces and other parts of the former Soviet Union. And Moscow – political capital, economic powerhouse and cultural innovator – continues to lead the way as the most fast-dealing, free-wheeling city in Russia.

ARTS

Moscow has always been known for the richness of its culture, ranging from the classic to the progressive. Whether a Tchaikovsky opera or an Ostrovsky drama, the classical performing arts in Moscow are among the best – and cheapest – in the world. The Tretyakov Gallery (p118) and Pushkin Fine Arts Museum (p115) house internationally famous collections of Russian and Impressionist art. But New Russia comes with new forms of art and entertainment. This bohemian side of Moscow – be it a beatnik band at an underground club or an avant-garde exhibit at a postindustrial gallery – provides a glimpse of Russia's future. Sometimes intellectual and inspiring, sometimes debauched and depraved, it is *always* eye-opening.

LITERATURE

The love of literature is an integral part of Russian culture, as most Ivans and Olgas will wax rhapsodic on the Russian classics without any hesitation. With the end of Soviet censorship, the literati are gradually figuring out what to do with their new-found freedom. Slowly but surely, new authors are emerging, exploring literary genres from historical fiction to science fiction.

For a tour of Moscow's literary sights, see p142.

Romanticism in the Golden Age

Among the many ways that Peter and Catherine the Greats brought Westernisation and modernisation to Russia was the introduction of a modern alphabet. As such, during the Petrine era, it became increasingly acceptable to use popular language in literature. This development paved the way for two centuries of Russian literary prolificacy.

Romanticism was a reaction against the strict social rules and scientific rationalisation of previous periods, exalting emotion and aesthetics. Nobody embraced Russian romanticism more than the national bard, Alexander Pushkin (1799–1837). Pushkin was born in Moscow. Here, he met his wife Natalia Goncharova. The two were wed at the Church of Grand Ascension (p101) and lived for a time on ul Arbat (p100).

Pushkin's most celebrated drama, *Boris Godunov,* takes place in medieval Muscovy. As per the title, the plot centres on the historical events leading up to the Time of Troubles and its resolution with the election of Mikhail Romanov as tsar. The epic poem *Yevgeny Onegin* is set, in part, in imperial Moscow. Pushkin savagely ridicules its foppish, aristocratic society, despite being a fairly consistent fixture of it himself.

What Pushkin is to poetry, so is Leo Tolstoy (1828–1910) to realist fiction. Tolstoy is one of the most celebrated novelists, not only in Russia, but in the world. The depth of his characters and the vividness of his descriptions evoke 19th-century Russia at its most passionate. His novels *War and Peace* and *Anna Karenina,* both of which are set in Moscow, express his scepticism with rationalism, espousing the idea that history is the sum of an infinite number of individual actions. This theme – that human beings can only cope with, but not control, the events of their lives – is consistent with his Buddhist-influenced world view.

top picks

HISTORY BOOKS

- Aleksandr Rodchenko: The New Moscow (Margarita Tupitsyn) See the capital through the eyes of the great Soviet photographer.
- The Greatest Battle (Andrew Nagorski) Provides a new perspective on the horrors and heroics of the turning-point WWII battle.
- Lenin's Tomb (David Remnick) The *Washington Post* Moscow correspondent's entertaining and award-winning first-hand account of the collapse of the Soviet Union.
- Midnight Diaries (Boris Yeltsin) A truly insider perspective on the Yeltsin years, recounting tales of oligarchs and alcohol.
- Moscow: Governing the Socialist Metropolis (Timothy Colton) A comprehensive (937-page!) history of modern Moscow.

In the course of writing these great works, Tolstoy underwent a conversion to Christianity and his later works reflect this change. His final novel, *Resurrection,* is the tale of a nobleman who seeks redemption for earlier sins.

Tolstoy spent most of his time at his estate in Yasnaya Polyana, but he also had property in Moscow (p117), and he was a regular parishioner at the Church of St Nicholas of Khamovniki (p117).

Although Fyodor Dostoevsky (1821–81) is more closely associated with St Petersburg, he was actually born in Moscow (p93). He was among the first writers to navigate the murky waters of the human subconscious, blending powerful prose with psychology, philosophy and spirituality. Dostoevsky's best-known works, such as *Crime and Punishment,* were all written (and to a large degree, set) in his adopted city of St Petersburg. But bibliophiles assert that his early years in Moscow profoundly influenced his philosophical development.

Amid the epic novels of Pushkin, Tolstoy and Dostoevsky, an absurdist short-story writer such as Nikolai Gogol (1809–52) sometimes gets lost in the annals of Russian literature. But his troubled genius created some of Russian literature's most memorable characters, including Akaki Akakievich, tragicomic hero of *The Overcoat.*

Gogol spent most of his years living abroad, but it was his hilarious satire of life in Russia that earned him the respect of his contemporaries. *Dead Souls* is his masterpiece. This 'novel in verse' follows the scoundrel Chichikov as he attempts to buy and sell deceased serfs, or 'dead souls', in an absurd money-making scam.

After the novel's highly lauded publication in 1841, Gogol suffered from poor physical and mental health. While staying with friends in Moscow (now the Gogol Memorial Rooms, p101), in a fit of depression, he threw some of his manuscripts into the fire, including the second part of *Dead Souls,* which was not recovered in its entirety (the novel ends midsentence). The celebrated satirist died shortly thereafter and he is buried at Novodevichy Cemetery (p113).

Symbolism in the Silver Age

The late 19th century saw the rise of the symbolist movement, which emphasised individualism and creativity, purporting that artistic endeavours were exempt from the rules that bound other parts of society. The outstanding figures of this time were the novelists Vladimir Solovyov (1853–1900), Andrei Bely (1880–1934) and Alexander Blok (1880–1921), as well as the poets Sergei Yesenin (1895–1925) and Vladimir Mayakovsky (1893–1930).

Although Bely lived in Moscow for a time (p101), he is remembered for his mysterious novel *Petersburg.* He was also respected for his essays and philosophical discourses, making him one of the most important writers of the symbolist movement.

Mayakovsky was a futurist playwright and poet, and he acted as the revolution's official bard. He lived near Lyubyanskaya pl, where his flat is now a museum (p79). He devoted his creative energy to social activism and propaganda on behalf of the new regime. But the romantic soul was unlucky in love and life. As is wont to happen, he became disillusioned with the Soviet Union, as reflected in his satirical plays. In one of his last letters, he wrote, 'She did devour me, lousy, snuffling dear Mother Russia, like a sow devouring her piglet'.

He shot himself in 1930 and is buried at Novodevichy Cemetery (p113). He is memorialised at Triumfalnaya pl, site of Mayakvoskaya metro.

Revolutionary Literature

The immediate aftermath of 1917 saw a creative upswing in Russia. Inspired by social change, writers carried over these principles into their work, pushing revolutionary ideas and groundbreaking styles.

The trend was temporary, of course. The Bolsheviks were no connoisseurs of culture, and the new leadership did not appreciate literature unless it directly supported the goals of communism. Some writers managed to write within the system, penning some excellent poetry and plays in the 1920s; however, most found little inspiration in the prevailing climate of art 'serving the people'. Stalin announced that writers were 'engineers of the human soul' and as such had a responsibility to write in a partisan direction.

The clampdown on diverse literary styles culminated in the late 1930s with the creation of socialist realism, a literary form created to promote the needs of the state, praise industrialisation and demonise social misfits. Alexey Tolstoy (1883–1945), for example, wrote historical novels comparing Stalin to Peter the Great and recounting the glories of the Russian civil war.

Literature of Dissent

While Stalin's propaganda machine was churning out novels with titles such as *How the Steel Was Tempered,* the literary community was secretly writing about life under a tyranny. Many accounts of Soviet life were printed in *samizdat* (underground) publications, secretly circulated among the literary community. Now-famous novels such as Rybakov's *Children of the Arbat* were published in Russia only with the loosening of censorship under *glasnost.*

Meanwhile, the Soviet Union's most celebrated writers were silenced in their own country, while their works received international acclaim. *Dr Zhivago,* for example, was published in 1956, but it was officially printed in the Soviet Union only 30 years later.

Boris Pasternak (1890–1960) lived in a country estate on the outskirts of Moscow (Peredelkino, p219). *Dr Zhivago's* title character is torn between two lovers, as his life is ravaged by the revolution and the civil war. The novel was unacceptable to the Soviet regime, not because the characters were antirevolutionary, but because they were apolitical, valuing their individual lives over social transformation. The novel was awarded the Nobel Prize for Literature in 1958 but Pasternak was forced to reject it.

Mikhail Bulgakov (1890–1940) was a prolific playwright and novelist who lived near Patriarch's Ponds (p92). He wrote many plays that were performed at the Moscow Art Theatre, some of which were apparently enjoyed by Stalin. But later his plays were banned, and he had difficulty finding work. Most of his novels take place in Moscow, including *Fatal Eggs, Heart of a Dog* and, most famously, *The Master and Margarita.*

The post*glasnost* era of the 1980s and 1990s uncovered a huge library of work that had been suppressed during the Soviet period. Authors such as Yevgeny Zamyatin, Daniil Kharms, Anatoly Rybakov, Venedict Erofeev and Andrei Bitov – banned in the Soviet Union – are now recognised for their cutting-edge commentary and significant contributions to world literature.

top picks

LITERARY SIGHTS

- Tolstoy Estate-Museum (p117)
- Bulgakov House-Museum (p92)
- Gogol Memorial Rooms (p101)
- Dostoevsky House-Museum (p93)
- Mayakovsky Museum (p79)
- Chekhov House-Museum (p98)

Contemporary Literature

Russia's contemporary literary scene is largely based in Moscow and, to some degree, abroad, as émigré writers continue to be inspired and disheartened by their motherland.

Check out what your neighbour is reading as she rides the metro: more than likely, it's a celebrity rag or a murder mystery. Action-packed thrillers and detective stories have become wildly popular in the 21st century, with Darya Dontsova, Alexandra Marinina and Boris Akunin ranking amongst the best-selling and most widely translated authors.

MOSCOW FICTION

- Anna Karenina (Leo Tolstoy) Tells of the tragedy of a woman who violates the rigid sexual code of her time, and offers a legitimate alternative for readers who don't have time for *War and Peace.*
- Dead Souls (Nikolai Gogol) A biting satire that gives a special, cynical insight into 19th-century provincial Russia.
- The Twelve (Alexander Blok) Pretty much a love letter to Lenin. Ironically, Blok later grew deeply disenchanted with the revolution, consequently fell out of favour and died a sad, lonely poet.
- The Ordeal (Alexey Tolstoy) A trilogy that takes place during the revolution and civil war. Alexey, not to be confused with his more famous ancestor, was one of the few Soviet authors who managed to produce serious literary work without being censored.
- Dr Zhivago (Boris Pasternak) Recounts the romantic tale of a doctor who is separated from his lover by the events of the revolution. The author was not allowed to accept the Nobel Prize that was awarded to this dramatic novel.
- The Master and Margarita (Mikhail Bulgakov) The Devil turns up in Moscow to cause all manner of anarchy and make idiots of the system and its lackeys. This darkly comic novel is the most telling fiction to come out of the Soviet Union.
- Children of the Arbat (Anatoly Rybakov) Based on the author's own experiences as an idealistic youth on the eve of the Great Purges. This tragic novel paints a vivid portrait of 1930s Russia.
- Moscow to the End of the Line (Venedict Erofeev) Written in 1970, this novel recounts a drunken man's train trip to visit his lover and child on the outskirts of the capital. As the journey progresses, the tale becomes darker and more hallucinogenic. *Moscow Stations*, by the same author, is another bleakly funny novella recounting alcohol-induced adventures.
- On the Golden Porch (Tatyana Tolstaya) A collection of short stories focusing on the domestic life of regular people – big souls in little flats – in the 1990s.
- The Slynx (Tatyana Tolstaya) The celebrated author's earlier, lesser-known novel, is set in a post–nuclear war Moscow that seems strangely similar to Moscow in the 1990s. In this dystopia, an uneducated scribe learns enough history to start his own revolution.
- Homo Zapiens (Viktor Pelevin) Tells the tale of a literature student who takes a job as a copywriter for New Russian gangsters, offering a darkly comic commentary on contemporary Russia. Pelevin won the 1993 Russian 'Little Booker' Prize for short stories.
- Russian Beauty (Victor Erofeyev) The tale of a wily beauty from the provinces who sleeps her way to the top of the Moscow social scene. She finds herself pregnant just about the same time she finds God. Caustically funny and overtly bawdy, this best seller in Russia has been translated into 27 languages.
- Day of the Oprichnik (Vladimir Sorokin) Describes Russia in the year 2028 as a nationalist country ruled with an iron fist that has shut itself off from the West by building a wall.
- The Winter Queen (Boris Akunin) One in the series of popular detective novels featuring the foppish Erast Fandorin as a member of the 19th-century Moscow police force. Several of these are now being made into movies (p49).
- Casual (Oksana Robsky) An autobiographical novel that became an instant best seller, providing a rare glimpse inside a world of gated mansions, bodyguards, luxury spas, chauffeured cars and all-night parties – a world that everybody in Moscow sees but few people actually experience.

Realist writers such as Tatyana Tolstaya and Ludmilla Petrushevskaya engage readers with their moving portraits of everyday people living their everyday lives. Meanwhile, social critics such as Viktor Pelevin, Dmitry Bykov and Vladimir Sorokin continue the Soviet literary tradition of using dark humour and fantastical storylines to provide scathing social commentary.

VISUAL ARTS

Icons

Up until the 17th century, religious icons were Russia's key art form. Originally painted by monks as a spiritual exercise, icons are images intended to aid the veneration of the holy subjects they depict, and are sometimes believed able to grant luck, wishes or even miracles. They're most commonly found on the iconostasis (screen) of a church.

Traditional rules decreed that only Christ, the Virgin, angels, saints and scriptural events could be painted on icons – all of which were supposed to be copies of a limited number of approved prototype images. Christ images include the Pantokrator (All-Ruler) and the Mandilion, the latter called 'not made by hand' because it was supposedly developed from the imprint of Christ's face on St Veronica's handkerchief. Icons were traditionally painted in tempera (inorganic pigment mixed with a binder such as egg yolk) on wood.

The beginning of a distinct Russian icon tradition came when artists in Novgorod started to draw on local folk art in their representation of people, producing sharply outlined figures with softer faces and introducing lighter colours, including pale yellows and

top picks

ART MUSEUMS

- Museum of Private Collections (p115)
- New Tretyakov Gallery (p119)
- Pushkin Fine Arts Museum (p115)
- Rerikh Museum (p116)
- Tretyakov Gallery (p118)

greens. The earliest outstanding painter was Theophanes the Greek (1340–1405), or Feofan Grek in Russian. Working in Byzantium, Novgorod and Moscow, Theophanes brought a new delicacy and grace to the form. His finest works are in the Annunciation Cathedral of the Moscow Kremlin (p71).

Andrei Rublyov (1370–1430), a monk at the Trinity Monastery of St Sergius and Andronikov Monastery, was the greatest Russian icon painter. His most famous work is the dreamy *Old Testament Trinity,* in Moscow's Tretyakov Gallery (p118).

The layperson Dionysius, the leading late-15th-century icon painter, elongated his figures and refined the use of colour. Sixteenth-century icons grew smaller and more crowded, their figures more realistic and Russian-looking. In 17th-century Moscow, Simon Ushakov (1626–86) moved towards Western religious painting with the use of perspective and architectural backgrounds.

Peredvizhniki

The major artistic force of the 19th century was the Peredvizhniki (Wanderers) movement, which saw art as a vehicle for promoting national awareness and social change. The movement gained its name from the touring exhibitions with which it widened its audience. These artists were patronised by the brothers Pavel and Sergei Tretyakov (after whom the Tretyakov Gallery is named). Artists included Vasily Surikov (1848–1916), who painted vivid Russian historical scenes; Nikolai Ghe (1831–94), who depicted biblical and historical scenes; and Ilya Repin (1884–1930), perhaps the best loved of all Russian artists, whose works ranged from social criticism *(Barge Haulers on the Volga),* to history *(Zaporozhie Cossacks Writing a Letter to the Turkish Sultan),* to portraits. Many Peredvizhniki masterpieces are on display at the Tretyakov Gallery (p118).

Later in the century, industrialist Savva Mamontov was a significant patron of the arts, promoting a Russian revivalist movement. His Abramtsevo estate (p221) near Moscow became an artists' colony. Victor Vasnetsov (1848–1926) was a Russian-revivalist painter and architect who is famous for his historical paintings with fairytale subjects. In 1894, Vasnetsov designed his own house in Moscow, which is now a small museum (p86). He also designed the original building for the Tretyakov Gallery. Nikolai Rerikh (1874–1947) – known internationally as Nicholas Roerich – was an artist whose fantastical artwork is characterised by rich, bold colours, primitive style and mystical themes. His paintings are on display at the Rerikh Museum (p116) and the Museum of Oriental Art (p100).

The late-19th-century genius Mikhail Vrubel (1856–1910) was unique in form and style. He was inspired by sparkling Byzantine and Venetian mosaics. His panels on the sides of Hotel Metropol are some of his best work (see the boxed text, p206).

Avant-garde

In the 20th century, Russian art became a mishmash of groups, styles and 'isms', as it absorbed decades of European change in a few years. It finally gave birth to its own avant-garde futurist movements.

BACKGROUND ARTS

43

Mikhail Larionov (1881–1964) and Natalya Goncharova (1881–1962) developed neoprimitivism, a movement based on popular arts and primitive icons. A few years later, Kazimir Malevich (1878–1935) announced the arrival of suprematism. His utterly abstract geometrical shapes (with the black square representing the ultimate 'zero form') finally freed art from having to depict the material world and made it a doorway to higher realities. Another famed futurist, who managed to escape subordinate 'isms', was Vladimir Mayakovsky, who was also a poet (see p40). Works by all of these artists are on display at the New Tretyakov Gallery (p119), as well as the Moscow Museum of Modern Art (p90).

An admirer of Malevich, Alexander Rodchenko (1891–1956) was one of the founders of the constructivist movement. He was a graphic designer, sculptor and painter, but he is best known for his innovative photography. Rodchenko often took his photos from unexpected or unusual angles to give his viewers a new perspective on the subject. His first published photomontage was an illustration of a Mayakovsky poem, the first of many collaborations with the artist-poet. Rodchenko's influence on graphic design is immeasurable, as many of his techniques were used widely later in the 20th century.

Soviet Era Art

Futurists turned to the needs of the revolution – education, posters and banners – with enthusiasm. They had a chance to act on their theories of how art shapes society. But, at the end of the 1920s, abstract art fell out of favour and was branded 'formalist'. The Communist Party wanted 'socialist realism', or realist art that advanced the goals of the glorious socialist revolution. Images of striving workers, heroic soldiers and inspiring leaders took over from abstraction. Plenty of examples of this realism are on display at the New Tretyakov Gallery (p119). Two million sculptures of Lenin and Stalin dotted the country – Malevich ended up painting penetrating portraits and doing designs for Red Square parades; Mayakovsky committed suicide.

After Stalin, an avant-garde 'conceptualist' underground was allowed to form. Ilya Kabakov (1933–) painted, or sometimes just arranged the debris of everyday life, to show the gap between the promises and realities of Soviet existence. Erik Bulatov's (1933–) 'Sotsart' style pointed to the devaluation of language by ironically reproducing Soviet slogans and depicting words disappearing over the horizon.

In 1962 the authorities set up a show of 'unofficial' art at the Manezh Exhibition Centre; Khrushchev called it 'dogshit' and sent it back underground. In the mid-1970s it resurfaced in the Moscow suburbs – only to be literally bulldozed back down. It became common practice for these artists to officially work as book illustrators and graphic designers, but to do their own more abstract work in secret.

Contemporary Art

In the immediate post-Soviet years contemporary painters of note abandoned Russia for the riches of the West. Today, with increased economic prosperity, many of the most promising young artists are choosing to stay put. There is unprecedented interest in contemporary art, as entrepreneurs are investing their new-found wealth in established and up-and-coming artists. Industrial space is being converted into art galleries such as Winzavod (p78) and Garazh Centre for Contemporary Culture (p130).

One of the best-known painters in Russia today is the religious artist Ilya Glazunov (1930–; see p116), who was a staunch defender of the Russian Orthodox cultural tradition. More notorious than popular is the artist and architect Zurab Tsereteli (1934–), whose monumental buildings and statues (many are also monumentally ugly) grace Moscow – see p113 and p117.

Artists are now freer than they ever were in the past to depict all aspects of Russian life (see the boxed text, opposite), with even the government pitching in to fund prestigious events such as the Moscow Biennale of Contemporary Art (p21). That said, contemporary artists and curators continue to be harassed, especially if they tackle such sensitive topics as the war in Chechnya, the Russian Orthodox Church or the Russian government (see the boxed text, p79).

THE ARTIST'S LIFE

Stanislav Shuripa is an artist who has been living and working in Moscow for 25 years. He acted as a curator at the Second Moscow Biennale of Contemporary Art and his sculptures have been exhibited at Winzavod, among other venues. We spoke with Stas about the artist's life in Moscow.

What's it like to live in Moscow as an artist? In recent years the life of artists in Moscow has become more interesting because there is a boom in public interest. The record growth in the art scene means a growth of institutions, media, up-and-coming artists and young curators. It is exciting when you feel like what you do is interesting for other people.

Does this also mean there's a boost in creative energy, producing new ideas and new forms of art? As for creative energy it is precisely true. There are a lot of possibilities for creative work, not only in my area of work but in many spheres. As for new ideas, it is more difficult to say. There are many ideas. Time will tell how new they are, and how important. It's an exciting environment, but it's also difficult because it's moving so fast.

How has Moscow's art scene changed in recent years? Ten years ago, nobody would have imagined that this would be happening. In the 1990s we had few structures or institutions – the art world was practically nonexistent. Now the scene takes on many different shapes – the art world has many levels. For example, right now there is the huge biennale of emerging art (p21), with many high-quality exhibitions of up-and-coming artists. There are new private museums, and other new structures showing exhibitions. So it means there are many more outlets for artists.

Do you feel that political pressure limits artistic expression? Personally, I do not feel this. In general, in terms of government oppression, nobody would say they feel it. There are incidents – you read about it in the newspapers. But the critical discussion arises between art and society, not between art and state. In general, all three players are trying to find a common language. The state sponsors exhibitions; it helps young artists to find studio space and funding.

I do notice the news – both here and in the West – that Russia is taking some steps toward dictatorship. We are not necessarily happy with the way things are progressing. But on a practical level, it's not an oppressive environment. Artists are more or less able to express whatever they want.

Where is the best place for visitors to Moscow to see and buy contemporary art? If they are thinking of buying, I would advise them to go to one of the leading galleries. Four of them are in Winzavod (p78). They are the most experienced and most professional galleries in Moscow. Art Strelka (p155) is a little bit different. It is also meant to be public, but it has a more festive atmosphere. They have openings every three weeks on Sundays. The kind of art is similar, but Winzavod is more upscale, and the events are more formal and prepared. Art Strelka is more democratic.

MUSIC

The classics never go out of style. This is certainly true for music in Moscow, where Mussorgsky, Stravinsky and especially Tchaikovsky still feature in concert halls on an almost-daily basis. The atmosphere in these places is a little stuffy, but the musicianship is first rate and the compositions are timeless. Music in Moscow takes many forms, however, and these days Western rock, blues and jazz are also ubiquitous in the capital.

Classical

The defining period of Russian classical music was from the 1860s to 1900. As Russian composers (and painters and writers) struggled to find a national identity, several influential schools formed, from which some of Russia's most famous composers and finest music emerged. The so-called Group of Five, which included Modest Mussorgsky (1839–81) and Nikolai Rimsky-Korsakov (1844–1908), believed that a radical departure was necessary, and they looked to *byliny* (folk music) for themes. Mussorgsky penned *Pictures at an Exhibition* and the opera *Boris Gudunov*; Rimsky-Korsakov is best known for *Scheherazade.*

Pyotr Tchaikovsky (1840–93) also embraced Russian folklore and music, as well as the disciplines of Western European composers. Tchaikovsky is widely regarded as the father of Russian national composers. His output, including the magnificent *1812 Overture;* his concertos and symphonies; the ballets *Swan Lake, Sleeping Beauty* and *The Nutcracker;* and his opera *Yevgeny Onegin* are among the world's most popular classical works. They are certainly the shows that are staged most often at the Bolshoi and other theatres around Moscow.

Following in Tchaikovsky's romantic footsteps was Sergei Rachmaninov (1873–1943) and the innovative Igor Stravinsky (1882–1971). Both fled Russia after the revolution. Stravinsky's *The Rite of Spring,* which created a furore at its first performance in Paris, and *The Firebird* were influenced by Russian folk music. Sergei Prokofiev (1891–1953), who also left Soviet Russia but returned in 1934, wrote the scores for Eisenstein's films *Alexander Nevsky* and *Ivan the Terrible,* the ballet *Romeo and Juliet,* and *Peter and the Wolf,* so beloved by music teachers of young children. His work, however, was condemned for 'formalism' towards the end of his life.

Similarly, the beliefs of Dmitry Shostakovich (1906–75) led to him being alternately praised and condemned by the Soviet government. He wrote brooding, bizarrely dissonant works, as well as accessible traditional classical music. After official condemnation by Stalin, Shostakovich's *7th Symphony* (also known as the *Leningrad Symphony*) brought him honour and international standing when it was performed by the Leningrad Philharmonic during the Siege of Leningrad. The authorities changed their minds again and banned his anti-Soviet music in 1948, then 'rehabilitated' him after Stalin's death.

Classical opera was performed regularly during the Soviet period, and continues to be popular. Nowadays, the top theatres – especially the Bolshoi – are attempting to showcase new works by contemporary composers, as well as unknown works that were censored or banned in the past.

top picks

MOSCOW ALBUMS

- **200km/h in the Wrong Lane** The English-language debut of the sexy, pseudo-lesbian duo tATu earned the Moscow natives the devotion of sugar-sweet pop lovers around the world.
- **Best of the Red Army Choir** The two-disc album uses classic folk songs and a few Soviet gems to show off the impressive vocals of Russia's celebrated choral group.
- **Eto bylo tak davno (That was so long ago)** The first studio recording of Moscow musicians Mashina Vremeni (Time Machine) made the legendary group the tsars of 'russky rock'.
- **Glubina** The latest album by rising stars Deti Picasso was named Best Russian Album of 2006 according to *Rolling Stone, Play* and *Afisha*.
- **Horowitz in Moscow** Both emotionally moving and musically magnificent, this live recording showcases the performance of world-renowned pianist Vladimir Horowitz when he returned to his homeland after almost 60 years away.
- **Mergers & Acquisitions** The insightful Ilya Lagushenko leads Moscow band Mumiy Troll in this album, providing sharp commentary and social criticism.
- **Moscow** The live album of heavy-metal rocker Valery Kipelov, who once fronted the group Aria, known as the 'Russian Iron Maiden'.
- **Peter & the Wolf** Each character in this children's classic is represented by a particular instrument and musical theme. Sergei Prokofiev wrote the masterpiece in 1936, after he returned to Moscow to live out his final years.

In March 2005 the Bolshoi premiered *Rosenthal's Children,* with music by Leonid Desyatnikov and words by Vladimir Sorokin, its first new opera in 26 years. The following year, in honour of the 100th anniversary of Dmitry Shostakovich's birthday, the Bolshoi ballet premiered the composer's ballet *Bolt.* Prior to that, the ballet was performed exactly once – in 1931 – before it was banned for its 'most serious formalist errors'. The next year again saw the previously unknown 'second version' of Mussorgsky's *Boris Godunov.* More often, though, Moscow theatres and performance halls feature classics from the 19th and 20th centuries that Russians know and love.

Rock

Russian music is not all about classical composers. Ever since the 'bourgeois' Beatles filtered through in the 1960s, Russians both young and old have been keen to sign up for the pop revolution. Starved of decent equipment and the chance to record or perform to big audiences, Russian rock groups initially developed underground. All music was circulated by illegal tapes known as *magizdat,* passed from listener to listener; concerts were held in remote halls in city suburbs. By the 1970s – the Soviet hippie era – the music had developed a huge following among the disaffected, distrustful youth.

Andrei Makarevich was the leader of Mashina Vremeni (Time Machine), now considered one of the patriarch groups of Soviet rock. Inspired by the Beatles, the band formed in 1968, playing simple guitar riffs and singable melodies. Even today, Mashina Vremeni remains popular across generations.

The god of Russian rock, though, was Viktor Tsoy, front person of the group Kino; the band's classic album is 1988's *Gruppa Krovi* (Blood Group). Tsoy's early death in a 1990 car crash sealed his legendary status. To this day, there is a graffiti-covered wall on ul Arbat that is dedicated to Tsoy, and fans gather on the anniversary of his death (August 15) to play his music.

Many contemporary favourites on the Russian rock scene have been playing together since the early days. One of the most notable Moscow bands (originally from Vladivostok) is Mumiy Troll, led by the literate, androgynous Ilya Lagushenko. After 25 years, the band continues to produce innovative stuff. Its latest studio album, AMBA, was released on the symbolic date of 7 July 2007.

Gaining worldwide renown is B-2, whose members, Shura and Leva, now reside in Australia. This 'post-punk' duo often appears at Moscow rock festivals, including the 2005 concert Live-8 on Red Square. The goth rocker Linda, a home-town favourite, also used the international event to show off her sound, which is an eclectic blend of world and dance music.

Also based in Moscow, Deti Picasso is an Armenian-Russian folk-rock band whose beautiful lead singer, Gaya Arutyunyan, has a haunting voice. The unique sound blends the vocals with acoustic guitar and a string quartet, adding in the occasional Armenian chant. Also making a name for herself in the folk scene, art-rock-folk vocalist Pelageya is apparently Putin's favourite.

The likes of techno-pop girl duo tATu and pretty-boy singer Dima Bilan (winner of 2008's Eurovision Song Contest) are the tame international faces of Russia's contemporary music scene. The former is from Moscow, host of the 2009 Eurovision Song Contest.

Meanwhile, Moscow clubs are filled with garage bands, new wave, punk, hard-rock and many Beatles cover bands.

BALLET

Ballet in Russia evolved as an offshoot of French dance combined with Russian folk and peasant dance techniques. As a part of his efforts toward Westernisation, Peter the Great invited artists from France to perform this new form of dance. In 1738 French dance master Jean Baptiste Lande established a school of dance in St Petersburg's Winter Palace, the precursor to the famed Vaganova School of Choreography. The Bolshoi Opera & Ballet Company was founded a few years later in 1776.

But the father of Russian ballet is considered to be the French dancer and choreographer Marius Petipa (1819–1910), who acted as principal dancer and premier ballet master of the Imperial Theatre. All told he produced more than 60 full ballets, including the classics *Sleeping Beauty* and *Swan Lake*.

At the turn of the 20th century, Sergei Diaghilev's Ballets Russes took Europe by storm. The stage decor was unlike anything seen before. Painted by artists such as Alexander Benois, Mikhail Larianov, Natalia Goncharova and Leon Bakst, it suspended disbelief and shattered the audience's sense of illusion.

During Soviet rule ballet enjoyed a privileged status, which allowed companies such as the Bolshoi to maintain a level of lavish production and high performance standards. In the 1960s, Yury Grigorovich emerged as a bright, new choreographer, with *Spartacus, Ivan the Terrible* and other successes.

Grigorovich directed the company for over 30 years, but not without controversy. In the late 1980s he came to loggerheads with some of his leading dancers. Stars such as Maya Plisetskaya, Ekaterina Maximova and Vladimir Vasiliev resigned, accusing him of being 'brutal' and 'Stalinist'. With encouragement from President Yeltsin, Grigorovich finally resigned in 1995, prompting his loyal dancers to stage the Bolshoi's first-ever strike.

Under artistic director Vladimir Vasiliev, the Bolshoi commenced a turnaround. During the years of his stewardship, productions included *Swan Lake* and *Giselle,* starring dancers such as Nina Anaiashvili, Sergei Filin and Svetlana Lunkina. Reviews were initially positive, but trouble was brewing. Politics and finances made Vasiliev's task near impossible, and he soon came under fire for mismanagement.

A power struggle ensued, with the ever-present Yury Grigorovich playing a leading role. Finally, in 2004, the rising star Alexey Ratmansky was appointed artistic director. Born in 1968 in Ukraine, Ratmansky is young but accomplished. Of his more than 20 ballets, *Dreams of Japan* was awarded a prestigious Golden Mask award in 1998. Yury Grigorovich continues to play an active role in Moscow's ballet scene, and the Bolshoi often performs his classic compositions. The Bolshoi's brightest star is currently Maria Alexandrova.

The Bolshoi is Moscow's most celebrated (and therefore most political) ballet company, but other companies in the city have equally talented dancers and directors. Both the Moscow Classical Ballet Theatre and the Stanislavsky and Nemirovich-Danchenko Musical Theatre (p190) stage excellent performances of the Russian classics.

The New Ballet (p189), directed by Aida Chernova and Sergei Starukhin, stages a completely different kind of dance. Dubbed 'plastic ballet', it combines dance with pantomime and drama. Productions vary widely, incorporating elements such as folk tales, poetry and improvised jazz. This bizarre, playful performance art is a refreshing addition to Moscow's dance scene.

CINEMA & TELEVISION
Cinema
Russian – or rather Soviet – cinema first flourished shortly after the revolution. Sergei Eisenstein's *Battleship Potemkin* (1925) remains one of the landmarks of world cinema, famous for its Odessa Steps sequence recreated in many other films, most notably Brian de Palma's *The Untouchables.* Charlie Chaplin described *Battleship Potemkin* as 'the best film in the world'. It and scores of other films made Moscow's film studios the most active in the country during the 20th century.

During the communist era the fate of any movie was decided by the vast bureaucracy of Moscow-based Goskino, which funded films and also distributed them. It was known for its aversion to risks (which, during the Stalin era, was undoubtedly smart).

During a 1986 congress of Soviet filmmakers held in Moscow, *glasnost* touched the USSR's movie industry. By a large vote the old and conservative directors were booted out of the leadership and renegades demanding more freedom were put in their place. During the remaining years of communism, over 250 previously banned films were released. For the first time, films began to explore real, contemporary issues.

By the time Nikita Mikhalkov's *Burnt by the Sun* won the best foreign movie Oscar in 1994, Russian film production was suffering. Funding had dried up during the economic chaos of the early 1990s and audiences couldn't afford to go to the cinema anyway.

Moscow's film industry has made a remarkable comeback since then. MosFilm, the successor to Goskino, is one of the largest production companies in the world, producing almost all of Russia's film, TV and video programming (see p108). Moscow is indeed the Russian Hollywood. Unfortunately, just like its American counterpart, the industry does not leave much room for artsy, independent films that are not likely to be blockbusters.

But there is no shortage of blockbusters. *The Turkish Gambit,* a drama set during the Russo-Turkish War, broke all post-Soviet box-office records in 2005. Another historical drama, *The State Counsellor* (2005), was based on a novel by Boris Akunin and produced by Mikhalkov, practically guaranteeing its success.

The glossy vampire thriller *Night Watch* (2004) struck box-office gold both at home and abroad, leading to an equally successful sequel, *Day Watch* (2006), and to Kazakhstan-born director Timur Bekmambetov being lured to Hollywood. *Twilight Watch,* the final part of the trilogy, was set for release in 2009.

Bekmambetov also directed *Irony of Fate: Continuation* (2007), a follow-up to the classic 1970s comedy. Simultaneously released on 1000 screens across the nation, the movie was

MOSCOW FILMS

- Irony of Fate (*Ironiya Sudby ili s Legkim Parom;* 1975) Directed by Eldar Ryazanov, this is a classic and national favourite screened on TV every New Year's eve. After a mind-bending party in Moscow, the protagonist wakes up (unbeknown to him) in St Petersburg. Lo and behold, his key fits into the lock of a building that looks exactly like his at the same address in a different town. Comedy ensues.

- Moscow Doesn't Believe in Tears (1980) Directed by Vladimir Menshov, this chick flick bagged the best foreign language film Oscar. Vera Alentova plays Katya, single mum and Soviet everywoman, battling through life in the capital between the late 1950s and late 1970s.

- Little Vera (1989) Vasily Pichul's ground-breaking film caused a sensation with its frank portrayal of a family in chaos (exhausted wife, drunken husband, rebellious daughter) and its sexual frankness – mild by Western standards but startling to the Soviet audience.

- Burnt by the Sun (1994) The story of a loyal apparatchik who becomes a victim of Stalin's purges. Mikhalkov's celebrated film won an Oscar for best foreign film.

- Brother (Brat; 1997) A gangster drama by Alexei Balabanov that portrays the harshness of post-Soviet Russia. A geeky kid – played by superstar Sergei Brodov – returns from his army service and joins his brother working as a hit man in St Petersburg. The sequel, *Brat 2* (2000), follows the star to the capital; like most sequels, it does not live up to the original.

- Night Watch (*Nochnoy Dozor;* 2004) and Day Watch (*Dnevnoy Dozor;* 2006) A Russian mix of *The Matrix* and *Dracula,* the glossy sci-fi fantasy thrillers were directed by Timur Bekmambetov. The third was due for a 2009 release.

- You I Love (*Ya Lyublu Tebya;* 2004) Directed by Olga Stolpovskaya and Dmitry Troitsky, this quirky, independent film is an offbeat and sometimes charming tale of modern love in Moscow.

- The State Councellor *(Statsky Sovetnik;* 2005) A blockbuster based on a tsarist thriller penned by Boris Akunin (see the boxed text, p42). It is directed by that old warhorse of Russian cinema Nikita Mikhailkov, who costars in it alongside Oleg Menshikov, heart throb of a million Russian housewives.

poorly reviewed but widely watched. The *Lord of the Rings*–style *Wolfhound* (2007) became an instant cult classic among Russian fantasy fanatics. These films helped Russian cinema clock up record takings of US$565 million in 2007.

Russian directors are still turning out challenging, art-house films. In 2003 Moscow director Andrei Zvyagintsev came home from Venice with the Golden Lion, awarded for his moody thriller *The Return.* His follow-up film, *The Banishment,* refers to the end of paradise for a couple whose marriage is falling apart. In 2006 stage director Ivan Vyrypaev won the small Golden Lion for his cinematic debut, the tragic love story *Euphoria.*

Released in 2007, Mikhalkov's latest, *12,* is based on Sidney Lumet's *12 Angry Men.* The Oscar-nominated film follows a jury deliberating over the trial of a Chechen teenager accused of murdering his father, who was an officer in the Russian army. Vladimir Putin is quoted as saying that it 'brought a tear to the eye'.

Every year in June, the Moscow International Film Festival (p22) offers a venue for directors of independent films from Russia and abroad to compete for international recognition. In 2007 the winning film, from Russian director Vera Storozheva, was *Travelling with Pets,* in which a recently widowed woman discovers a new life for herself.

TELEVISION

Entertainment programming on TV is dominated by crime series, in which shaven-headed veterans of the war in Chechnya pin down conspiring oligarchs and politicians. That said, Russian TV does provide a wide choice of programs, some of which are modelled on Western formats. Reality TV, for example, has spawned Russian versions of American Idol (*Fabrika Zvyozd,* or 'Star Factory'), the Real World (*Dom,* or 'House') and Survivor (*Posledny Geroy,* or 'The Last Hero').

Programs do include high-quality, educational shows – documentaries shown have been especially good in the last few years. Kultura is an excellent national, noncommercial channel dedicated to arts and culture.

Other unconventional channels have recently emerged, reflecting social trends. Zvezda (Star) belongs to the Defence Ministry and is supposed to encourage young people to serve in the army. Spas TV is designed to summon lost souls under the auspices of the Orthodoxy. And the English-language Russia Today has launched an onslaught of Kremlin propaganda for Western audiences.

THEATRE

Moscow's oldest theatre, the Maly Theatre, was established in 1756 upon the decree of Empress Elizabeth. But Russia's theatre really started to flourish under the patronage of drama-lover Catherine the Great, who set up the Imperial Theatre Administration and herself penned several plays. During her reign Moscow playwright Denis Fonvizin wrote *The Brigadier* (1769) and *The Minor* (1791), satirical comedies that are still performed today.

Alexander Ostrovsky (1823–1886) was a prominent playwright who lived in Zamoskvorechie (see p124) and based many of his plays on the merchants and nobles who were his neighbours. As the director of the Maly Theatre, he is credited with raising the reputation of that institution as a respected drama theatre and school. Other 19th-century dramatists included Alexander Pushkin, whose drama *Boris Godunov* (1830) later was used as the libretto for the Mussorgsky opera; Nikolai Gogol, whose tragic farce *The Government Inspector* (1836) was said to be a favourite play of Nicholas I; and Ivan Turgenev, whose languid *A Month In The Country* (1849) laid the way for most famous Russian playwright of all: Anton Chekhov (1860–1904).

Chekhov lived on the Garden Ring in Presnya (see p98), though he spent much of his time at his country estate in Melikhovo (p219). In 1898 Konstantin Stanislavsky implemented his innovative approach of method acting and made Anton Chekhov a success (see the boxed text, p192). Chekhov's *The Seagull, The Three Sisters, The Cherry Orchard* and *Uncle Vanya*, all of which take the angst of the provincial middle class as their theme, owed much of their success to their 'realist' productions at the Moscow Art Theatre.

Through the Soviet period, theatre remained popular, not least because it was one of the few areas of artistic life where a modicum of freedom of expression was permitted. Stalin famously said of Bulgakov's play *White Guard* that, although it had been written by an enemy, it still deserved to be staged because of the author's outstanding talent. Bulgakov is perhaps the only person dubbed an 'enemy' by Stalin and never persecuted.

Others were not so fortunate. The rebellious director of the Taganka Theatre, Yury Lyubimov, was sent into exile as a result of his controversial plays. The avant-garde actor-director Vsevolod Meyerhold suffered an even worse fate. Not only was his Moscow theatre closed down, but he was imprisoned and later tortured and executed as a traitor.

Today, Moscow's theatre scene is as lively as those in London and New York. The capital hosts over 40 theatres, which continue to entertain and provoke audiences. Notable directors include Kama Gingkas, who works with the Moscow Art Theatre (p192) and Pytor Fomenko, who heads up Moscow's Fomenko Studio Theatre (p192).

Gaining an international reputation are brothers Oleg and Vladimir Presnyakov, who cowrite and direct their plays under the joint name Presnyakov Brothers; they've been praised for their plays' natural-sounding dialogue and sardonic wit. *Terrorism,* their best-known work, has played around the world.

CIRCUS

While Western circuses grow smaller and scarcer, the Russian versions are like those from childhood stories – prancing horses with acrobats on their backs, snarling lions and tigers, heart-stopping high-wire artists and hilarious clowns. No wonder the circus remains highly popular, with around half the population attending a performance once a year.

The Russian circus has its roots in the medieval travelling minstrels *(skomorokhi)*, and circus performers today still have a similar lifestyle. The Russian State Circus company, RosGosTsirk, assigns its members to a particular circus for a performance season, then rotates them around to other locations. What the members give up in stability, they gain in job security. RosGosTsirk ensures them employment throughout their circus career.

Many circus performers find their calling not by chance, but by ancestry. It is not unusual for generations of one family to practice the same circus skill, be it tightrope walking or lion taming. As one acrobat explained quite matter of factly: 'We can't live without the circus. There are very few who leave'.

Moscow is home to several circuses, including the acclaimed Nikulin Circus on Tsvetnoy bulvar (see p194). Its namesake is the beloved clown Yury Nikulin, who is described as 'the honour and conscience of the Russian circus'.

Speaking of honour and conscience, most of the major troupes have cleaned up their act with regard to the treatment of animals. In Moscow circuses, it is unlikely you will see animals treated cruelly or forced to perform degrading acts.

ARCHITECTURE

The Russian capital is an endless source of amusement and amazement for the architecture aficionado. The city streets are a textbook of Russian history, with churches, mansions, theatres and hotels standing as testament to the most definitive periods. Despite the tendency to demolish and rebuild (exhibited both in the past and in the present), Moscow has so far managed to preserve an impressive array of architectural gems.

MEDIEVAL MOSCOW

Moscow's oldest architecture has its roots in Kyivan Rus. The quintessential structure is the Byzantine cross-shaped church, topped with vaulted roofs and a central dome. As Russian culture moved north from Kyiv in the 11th and 12th centuries, the towns of the Golden Ring copied this architectural design, developing their own variations on the pattern. Roofs grew steeper to prevent the crush of heavy snow; windows grew narrower to keep out the cold.

In many cases, stone replaced brick as the traditional building material. For example the white stone Assumption Cathedral (p225) and Golden Gate (p227), both in Vladimir, are close copies of similar brick structures in Kyiv. In some cases, the stone facade became a tableau for a glorious kaleidoscope of carved images, such as the Cathedral of St Dmitry (p226) in Vladimir and the Church of the Intercession on the Nerl (p228) in Bogolyubovo.

STALIN'S SEVEN SISTERS

The foundations for seven large skyscrapers were laid in 1947 to mark Moscow's 800th anniversary. Stalin had decided that Moscow suffered from a 'skyscraper gap' when compared to the USA, and ordered the construction of these seven behemoths to jump-start the city's skyline.

One of the main architects, Vyacheslav Oltarzhevsky, had worked in New York during the skyscraper boom of the 1930s, and his experience proved essential. (Fortunately, he'd been released from a Gulag in time to help.)

In addition to the 'Seven Sisters' listed here, there were plans in place to build an eighth Stalinist skyscraper in Zaryadie (near Kitay Gorod). The historic district was razed in 1947 and a foundation was laid for a 32-storey tower. It did not get any further than that – for better and for worse – and the foundation was later used for the gargantuan Hotel Rossiya (demolished in 2006).

With their widely scattered locations, the towers provide a unique visual look and reference for Moscow. Their official name in Russia is *vysotky* (high-rise) as opposed to *neboskryob* (foreign skyscraper). They have been nicknamed variously 'Seven Sisters', 'wedding cakes', 'Stalin's sisters' and more.

Foreign Affairs Ministry (Map pp102–3; Smolenskaya-Sennaya pl 32/34; Ⓜ Smolenskaya)

Hilton Leningradskaya Hotel (Map pp84–5; Kalanchevskaya ul 21/40; Ⓜ Komsomolskaya) See p208.

Hotel Ukraina (Map p107; Kutuzovsky pr 2/1; Ⓜ Kievskaya) See p211.

Kotelnicheskaya apartment block (Map pp128–9; Kotelnicheskaya nab 17/1; Ⓜ Taganskaya) The Illuzion cinema (p190) is here.

Kudrinskaya apartment block (Map pp96–7; Kudrinskaya pl 1; Ⓜ Barrikadnaya) The Real McCoy (p184) eatery and bar is here.

Moscow State University (Map pp60–1; Universitetskaya pl 1; Ⓜ Universitetskaya) See p132.

Transport Ministry (Map pp84–5; ul Sadovaya-Spasskaya; Ⓜ Krasnye Vorota)

Early church-citadel complexes required protection, so all of these settlements had sturdy, fortress-style walls replete with fairytale towers – Russia's archetypal kremlins. They are still visible in Rostov-Veliky (p223) and Suzdal (p228) – and of course Moscow (see the boxed text, p68).

At the end of the 15th century, Ivan III imported architects from Italy to build two of the three great cathedrals in the Moscow Kremlin: Assumption Cathedral (p67) and Archangel Cathedral (p70). Nonetheless, the outsider architects looked to Kyiv for their inspiration, again copying the Byzantine design.

It was not until the late 16th century that architects found inspiration in the tent roofs and onion domes on the wooden churches in the north of Russia. Their innovation was to construct these features out of brick, which contributed to a new, uniquely Russian style of architecture. The iconic illustration is St Basil's Cathedral (p73), although there are other examples around Moscow, such as the Ivan the Great Bell Tower (p69) in the Kremlin, and the Ascension Church (p132) at Kolomenskoe.

In the 17th century, merchants financed smaller churches bedecked with tiers of *kokoshniki* (gables), colourful tiles and brick patterning. The Church of St Nicholas in Khamovniki (p117) and the Church of the Trinity in Nikitniki (p77) are excellent examples, as are most of the churches in Suzdal (p228) and Yaroslavl (p233). Patriarch Nikon outlawed such frippery shortly after the construction of the Church of the Nativity of the Virgin in Putinki (p92).

IMPERIAL MOSCOW

Embellishments returned at the end of the 17th century with the Western-influenced Moscow baroque. This style featured ornate white detailing against red-brick walls, such as at the Epiphany Cathedral (p77) in the monastery with the same name in Kitay Gorod. Zamoskvorechie (p118) is a treasure chest of Moscow baroque churches.

In 1714 it all came to a halt. Peter the Great's edict banned stone construction in Moscow and everywhere else in Russia, as all the resources were needed for the new city of St Petersburg. But frequent fires and a general outcry from Moscow's wealthy elite meant that the order was rescinded in 1722.

Tsar Alexander I favoured the grandiose Russian Empire style, commissioning it almost exclusively. Moscow abounds with Empire-style buildings, since much of the city had to be

---

ENDANGERED ARCHITECTURE

The urban development taking place in Moscow is an exciting sign of the city's sense of prosperity and possibility. It is also a source of contention among architects, historians and other critics, who claim that Moscow is losing its architectural heritage.

The nonprofit group Moscow Architectural Preservation Society (MAPS; www.maps-moscow.com) estimates that more than 400 buildings have been razed since 1989, including as many as 60 buildings of historical interest. The latter are supposed to be protected by federal law, but critics claim that the laws are useless in the face of corruption and cash.

Activists go so far as to compare Luzhkov to Stalin when it comes to development, claiming that the city has lost more buildings during the contemporary period than any time since the 1930s. That the mayor's wife is a prominent developer who has made millions from city contracts only adds fuel to their fire.

Preservationists are distressed about the tendency to tear down and build up, as opposed to preserve, but architects and artists are challenging this trend. Recent projects include Winzavod (p78), an art centre housed in a former wine factory, and the Garazh Centre of Contemporary Culture (p130), housed – you guessed it – in a former garage. Most prominently, the Krasny Oktyabr chocolate factory (p122), occupying a prime spot opposite the Kremlin, is now being revamped into residential and retail space with an emphasis on preserving the historic building.

Critics insist, however, that these examples are anomalies. Many buildings might look old, but they are mere replicas, as for example along the Arbat (p100). Or, developers maintain the historic facade, but destroy the building behind it, such as the complex that houses the Café Pushkin (p167) and Turandot (p167). As one critic observed, 'It is…like the Bolsheviks in the 1920s, but at least they had an ideal for the city'.

rebuilt after the fire of 1812. The flamboyant decorations of earlier times were used on the huge new buildings erected to proclaim Russia's importance, such as the Triumphal Arch (p106) and the Bolshoi Theatre (p87).

The Russian revival of the end of the 19th century extended to architecture. The Cathedral of Christ the Saviour (p109) was inspired by Byzantine Russian architecture. The State History Museum (p75) and the Leningradsky vokzal (Leningrad station) were inspired by medieval Russian styles. The extraordinary Kazansky vokzal (Kazan station) embraces no fewer than seven earlier styles.

Meanwhile, Russia's take on Art Nouveau – Style Moderne – added wonderful curvaceous flourishes to many buildings across Moscow. Splendid examples include Yaroslavsky vokzal and the Hotel Metropol (p206).

SOVIET MOSCOW

The revolution gave rein to young constructivist architects, who rejected superficial decoration; they designed buildings whose appearance was a direct function of their uses and materials – a new architecture for a new society. They used lots of glass and concrete in uncompromising geometric forms.

Konstantin Melnikov was probably the most famous constructivist, and his own house (see the boxed text, p105) off ul Arbat is one of the most interesting and unusual examples of the style. The former bus depot that now houses the Garazh Centre for Contemporary Culture (p130) is a more utilitarian example. In the 1930s, constructivism was denounced, as Stalin had much grander predilections.

Stalin favoured neoclassical architecture, which echoed ancient Athens ('the only culture of the past to approach the ideal,' according to Anatoly Lunacharsky, the first Soviet Commissar of Education). Stalin also favoured building on a gigantic scale to underline the might of the Soviet state. Monumental classicism inspired a 400m-high design for Stalin's pet project, a Palace of Soviets, which (mercifully) never got off the ground.

Stalin's architectural excesses reached their apogee in the seven wedding-cake-style skyscrapers that adorn the Moscow skyline, also known as the 'Seven Sisters' (p51).

In 1955 a schizophrenic decree ordered architects to avoid 'excesses'. A bland modern style was introduced, stressing function over form. The State Kremlin Palace (p65) is representative of this period. The White House (p98) was built later, but harks back to this style.

MODERN PLANNING & DEVELOPMENT

At the end of the Soviet Union, architectural energies and civic funds were initially funnelled into the restoration of decayed churches and monasteries, as well as the rebuilding of structures such as the Cathedral of Christ the Saviour (p109) and Kazan Cathedral (p75).

In more recent years Moscow has been a hotbed of development. Skyscrapers and steeples are changing the city skyline; the metro is expanding in all directions; and office buildings, luxury hotels and shopping centres are going up all over the city.

The latest target for intensive urban development is Moskva-City, the area west of Krasnaya Presnya Park and the World Trade Centre. Mayor Luzhkov has slated this neighbourhood as the future location of the city administration, and a new mini metro line is up and running.

Developers have followed suit, building shiny glass and metal buildings on either side of the Moscow River and a cool pedestrian bridge connecting them. Federation Tower (www.federationtower.ru) gained the claim of tallest building in Europe at its 2009 opening.

Moskva-City is the first of many dramatic developments, some of which are still in the planning stages. On the southern outskirts of the city, the Norman Foster–designed US$4 billion Crystal Island complex will be the world's largest building – 2.5 sq km – when completed.

GOVERNMENT & POLITICS

In December 1993, two years after the collapse of the Soviet Union, Russia finally adopted a new constitution. The circumstances of its enactment were less than desirable. Russia's early transition away from Communist Party rule was marked by power conflicts between the president, Boris Yeltsin, and parliament, as well as between central and regional governments.

In the autumn of 1993 the contest turned violent, when Boris Yeltsin ordered the defiant parliament to be shut down. Under siege in their offices in Russia's White House (p98), Yeltsin's left-wing opponents issued a nationwide summons for people to take to the streets in protest. But their call to arms went unheeded and their resistance was bombarded into submission. The president had prevailed.

The resultant 1993 constitution created a strong executive system. The president is charged with selecting the prime minister and forming the government, and he is entitled to bypass the legislature and rule by executive decree if deemed necessary. Moreover, the president possesses access to a wide array of bureaucratic, economic and coercive resources with few restraints. President Yeltsin's leadership style was to broker deals with his political rivals, using force only in exceptional cases. President Putin, on the other hand, was more willing to use the coercive powers inherent in the office to cower his would-be opponents.

The parliament, or Federal Assembly, contains a lower house, or Duma (p92), based on popular representation, and an upper house, or Senate (p65), based on regional representation. Under the polarising and unpredictable Yeltsin, the Duma made the most of its mandate, opposing the president's policies and organising impeachment inquiries. But under the popular and determined Putin, the legislature became a more compliant branch, passing the president's initiatives while fearing his retribution.

The constitution also established a federal system composed of 89 territorial subjects, including the city of Moscow. During Yeltsin's tenure, Russia's regions enjoyed greater autonomy over local political and economic affairs. But this trend was reversed under Putin; after a brief experiment with direct elections, the president reassumed the right to appoint and dismiss regional governors.

The 1993 constitution created the institutional framework of a democratic system, but it also contained the seeds of creeping authoritarianism. Since the constitution's inception, the unchecked powers of the executive have been increasingly deployed to the detriment of Russian democracy. Press freedoms, civil society and electoral competition have all been significantly constrained. Meanwhile, corruption, coercion and incompetence contaminate the public sector. As a result, Russia has evolved into a kind of illiberal democracy. There is little indication that these trends will change under President Medvedev.

Moscow reflects these larger developments of Russian politics. The capital has known but one boss since 1992, Yury Luzhkov. The mayor is a big-city boss in the grandest of traditions. Through a web of financial arrangements, ownership deals and real-estate holdings, Luzhkov is as much a CEO as he is mayor. Most of the large Western hotels can boast the Moscow government as an investor, an arrangement that obviously has its advantages when city inspectors call. Luzhkov is also seen as the driving force behind myriad construction (and reconstruction) projects, which have raised the protests of preservationists (see the boxed text, p52).

Rarely seen in public without his working-class cap, Luzhkov plays the part of populist with aplomb, cleaning streets, planting flowers, hosting beer festivals, cheering for FC Spartak and bashing gay paraders (see p249 for more information). He consistently supports patriotic causes and is strongly identified with Russian nationalist themes. He has been generous with the city's money in the restoration of the long-neglected churches and historic monuments. His 'bread and circus' strategy has included hosting spectacular city celebrations, especially the over-the-top 850th anniversary fete in 1997.

Blessed with the riches of Moscow, the mayor delivers the goods. He won reelection in 1996, 1999 and again in 2003. Luzhkov then began to talk about retirement; in 2005, city legislators promised retired chief executives a dacha, a car, a guard and a generous pension. But Putin would not hear of it. The former political rivals have found mutually beneficial coexistence. And, in 2007, Luzhkov was reappointed for a fifth term. Quite a run for the 'Mayor in the Cap'.

MEDIA
NEWSPAPERS

While genuine freedom of speech is absent from TV (see below), the best newspapers offer editorial opinions largely independent of their owners' or the government's views. This said, both the leading paper, and one of the most respected, Kommersant (www.kommersant.com), and its main rival Izvestia (http://izvestia.com) have financial ties with Gazprom, the state-owned gas monopoly, and so are muted in their criticism of the government. Gazeta (www.gzt.ru) has ties with the UK's *Daily Telegraph* and *Sunday Telegraph,* while Vedomosti (www.vedomosti.ru/eng), a joint venture by the *Financial Times* and *Wall Street Journal,* is a highly professional business daily.

Novaya Gazeta (www.novayagazeta.ru) is a well-known liberal rag that is published in Moscow. It was famous mainly for its column by investigative reporter Anna Politkovskaya, who was tragically murdered in 2006. She gained notoriety after playing an active role in negotiations with Chechen rebels during hostage crises in 2002 and 2004, as well as for her fervent opposition to the Chechen war. Her controversial book *Putin's Russia* was published in the UK in 2004, while *A Russian Diary: A Final Account* was published posthumously.

TELEVISION

With a population habituated for decades to receiving the party line through the tube, conventional wisdom has it that in Russia, whoever controls the TV rules the country. Ex-president Putin grasped this fact. Through a variety of takeovers and legal challenges, he succeeded in putting practically all TV channels under the Kremlin's direct or indirect control. In an effort to present Russia's viewpoint to the outside world, the state also set up the digital channel Russia Today (www.russiatoday.ru) in 2005, a CNN/BBC-style news and current affairs station that even broadcasts in Arabic to cover the Al Jazeera audience.

DEMSCHIZA Leonid Ragozin

All my journalist friends are 'demschiza' – democratic schizophrenics. This is a web slang word initially used to describe the most hysterical Kremlin bashers, who tend to see a KGB conspiracy behind any snowfall. But as Putin's grip on power got stronger, the demschiza ranks widened and the lists of offences sufficient for someone to be dubbed a public enemy multiplied. I am sure that whoever invented the term in the first place is a perfect demschiza these days. There is no censorship in Russia in the sense that there is no guy with scissors cutting out your most subversive thoughts, but there is a commonly accepted attitude to what is normal and what is, well, schizophrenic.

If you've read or seen *One Flew over the Cuckoo's Nest,* you know how relative normality is, especially in a country with an ancient tradition of punitive psychiatry. Of course most mainstream media editors tend to stick to the mainstream opinion. You write: 'Elections in Western countries are generally fair'. What a demschiza statement! Everybody knows Bush cheated in 2000. Or you may say: 'The US is not always hypocritical, sometimes it is serious about promoting democracy'. Outrageous demschiza! Western democracy is just a cover for the American dictatorship. Now, how about this one: 'The West is not a threat to Russia, at least not as much as its own leadership'. Breath deep, ambulance is on the way.

As the number of media outlets where you can make such statements and get away with it has been reduced to a historical low since the fall of communism, the real public discussion has shifted from TV and newspapers to web communities. Livejournal (www.livejournal.com) has been the main platform for a decade. All the demschiza are here. So is the other side, for which there is another term – *gebnya* (GB, standing for *gosudarstvenny bezopastnost* or 'state security', as in KGB). *Gebnya* is usually coupled with the adjective *krovavaya* (bloody). I find all that a bit too demoschizophrenic.

For journalists and politicians *Livejournal* is the main and often the only source of news, rumours and opinions, as well as the place to chat with someone from the other side of the barricades. Everybody who is anybody has an account here, openly or secretly – Kremlin spin doctors, opposition leaders, political emigrants, Chechen separatists and, of course, almost every journalist. There are several places in the city where all these people meet offline – notably Jean-Jacques (p172), Mayak (p172) and bilingua (see the boxed text, p183). Come for a drink to one of these places on a Friday night and amid all the seemingly amiable beer-fuelled chat, you might see history in the making.

Leonid Ragozin is a world correspondent at Russian Newsweek.

PEDICURES, PANTIES & POODLES Alan & Julia Thompson

Olga and Masha, two New Russian women, meet at a party, clutching identical Prada handbags.

'Paris, US$300,' Olga confidently reports.

'Moscow, US$500!' Masha trumps.

This popular anecdote chides the perversely status-conscious New Russians, whose social world is awash with exclusive designer labels and conspicuous price tags. Russia's newly rich have abandoned the austerity of the old Soviet regime and become adoring patrons of Europe's fashion houses. So now Moscow boasts boutiques for Louis Vuitton, Jimmy Choo, Hermes, Cartier, Dior, Tiffany and more. In fact, Moscow's Armani store does more business than any other in the world, apart from Tokyo.

To view Moscow's show ponies in their natural habitat, check out Tretyakovsky proezd (see the boxed text, p149). Here, the high fashionistas gather in full regalia. It is not always a pretty sight. The desire to coordinate often goes to extremes, even if it means head-to-toe Burberry plaid. Manicures, pedicures, lipstick, brassieres, panties and high heels are all made to match as if by Milan mandate. Keeping up with the Hiltons, temperamental lapdogs – sometimes supporting designer poodle-wear – have become an accessory essential.

Alan and Julia Thompson are members of the Fashion GAI.

Not that Russian TV is managed by some Soviet-style spooks. In fact the heads of the main state channels – Channel 1 and Rossiya – were among those young journalists who gave Russian audiences a taste of editorial freedom in the 1990s. Many faces on the screen are still the same, but news and analysis is generally uncontroversial. RenTV (www.ren-tv.com) has coverage that tends to be more objective than the norm.

FASHION

On first impression, conspicuous consumption seems to be the theme of Russian fashionistas (see the boxed text, above). Connoisseurs argue, however, that *la mode* in Moscow is becoming more sophisticated, creatively mixing well-known Western brands with up-and-coming local designers.

Russian models have certainly taken the fashion world by storm, with beauties such as Natalya Vodianova and Evgenia Volodina dominating the pages of *Vogue* and *Elle*. Moscow designers are also attracting increasing attention, both at home and abroad. The best-known Moscow designers are Valentin Yudashkin (p154), known for his refined style that suits prominent personalities such as the president; and Denis Simachyov (p152), whose designs appeal to a younger class of rich and reckless.

Igor Chapurin (p152) has also earned international recognition as the first Russian designer to show a prêt-à-porter collection in Paris. With boutiques in Paris and Milan (and Moscow), Chapurin manages to blend feminine frills with seductive styles. Another name to look out for in Moscow is Darya Zhukova, the girlfriend of Roman Abramovich, whose designs have made it to Hollywood.

Moscow hosts two major fashion events: Fashion Week in Moscow (p21), held at Gostiny Dvor, and Russian Fashion Week (p22), held at the World Trade Centre. Both events take place twice a year (spring and autumn).

Such high fashion is not so interesting to the average Ivan or Tatiana on the street, though. These days most Russians shop at the same stores and wear the same clothes as their counterparts in the West: blue jeans, business suits, or anything in between. Moscow's many shopping centres are filled with the same stores you might find anywhere in Europe.

Only winter differentiates Russian style, bringing out the best or the worst of it, depending on your perspective. Fur is still the most effective and most coveted way to stay warm. Some advice from a local fashion connoisseur: 'Your protests that fur is cruel are likely to be met by blank stares and an uncomfortable shifting of feet. Don't come in winter if this offends you.' If you think you might want to do as the Muscovites do when in Moscow, stop by Yekaterina (p152) and pick out a fur hat.

NEIGHBOURHOODS

top picks

- Art Muzeon Sculpture Park (p119)
- Ice Sculpture Gallery (p98)
- Armoury (p72)
- Lenin's Tomb (p74)
- Moscow Museum of Modern Art (p90)
- Moscow Zoo (p95)
- Novodevichy Convent & Cemetery (p112)
- Gallery of European & American Art of the 19th & 20th Centuries (p115)
- Rerikh Museum (p116)
- ZKP Tagansky Cold War Museum (p126)

NEIGHBOURHOODS

Moscow is an ancient city, founded almost 900 years ago and then developed organically over the course of centuries. But you wouldn't know it to look at a map. With the Kremlin at the centre, circled by ring roads and bisected by radial roads, the view is of an orderly, well-planned city. For this book's purposes, we've broken the capital into 10 digestible districts, each defined by its geography, activities and atmosphere.

Imagine the Russian capital as a *pirog,* or a pie, with the oldest part of the city – the Kremlin and Kitay Gorod – occupying the juicy central heart of it. The Moscow River flows to the south, while the other three sides are surrounded by the Inner Ring Rd, made up of Mokhovaya ul, Okhotny Ryad, Tverskaya proezd, Novaya pl and Staraya pl. This central heart was ancient Moscow.

> 'Each neighbourhood is a roughly triangular wedge, delineated by radial roads and – in some cases – rivers.'

From this core, Moscow developed outward – at first as far as the Boulevard Ring, about 1km from the Kremlin. This ring road used to be ramparts that protected the city, with gates at each of the intersections. Later, it was the Garden Ring – about 2km out – that acted as the dividing line between the upper classes in the city and the poorer masses outside. Nowadays, a multilane highway known as MKAD, 15km to 20km from the Kremlin, is the boundary between Moscow proper and the *zagorod,* or suburbs. The majority of the city sights, however, are still located within the Garden Ring.

Successive neighbourhoods form a circle around the Kremlin and Kitay Gorod, following the Boulevard Ring and the Garden Ring roads. Each neighbourhood is a roughly triangular wedge, delineated by radial roads and – in some cases – rivers. The pie pieces fit together in a circle around the centre, with a few outliers such as Presnya and Dorogomilovo.

To the east is Basmanny, its primary landmark being the Chistye Prudy, the 'clean ponds' that sparkle with sunlight on the main boulevard. North of here is Krasnoselsky and Meshchansky, a mostly industrial area dwarfed by chaotic Komsomolskaya pl.

Directly north of the Kremlin is Tverskoy, Moscow's most prominent commercial district, named for the main drag Tverskaya ul. Southwest of Tverskoy is Presnya, a vast area that contains the new business development at Moskva-City.

West of the Kremlin, Arbat is home to (and namesake of) the famous street that came alive with artists in the 1960s. Further west, the Moscow River loops around the district of Dorogomilovo, site of the monumental Park Pobedy (Victory Park). In the far south of Dorogomilovo, 6km south of the Kremlin, an unfamiliar sight rises on the landscape: hills. This is Vorobyovy Gory (Sparrow Hills), the city's only elevation of note. It is topped by the Moscow State University skyscraper, a landmark visible for miles in all directions.

South of the Kremlin, the Moscow River acts as a natural boundary between districts. To the southwest, tucked into a river bend, Khamovniki is rich with museums, stretching all the way to Novodevichy Convent. Directly south of the Kremlin is Zamoskvorechie, which means 'Beyond the Moscow River'. Surrounded on three sides, it's another historic part of Moscow with church-lined streets. Taganka sits to the southeast, isolated by the Moscow River and the smaller Zauzie River, which winds northeast from here.

Moscow is greater than these 10 areas. Located about 4.5km from the Kremlin, the Third Ring is a new eight-lane, high-speed motorway, built to absorb some of the traffic from Moscow streets, providing motorists with a speedy route across (or rather, around) town. Outer Moscow sprawls all the way out to the Outer Ring Rd (MKAD), about 15km to 20km from the Kremlin.

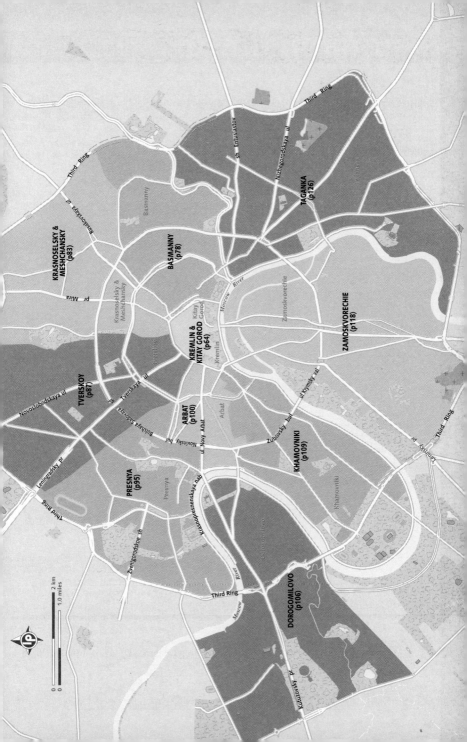

NEIGHBOURHOODS OUTER MOSCOW

OUTER MOSCOW

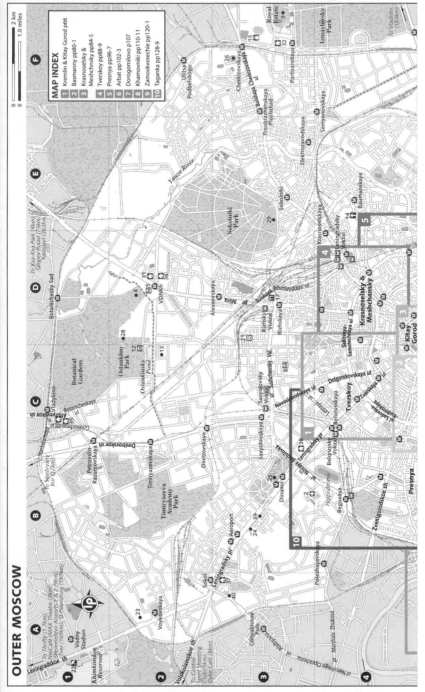

MAP INDEX

1	Kremlin & Kitay Gorod p66
2	Basmanny pp80-1
3	Krasnoselsky & Meshchansky pp84-5
4	Tverskoy pp88-9
5	Presnya pp96-7
6	Arbat pp102-3
7	Dorogomilovo p107
8	Khamovniki pp110-11
9	Zamoskvorechie pp120-1
10	Taganka pp128-9

0 — 2 km
0 — 1.0 miles

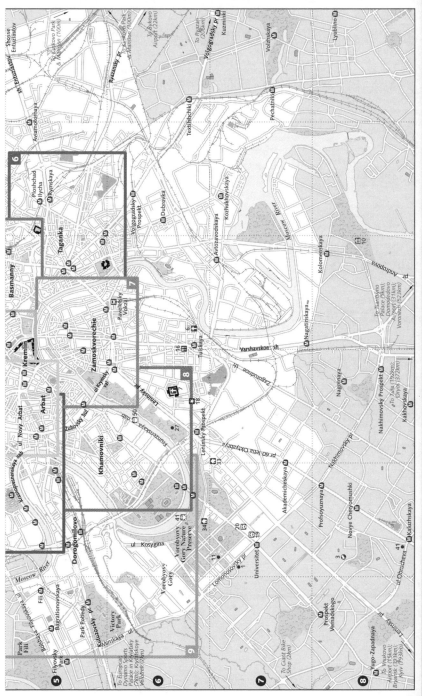

OUTER MOSCOW (pp60-1)

ITINERARY BUILDER

The table below allows you to plan a day's worth of activities in any area of the city. Simply select which area you wish to explore, and then mix and match from the corresponding listings to build your day. The first item in each cell represents a well-known highlight of the area, while the other items are more off-the-beaten-track gems.

ACTIVITIES	Sights	Eating	Drinking & Nightlife
Kremlin & Kitay Gorod	St Basil's Cathedral (p73) Lenin's Tomb (p74) Kitay Gorod (p76)	Red Square, 1 (p162) Loft Café (p162) Drova (p164)	Club Che (p180)
Basmanny	Polytechnical Museum (p78) Sakharov Museum (p78) Winzavod (p78)	Kovchyog Noyev (p163) Avocado (p163) Prime Star (p164)	Art Garbage (p183) Krizis Zhanra (p183) Petrovich (p180)
Tverskoy	Moscow Museum of Modern Art (p90) Upper St Peter Monastery (p91) Gulag History Museum (p87)	Café Pushkin (p167) Botanika (p170) Gallery (p166)	Chaikhona No 1 (p180) Gogol (p183) Vremya Yest (p180)
Presnya	Patriarch's Ponds (p95) Moscow Zoo (p95) Ice Sculpture Gallery (p98)	Il Cucinino (p171) Correa's (p170) Shinok (p170)	Real McCoy (p184) Sixteen Tons (p186)
Arbat	Museum of Oriental Art (p100) Melnikov House (p105) Gogol Memorial Rooms (p101)	Coffee Mania (p172) Genatsvale on Arbat (p172) Mayak (p172)	Kvartira 44 (p182) Zhiguli (p181) Tinkoff (p181)
Dorogomilovo	Park Pobedy (p106) Vorobyovy Gory Nature Preserve (p132) Moscow State University (p132)	Pinocchio (p173)	Probka (p182)
Khamovniki	Novodevichy Convent & Cemetery (p112) Gallery of Euro. & Am. Art of 19th & 20th Cent. (p115) Rerikh Museum (p116)	Stolle (p174) Skazka Vostoka (p174) Tiflis (p174)	Roadhouse (p186) Soho Rooms (p184)
Zamosk-vorechie	Tretyakov Gallery (p118) Krasny Oktyabr Chocolate Factory & Museum (p122) Art Muzeon Sculpture Park (p119)	Suliko (p175) Grably (p175) Pelmeshka (p175)	Apshu (p182) Lebedinoe Ozero (p180) GQ Bar (p182)

KREMLIN & KITAY GOROD

Drinking p179; Eating p162; Shopping p148; Sleeping p205

Moscow started in the 12th century as a triangular plot of land – a smallish fort – perched atop Borovitsky Hill. Surrounded by a wall for protection, the fort contained the earliest settlement, while ceremonies and celebrations were held on the plaza outside. The fort, of course, is the Kremlin, while the ceremonial plaza is Red Square – still at the heart of Moscow historically, geographically and spiritually. Immediately east of Red Square, Kitay Gorod was the first settlement outside the Kremlin walls in the 13th and 14th centuries, an era that is still remembered for its architecture. This whole area, Moscow's historic heart, lies inside an arc bound by the Inner Ring Rd.

In the early days, all the residents lived within the low wall that surrounded the Kremlin, or fortress. These days, nobody lives in this central district. Official buildings, historic museums, grand theatres, luxury hotels and shopping centres line the streets. The wide boulevards and ceremonial squares are best suited for parades, rallies, concerts and other pomp and circumstance. Only the picturesque, walkable streets of Kitay Gorod are lined with shops and cafés to cater to the people.

Otherwise, this is the domain of officialdom, which visitors will perceive immediately. The police presence is very visible, directing cars and pedestrians in an orderly fashion. Official events often cause the closure of Red Square, if not the surrounding streets. The atmosphere is befitting Russia's authoritarian image. The powerful Kremlin walls, the stately buildings and the proliferation of police emphasise the idea that this regime takes itself seriously (as have all regimes that have ruled from the Kremlin).

Nonetheless, this is the area where visitors to Moscow spend most of their time, and rightly so. The historical significance and architectural magnificence of this 1-sq-km space is truly awe inspiring.

The Kremlin is a north-pointing triangle with 750m-long sides. Red Square lies outside its eastern wall (accessible via Ploshchad Revolyutsii metro station), while Alexandrovsky Garden flanks the western wall (accessible via Aleksandrovsky Sad or Biblioteka imeni Lenina stations). The Moscow (Moskva) River flows to the south, so the best views of the Kremlin are from Sofiyskaya nab, across the river. North of the Kremlin, above the apex, is Manezhnaya pl, named after the royal stables that once occupied this spot. Manezhnaya pl is also the site of Okhotny Ryad metro station. East of here, Kitay Gorod is accessible by Ploshchad Revolyutsii or Kitay-Gorod metro stations.

KREMLIN

Ever since 1147, when Yury Dolgoruky summoned his allies to this spot, the Kremlin (Map p66; ☎ 495-202 3776; www.kremlin.museum.ru; adult/student R300/50, audio guide R150; ⊗ 9.30am-4pm Fri-Wed; Ⓜ Aleksandrovsky Sad) has served as the symbol of the Russian state. From here Ivan the Terrible unleashed his terror, Napoleon watched Moscow burn, Lenin fashioned the dictatorship of the proletariat, Gorbachev orchestrated *perestroika* (restructuring) and Yeltsin concocted the New Russia.

A kremlin – or fortified stronghold – has existed on this site since Moscow's earliest years. When the city became the capital of medieval Rus in the 1320s, the Kremlin served as the headquarters of the Russian Orthodox Church and the seat of the prince. The 'White Stone Kremlin', which had limestone walls, was built shortly thereafter.

After Ivan III (the Great) married the Byzantine princess Sofia Paleologue in 1469, his ambition was to build a capital that would equal the fallen Constantinople in grandeur, political power, achievements and architecture. In an effort to build the 'Third Rome', Ivan brought stonemasons and architects from Italy, who built new walls, three great cathedrals, and other structures. Most of the present-day buildings date from this period.

Although Peter I (the Great) shifted the capital to St Petersburg, the tsars still showed up here for coronations and other celebrations. The fortress was threatened by Napoleon, who inflicted serious damage before making his retreat in 1812. But still the ancient symbol endured. The citadel wouldn't be breached again until the Bolsheviks stormed the place in November 1917.

Make advanced arrangements for the 'One Day at the Kremlin' tour at the Kremlin Excursion

Office (Map p66; ☎ 495-290 3094; Ⓜ Alexandrovsky Sad) in Alexandrovsky Garden. Capital Tours (p252) offers standard daily tours of the Kremlin and Armoury, while Dom Patriarshy Tours (p252) offers more in-depth tours of the Kremlin cathedrals, sometimes including a visit to the otherwise off-limits palaces. Numerous freelance guides also tout their services near the Kutafya Tower.

The main ticket office is in Alexandrovsky Garden, just off Manezhnaya ul. The ticket to the 'Architectural Ensemble of Theatre Square' covers entry to all five church-museums, as well as Patriarch's Palace and exhibits in the Ivan the Great Bell Tower. It does not include the Armoury or the Diamond Fund Exhibition. In any case, you can and should buy tickets for the Armoury here. Arrive early before tickets sell out. There's also an entrance at the southern Borovitskaya Tower, mainly used by those heading straight to the Armoury or Diamond Fund Exhibition.

Before entering the Kremlin, deposit bags at the left-luggage office (Map p66; per bag R60; ☺ 9am-6.30pm Fri-Wed), beneath the Kutafya Tower near the main ticket office. Inside the Kremlin, police will keep you from straying into out-of-bounds areas. Visitors wearing shorts will be refused entry. Photography is not permitted inside the Armoury or any of the buildings on Sobornaya pl (Cathedral Square).

Visiting the Kremlin buildings and the Armoury is at least a half-day affair. If you intend to visit the Diamond Fund or other special exhibits, plan on spending most of the day here. If you are short on time, skip the Armoury and the Diamond Fund and dedicate a few hours to admiring the amazing architecture and historic buildings around Sobornaya pl.

top picks

KREMLIN & KITAY GOROD

- Armoury (p72) Museum of royal treasures.
- Assumption Cathedral (p67) Golden domes glistening in the sun.
- Lenin's Tomb (p74) Pay your respects to the communist leader.
- State History Museum (p75) Exhibits from the Stone Age to the present.
- St Basil's Cathedral (p73) Famous onion domes and spires.

ENTRANCE TOWERS Map p66

The Kutafya Tower (Kutafya bashnya), which forms the main visitors' entrance today, stands apart from the Kremlin's west wall, at the end of a ramp over the Alexandrovsky Garden. The ramp was once a bridge over the Neglinnaya River and used to be part of the Kremlin's defences; this river has been diverted underground, beneath the Alexandrovsky Garden, since the early 19th century. The Kutafya Tower is the last of a number of outer bridge towers that once stood on this side of the Kremlin.

From the Kutafya Tower, walk up the ramp and pass through the Kremlin walls beneath the 1495 Trinity Gate Tower (Troitskaya bashnya), the tallest of the Kremlin's towers at 80m. Right below your feet were the cells for prisoners in the 16th century. On your way to Sobornaya pl you pass the government buildings described following, which are closed to visitors.

GOVERNMENT BUILDINGS Map p66

The lane to the right (south), immediately inside the Trinity Gate Tower, passes the 17th-century Poteshny Palace (Poteshny dvorets), where Stalin lived. The yellow palace was built by Tsar Alexey Mikhailovich and housed the first Russian theatre. Here, Tsar Alexey enjoyed various comedic performances. In keeping with conservative Russian Orthodox tradition, however, after the shows he would go to the *banya* (Russian bathhouse), then attend a church service to repent his sins.

The bombastic marble, glass and concrete State Kremlin Palace (Gosudarstvenny Kremlyovsky dvorets), built between 1960 and 1961 for Communist Party congresses, is now also known as the Kremlin Ballet Theatre (p189). North of the State Kremlin Palace is the 18th-century Arsenal, commissioned by Peter the Great to house workshops and depots for guns and weaponry. An unrealised plan at the end of the 19th century was to open a museum of the Napoleonic Wars in the Arsenal. Now housing the Kremlin Guard, the building is ringed with 800 captured Napoleonic cannons.

The offices of the president of Russia, the ultimate seat of power in the modern Kremlin, are in the yellow, triangular former Senate building, a fine 18th-century neoclassical edifice, east of the Arsenal. Built in 1785 by architect Matvei Kazakov, it was noted for its huge cupola. In the 16th and

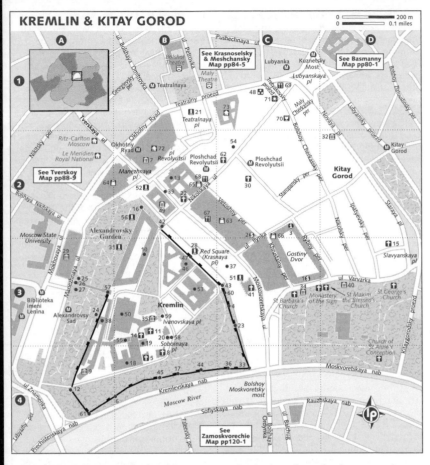

KREMLIN & KITAY GOROD

0 —————— 200 m
0 —————— 0.1 miles

17th centuries this area was where the *boyars* (high-ranking Russian nobles) lived. Next to the Senate is the 1930s Supreme Soviet (Verkhovny Soviet) building.

PATRIARCH'S PALACE Map p66

This palace (Patriarshy dvorets) was mostly built in the mid-17th century for Patriarch Nikon, whose reforms sparked the break with the Old Believers (p127). The palace contains an exhibit of 17th-century household items, including jewellery, hunting equipment and furniture. From here you can access the five-domed Church of the Twelve Apostles, which has a gilded wooden iconostasis and a collection of icons by the leading 17th-century icon painters.

The highlight of the Patriarch's Palace is perhaps the ceremonial Cross Hall (Krestovaya palata), where feasts for the tsars and ambassadors were held. From the 18th century the room was used to produce *miro* (a holy oil used during church services, which contains over 30 herbal components); the oven and huge pans from the production process are on display.

Now quiet, the palace in its heyday was a busy place. Apart from the Patriarch's living quarters, it had huge kitchens, warehouses and cellars stocked with food, workshops, a school for high-born children, offices for scribes, dormitories for those waiting to be baptised, stables and carriage houses.

The Patriarch's Palace often holds special exhibits (adult/student R100/50), which can be visited individually, without access to the other buildings on Sobornaya pl.

KREMLIN & KITAY GOROD (p66)

ASSUMPTION CATHEDRAL Map p66

On the northern side of Sobornaya pl, with five golden helmet domes and four semi-circular gables facing the square, the Assumption Cathedral (Uspensky sobor) was the focal church of prerevolutionary Russia, and the burial place of most of the heads of the Russian Orthodox Church from the 1320s to 1700. A striking 1660s fresco of the Virgin Mary faces Sobornaya pl, above the door once used for royal processions. If you have limited time in the Kremlin, come straight here. The visitors' entrance is at the western end.

TOWERS OF POWER

The present Kremlin walls were built between 1485 and 1495, replacing the limestone walls from the 14th century. The walls are 6m to 17m tall, depending on the landscape, and 2m to 5m thick. They stretch for 2235m. Originally, a 32m-wide moat encircled the northern end of the Kremlin, connecting the Moscow and Neglinnaya Rivers.

The 20 distinctive towers were built mostly between 1485 and 1500, with tent roofs added in the 17th century. Originally, the towers had lookout posts and were equipped for heavy fighting. Most were designed by Italian masons. The more interesting towers are on the eastern and southern sides. Starting at the northern corner and going clockwise, the towers are as following:

Corner Arsenal Tower (Arsenalnaya bashnya) The stronghold of the Kremlin with walls 4m thick. A well built into the basement to provide water during sieges still survives today.

St Nicholas Tower (Nikolskaya bashnya) Previously a gated defensive tower on the northeastern flank. Through this gate, Dmitry Pozharsky and Kuzma Minin (as depicted in the statue in front of St Basil's Cathedral) led a civilian army and drove out the Polish occupiers.

Senate Tower (Senatskaya bashnya) Originally a nameless, gateless tower, and finally named after the construction of the Senate in the 18th century.

Saviour Gate Tower (Spasskaya bashnya) The Kremlin's 'official' exit onto Red Square. This gate – considered sacred – was used for processions in tsarist times. The two white-stone plaques above the gate commemorate the tower's construction. Between the tower's double walls, a staircase links five of its 10 levels. The current clock was installed in the gate tower in the 1850s. Hauling 3m-long hands and weighing 25 tonnes, the clock takes up three of the tower's levels. Its melodic chime sounds every 15 minutes across Red Square and across the country (on the radio).

Tsar Tower (Tsarskaya bashnya) A later addition (1680), which sits on top of the Kremlin wall. Legend has it that Ivan the Terrible watched executions and other Red Square activities from the old wooden tower that previously stood on this site.

Alarm Tower (Nabatnaya bashnya) Housed the Spassky Alarm Bell, which was used to warn of enemy attacks and to spur popular uprisings. After quashing one uprising, Catherine the Great was so outraged that she had the clapper removed from the bell, so it could sound no more. The bell remained mute in the tower for 30 years before it was finally removed.

Konstantin & Yelena Tower (Konstantino-Yeleninskaya bashnya) Built to protect the settlements outside the city, it is complete with firing platforms and a drawbridge over the moat. During the 17th century this tower was used as a prison, earning it the nickname 'torture tower'.

Moskvoretskaya Tower The round tower at the southeastern corner.

Petrovskaya Tower (Petrovskaya bashnya) A service entrance used by Kremlin gardeners. Petrovskaya Tower was destroyed first by the Poles in 1612, then again by the French 200 years later, but it was rebuilt each time.

First & Second Nameless Towers Both destroyed in 1771 because they interfered with the construction of the Kremlin Palace, but rebuilt after its completion.

Secret Tower (Taynitskaya bashnya) The first tower built (1485), it is named after a secret passageway leading down to the river.

Annunciation Tower (Blagoveshchenskaya bashnya) Named for the miracle-working icon on the facade. In 1633 the so-called Laundry Gate was constructed nearby for Kremlin washerwomen to go down to the Moscow River, but it was later bricked up.

Water Tower (Vodovzvodnaya bashnya) A circular tower erected at the confluence of the Moscow and Neglinnaya Rivers. From 1633 a water lift in the tower pumped water to a reservoir and supplied a system of underground piping for the Kremlin.

In 1470 Russian architects Krivtsov and Myshkin were commissioned by Ivan the Great to replace the old dilapidated cathedral, which dated from 1326. As soon as the ceiling was put up, one of the walls collapsed. During Soviet times, history books said this calamity was the result of bad handiwork but, today, revisionist history indicates that an earthquake caused the collapse. Either way, Krivtsov and Myshkin lost their jobs, and Italian architect Aristotle Fioravanti was given a crack at it. After the foundation was completed, Aristotle toured Novgorod, Suzdal and Vladimir to acquaint himself with Russian architecture. His design is a more spacious version of the Assumption Cathedral (p225) at Vladimir, with a Renaissance twist.

In 1812 French troops used the cathedral as a stable; they looted 295kg of gold and over five tonnes of silver from here, but much of it was recovered. The church closed in 1918. According to some accounts, in 1941, when the Nazis were on the outskirts of Moscow, Stalin secretly ordered a service in the cathedral to protect the city from the enemy. The cathedral was officially returned to the Church in 1989, but it operates as a museum.

The interior of the Assumption Cathedral is unusually bright and spacious, full of warm golds, reds and blues. The west wall features a scene of the Apocalypse, a favourite theme of the Russian Church in the Middle Ages. The pillars have pictures of martyrs, considered to be the pillars of faith. Above the southern gates there are frescoes of Yelena and Constantine, who brought Christianity to Greece and the south of Russia. The space above the northern gate depicts Olga and Vladimir, who brought Christianity to the north.

Most of the existing murals on the cathedral walls were painted on a gilt base in the 1640s, with the exception of three grouped together on the south wall: *The Apocalypse (Apokalipsis)*, *The Life of Metropolitan Pyotr (Zhitie Mitropolita Petra)* and *All Creatures Rejoice in Thee (O tebe raduetsya)*. These are attributed to Dionysius and his followers, the cathedral's original 15th-century mural painters. The tombs of many leaders of the Russian Church (metropolitans up to 1590, patriarchs from 1590 to 1700) are against the north, west and south walls.

Near the south wall is a tent-roofed wooden throne made in 1551 for Ivan the Terrible, known as the Throne of Monomakh. Its carved scenes highlight the career of 12th-

century Grand Prince Vladimir Monomakh of Kiev. Near the west wall there is a shrine with holy relics of Patriarch Hermogen, who was starved to death during the Time of Troubles in 1612.

The iconostasis dates from 1652, but its lowest level contains some older icons. The 1340s *Spas yaroe oko (Saviour with the Angry Eye)* is second from the right. On the left of the central door is the *Vladimirskaya Bogomater (Virgin of Vladimir)*, an early-15th-century Rublyov school copy of Russia's most revered image, the *Vladimirskaya Ikona Bogomateri (Vladimir Icon of the Mother of God)*. The 12th-century original, now in the Tretyakov Gallery (p118), stood in the Assumption Cathedral from the 1480s to 1930. One of the oldest Russian icons, the 12th-century red-clothed *Svyatoy Georgy (St George)* from Novgorod, is by the north wall.

The original icons of the lower, local tier are symbols of victory brought from Vladimir, Smolensk, Veliky Ustiug and other places. The south door was brought from the Nativity of the Virgin Cathedral (p228) in Suzdal.

CHURCH OF THE DEPOSITION OF THE ROBE Map p66
This delicate single-domed church (Tserkov Rizpolozhenia), beside the west door of the Assumption Cathedral, was built between 1484 and 1486 in exclusively Russian style. It was the private chapel of the heads of the Church, who tended to be highly suspicious of such people as Italian architects.

Originally an open gallery or porch surrounded the church; it was later removed and the church was connected with the Great Kremlin Palace for the convenience of the tsars. The interior walls, ceilings and pillars are covered with 17th-century frescoes. It houses an exhibition of 15th- to 17th-century woodcarvings.

IVAN THE GREAT BELL TOWER Map p66
With its two golden domes rising above the eastern side of Sobornaya pl, the Ivan the Great Bell Tower (Kolokolnya Ivana Velikogo) is the Kremlin's tallest structure – a landmark visible from 30km away. Before the 20th century it was forbidden to build any higher than this tower in Moscow.

Its history dates back to the Church of Ioann Lestvichnik Under the Bells, built on this site in 1329 by Ivan I. In 1505 the Italian Marco Bono designed a new belfry, originally with only two octagonal tiers beneath a drum and a dome. In 1600 Boris Godunov raised it to 81m, a public works project designed to employ the thousands of people who had come to Moscow during a famine.

The building's central section, with a gilded single dome and a 65-tonne bell, dates from between 1532 and 1542. The tent-roofed annexe, next to the belfry, was commissioned by Patriarch Filaret in 1642 and bears his name. Exhibitions from the Kremlin collections are shown on the ground level.

TSAR CANNON & BELL Map p66

North of the bell tower is the 40-tonne Tsar Cannon (Tsar Pushka). It was cast in 1586 by the blacksmith Ivan Chokhov for Fyodor I, whose portrait is on the barrel. Shot has never sullied its 89cm bore and certainly not the cannonballs beside it, which are too big even for this elephantine firearm.

Beside (not inside) the bell tower stands the world's biggest bell, a 202-tonne monster that has never rung. An earlier version, weighing 130 tonnes, fell from its belfry during a fire in 1701 and shattered. Using these remains, the current Tsar Bell (Tsar Kolokol) was cast in the 1730s for Empress Anna Ivanovna. The bell was cooling off in the foundry casting pit in 1737 when it came into contact with water, causing an 11-tonne chunk to break off. One hundred years later, the architect Monferrand took the damaged bell out of the pit and put it on a pedestal. The bas-reliefs of Empress Anna and Tsar Alexey, as well as some icons, were etched on its sides.

South of the bell, the pleasant park of Ivanovskaya pl offers spectacular views south over Moscow.

ARCHANGEL CATHEDRAL Map p66

The Archangel Cathedral (Arkhangelsky sobor) at the southeastern corner of Sobornaya pl was for centuries the coronation, wedding and burial church of tsars. It was built by Ivan Kalita in 1333 to commemorate the end of the great famine, and dedicated to Archangel Michael, guardian of the Moscow princes. By the turn of the 16th century it had fallen into disrepair and was rebuilt between 1505 and 1508

by the Italian architect Alevisio Novi. Like the Assumption Cathedral (p67), it is five-domed and essentially Byzantine-Russian in style. However, the exterior has many Venetian Renaissance features, notably the distinctive scallop-shell gables and porticoes.

The tombs of all Muscovy's rulers from the 1320s to the 1690s are here, bar one (the absentee is Boris Godunov, whose body was taken out of the grave on the order of a 'False Dmitry' and buried at Sergiev Posad in 1606). The bodies are buried underground, beneath the 17th-century sarcophagi and 19th-century copper covers. Tsarevitch Dmitry (a son of Ivan the Terrible), who died mysteriously in 1591, lies beneath a painted stone canopy. It was Dmitry's death that sparked the appearance of a string of impersonators, known as False Dmitrys, during the Time of Troubles. Ivan's own tomb is out of sight behind the iconostasis, along with those of his other sons, Ivan (whom he killed) and Fyodor I (who succeeded him). From Peter the Great onwards, emperors and empresses were buried in St Petersburg; the exception being Peter II, who died in Moscow and is here.

Some 17th-century murals were uncovered during restorations in the 1950s. The south wall depicts many of those buried here; on the pillars are some of their predecessors, including Andrei Bogolyubsky, Prince Daniil and Alexander Nevsky.

HALL OF FACETS Map p66

Named for its Italian Renaissance stone facing, the Hall of Facets (Granovitaya palata) was designed and built by Marco Ruffo and Pietro Solario between 1487 and 1491, during the reign of Ivan the Great. Its upper floor housed the tsars' throne room, scene of banquets and ceremonies. Access to the Hall of Facets was via an outside staircase from the square below. During the Streltsky Rebellion of 1682, several of Peter the Great's relatives were tossed down the exterior Red Staircase, so called because it ran red with their blood. (It's no wonder that Peter hated Moscow and decided to start afresh with a new capital in St Petersburg.) Stalin destroyed the staircase, but it was rebuilt in 1994.

The hall is 500 sq metres, with a supporting pillar in the centre. The walls are decorated with gorgeous murals of biblical and historical themes, although none is original.

Alas, the building is closed to the public, although some special tours with Dom Patriarshy Tours (p252) allow access.

TEREM PALACE Map p66
The 16th- and 17th-century Terem Palace (Teremnoy dvorets) is the most splendid of the Kremlin palaces. Made of stone and built by Vasily III, the palace's living quarters include a dining room, living room, study, bedroom and small chapel. Unfortunately, the palace is closed to the public, but you can glimpse its cluster of 11 golden domes and chequered roof behind and above the Church of the Deposition of the Robe.

ANNUNCIATION CATHEDRAL Map p66
The Annunciation Cathedral (Blagoveshchensky sobor), at the southwest corner of Sobornaya pl, contains the celebrated icons of master painter Theophanes the Greek (Feofan Grek in Russian).

Vasily I built the first wooden church on this site in 1397. Between 1484 and 1489, Ivan the Great had the Annunciation Cathedral rebuilt to serve as the royal family's private chapel. Originally the cathedral had just three domes and an open gallery around three sides. Ivan the Terrible, whose tastes were more elaborate, added six more domes and chapels at each corner, enclosed the gallery and gilded the roof.

Under Orthodox law, Ivan's fourth marriage disqualified him from entering the church proper, so he had the southern arm of the gallery converted into the Archangel Gabriel Chapel (Pridel Arkhangela Gavriila), from where he could watch services through a grille. The chapel has a colourful iconostasis, dating from its consecration in 1564, and an exhibition of icons.

Many murals in the gallery date from the 1560s. Among them are *Capture of Jericho* in the porch, *Jonah and the Whale* in the northern arm of the gallery, and the *Tree of Jesus* on its ceiling. Other murals feature ancient philosophers such as Aristotle, Plutarch, Plato and Socrates holding scrolls with their own wise words. Socrates' scroll reads: 'No harm will ever come to a good man. Our soul is immortal. After death the good shall be rewarded and the evil punished'. Plato's says: 'We must hope God shall send us a heavenly Teacher and a Guide'.

The small central part of the cathedral has a lovely jasper floor. The 16th-century frescoes include Russian princes on the north pillar and Byzantine emperors on the south, both with Apocalypse scenes above them. But the cathedral's real treasure is the iconostasis, where in the 1920s restorers uncovered early-15th-century icons by three of the greatest medieval Russian artists.

It was most likely Theophanes who painted the six icons at the right-hand end of the biggest row of the six tiers of the iconostasis. From left to right, these are the Virgin Mary, Christ Enthroned, St John the Baptist, the Archangel Gabriel, the Apostle Paul and St John Chrysostom. Theophanes was a master of portraying pathos in the facial expressions of his subjects, setting these icons apart from most others.

The third icon from the left, Archangel Michael, is ascribed to Andrei Rublyov, who may also have painted the adjacent St Peter. Rublyov is also reckoned to be the artist of the first, second, sixth and seventh (and probably the third and fifth) icons from the left of the festival row, above the deesis (biggest) row. The seven icons at the right-hand end are attributed to Prokhor of Gorodets.

GREAT KREMLIN PALACE Map p66
Housing the Armoury and much more, the 700-room Great Kremlin Palace (Bolshoy Kremlyovsky dvorets) was built between 1838 and 1849 by architect Konstantin Thon as an imperial residence for Nicholas I. It is now an official residence of the Russian president, used for state visits and receptions. However, unlike Russian tsars, the president doesn't have living quarters here.

The huge palace incorporates some of the earlier buildings such as the Hall of Facets, Terem Palace and several chapels. Although vast, the building has never received great praise, being criticised as 'barracklike' and 'pretentious'. Several ceremonial halls are named after saints, including St George, St Vladimir, St Andrew, St Catherine and St Alexander. St George's Hall is mainly used for state awards ceremonies, while major international treaties are signed in St Vladimir's Hall. To save you the trouble, the Great Kremlin Palace (apart from the Armoury, p72) is closed to tourists, except those on an official state visit. From time to time Dom Patriarshy Tours (p252) brings tourists here.

ARMOURY Map p66

Oruzheynaya palata; adult/student R350/70, audio guide R200; 🕙 **10am, noon, 2.30pm, 4.30pm;** Ⓜ **Aleksandrovsky Sad**

The Armoury dates back to 1511, when it was founded under Vasily III to manufacture and store weapons, imperial arms and regalia for the royal court. Later it also produced jewellery, icon frames and embroidery.

During the reign of Peter the Great all craftspeople, goldsmiths and silversmiths were sent to St Petersburg, and the armoury became a mere museum storing the royal treasures. A fire in 1737 destroyed many of the items. In the early 19th century, new premises were built for the collection. Much of it, however, never made it back from Nizhny Novgorod, where it was sent for safekeeping during Napoleon's invasion in 1812.

Another building to house the collection was completed in 1851, but it was later demolished to make way for the Palace of Congresses, now the State Kremlin Palace (p65). So the Armoury is now housed in the Great Kremlin Palace. Despite the disasters that have befallen this collection throughout the centuries, the Armoury still contains plenty of treasures for ogling, and remains a highlight of any visit to the Kremlin.

The exhibit starts upstairs; your ticket will specify a time for entry. Here's what you'll find:

Rooms 1 Stuffed to the gills with bling, especially gold and silver objects from the 12th to the 20th centuries. Don't overdose, as there is plenty more to come.

Room 2 Houses the renowned Easter eggs made from precious metals and jewels by St Petersburg jeweller Fabergé. The tsar and tsarina traditionally exchanged these gifts each year at Easter. Most famous is the Grand Siberian Railway egg, with gold train, platinum locomotive and ruby headlamp, created to commemorate the completion of the Moscow–Vladivostok line.

Rooms 3 and 4 Armour, weapons and more armour and more weapons.

Room 5 Here you will find all those gifts proffered by visiting ambassadors over the years. Each piece of gold or silver is yet another reason why the average peasant trying to coax some life out of a mouldy seed might get a little miffed. Ignoring the plight of the masses, you can enjoy the skill of the craftspeople who made these items.

Room 6 Coronation dresses of 18th-century empresses (Empress Elizabeth, we're told, had 15,000 other dresses).

Room 7 Contains the joint coronation throne of boy-tsars Peter the Great and his half-brother Ivan V (with a secret compartment from which Regent Sofia prompted them), as well as the 800-diamond throne of Tsar Alexey, Peter's father. The gold Cap of Monomakh, jewel-studded and sable-trimmed, was used for two centuries at coronations.

Room 8 Only the best royal harnesses and equestrian gear.

Room 9 Centuries' worth of royal carriages and sledges line the aisles in this huge room, one of which surely could have kept a village of potential revolutionaries fed for several years. Look for the sleigh in which Elizabeth rode from St Petersburg to Moscow for her coronation, pulled by 23 horses at a time – about 800 in all for the trip.

DIAMOND FUND EXHIBITION Map p66

☎ **495-629 2036; admission R500;** 🕙 **10am-1pm, 2-5pm Fri-Wed;** Ⓜ **Aleksandrovsky Sad**

If the Armoury hasn't sated your lust for diamonds, there are more in the separate Diamond Fund Exhibition in the same building. The collection, mainly precious stones and jewellery garnered by tsars and empresses, includes such weighty beasts as the 190-carat diamond given to Catherine the Great by her lover Grigory Orlov. The displays of unmounted diamonds are stunning, revealing the real beauty of these gems.

There are almost no signs, even in Russian, as the locals are only allowed in as part of a guided tour. No tours are offered in other languages, which is to your advantage, since you do not have to wait as the Russian visitors do.

ALEXANDROVSKY GARDEN Map p66

Aleksandrovsky sad; Ⓜ **Aleksandrovsky Sad**

The first public park in Moscow, Alexandrovsky Garden sits along the Kremlin's western wall. Colourful flower beds and impressive Kremlin views make it a favourite strolling spot for Muscovites and tourists alike. Back in the 17th century, the Neglinnaya River ran through the present gardens, with dams and mills along its banks. When the river was diverted underground, the garden was founded by architect Osip Bove, in 1821. Enter through the original gates at the northern end.

The Tomb of the Unknown Soldier (Mogila neizvestnogo soldata) at its north end is a kind of national pilgrimage spot, where newlyweds bring flowers and have their pictures taken. The tomb contains the remains of one soldier who died in December 1941 at Km 41 of Leningradskoe sh – the nearest the Nazis came to Moscow. The inscription reads: 'Your name is unknown, your deeds immortal.' There's an eternal flame, and other inscriptions listing the Soviet hero cities of WWII – those that withstood the heaviest fighting – and honouring 'those who fell for the motherland' between 1941 and 1945. South of the tomb, a row of red urns contains earth from the 'hero cities'. The changing of the guard happens every hour.

Further south, the obelisk was originally a monument to commemorate the House of Romanovs. In 1918 it had a dramatic change in mission when it was redesignated the Monument to Revolutionary Thinkers, in honour of those responsible for the spread of communism in Russia.

RED SQUARE

The first time you set foot on Red Square, or Krasnaya pl, is a guaranteed awe-striker. For starters, the vast rectangular stretch of cobblestones, surrounded by architectural marvels, is jaw-dropping gorgeous. In fact, in old Russian *'krasny'* was the word for 'beautiful'; and it does live up to the original meaning of its name. Further, it evokes an incredible sense of import to stroll across a place where so much of Russian history unfolded.

Red Square used to be a market square adjoining the merchants' area in Kitay Gorod. It has always been a place where occupants of the Kremlin chose to congregate, celebrate and castigate for all the people to see. Back in the day, Red Square was the top spot for high-profile executions such as the Cossack rebel Stepan Razin in 1671 and the Streltsy (Peter the Great's mutinous palace guard) in 1698.

Soviet rulers chose Red Square for their military parades, perhaps most poignantly on 7 November 1941, when tanks rolled straight off to the frontline outside Moscow; and during the Cold War, when lines of ICBMs (intercontinental ballistic missile) rumbled across the square to remind the West of Soviet military might. On Victory Day in 2008, tanks rolled across Red Square for the first time since the collapse of the Soviet Union.

Red Square is closed to traffic, which means the square is filled with tourists, bridal parties and business people snapping photos and marvelling at their surroundings. The square empties out at night, but this is when the square is most atmospheric. The Kremlin towers and St Basil's domes, illuminated by floodlights and set against the night sky, create a spectacular panorama (even better in person than on a postcard).

From Manezhnaya pl (Okhotny Ryad metro station), enter Red Square through the Resurrection Gate, with its twin red towers topped by green tent spires. The first gateway, built in 1680, was destroyed because Stalin thought it an impediment to the parades and demonstrations held in Red Square. This exact replica was built in 1995. Through the gateway is the bright Chapel of the Iverian Virgin, originally built in the late 18th century to house the icon of the same name.

ST BASIL'S CATHEDRAL Map p66

Intercessional Cathedral; ☎ 495-698 3304; adult/student R100/50; ⊙ 11am-5pm Wed-Mon; Ⓜ Ploshchad Revolyutsii

At the southern end of Red Square, framed by the massive facades of the Kremlin and GUM, stands the icon of Russia: St Basil's Cathedral. This crazy confusion of colours, patterns and shapes is the culmination of a style that is unique to Russian architecture. Before St Basil's, this style of tent roofs and onion domes had been used to design wooden churches.

In 1552 Ivan the Terrible captured the Tatar stronghold of Kazan on the feast of Intercession. He commissioned this landmark church, officially the Intercession Cathedral, to commemorate the victory. From 1555 to 1561 architects Postnik and Barma created this masterpiece that would become the ultimate symbol of Russia.

The cathedral's apparent anarchy of shapes hides a comprehensible plan of nine main chapels: the tall, tent-roofed one in the centre; four big, octagonal-towered ones, topped with the four biggest domes; and four smaller ones in between.

Legend has it that Ivan had the architects blinded so they could never build anything comparable. This is a myth, however, as records show that they were employed a quarter of a century later (and four years after Ivan's death) to add an additional chapel to the structure.

The misnomer St Basil's actually refers only to this extra northeastern chapel. It was built over the grave of the barefoot holy fool Vasily (Basil) the Blessed, who predicted Ivan's damnation. Vasily, who died while Kazan was under siege, was buried beside the church that St Basil's soon replaced. He was later canonised.

LENIN UNDER GLASS

Red Square is home to the world's most famous mummy, that of Vladimir Ilych Lenin. When he died of a massive stroke on 22 January 1924, aged 53, a long line of mourners patiently gathered in the depths of winter for weeks to glimpse the body as it lay in state. Inspired by the spectacle, Stalin proposed that the father of Soviet communism should continue to serve the cause as a holy relic. So the decision was made to preserve Lenin's corpse for perpetuity, against the vehement protests of his widow, as well as Lenin's own expressed desire to be buried next to his mother in St Petersburg.

Boris Zbarsky, a biochemist, and Vladimir Voribov, an anatomist, were issued a political order to put a stop to the natural decomposition of the body. The pair worked frantically in a secret laboratory in search of a long-term chemical solution. In the meantime the body's dark spots were bleached, and the lips and eyes sewn tight. The brain was removed and taken to another secret laboratory, to be sliced and diced by scientists for the next 40 years in the hope of uncovering its hidden genius.

In July 1924 the scientists hit upon a formula to successfully arrest the decaying process, a closely guarded state secret. This necrotic craft was passed on to Zbarsky's son, who ran the Kremlin's covert embalming lab for decades. After the fall of communism, Zbarsky came clean: the body is wiped down every few days and then, every 18 months, thoroughly examined and submerged in a tub of chemicals, including paraffin wax. The institute has now gone commercial, offering its services and secrets to wannabe immortals for a mere million dollars.

In the early 1990s Boris Yeltsin expressed his intention to heed Lenin's request and bury him in St Petersburg, setting off a furore from the political left as well as more muted objections from Moscow tour operators. It seems that the mausoleum, the most sacred shrine of Soviet communism, and the mummy, the literal embodiment of the Russian Revolution, will remain in place for at least several more years.

Only in the 1670s were the domes patterned, giving St Basil's its multicoloured appearance. Between 1772 and 1784 the cathedral received a metal roof and a whitewashing; its domes were gold-leafed in keeping with the fashion of the time. Although Napoleon ordered it to be destroyed in 1812, his troops did not have enough time to complete the task. In 1817 the cathedral returned to its present colourful appearance, the cemetery was closed and the houses and moat surrounding the cathedral were removed.

The interior is open to visitors. Besides a small exhibition on the cathedral itself, it contains lovely frescoed walls and loads of nooks and crannies to explore. A collective ticket (adult/student R230/90) with the State History Museum (opposite) is available.

Out front of St Basil's is the statue of Kuzma Minin and Dmitry Pozharsky, one a butcher and the other a prince, who together raised and led the army that ejected occupying Poles from the Kremlin in 1612. Up the slope is the round, walled Place of Skulls, where Peter the Great executed the Streltsy.

LENIN'S TOMB Map p66

Mavzoley Lenina; ☎ 495-623 5527; admission free; ☯ 10am-1pm Tue-Thu, Sat & Sun; Ⓜ Ploshchad Revolyutsii

Although Vladimir Ilych requested that he be buried beside his mum in St Petersburg, he still lies in state at the foot of the Kremlin wall, receiving visitors who come to pay their respects to the founder of the Soviet Union. The embalmed leader has been here since 1924 (apart from a retreat to Siberia during WWII). See the boxed text, above, to learn how he keeps his waxy demeanour.

Before joining the queue at the northwestern corner of Red Square, drop your camera at the left-luggage office in the State History Museum, as you will not be allowed to take it with you. Humourless guards ensure that visitors remain respectful.

After trouping past the embalmed figure, emerge from the mausoleum and inspect the Kremlin wall, where other communist heavy hitters are buried:

Josef Stalin From 1953 to 1961, Lenin shared his tomb with Stalin. In 1961, during the 22nd Party Congress, the esteemed and by then ancient Bolshevik Madame Spiridonova announced that Vladimir Ilych had appeared to her in a dream, insisting that he did not like spending eternity with his successor. With that, Stalin was removed and given a place of honour immediately behind the mausoleum.

Leonid Brezhnev The fourth general secretary, successor to Khrushchev.

Felix Dzerzhinsky The founder of the Cheka (forerunner of the KGB).

Yakov Sverdlov A key organiser of the revolution and the first official head of the Soviet state.

Andrei Zhdanov Stalin's cultural chief and the second most powerful person in the USSR immediately after WWII.

Mikhail Frunze The Red Army leader who secured Central Asia for the Soviet Union in the 1920s.

Inessa Armand Lenin's rumoured lover. She was a respected Bolshevik who was the director of Zhenotdel, an organisation fighting for equality for women within the Communist Party.

John Reed The American author of *Ten Days that Shook the World*, a first-hand account of the revolution.

STATE HISTORY MUSEUM Map p66
☎ 495-692 3731; www.shm.ru; adult/student R150/60, audio guide R110; ☼ 10am-5pm Wed-Sat & Mon, 11am-7pm Sun; Ⓜ Ploshchad Revolyutsii
At the northern end of the square, the State History Museum has an enormous collection covering the whole Russian empire from the time of the Stone Age. The building, dating from the late 19th century, is itself an attraction – each room is in the style of a different period or region, some with highly decorated walls echoing old Russian churches. Reopened in 1997, each year sees the addition of a few more galleries. A joint ticket (adult/student R230/90) allowing access to the museum and St Basil's Cathedral is available at either spot.

GUM Map p66
☎ 495-788 4343; www.gum.ru; Krasnaya pl 3; ☼ 10am-10pm; Ⓜ Ploshchad Revolyutsii
The elaborate 19th-century facade on the northeastern side of Red Square is the Gosudarstvenny Universalny Magazin (State Department Store). GUM once symbolised all that was bad about Soviet shopping: long queues and shelves empty of all but a few drab goods. A remarkable transformation has taken place since *perestroika,* and today GUM is a bright, bustling place with over 1000 fancy shops (p149).

KAZAN CATHEDRAL Map p66
Kazansky Sobor; Nikolskaya ul 3; admission free; ☼ 8am-7pm, evening service 8pm Mon; Ⓜ Ploshchad Revolyutsii
The original Kazan Cathedral was founded on this site at the northern end of Red Square in 1636 in thanks for the 1612 expulsion of Polish invaders (for two centuries it housed the Virgin of Kazan icon, which supposedly helped to rout the Poles). From here, the archpriest Avvakum Petrov led

the opposition against Patriarch Nikon's 17th-century reforms of the Russian Orthodox Church, thus starting the separatist Old Believers' (p127) movement.

Three hundred years later, the cathedral was completely demolished, allegedly because it impeded the flow of celebrating workers in May Day and Revolution Day parades. The little church that occupies the site today is a 1993 replica.

MANEZHNAYA PLOSHCHAD
At the north end of Red Square, through the Resurrection Gate, is Manezhnaya pl (Manezh Square), named after the Kremlin's stables that once occupied this area. The Soviet Union's most successful WWII commander, Marshall Zhukov, presides over the square, mounted on his horse and appearing much like he did at the Victory Day parade in Red Square on 24 June 1945.

In the 1990s Manezhnaya pl was transformed with the vast underground Okhotny Ryad shopping mall (p149). From the square, it appears as a series of half-domes and balustrades, and a network of fountains and sculptures. It also contains the entrance to the Okhotny Ryad metro station.

This square has long been dominated by huge hotels, which have gone decidedly upscale in recent years. The historic National Hotel, now known as Le Royal Meridien National (p209), still dominates the corner opposite Alexandrovsky Garden. The National has been joined by the Ritz-Carlton (p209) on the former site of the much-maligned Intourist Hotel. The newest addition to the square is the Four Seasons Hotel Moskva (p205), occupying the site of the old Hotel Moskva.

The fine old edifices to the southwest of the square are the Russian State Library (p251), including the classical Paskkov House dating from 1787; and the old Moscow State University building, constructed in 1793 and named after the celebrated scientist Mikhail Lomonosov.

ARCHAEOLOGICAL MUSEUM Map p66
☎ 495-692 4171; www.mosmuseum.ru; Manezhnaya pl 1; admission R60; ☼ 10am-5.30pm Tue-Sun; Ⓜ Okhotny Ryad
An excavation of Voskresensky most (Voskresensky Bridge), which used to span the Neglinnaya River and commence the road to Tver, uncovered coins, clothing and other artefacts from old Moscow. The

museum displaying these treasures is situated in a 7m-deep underground pavilion that was formed during the excavation itself. The entrance is at the base of the Four Seasons. It was closed at the time of research, but expected to reopen with the hotel.

CENTRAL LENIN MUSEUM Map p66
pl Revolyutsii 2; Ⓜ Ploshchad Revolyutsii
The former Central Lenin Museum was once the big daddy of all the Lenin museums, but was closed in 1993 after the White House shoot out. It is sometimes used for special exhibits or communist rabble rousing. More often, it is simply a backdrop for rows of souvenir kiosks.

MANEZH EXHIBITION CENTRE Map p66
☎ 495-692 4459; Manezhnaya ul; exhibits R200-300; ⏱ 11am-8pm Tue-Sun; Ⓜ Biblioteka imeni Lenina
The long, low building on the southwestern side of the square is the Manezh, housing art exhibitions. This neoclassical landmark was badly damaged by a fire in 2004, sparking much speculation that it was not an accident. It is newly renovated and reopened, and now with an underground parking garage. Exhibits range from contemporary art and photography to lingerie and lilies.

TEATRALNAYA PLOSHCHAD
The aptly named Teatralnaya pl, or Theatre Square, opens out on both sides of Okhotny ryad, 200m northeast of Manezhnaya pl. In the early 18th century, the Neglinnaya River ran through here and powered water mills where the Hotel Metropol is now. Only in the early 19th century did the square receive its grand appearance, with the construction of the Bolshoi Theatre (p87) and the Maly Theatre (p192). The 1835 fountain by Vitali – now partially blocked by Karl Marx – marks the centre of the square. The Art Nouveau masterpiece Hotel Metropol (p206) was added in 1901. The metro station Teatralnaya provides easy access to these sights.

STARYE POLYA Map p66
Old Fields; Teatralny proezd; Ⓜ Lubyanka or Teatralnaya
Along Teatralny proezd, archaeologists uncovered the 16th-century fortified wall that used to surround Kitay Gorod, as well

as the foundations of the 1493 Trinity Church. Coins, jewellery and tombstones were also excavated here. Besides the remains of the wall and the church, you can now see a statue of Ivan Fyodorov, the 16th-century printer responsible for Russia's first book.

The gated walkway of Tretyakovsky proezd leads into Kitay Gorod. The archway, built in the 1870s, was apparently financed by the Tretyakov brothers, founders of the namesake gallery (p118). Apparently, the construction of the medieval-style gate and the opening of the passageway was an attempt to relieve traffic on Nikolskaya ul. Since its reopening in 2000, Tretyakovsky proezd is lined with exclusive shops, including Mercury, which financed much of the restoration.

KITAY GOROD
The narrow old streets east of Red Square are among the oldest in Moscow, established in the 13th century as an early trade and financial centre. Kitay Gorod means – literally – 'Chinatown', but actually has nothing to do with China. The name derives from *kita*, which means 'wattle', after the palisades that reinforced the earthen ramp erected around this early Kremlin suburb. The area's ancient, bustling streets and exquisite, tiny churches make it an ideal place for an enjoyable stroll (see p134 for details).

Kitay Gorod is bound, quite definitively, by Red Square in the west (close to Ploshchad Revolyutsii metro station) and by Novaya pl and Staraya pl in the east (close to Kitay-Gorod station). The Moscow River forms the southern boundary, while Teatralnaya proezd forms the northern limit.

MOSCOW CITY HISTORY MUSEUM
Map p66
☎ 495-624 8490; www.mosmuseum.ru; Novaya pl 12; admission R70; ⏱ 11am-5.30pm Tue-Sun; Ⓜ Lubyanka
This elaborate Russian Empire–style building dates from 1825. Formerly the John the Baptist Church, it now houses a small history museum, demonstrating how the city has spread from its starting point at the Kremlin. Exhibits are heavy on artefacts from the 13th and 14th centuries, especially household items, weapons and other representations of medieval Moscow.

ROMANOV CHAMBERS IN ZARYADIE

Map p66

Palaty Romanovikh v Zaryadye; ☎ 495-692 1256; **ul Varvarka 10; admission R100;** ☯ 10am-5pm Thu-Mon, 11am-6pm Wed; Ⓜ Kitay-Gorod
This small but interesting museum is devoted to the lives of the Romanov family, who were mere *boyars* (nobles) before they became tsars. The house was built by Nikita Romanov, whose grandson Mikhail later became the first tsar of the 300-year Romanov dynasty. Exhibits (with descriptions in English) show the house as it might have been when the Romanovs lived here in the 16th century. Some of the artistic detail, such as the woodwork in the women's quarters, is amazing. Enter from the rear of the building.

OLD ENGLISH COURT Map p66

Stary Angliisky Dvor; ☎ 495-698 3952; www .mosmuseum.ru; **ul Varvarka 4a; admission R35;** ☯ 11am-6pm Tue-Sun; Ⓜ Kitay-Gorod
This reconstructed 16th-century house, white with peaked wooden roofs, was the residence of England's first emissaries to Russia (sent by Elizabeth I to Ivan the Terrible). It also served as the base for English merchants, who were allowed to trade duty free in exchange for providing military supplies to Ivan. Today, it houses a small exhibit dedicated to this early international exchange.

SYNOD PRINTING HOUSE Map p66

Nikolskaya ul 15; Ⓜ Ploshchad Revolyutsii
This is where Ivan Fyodorov reputedly produced Russia's first printed book, *The Apostle*, in 1563. (You can see the man himself at Starye Polya, opposite.) In 1703 the first Russian newspaper, *Vedomosti*, was also printed here. Up until the early 19th century, Kitay Gorod was something of a printing centre, home at the time to 26 of Moscow's 31 bookshops.

ZAIKONOSPASSKY MONASTERY

Map p66

Nikolskaya ul 7-9; Ⓜ Ploshchad Revolyutsii
This monastery was founded by Boris Godunov in 1600, although the church was built in 1660. The name means 'Behind the Icon Stall', a reference to the busy icon trade that once took place here. On the orders of Tsar Alexey, the Likhud brothers, scholars of Greek, opened the Slavonic Greek and Latin Academy on the monastery premises in 1687. (Mikhail Lomonosov was a student here.) The academy later became a divinity school and was transferred to the Trinity Monastery of St Sergius (p218) in 1814.

MONASTERY OF THE EPIPHANY

Map p66

Bogoyavlensky per 2; Ⓜ Ploshchad Revolyutsii
This monastery is the second-oldest in Moscow; it was founded in 1296 by Prince Daniil, son of Alexander Nevsky. Stefan, one of the first abbots of the monastery, was the brother of Sergei Radonezhsky, who was patron saint of Russia and founder of the Trinity Monastery of St Sergius. The current Epiphany Cathedral was constructed in the 1690s in the Moscow baroque style.

CHURCH OF THE TRINITY IN NIKITNIKI

Map p66

Ipatyevsky per; Ⓜ Kitay-Gorod
This little gem of a church, built in the 1630s, is an exquisite example of Russian baroque. Its onion domes and tiers of red and white spade gables rise from a square tower. Its interior is covered with 1650s gospel frescoes by Simon Ushakov and others. A carved doorway leads into St Nikita the Martyr's Chapel, above the vault of the Nikitnikov merchant family, one of the patrons who financed the construction of the church.

BASMANNY

Drinking p179; Eating p162; Shopping p149; Sleeping p206

The most central part of the Basmanny district, just east of Kitay Gorod, is a bustling, atmospheric neighbourhood that has existed since the 16th century. From this time, the main thoroughfare, now ul Maroseyka and ul Pokrovka, was the route to the royal estate at Izmaylovsky Park (p131) and was lined with mansions. Peter the Great gave this territory to his pal and political protégé Alexander Menshikov, who established his estate here.

Not much architecture remains from this early period, thanks to the fire of 1812, but the main drag is still a lively strip, packed with shops, restaurants and cafés. The surrounding residential area is a maze of winding, one-way streets that are filled with surprises. The district is home to Moscow's first post office, founded in 1783 in one of the houses of the former Menshikov estate. These streets were also home to architect Matvey Kazakov and poet Alexander Pushkin.

The outlying areas also have a colourful history. The district takes its name from Basmannaya sloboda, or 'basman village'. In old Russian, *basman* was the bread that was provided to troops and workers, so the name refers to a sort of bakers' district that surrounded the present-day Staraya Basmannaya ul. Further northeast, Baumanskaya ul was formerly known as German street. It was in fact the centre of a German district, where all Catholics and Lutherans were forced to relocate in the mid-17th century. Nowadays, the area outside the Garden Ring does not draw many visitors, except perhaps to catch the train at Kursky vokzal. However, Moscow developers are getting creative with the surrounding industrial buildings, which now house some cool postmodern galleries and clubs. The easiest way to get here is by the Kurskaya or Chkalovskaya metro stations.

CHISTYE PRUDY Map pp80–1
Chistoprudny bul; Ⓜ Chistye Prudy

Chistye Prudy (Clean Ponds) refers to the lovely little pond that graces the Boulevard Ring at the ul Pokrovka intersection. The Boulevard Ring is always a prime location for strolling (see the walking tour, p140) but the addition of the quaint pond makes this a desirable address indeed. Paddleboats in summer and ice skating in winter are essential parts of the ambience. Pick a café and (season dependent) sip a beer or a coffee while watching strollers or skaters go by.

WINZAVOD Map pp80–1
☎ 495-917 4646, www.winzavod.ru; 4-Siromyatnichesky per 1; Ⓨ noon-8pm Tue-Sun; Ⓜ Chkalovskaya

You might not expect to find a cutting-edge art gallery amid the semi-sketchy streets behind Kursky vokzal. Then again, considering Soho before the 1980s, maybe you would. This former wine-bottling factory was converted into exhibit and studio space for Moscow artists, and opened in 2007. The postindustrial complex is now home to Moscow's most prestigious art galleries, including M&J Guelman, Aidan and XL. At the time of research, the complex also contained three photo galleries, as well as an avant-garde clothing store and a small café. This is the newest thing in the Moscow art world: it's worth checking out even if you're not in the market for the next Black Square.

SAKHAROV MUSEUM Map pp80–1
☎ 495-623 4401; www.sakharov-center.ru; Zemlyanoy val 57; admission free; Ⓨ 11am-7pm Tue-Sun; Ⓜ Chkalovskaya

South of Kursky vokzal, by the Yauza River, is a small park with a two-storey house containing the Andrei Sakharov Museum. The park is dotted with unusual sculptures, most built from weapons and other military-industrial waste. Look out for a piece of the Berlin Wall that has been repurposed in a poignant display. The exhibits recount the life of Sakharov, the nuclear-physicist-turned-human-rights-advocate, detailing the years of repression in Russia and providing a history of the courage shown by the dissident movement. Temporary expositions cover current human-rights issues and contemporary art. Curators at the Sakharov are frequently in the news for the controversy surrounding their exhibits (see the boxed text, opposite).

POLYTECHNICAL MUSEUM Map pp80–1
☎ 495-623 0756; www.polymus.ru; Novaya pl 3/4; adult/child R200/80, guided tour in Russian R300; Ⓨ 10am-5pm Tue-Sat; Ⓜ Lubyanka

Occupying the entire block of Novaya pl, this giant museum covers the history of Russian science, technology and industry. Indeed, the museum claims to be the largest science museum in the world. The permanent exhibits cover just about every aspect of Soviet scientific achievement, from a model of Lomonosov's laboratory to Mendeleev's development of the periodic table to Popov's first radio receiver. It is not as interactive or up to date as you might hope, but there is a new hands-on exhibit, *Igroteka*, which allows visitors to conduct their own experiments.

While the museum's focus is scientific, the building is also architecturally interesting and visually appealing. Three different parts of the structure were built at different times and in different styles: the oldest, central section (1877) represents the Russian Byzantine era; the eastern section (1896) is inspired by 17th-century Russian styles; and the western section (1907) is Art Nouveau.

MAYAKOVSKY MUSEUM Map pp80–1
☎ 495-621 6591; www.mayakovsky.info; Lubyansky proezd 3/6; admission R100; ⏰ 1-8pm Thu, 10am-5pm Fri-Tue; Ⓜ Lubyanka

The startling postmodern entrance on this prerevolutionary mansion is appropriate for a museum dedicated to the revolutionary, futurist poet Vladimir Mayakovsky. The building is actually where Mayakovsky lived in a communal apartment during the last years of his life. The room where he worked – and shot himself in 1930 – has been preserved. Run by the poet's granddaughter, the museum contains an eclectic collection of his manuscripts and sketches, as well as the requisite personal items and family photographs.

MENSHIKOV TOWER Map pp80–1
Menshikova Bashnya; Arkhangelsky per;
Ⓜ **Chistye Prudy**
In the late 17th century Peter the Great gifted much of the land in Basmanny to his pal Alexander Menshikov, who invested his time and money to clean up the area. Hidden behind the post office, this famous tower was built between 1704 and 1706 on the order of Menshikov from his

CAUTION: CENSORSHIP

By some accounts artists are freer than ever before to depict all aspects of Russian life (see the boxed text, p45). The fact remains, however, that certain subjects appear to be off limits. According to Marat Guelman, owner of the M&J Guelman gallery (opposite), as quoted in *Russia!* magazine, 'there are four completely taboo subjects in Russian art today: the government, the Orthodox Church, Chechnya and Putin'. While some artists and curators are able to work within these boundaries, others find themselves coming into conflict with the powers that be.

In 2003 Yury Samodurov, director of the Sakharov Museum (opposite), premiered a contemporary-art exhibit entitled 'Caution: Religion'. The exhibit cast a critical eye on the clash between the nascent Orthodox revival and the emerging mass-consumer culture in Russia. It depicted, among other things, the image of Jesus on a Coke can and the seven deadly sins being committed by an average Russian family in daily life. The exhibit elicited a shrill reaction from the Russian Orthodox Church, nationalist politicians and some patriotic hooligans, who were so offended that they vandalised the museum. The prosecutor found Samodurov and his deputy guilty of inciting ethnic hatred and offending true believers.

The sentence, apparently, did not scare Samodurov into submission. In 2007, the Sakharov Museum hosted an exhibit of artwork that had been banned from other museums. Appropriately, it was entitled 'Forbidden Art 2006'. The exhibit featured work by some of Russia's best-known contemporary artists, such as Ilya Kabakov, Aleksandr Kosolapov, the Siberian collective Blue Noses and Mikhail Roginskii. The exhibit touched on all the taboo subjects mentioned above, so it certainly caught the attention of the authorities. In 2008 Amnesty International called on the Russian authorities to respect the right to freedom of expression and to stop the criminal prosecution of Samodurov and his colleagues, but it's not clear if anyone is listening.

Later in 2007, 17 works of art were pulled from 'Sots-Art: Political Art in Russia', which was on its way to an exhibition in Paris. The banned artwork included several pieces from the aforementioned exhibits. Other offending items included a series entitled *Slava Rossii*, or 'Glory to Russia', depicting the seamier sides of life in Russia; and *The Era of Mercy*, an image of two kissing policemen. 'This art disgraces Russia,' the Minister of Culture apparently claimed.

These episodes are revealing of the way in which Russia's long tradition of dissent has evolved in postcommunist times. Throughout the Soviet period, dissent most often took political forms, correcting the lies of the regime and exposing its brutalities. As a prime example, the museum's inspiration and namesake, Andrei Sakharov, spent nearly six years under house arrest in Nizhny Novgorod for criticising Soviet policy. When communism collapsed, some wondered if Russia's long tradition of dissent would fade away with the commissars. As evidenced by these incidents, dissent in post-Soviet Russia has not disappeared, but it is taking on new cultural forms. The communist dictatorship may have fallen, but the ghost of Andrei Sakharov still haunts the Kremlin.

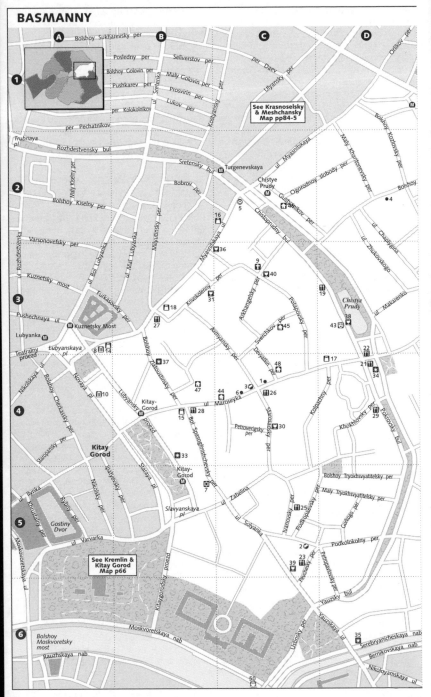

BASMANNY

NEIGHBOURHOODS **BASMANNY**

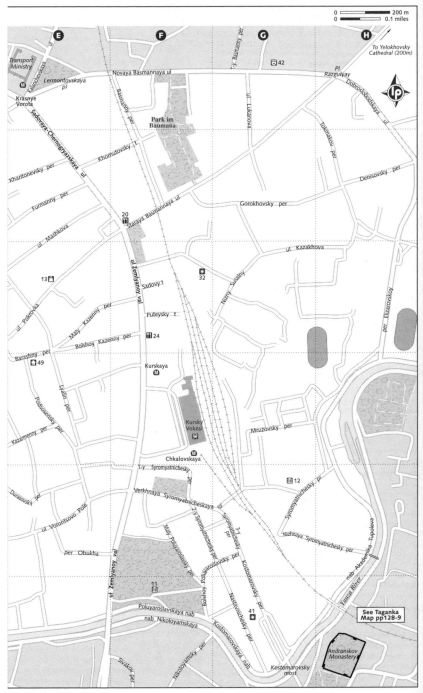

0   200 m
0   0.1 miles

E   **F**   **G**   **H**

To Yelokhovsky
Cathedral (200m)

Transport
Ministry

Lermontovskaya
pl

Krasnye
Vorota

Novaya Basmannaya ul

42

Pl.
Razgulyay

Dobroslobodskaya

ul Lukanova

Khomutovsky t.

Park im
Baumana

Basmanny per

Sadovaya-Chernogryazskaya ul

Kharitonevsky per

Furmanny per

ul Mashkova

Staraya Basmannaya ul

20

Tokmakov per

Denisovsky per

Gorokhovsky per

ul Kazakhova

13

ul Zemlyanoy val

Sadovy t.

32

Nizhny Susalny

ul Pokrovka

Maly Kazenny per

Puteysky t.

Bolshoy Kazenny per

24

per Elizarovsky

Barashny per

49

Lyalin per

Kurskaya

Podsosensky per

Kazarmenny per

Kursky
Vokzal

Mruzovsky per

Durasovsky per

Chkalovskaya

1-y Syromyatnichesky

12

ul Vorontsovo Pole

Verkhnaya Syromyatnicheskaya ul

Syromyatnichesky
per

3-y
per

Syromyatnichesky pr

Nizhnyaya Syromyatnichesky per

nab. Akademika-Tupoleva

per Obukha

Maly Poluyaroslavsky per

2-y Syromyatnichesky per

Bolshoy Poluyaroslavsky per

Nastavnichesky per

Kostomarovsky per

Yauza River

ul Zemlyanoy val

11

41

Poluyaroslavskaya nab

nab Nikoloyamskaya

Kostomarovskaya nab

Kostomarovsky
most

See Taganka
Map pp128-9

Sivakov per

Nikoloyamsky per

Andronikov
Monastery

BASMANNY (pp80–1)

newly founded estate. The tower – one of Moscow's first baroque buildings – was originally 3m taller than the Ivan the Great Bell Tower. A thunderstorm in 1723 saw it hit by lightning and seriously damaged by fire. Trouble plagued the owner as well. Menshikov fell from grace after the death of Peter the Great, and he was exiled to Siberia. The tower was neglected. When finally repaired in the 1780s, it lost much of its height and elegance. Today, it houses the working Church of Archangel Gabriel.

CHORAL SYNAGOGUE Map pp80–1

☎ 495-940 5557; www.keroor.ru/ru/synagogue; Bolshoy Spasoglinishchevsky per 10; ☽ 9am-6pm; Ⓜ Kitay-Gorod

Construction of a synagogue was banned inside Kitay Gorod, so Moscow's oldest and most prominent synagogue was built just outside the city walls, not far from the Jewish settlement of Zaryadye. Construction started in 1881 but dragged on due to roadblocks by the anti-Semitic tsarist government. It was completed in 1906 and was the only synagogue that continued to operate throughout the Soviet period, in spite of Bolshevik demands to convert it into a workers'

club. Apparently, Golda Meir shocked the authorities when she paid an unexpected visit here in 1948. These days the exquisite interior has been completely restored and is open for visitors. The building hosts the International Jewish Social Club (☽ 2-5pm Sun).

YELOKHOVSKY CATHEDRAL Map pp60–1

Church of the Epiphany in Yelokhovo; www.mospat .ru; Spartakovskaya ul 15; Ⓜ Baumanskaya

On the outskirts of Moscow, Spartakovskaya ul is the unlikely address of Moscow's senior Orthodox cathedral. This role was given to the Church of the Epiphany in Yelokhovo in 1943 (the Patriarch had been evicted from the Kremlin's Assumption Cathedral in 1918), and the Patriarch now leads important services here.

Built between 1837 and 1845 with five domes in a Russian eclectic style, the cathedral is full of gilt and icons, not to mention old women kneeling, polishing, lighting candles, crossing themselves and kissing the floor. In the northern part is the tomb of St Nicholas the Miracle Worker (Svyatoy Nikolay Ugodnik). A shrine in front of the right side of the iconostasis contains the remains of St Alexey, a 14th-century metropolitan.

KRASNOSELSKY & MESHCHANSKY

Drinking p180; Eating p163; Shopping p150; Sleeping p207

These two side-by-side districts contrast in every way. Krasnoselsky is a mostly industrial neighbourhood, dominated by the train stations and railway yards surrounding Komsomolskaya pl. Meshchansky is more commercial and residential, with vast parks and palaces in its northern reaches. It is ironic, then, that the name Krasnoselsky originates from *krasnoye selo*, or 'beautiful village'; while Meshchansky takes its name from *meshchane*, an old word for the lower classes.

Taken together, the districts stretch north-east from Lubyanka Square, or Lubyanskaya pl. Myastnitskaya ul, Lermontovskaya pl and Novaya Basmannaya ul form the border in the south, while Neglinnaya ul, Tsvetnoy bul and Samotechnaya ul do the same in the west. Metro stations ring the pie-shaped area, including Lubyanka at the southern point, Sretensky Bulvar and Krasnye Vorota along the south-eastern edge, and Trubnaya and Tsvetnoy Bulvar along the western edge. Additional stations – Sukharevskaya and Krasnye Vorota – are along the Garden Ring, while Prospekt Mira and Komsomolskaya are further out.

For decades Lubyanka Square was a chilling symbol of the KGB, or Komitet Gosudarstvennoy Bezopasnosti (Committee for State Security), thanks to the monolithic Lubyanka Prison that still dominates the intersection. From 1926 to 1990, it was called pl Dzerzhinskogo, after Felix Dzerzhinsky, who founded the Cheka, the KGB's forerunner. A tall statue of Dzerzhinsky once stood here.

When the 1991 coup collapsed, the statue was memorably removed by angry crowds, with the assistance of a couple of cranes. There was a recent proposal – backed by Mayor Luzhkov, strangely enough – to resurrect 'Iron Felix' and return him to his place of honour, but these Felix fans did not get very far. Now you can see the statue in all its (somewhat reduced) glory in the Art Muzeon Sculpture Park (p119), where it stands among others fallen from grace.

The streets west of Lubyanka Square are crammed with shops, hotels and restaurants, as well as Moscow's favourite Soviet-era retro clubs. Once a popular – and populist – area for eating, drinking and shopping, this neighbourhood is quickly going the way of other swanky, central Moscow districts, with upscale venues crowding out the more democratic options. (They are easily accessible via Kuznetsky Most metro station.)

North-east of here, the atmosphere changes radically at Komsomolskaya pl. The three main train stations surrounding the square, and the diverse and dubious crowds that frequent them, make this one of Moscow's hairiest places.

This one square captures not only Moscow's social diversity, but also its architectural diversity. Kazansky vokzal (Kazan station), on the south side of the square, was built by architect Alexey Shchusev between 1912 and 1926. It is a retrospective of seven building styles that date back to a 16th-century Tatar tower in Kazan. Leningradsky vokzal (Leningrad station), with the tall clock tower on the northern side of the square, is Moscow's oldest station, built in 1851. Yaroslavsky vokzal (Yaroslavl station) is a 1902–04 Art Nouveau fantasy by Fyodor Shekhtel. Overseeing the whole square is one of Stalin's 'Seven Sisters' (see boxed text, p51), the 26-storey Hilton Leningradskaya Hotel (p208).

LUBYANKA PRISON Map pp84–5
Lubyanskaya pl; Ⓜ Lubyanka
In the 1930s Lubyanka Prison was the feared destination of thousands of innocent victims of Stalin's purges. Today the grey building looming on the northeastern side of the square is no longer a prison, but is the headquarters of the newly named Federal Security Service, or *Federalnaya Sluzhba Beopasnosti*. The FSB keeps a pretty good eye on domestic goings on. The building is not open to the public.

The much humbler Memorial to the Victims of Totalitarianism stands in the little garden on the southeastern side of the square. This single stone slab comes from the territory of an infamous 1930s labour camp situated on the Solovetsky Islands in the White Sea.

FSB MUSEUM Map pp84–5
☎ 495-224 1982; ul Bolshaya Lubyanka 12/1;
🕑 by appointment; Ⓜ Lubyanka
It calls itself the FSB Museum, named for the Federal Security Service, the successor to the KGB. But this four-room museum is

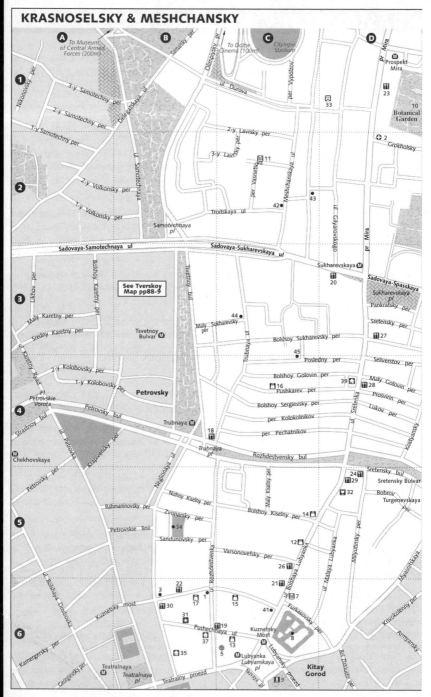

KRASNOSELSKY & MESHCHANSKY

To Museum
of Central Armed
Forces (200m)

To Dome
Cinema (100m)

Olimps
Stadium

Nikolaevsky per
3-y Samotechny per
2-y Samotechny per
1-y Samotechny per
2-y Volkonsky per
1-y Volkonsky per
Delegatskaya ul
Samotechnaya
Samotechnaya
Samotechnaya
Samotechnaya pl
Sadovaya-Samotechnaya ul

Olimpysky pr
Simacky per
ul Durova
2-y Lavrsky per
3-y Lavrsky per
per Vasnetsova
11
Meshchanskaya ul
42
43
Troitskaya ul
pr Vypolzov

pr Mira
Prospekt Mira
23
10
Botanical Garden
2
Grokholsky

Sadovaya-Sukharevskaya ul
Sukharevskaya
20
Sadovaya-Spasskaya
Sukharevskaya pl
Pankratsky per
Sretensky per
27

See Tverskoy
Map pp88-9

Likhov per
Bolshoy Karetny per
Maly Karetny per
Sredny Karetny per
S Karetny Ryad
2-y Kolobovsky per
1-y Kolobovsky per
Tsvetnoy Bulvar
Tsvetnoy bul
Petrovsky
Pl Petrovskie Vorota
Petrovsky bul
Strastnoy bul
Petrovka
Petrovsky per
Chekhovskaya
Petrovsky per
Krapivensky per
Neglinnaya ul

44
Maly Sukharevsky per
Trubnaya ul
Bolshoy Sukharevsky per
45
Posledny per
Bolshoy Golovin per
16
Pushkarev per
Bolshoy Sergievsky per
per Kolokolnikov
per Pechatnikov
Rozhdestvensky bul
18
Trubnaya
Trubnaya pl
Seliverstov per
Maly Golovin per
28
Prosvirin per
Lukov per
Sretenka ul
39
Krasnoselsky

ul Giljarovskogo

Rahmaninovsky per
Zvonarsky per
Petrovskie linii
Sandunovsky per
Varsonovefsky per
34
Nizhny Kiselny per
Maly Kiselny per
Bolshoy Kiselny per
14
12
26
21
7
41
Bolshaya Lubyanka
Rozhdestvenka
Sretensky bul
24
29
32
Bobrov per
Turgenevskaya
Milyutinsky per
Maly Zlatoustin per
Krivokolenny per
Armyansky
Myasnitskaya

ul Bolshaya Dmitrovka
Kuznetsky most
3
22
30
17
1
15
31
35
Pushechnaya ul
37
19
13
5
Kuznetsky Most
8
Lubyanka
Lubyanskaya pl
Furkasovsky per
Malaya Lubyanka
Novaya pl
Kitay Gorod
9
Kamergersky per
Georgievsky per
Teatralnaya
Teatralnaya pl
Teatralny proezd
Bol Zlatoustin per

84

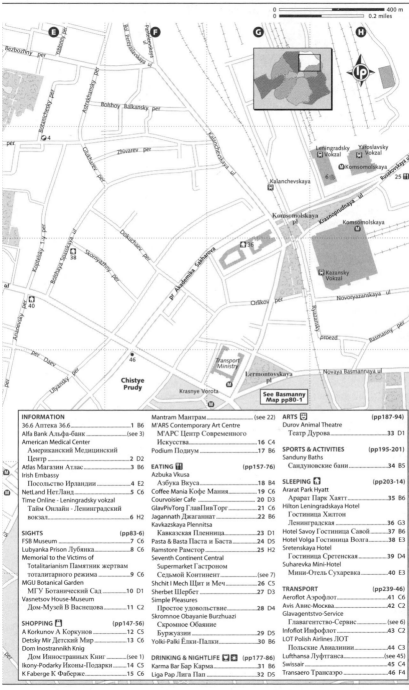

NEIGHBOURHOODS KRASNOSELSKY & MESHCHANSKY

See Basmanny Map pp80-1

top picks

IT'S FREE

- Lenin's Tomb (p74) Pay your respects to the founder of the Soviet state.
- Cathedral of Christ the Saviour (p109) Glitter and gold on a huge scale.
- Winzavod (p78) and Garazh Centre for Contemporary Art (p130) Contemporary art in post-industrial settings.
- Kolomenskoe Museum-Reserve (p132) and Tsaritsyno Palace (p133) Pay to enter the museums, but seeing the beautiful grounds and churches will cost you nothing.
- Gorky House-Museum (p101) A tribute to a literary mastermind, housed inside an Art Nouveau masterpiece.
- Sakharov Museum (p78) Political and artistic exhibits, as well as information about the life and times of the dissident.

devoted to the history, propaganda and paraphernalia of the Soviet intelligence services, from the Cheka to the KGB (you won't find much in-depth info on the operations of the current security service!). An FSB agent leads a small group, room by room, recounting Cold War–era espionage anecdotes. Exhibits include a few fun spy tools, but nothing to really impress a technologically advanced audience.

The museum was closed for renovation at the time of research, with the close-lipped security service giving no indication of when it might reopen. Even under normal circumstances, security at this place is supertight, and it is open only by appointment.

VASNETSOV HOUSE-MUSEUM
Map pp84–5

☎ 495-681 1329; per Vaznetsova 13; admission R80; ☼ 10am-5pm Wed-Sun; Ⓜ Sukharevskaya

Victor Vasnetsov (1848–1926) is a Russian-revivalist painter and architect who is famous for his historical paintings with mystical and fairytale subjects. In 1894 Vasnetsov designed his own house in Moscow, which is now a small museum. Fronted by a colourful gate, it is a charming home, still filled with the original wooden furniture, tiled stove and many of the artist's paintings. The attic studio, where he once painted, is now hung with paintings depicting Baba Yaga and other characters from Russian fairytales.

Early on, Vasnetsov was scorned for his fantastical style, as it was such a startling contrast to the realism of the Peredvezhniki. Even Pavel Tretyakov, the most prominent patron of the arts at the time, refused to buy his paintings. However, by the turn of the century, he found a source of support in Savva Mamontov, whose financing drove the Russian revivalist movement.

MGU BOTANICAL GARDEN Map pp84–5
☎ 495-680 5880; www.hortus.ru, in Russian; pr Mira 26; adult/child R50/10; ☼ 10am-10pm; Ⓜ Prospekt Mira

When you need an escape from the city's hustle and bustle, the MGU Botanical Garden offers a wonderful retreat. There have been gardens on this site for hundreds of years. Established in 1706, it was owned by the Moscow general hospital to grow herbs and other medicinal plants. These days it is operated by the university. Visitors can wander along the trails, enjoy an exhibition of ornamental plants and explore three greenhouses containing plants from various climate zones.

Drinking p180; Eating p165; Shopping p151; Sleeping p208

The streets around Tverskaya ul comprise the vibrant Tverskoy district, characterised by old architecture and new commerce. Tverskaya ul dates back to the 12th century, although this district developed significantly when Peter the Great moved to St Petersburg and this became the main route for the journey between the two capitals.

Tverskoy has always been a theatre district, home to the capital's first theatre, the Petrovka, later replaced by the Bolshoi and the other landmarks around Theatre Square. In 1882 the State lifted a ban on private theatres, contributing to the district's cultural capital with the opening of Moscow Art Theatre (p192) and others. Currently, Tverskoy is home to 19 theatres, as well as the Tchaikovsky Concert Hall (p188) and the Nikulin Circus on Tsvetnoy Bulvar (p194).

Aside from being a cultural centre, Tverskoy is certainly the city's liveliest commercial district. Its streets are lined with restaurants, bars, theatres and shops, giving it a modern bright-lights-big-city atmosphere. Small lanes such as Kamergersky per and Stoleshnikov per are among Moscow's trendiest places to sip a coffee or a beer and watch the bustle. To get a taste of Tverskoy, follow the walking tour on p135.

The radial lines that run roughly parallel to Tverskaya ul are ul Malaya Dmitrovka and ul Bolshaya Dmitrovka to the east; and ul Petrovka and ul Karetny Ryad further east. Neglinnaya ul, Tsvetnoy bul and Samotechnaya ul form the eastern boundary. For the purposes of this book, Malaya Bronnaya ul and Bolshaya Nikitskaya ul and ul Krasina form the southwestern boundary.

ULITSA PETROVKA

Now restored to its fashionable prerevolutionary status, ul Petrovka is at the centre of Moscow's glossiest central shopping area. Petrovsky Passage was one of the earliest converts to the consumer culture, when it was transformed into a light- and fountain-filled shopping centre, bursting with upscale shops. The Central Department Store (TsUM; p153), once a source of drab Soviet products, is now Moscow's finest department store, selling top-of-the-line name brands at out-of-this-world prices. Cobblestoned Stoleshnikov per – closed to road traffic – is one of Moscow's sleekest streets, home to the most exclusive (and expensive) boutiques. If you don't come to shop, come to watch the shoppers. This is the place to see the gaudy and the glamour of Moscow's New Russians.

Just to prove that New Russia is not without culture or conviction, ul Petrovka commences at Theatre Square, home to the celebrated Bolshoi. Petrovka also contains the funky and fanciful Moscow Museum of Modern Art and the poignant and provocative Gulag History Museum. Further north, the magnificent New Opera stands amid the verdant splendour of the Hermitage Gardens.

To reach ul Petrovka, take the metro to Teatralnaya or walk east from Chekhovskaya metro station.

BOLSHOI THEATRE Map pp88–9

☎ 495-250 7317, hot line 8-800-333 1333; www
.bolshoi.ru; Teatralnaya pl 1; tickets R200-2000;
Ⓜ Teatralnaya

Theatre Square anchors ul Petrovka with its three grand theatres surrounding a wide plaza and flowing fountain. The centrepiece, of course, is the world-renowned Bolshoi Theatre. The present pink-and-white beauty was built in 1824, replacing the Petrovka Theatre that previously stood on this site. This historic theatre saw the premier of Tchaikovsky's *Swan Lake* in 1877 and *The Nutcracker* in 1919. The main stage has recently reopened after much-needed renovations, while the New Stage continues to put on performances (see p189 for details).

Across and down ul Petrovka from the 'grand' Bolshoi is the 'lesser' Maly Theatre (p192), also built in 1824. Back in the day, when there were only two theatres in Moscow, the custom was to label the opera theatre the *bolshoi* and the drama theatre the *maly*. On the west side of the square is the National Youth Theatre.

GULAG HISTORY MUSEUM Map pp88–9

☎ 495-621 7346; www.museum-gulag.narod.ru,
in Russian; ul Petrovka 16; 🕐 11am-4pm Tue-Sat;
Ⓜ Chekhovskaya

In the midst of all the swanky shops on ul Petrovka, an archway leads to a courtyard

NEIGHBOURHOODS TVERSKOY

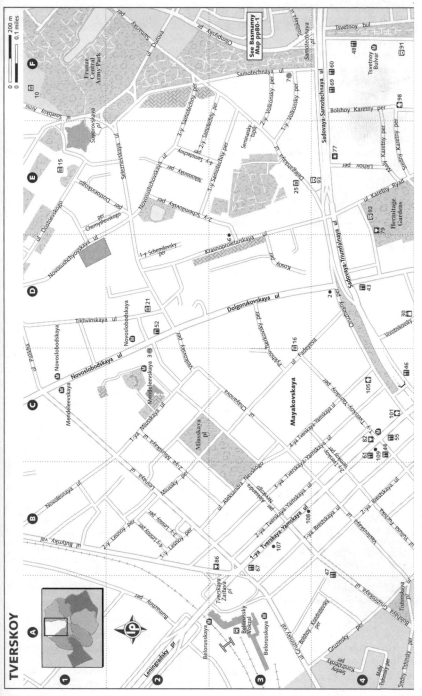

lonelyplanet.com

NEIGHBOURHOODS TVERSKOY

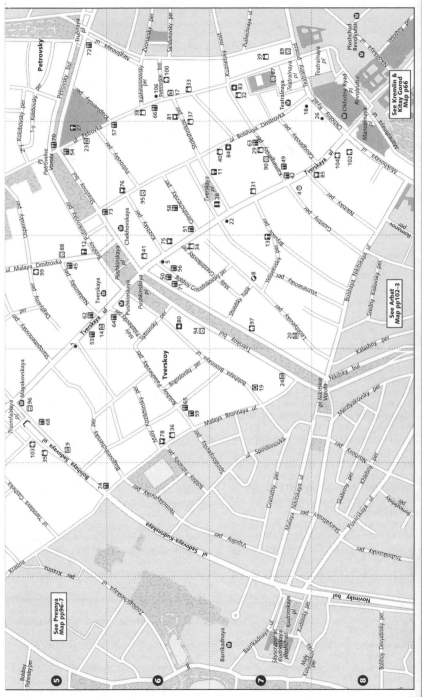

See Kremlin & Kitay Gorod Map p66

See Arbat Map pp102–3

See Presnya Map pp96-7

TVERSKOY (pp88-9)

that is strung with barbed wire and hung with portraits of political prisoners. This is the entrance to a unique museum dedicated to the Chief Administration of Corrective Labour Camps and Colonies, better known as the GULAG. Guides dressed like guards describe the vast network of labour camps that once existed in the former Soviet Union and recount the horrors of camp life.

Millions of prisoners spent years in these labour camps, made famous by Alexander Solzhenitsyn's book *The Gulag Archipelago*. More than 18 million people passed through this system during its peak years, from 1929 to 1953, although many camps remained in operation until the end of the 1980s. The gulag became a chilling symbol of political repression, as many of the prisoners were serving time for 'antisocial' or 'counter-revolutionary' behaviour. The museum serves as a history lesson about the system, as well as a memorial to its victims.

MOSCOW MUSEUM OF MODERN ART Map pp88–9

MMOMA; ☎ 495-694 2890; www.mmoma.ru; ul Petrovka 25; adult/student R200/100; ☽ noon–7pm; Ⓜ Chekhovskaya

A pet project of the ubiquitous Zurab Tsereteli (see the boxed text, p113), this museum is housed in a classical 18th-century merchant's home, originally designed by Matvei Kazakov (architect of the Kremlin Senate). It is the perfect light-filled setting for an impressive collection of 20th-century paintings, sculptures and graphics, which includes both Russian and foreign artists. The highlight is the collection of avant-garde art, with works by Chagall, Kandinsky and Malevich. Unique to this museum is its exhibit of 'nonconformist' artists from the 1950s and '60s – those whose work was not acceptable to the Soviet regime. The gallery also hosts temporary exhibits that often feature contemporary artists. Be sure not to bypass the whimsical sculpture garden in the courtyard. There are additional MMOMA outlets, used primarily for temporary exhibits, on Tverskoy bul (p93) and Ermolaevsky per (p95).

UPPER ST PETER MONASTERY
Map pp88–9

Petrovsky monastyr; cnr ul Petrovka & Petrovsky bul; admission free; ⏰ **8am-8pm;** Ⓜ **Chekhovskaya**
The Upper St Peter Monastery was founded in the 1380s as part of an early defensive ring around Moscow. The grounds are pleasant in a peaceful, near-deserted way. The main, onion-domed Virgin of Bogolyubovo Church dates from the late 17th century. The loveliest structure is the brick Cathedral of Metropolitan Pyotr, restored with a shingle roof. (When Peter the Great ousted the Regent Sofia in 1690, his mother was so pleased she built him this church.)

TVERSKAYA ULITSA & TVERSKOY BULVAR

Moscow's main drag is Tverskaya ul – the start of the road to Tver and on to St Petersburg. It is a wide highway, crowded with cars whizzing by (or creeping, as the case may be). The pavements are crowded with shoppers, and the selection of stores is vast. This busy street lacks the personality of some of Moscow's other districts, due in part to the soulless reconstruction in the 1930s. Residents also claim that recent development has driven out local shops that used to cater to the community.

The bottom of Tverskaya ul, at Manezhnaya pl (p75), is the city's hub. From here, the busy street heads northwest, past the trendy pedestrian side street Kamergersky per, a prime people-watching spot – its cafés and restaurants provide perfect vantage points for Moscow's most beautiful people to don their shades and check each other out.

Heading north, each busy intersection has its own unique personality, crowded shopping centres, metro stop and traffic jams. The first of the prominent squares along the main road is known, appropriately, as Tverskaya pl. Further along, a statue of Alexander Pushkin surveys his domain from the square that bears his name. From here, the Boulevard Ring turns south. Peaceful, pleasant and blooming with

top picks

TVERSKOY

- **Contemporary History Museum** (right) Feeling nostalgic for the Soviet Union?
- **Glinka Museum of Musical Culture** (p94) Musical instruments from around the world and across the ages.
- **Gulag History Museum** (p87) Learn about the horrors of the Soviet prison camps.
- **Moscow Museum of Modern Art** (p90) The best collection of Russian art from the 20th century.

trees, Tverskoy bul is possibly the loveliest stretch of the Boulevard Ring.

Further north, the revolutionary poet Vladimir Mayakovsky overlooks Triumfalnaya pl, while Belorussky vokzal is the centrepiece of the crazy intersection at the top of Tverskaya ul. The green Zamoskvoretskaya metro line runs beneath Tverskaya ul, providing easy access to each of these squares.

HOUSE OF UNIONS & STATE DUMA
Map pp88–9

Okhotny ryad 2/1; Ⓜ **Teatralnaya**

The buildings lining Okhotny ryad, just north of Tverskaya ul, serve official functions. The glowering State Duma was erected in the 1930s for Gosplan (Soviet State Planning Department), source of the USSR's Five-Year Plans, but it is now the seat of the Russian parliament. The green-columned House of Unions dates from the 1780s. Its ballroom, called the Hall of Columns, is the famous location of one of Stalin's most grotesque show trials, that of Nikolai Bukharin, a leading Communist Party theorist who had been a close associate of Lenin. Both buildings are closed to the public.

TVERSKAYA PLOSHCHAD Map pp88–9

A statue of the founder of Moscow, Yury Dolgoruky, presides over this prominent square near the bottom of Tverskaya ul. So does Mayor Luzhkov, as the buffed-up five-storey building opposite is the Moscow mayor's office. Many ancient churches are hidden in the back streets, including the 17th-century Church of SS Kosma & Damian. West of here, through the arch across Bryusov

per, is the unexpected, gold-domed Church of the Resurrection, which is full of fine icons rescued from churches torn down during the Soviet era.

CHURCH OF THE NATIVITY OF THE VIRGIN IN PUTINKI Map pp88–9

ul Malaya Dmitrovka 4; Ⓜ **Pushkinskaya**

When this church was completed in 1652, the Patriarch Nikon responded by banning tent roofs like the ones featured here. Apparently, he considered such architecture too Russian, too secular and too far removed from the Church's Byzantine roots. Fortunately, the Church of the Nativity has survived to grace this corner near Pushkinskaya pl.

CONTEMPORARY HISTORY MUSEUM
Map pp88–9

☎ 495-699 6724; www.sovr.ru; Tverskaya ul 21; adult/student R100/70; ☉ 10am-6pm Tue-Sun; Ⓜ Pushkinskaya

Formerly known as the Revolution Museum, this retro exhibit traces Soviet history from the 1905 and 1917 revolutions up to the 1980s. The highlight is the extensive collection of propaganda posters, in addition to all the Bolshevik paraphernalia. Look for the picture of the giant Palace of Soviets (Dvorets Sovietov) that Stalin was going to build on the site of the blown-up – and now rebuilt – Cathedral of Christ the Saviour. English-language tours are available with advance notice.

BULGAKOV HOUSE-MUSEUM Map pp88–9

☎ 495-970 0619; www.dombulgakova.ru, in Russian; Bolshaya Sadovaya ul 10; admission free; ☉ 1-11pm Sun-Thu, 1pm-1am Fri & Sat; Ⓜ Mayakovskaya

Author of *The Master and Margarita* and *Heart of a Dog*, Mikhail Bulgakov was a Soviet-era novelist and playwright who was labelled a counter-revolutionary and censored throughout most of his life. His most celebrated novels were published posthumously, earning him a sort of cult following in the late Soviet period. Bulgakov lived with his third wife Yelena Shilovskaya (the inspiration for Margarita) in a flat on the Garden Ring from 1931 until his death in 1940.

Back in the 1990s the empty flat was a hang-out for dissidents and hooligans, who painted graffiti and wrote poetry on the walls. Nowadays, the walls have been whitewashed and the doors locked, but there is a small museum and café on the ground floor. The exhibit features some of his personal items, as well as posters and illustrations of his works. More interesting are the readings and concerts that are held here (check the website), as well as the offbeat tours on offer. A black cat hangs out in the courtyard.

MOSCOW MUSEUM OF MODERN ART Map pp88–9
MMOMA; ☎ 495-694 2890; www.mmoma.ru; Tverskoy bul 9; ☽ noon-8pm; Ⓜ Pushkinskaya
This is a branch of the main MMOMA outlet on ul Petrovka (p90), and is utilised for temporary exhibits of paintings, sculpture, photography and multimedia pieces. Be sure to check the website to see what's on, as the museum often closes in between shows.

LYUBAVICHESKAYA SYNAGOGUE
Map pp88–9
☎ 495-202 4530; Bolshaya Bronnaya ul 6; Ⓜ Pushkinskaya
Converted to a theatre in the 1930s, this building was still used for gatherings by the Jewish community throughout the Soviet period. The rug on the altar hides a trapdoor leading to a small cell where Jews used to hide from the communists. Today the building serves as a working synagogue, as well as a social centre for the small but growing Jewish community in Moscow.

MATRYOSHKA MUSEUM Map pp88–9
☎ 495-291 9645; Leontevsky per 7; admission free; ☽ 10am-6pm Mon-Thu, 10am-5pm Fri; Ⓜ Pushkinskaya
On a quiet side street, the Matryoshka Museum – formerly the Museum of Folk Art – is a two-room museum showcasing designer *matryoshka* dolls and different painting techniques. The centrepiece is a 1m-high *matryoshka* with 50 dolls inside. The exhibit demonstrates the history of this favourite Russian souvenir. Don't come looking for modern-day, pop-culture-inspired dolls because the museum takes a traditionalist tact. Downstairs, an excellent souvenir shop offers a wide selection of handicrafts, including hand-painted *matryoshki*.

OUTER TVERSKOY
Beyond the Garden Ring, Tverskoy district is mostly residential, with clusters of industrial development around the railway terminals, Belorussky vokzal and Savelovsky vokzal. Tverskaya ul changes name to Tverskaya-Yamskaya ul and, beyond Belorussky vokzal, to Leningradsky pr and eventually to Leningradskoe sh, as this highway heads out of town. The green Zamoskvoretskaya metro line follows this road almost all the way to MKAD, finally terminating at Rechnoy Vokzal.

Further east, the road that was ul Bolshaya Dmitrovka and Malaya Dmitrovka changes to the multilane Novoslobodskaya ul. This northeastern corner of Tverskoy district is accessible via the connecting metro stations at Novoslobodskaya or Mendeleevskaya.

In recent years, major roads such as Leningradsky pr and Novoslobodskaya ul have been built up with high-rise apartment and office buildings. They are often choked with cars, which might be alleviated by the ongoing widening of the roads, but it is doubtful. This is your route to Sheremetyevo airport; if you intend to travel by car, be sure to allow extra time for traffic jams.

CENTRAL MUSEUM OF THE ARMED FORCES Map pp88–9
Tsentralny Muzey Vooruzheny Sil; ☎ 495-681 6303; www.cmaf.ru, in Russian; ul Sovetskoy Armii 2; admission R70; ☽ 10am-4.30pm Wed-Sun; Ⓜ Novoslobodskaya
Covering the history of the Soviet and Russian military since 1917, this massive museum occupies 24 exhibit halls plus open-air exhibits. Over 800,000 military items, including uniforms, medals and weapons, are on display. Among the highlights are remainders of the American U2 spy plane (brought down in the Urals in 1960) and the victory flag raised over Berlin's Reichstag in 1945. Take trolleybus 69 (or walk) 1.3km east from the Novoslobodskaya metro.

DOSTOEVSKY HOUSE-MUSEUM
Map pp88–9
☎ 495-681 1085; ul Dostoevskogo 2; admission R40; ☽ 11am-6pm Thu, Sat & Sun, 2-7pm Wed & Fri; Ⓜ Novoslobodskaya
While this renowned Russian author is more closely associated with St Petersburg, Fyodor Dostoevsky was actually born in Moscow, and his family lived in a tiny

apartment on the grounds of Marinsky Hospital. He lived here until the age of 16, when he went to St Petersburg to enter a military academy. The family's Moscow flat has been re-created according to descriptions written by Fyodor's brother. Visitors can see the family's library, toys and many other personal items, including Fyodor's quill pen and an original autograph.

GLINKA MUSEUM OF MUSICAL CULTURE Map pp88–9

☎ 495-639 6226; ul Fadeeva 4; admission R50; ☽ noon-7pm Tue-Sun; Ⓜ Mayakovskaya

Musicologists will be amazed by this massive collection of musical instruments from all over the world. The museum boasts over 3000 instruments – handcrafted works of art – from the Caucasus to the Far East. Russia is very well represented – a 13th-century *gusli* (traditional instrument similar to a dulcimer) from Novgorod, skin drums from Yakutia, a *balalaika* (triangular instrument) by the master Semyon Nalimov – but you can also see such classic pieces as a violin made by Antonio Stradivari. Recordings accompany many of the rarer instruments, allowing visitors to experience their sound.

This incredible collection started with a few instruments that were donated by the Moscow Tchaikovsky Conservatory at the end of the 19th century. The collection grew exponentially during the Soviet period. It was named after Mikhail Glinka in 1945, in honour of the nationalist composer's 150th birthday.

MOSCOW HOUSE OF PHOTOGRAPHY
Map pp88–9

Moskovsky Dom Fotografii (MDF); ☎ 495-231 3325; www.mdf.ru; Sushchevskaya ul 14; admission free; ☽ 11am-6pm; Ⓜ Mendeleevskaya

With impressive archives of contemporary and historic photography, the Moscow

House of Photography organises occasional exhibits at its small on-site museum, often featuring works from prominent photographers from the Soviet period. You can also see its exciting and innovative contemporary exhibits around town, especially at Manezh Exhibition Centre (p76) and Winzavod (p78). MDF is also responsible for several month-long photography festivals, Photobiennale (held in even-numbered years) and Fashion & Style in Photography (held in odd-numbered years).

MUSEUM OF DECORATIVE & FOLK ART Map pp88–9

☎ 495-623 7725; Delegatskaya ul 3 & 5; ☽ 10am-5pm Sat-Thu; Ⓜ Tsvetnoy Bulvar

Just beyond the Garden Ring, this museum showcases the centuries-old arts and crafts traditions from all around Russia and the former Soviet republics. It includes all the goodies you might find in souvenir shops or at the Izmaylovo Market (p156), but these antique pieces represent the crafts at their most traditional and their most authentic. Of the 40,000 pieces in the collection, you might see painted Khokhloma woodwork from Nizhny Novgorod, including wooden toys and *matryoshka* dolls; baskets and other household items made from birch bark, a traditional Siberian technique; intricate embroidery and lacework from the north, as well as the ubiquitous Pavlov scarves; and playful Dymkovo pottery and Gzhel porcelain. Look also for the so-called 'propaganda porcelain' – fine china decorated with revolutionary themes.

The museum is known for its impressive collection of Palekh – black lacquer boxes and trays painted with detailed scenes from Russian fairytales. The collection fills two rooms. It features, among others, pieces by Ivan Golikov and Ivan Markichev, often considered the originators of the Palekh style.

Eating p170; Sleeping p210

The vast, diverse Presnensky (Presnya) district stretches from Malaya Bronnaya ul in the east all the way to the Third Ring Rd in the west. It literally spans the centuries, taking in the area around Patriarch's Ponds, which is a ritzy residential area that developed in the 19th century; the traffic-jammed Kudrinskaya pl, dominated by the very 20th-century Stalinist skyscraper (see the boxed text, p51); and the huge new business development at Moskva-City, one of Moscow's largest ongoing urban projects, which is bringing the capital into the 21st century. (At the time of research, Moskva-City was not much more than a gigantic construction site – but an impressive one.)

Moskva-City is well and truly up-and-coming, with an emphasis on 'up'. Skyscrapers of glass and steel tower 20 stories over the rest of the city, shining like beacons to Moscow's wheelers, dealers and fortune seekers. The northern bank of the river is marked by the impressive facades of the White House and the World Trade Centre (WTC), with more tall glass-and-steel structures on the way.

Mayor Luzhkov has grand plans to move much of the city administration to this new urban centre, which the WTC and the exhibition centres have made into a hotbed of business activity. Already, a fancy new pedestrian bridge connects two shiny skyscrapers on either side of the river.

Presnya is named for the Presnya River, which used to flow through this area. Alas, the river has been diverted underground, through a pipe, which empties into the Moscow River along Krasnopresnensky nab. But its remnants are still visible, as Patriarch's Ponds and the small lakes on the grounds of the Moscow Zoo were originally formed by the Presnya River, as were the waterways in Krasnaya Presnya Park.

The most central metro stations are at Kudrinskaya pl (Barrikadnaya or Krasnopresnenskaya stations) and ul 1905 goda (Ulitsa 1905 Goda station), but Patriarch's Ponds are more easily accessed from Mayakovskaya station. The new development around Moskva-City has its own minimetro spur branching off from Kievskaya station, with a convenient stop at Delovoy Tsentr.

PATRIARCH'S PONDS Map pp96–7

Patriarshy Prudy; Bolshoy Patriarshy per;
Ⓜ Mayakovskaya

Patriarch's Ponds harks back to Soviet days, when the parks were populated with children and babushky. You'll see grandmothers pushing strollers, and lovers kissing on park benches. In summer children romp on the swings and monkey bars, while winter sees them ice skating on the pond. The small park has a huge statue of 19th-century Russian writer Ivan Krylov, known to Russian children for his didactic tales. Once this area contained several ponds that kept fish for the Patriarch's court (hence the name).

Patriarch's Ponds were immortalised by writer Mikhail Bulgakov, who had the devil appear here in *The Master and Margarita*. The initial paragraph of the novel describes the area to the north of the pond, where the devil enters the scene and predicts the rapid death of Berlioz. Contrary to Bulgakov's tale, a tram line never ran along the pond. Bulgakov's flat (p92), where he wrote the novel and lived up until his death, is around the corner on the Garden Ring.

MOSCOW MUSEUM OF MODERN ART Map pp96–7

MMOMA; ☎ 495-694 2890; www.mmoma.ru; Ermolaevsky per 17; adult/student R200/100; ◷ noon-8pm; Ⓜ Mayakovskaya

This is a branch of the main outlet on ul Petrovka (p90), which is utilised for temporary exhibits of paintings, sculpture, photography and multimedia pieces. Be sure to check the website to see what's on, as the museum often closes in between shows.

MOSCOW ZOO Map pp96–7

☎ 499-255 5375; www.moscowzoo.ru, in Russian; cnr Barrikadnaya & Bolshaya Gruzinskaya uls; adult/child R150/free; ◷ 10am-7pm Tue-Sun May-Sep, 10am-5pm Tue-Sun Oct-Apr; Ⓜ Barrikadnaya

Popular with families, this big zoo is surprisingly well maintained and populated with lots of wildlife, though enclosures are often too close for animal comfort. The highlight is the big cats exhibit, starring several Siberian tigers. Huge flocks of feathered friends populate the central pond, making for a pleasant stroll for birdwatchers. For a new perspective on Moscow's nightlife,

PRESNYA

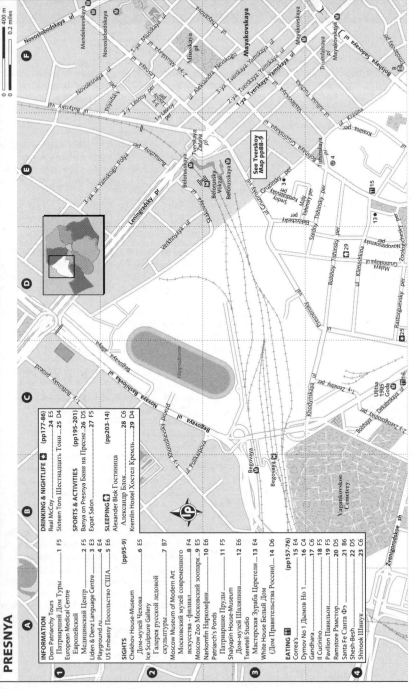

INFORMATION
Dom Patriarchy Tours
Патриарший Дом Туры 1 F5
European Medical Centre
Европейский
Медицинский Центр 2 F5
Liden & Denz Language Centre 3 E3
Playground.ru 4 E4
US Embassy Посольство США 5 E6

SIGHTS (pp95–9)
Chekhov House-Museum
Дом-музей Чехова 6 E5
Ice Sculpture Gallery
Галерея русской ледовой
скульптуры 7 B7
Moscow Museum of Modern Art
Московский музей современного
искусства – филиал................................8 F4
Moscow Zoo Московский зоопарк 9 E5
Narkomfin Наркомфин 10 E6
Patriarch's Ponds
Патриаршие Пруды 11 F5
Shalyapin House-Museum
Дом-музей Шаляпина 12 E6
Tsereteli Studio
Мастерская Зураба Церетели 13 E4
White House Белый Дом
(Дом Правительства России) 14 D6

EATING (pp157–76)
Correa's 15 E4
Dymov No 1 Дымов No 1 ....16 C4
Gandhara 17 C6
Il Cucinino 18 F5
Pavilion Павильон 19 F5
Ramstore Рамстор 20 D5
Santa Fe Санта Фэ 21 B6
Shesh-Besh 22 D5
Shinook Шинук 23 C6

DRINKING & NIGHTLIFE (pp177–86)
Real McCoy 24 E5
Sixteen Tons Шестнадцать Тонн 25 D4

SPORTS & ACTIVITIES (pp195–201)
Banya on Presnya Баня на Пресне 26 D5
Expat Salon 27 F5

SLEEPING (pp203–14)
Alexander Blok Гостиница
Александр Блок 28 C6
Kremlin Hostel Хостел Кремль 29 D4

See Tverskoy
Map pp88–9

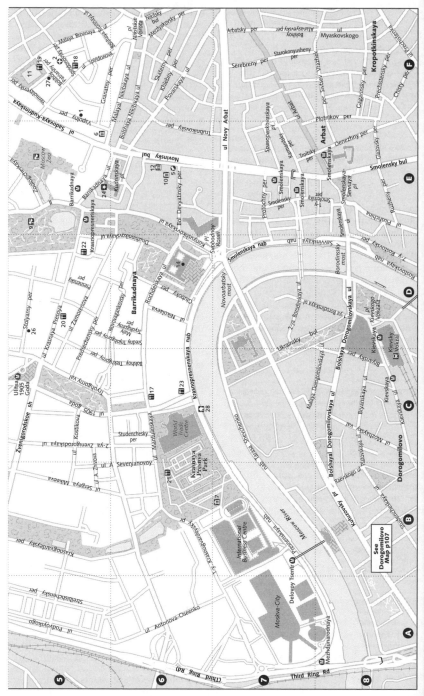

check out the nocturnal animal exhibit. At night this interior space is artificially lit so that the animals remain awake. By day the black lighting allows visitors to see them prowling around as they would during the darkest hours. For more four-legged fun, follow the footbridge across Barrikadnaya ul to see the exhibits featuring animals from each continent.

CHEKHOV HOUSE-MUSEUM Map pp96–7
☎ 495-291 6154; ul Sadovaya-Kudrinskaya 6; admission R80; ⏰ 11am-5pm Tue-Sun; Ⓜ Barrikadnaya
'The colour of the house is liberal, ie red', Anton Chekhov wrote of his house on the Garden Ring, where he lived from 1886 to 1890. The red house now contains the Chekhov House-Museum, with bedrooms, drawing room and study all intact. The overall impression is one of a peaceful and cultured family life. The walls are decorated with paintings that were given to Chekhov by Levitan (painter) and Shekhtel (Art Nouveau architect), who often visited him here. Photographs depict the playwright with literary greats Leo Tolstoy and Maxim Gorky. One room (p219) is dedicated to Chekhov's time in Melikhovo, showing photographs and manuscripts from his country estate.

WHITE HOUSE Map pp96–7
Krasnopresnenskaya nab 2; Ⓜ Krasnopresnenskaya
Moscow's White House, scene of two crucial episodes in recent Russian history, stands just north of Novoarbatsky most. It was here that Boris Yeltsin rallied the opposition that confounded the 1991 hard-line coup, then two years later sent in tanks and troops to blast out conservative rivals, some of them the same people who backed him in 1991. The images of Yeltsin climbing on a tank in front of the White House in 1991, and

of the same building ablaze after the 1993 assault, are among the most unforgettable from those tumultuous years. These days, things are relatively stable around the White House, where Prime Minister Putin now has his office.

The White House – officially called the House of Government of the Russian Federation (Dom pravitelstva Rossiyskoy federatsii) – fronts a stately bend in the Moscow River, with the Stalinist Hotel Ukraina rising on the far bank. This corner of Moscow is particularly appealing when these buildings and Novoarbatsky most are lit up at night.

ICE SCULPTURE GALLERY Map pp96–7
☎ 495-220 4619; Krasnaya Presnya Park; adult/student/child R470/250/250; ⏰ 11am-8pm; Ⓜ Ulitsa 1905 Goda
Ice sculpture has a long history in Russia, but it's not usually a year-round attraction. Until now. Cool off in the first-ever year-round Ice Sculpture Gallery, which is housed in a refrigerated winter-wonderland tent at the west end of Krasnaya Presnya Park. The changing exhibit is small but spectacular – the frozen masterpieces enhanced by colourful lights and dreamy music. At the time of research, sculptures depicted elaborate scenes from Russian fairytales, but the exhibit is expected to change on a biannual basis. The admission price includes a special down vest and warm fuzzy foot-covers to protect you from the -10°C climate.

NARKOMFIN Map pp96–7
Novinsky bul 25; Ⓜ Barrikadnaya
The model for Le Corbusier's Unitè D'Habitation, this architectural landmark is set slightly back from the Garden Ring, wedged between the US embassy and Novinsky Passage shopping centre. On the World Monuments Fund Watch List since 2002, this building is an early experiment in semicommunal living, and a prototype for contemporary apartment blocks. Designed and built between 1928 and 1930 by Moisei Ginzburg and Ignatii Milinis Narkomfin, the building offered housing for members of the Commissariat of Finances. There was room for 52 families in duplex apartments and a penthouse on the roof for the Commissar of Finances. In following with constructivist ideals (see p105), communal space was maximised and individual space was minimised. Apartments had minute

top picks
PRESNYA
- Moscow Zoo (p95) Visit the not-quite-wild-but-still-wonderful animal world.
- Ice Sculpture Gallery (right) Moscow's coolest art exhibit.
- Patriarch's Ponds (p95) Bring your copy of The Master and Margarita and settle into a sunny spot.

top picks

FOR CHILDREN

Got kids with you in Moscow? They might not appreciate an age-old icon or a Soviet hero, but Moscow has plenty to offer the little ones.

- **Patriarch's Ponds** (p95) Has a small playground area and plenty of room for the kids to run around.
- **All-Russia Exhibition Centre** (p130) Amusement-park rides and video games in a socialist-realist setting.
- **Central Museum of the Armed Forces** (p93) Let the kids climb around on army tanks, as opposed to monkey bars.
- **Gorky Park** (p119) Thrilling rides in summer and ice skating in winter make it the ultimate Russian experience.
- **Matryoshka Museum** (p93) Dolls and more dolls.
- **Moscow Zoo** (p95) Big cats for little kids.
- **Art Muzeon Sculpture Park** (p119) See all the Soviet heroes and climb around on them, too.

kitchens and people were encouraged to eat in the communal dining room in the neighbouring utilities block.

Narkomfin was built strictly on Corbusian principles: pillar supports, supporting frames, wall screens, horizontal windows, open planning and flat, functional roofs. Yet it predated Le Corbusier's vertical city. It is said that the young architect asked Ginzburg for copies of the layouts of the duplex apartments, which he took back to Paris and developed into his own revolutionary designs.

Having been in a semiruinous state for many years, Russian property development group MIAN Companies is now buying up apartments in the building in order to open an 'Art Hotel'. Good news, says the founder of the Moscow Architectural Preservation Society Clementine Cecil, as it represents an opportunity to set a positive precedent for the conversion and use of constructivist buildings.

SHALYAPIN HOUSE-MUSEUM Map pp96–7
☎ 495-205 6326; Novinsky bul 25; admission R50; ⏱ 10am-5pm Tue & Sat, 11.30am-6pm Wed & Thu, 10am-3.30pm Sun; Ⓜ Barrikadnaya
The world-famous opera singer Fyodor Shalyapin (also spelt Chaliapin) lived in this quaint cottage from 1910 to 1920 with his Italian wife and five children. In Russian cultural life, the eminent bass stands alongside icons such as Konstantin Stanislavsky and Maxim Gorky. Indeed, his stature is evident from the museum exhibit, which features photographs of the singer in such admirable company, as well as gifts and correspondence that they exchanged. More interesting for theatre buffs are the posters featuring Shalyapin's most celebrated performances, original stage costumes and recordings of his performances. Occasional concerts are held in the museum's white room.

Next door to Shalyapin's house, the small art gallery (☎ 495-255 5787; admission R50; ⏱ 11am-7pm Wed-Mon) holds temporary exhibits by local artists, most of whom have some historical association with Shalyapin or the surrounding neighbourhood.

ARBAT

Drinking p181; Eating p171; Shopping p153; Sleeping p210

Moscow's most famous street, ul Arbat, is something of an art market, complete with instant-portrait painters, soapbox poets, jugglers and buskers (as well as some pickpockets). It is undeniable that the Arbat today has been taken over by souvenir stands and pavement cafés. Nonetheless, it still evokes a free-thinking artistic spirit. Near ul Arbat's eastern end, the Wall of Peace is composed of hundreds of individually painted tiles on a theme of international friendship; a statue of the bard Bulat Okudzhava (see the boxed text, opposite) stands near the western end.

Just off the well-worn cobblestones of the Arbat lie the quiet lanes of old Moscow, a city once inhabited by writers and their heroes, old nobles and the nouveau rich. The era and its people are long gone, but you can still sense them in the grand houses they left behind. Evocative street names identify the area as an old settlement of court attendants: Khlebny (bread), Skatertny (tablecloth), Serebryany (silver) and Plotnikov (carpenters). Aristocrats and artists eventually displaced the original residents, and the mansions that line the streets reflect that change.

In the back streets around Bolshaya Nikitskaya ul, especially, many old mansions have survived – some renovated, others dilapidated. Most of those inside the Boulevard Ring were built by the 18th-century aristocracy; those outside, by rising 19th-century industrialists. These days many of these buildings are occupied by embassies and cultural institutions. With little traffic, Bolshaya Nikitskaya ul is excellent for a quiet ramble (see the Literary Sojourn walking tour, p142).

Bolshaya Nikitskaya ul runs almost parallel to Tverskaya from the Moscow State University building to the Garden Ring. Pl Nikitskie Vorota, where Bolshaya Nikitskaya ul crosses the Boulevard Ring, is named after the Nikitsky Gates in the old city walls, which the ring has replaced.

Until the 1960s, ul Arbat was Moscow's main westward artery. Then a swathe was bulldozed through the streets to its north, taking out the old Arbatskaya pl, a monastery and half a dozen churches. The result was present-day ul Novy Arbat – wide, fast and filled with traffic.

The Arbat district centres on Arbatskaya pl, the square formed at the intersection of Vozdvizhenka ul (which runs west from the Kremlin), ul Novy Arbat (which continues west to become the road to Smolensk) and the Boulevard Ring (here, Nikitsky bul). Wide, busy Novy Arbat slices the district almost in half. The metro station Arbatskaya, on the light-blue Filyovskaya line, is at Arbatskaya pl.

Just south of the square, ul Arbat (sometimes called '*stary* Arbat', or 'old Arbat') is a 1.3km pedestrian mall that stretches to Smolenskaya-Sennaya pl on the Garden Ring. On this square is one of Stalin's 'Seven Sisters', the Foreign Affairs Ministry (see the boxed text, p51). Reach Smolenskaya-Sennaya pl via Solenskaya station on the dark-blue Arbatsko-Pokrovskaya metro line.

'*Stary*' Arbat defines the character of the neighbourhood, but it is sadly isolated by the busyness and traffic around Smolenskaya-Sennaya pl and Arbatskaya pl.

MUSEUM OF ORIENTAL ART Map pp102–3
☎ 495-291 0212; Nikitsky bul 12a; admission R100; ⏲ 11am-7pm Tue-Sun; Ⓜ Arbatskaya

This impressive museum on the Boulevard Ring holds three floors of exhibits, spanning the Asian continent. Of particular interest is the 1st floor, dedicated mostly to the Caucasus, Central Asia and North Asia (meaning the Russian republics of Cukotka, Yakutiya and Priamurie). But the entire continent is pretty well represented, even the countries that were not part of the Russian or Soviet empires. The collection covers an equally vast time period, from ancient times to the 20th century, including paint-ing, sculpture and folk art. One unexpected highlight is a special exhibit on Nikolai Rerikh (p116), the Russian artist and explorer who spent several years travelling and painting in Asia.

PUSHKIN HOUSE-MUSEUM Map pp102–3
☎ 499-241 9293; www.pushkinmuseum.ru, in Russian; ul Arbat 53; admission R80; ⏲ 10am-5pm Wed-Sun; Ⓜ Smolenskaya

After Alexander Pushkin married Natalya Goncharova at the nearby Church of the Grand Ascension (opposite), they moved to this charming blue house on the old Arbat. The museum provides some insight into the couple's home life, a source of much Russian romanticism. (The lovebirds are also featured in a statue across the street.) Literary buffs will appreciate the poetry readings and other performances that take place here. This place should not be confused with the Pushkin Literary Museum (p116), which focuses on the poet's literary influences.

Just next door is the Memorial Apartment of Andrei Bely (☎ 499-241 9293; ul Arbat 55; admission R80; ⏰ 10am-5pm Wed-Sun), Silver Age author of the surreal novel *Petersburg*.

CHURCHES OF THE GRAND & SMALL ASCENSION Map pp102–3
Bolshaya Nikitskaya ul; Ⓜ Arbatskaya

In 1831 the poet Alexander Pushkin married Natalya Goncharova in the elegant Church of the Grand Ascension, on the western side of pl Nikitskie Vorota. Six years later he died in St Petersburg, defending her honour in a duel. Such passion, such romance… The church is frequently closed, but the celebrated couple is featured in the Rotunda Fountain, erected in 1999 to commemorate the poet's 100th birthday.

Down the street, the festive Church of the Small Ascension sits on the corner of Voznesensky per. Built in the early 17th century, it features whitewashed walls and stone embellishments carved in a primitive style.

GORKY HOUSE-MUSEUM Map pp102–3
☎ 495-690 5130; Malaya Nikitskaya ul 6/2; admission free; ⏰ 11am-6pm Wed-Sun; Ⓜ Pushkinskaya

This fascinating 1906 Art Nouveau mansion was designed by Fyodor Shekhtel and gifted to celebrated author Maxim Gorky in 1931. The house is a visual fantasy with sculpted doorways, ceiling murals, stained glass, a carved stone staircase and exterior tile work. Besides the fantastic decor it contains many of Gorky's personal items, including his extensive library. A small room in the cupola houses random, rotating exhibits of contemporary or quixotic artwork.

GOGOL MEMORIAL ROOMS Map pp102–3
☎ 495-291 1224; Nikitsky bul 7; admission free; ⏰ noon-7pm Mon & Wed-Fri, noon-5pm Sat & Sun; Ⓜ Arbatskaya

The 19th-century writer Nikolai Gogol spent his final tortured months here. The rooms – now a small but captivating museum – are arranged as they were when Gogol lived here. You can even see the fireplace where he famously threw his manuscript of *Dead Souls*. An additional reading room contains a library of Gogol's work and other reference materials about the author. The quiet courtyard contains a statue of the emaciated, sad author surrounded by some of his better-known characters in bas-relief.

ARBAT, MY ARBAT Clementine Cecil
Arbat, my Arbat, You are my calling. You are my happiness and my misfortune.

Bulat Okudzhava

For Moscow's beloved bard Bulat Okudzhava, the Arbat was not only his home, it was his inspiration. Although he spent his university years in Georgia dabbling in harmless verse, it was only upon his return to Moscow – and to his cherished Arbat – that his poetry adopted the free-thinking character for which it is known.

He gradually made the transition from poet to songwriter, stating that, 'Once I had the desire to accompany one of my satirical verses with music. I only knew three chords; now, 27 years later, I know seven chords, then I knew three'. While Bulat and his friends enjoyed his songs, the composers, singers and guitarists did not, resenting the fact that somebody with no musical training was writing songs. The ill feeling subsided when a well-known poet announced that '…these are not songs. This is just another way of presenting poetry'.

And so a new form of art was born. The 1960s were heady times, in Moscow as elsewhere, and Okudzhava inspired a whole movement of liberal-thinking poets to take their ideas to the streets. Vladimir Vysotsky and others – some political, others not – followed in Okudzhava's footsteps, their iconoclastic lyrics and simple melodies drawing enthusiastic crowds all around Moscow.

The Arbat today, crowded with tacky souvenir stands and overpriced cafés, bears little resemblance to the hallowed haunt of Okudzhava's youth. But its memory lives on in the bards and buskers, painters and poets who still perform for strolling crowds on summer evenings.

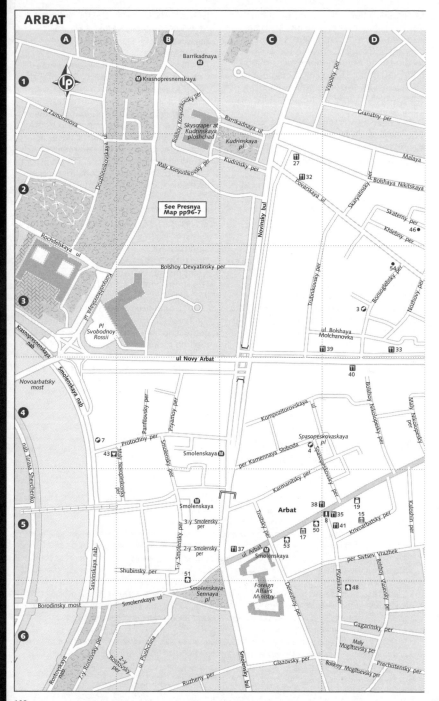

ARBAT

Barrikadnaya

Krasnopresnenskaya

ul Zamorenova

Bolshoy Konyushkovsky per

Barrikadnaya ul

Skyscraper at
Kudrinskaya
ploshchad

Kudrinskaya
pl

Kudrinsky per

Maly Konyushkovsky per

Granatny per

Malaya

27

32

Tovarskaya ul

Skaryatinsky per

Bolshaya Nikitskaya

See Presnya
Map pp96-7

Novinsky bul

Skatery per

46

Khlebny per

Rochdelskaya ul

Druzhinnikovskaya ul

Bolshoy Devyatinsky per

Trubnikovsky per

Borisoglebsky per

Nozhovy per

54

3

Konyushkovskaya ul

Pl
Svobodnoy
Rossii

ul Bolshaya
Molchanovka

39

33

ul Novy Arbat

40

Krasnopresnenskaya nab

Novoarbatsky
most

Smolenskaya nab

Kompozitorskaya ul

Bolshoy Nikolopesky per

Maly Nikolopesky per

Panfilovsky per

Pryanoy per

Spasopeskovaskaya
pl

nab Tarasa Shevchenko

7

43

Protochny per

Maly Nikolopeskovsky per

Smolensky per

Smolenskaya

per Kamennaya Sloboda

4

Spasopeskovsky per

Karmanitsky per

Arbat

38

35

19

15

8

50

41

Krivoarbatsky per

Kaloshin per

Savvinskaya nab

Smolenskaya

3-y Smolensky
per

2-y Smolensky
per

1-y Smolensky per

Plotnikov per

17

53

37

ul Arbat

Smolenskaya

Denezhny per

51

Shubinsky per

Borodinsky most

Smolenskaya ul

Smolenskaya-
Sennaya
pl

Foreign
Affairs
Ministry

48

per Sivtsev Vrazhek

Bolshoy Vlasevsky per

Rostovskaya nab

1-y Rostovsky
per

2-y Rostovsky
per

ul Plushchina

Ruzheny per

Smolensky bul

Glazovsky per

Bolshoy Mogiltsevsky per

Gagarinsky per

Maly
Mogiltsevsky per

Prechistensky per

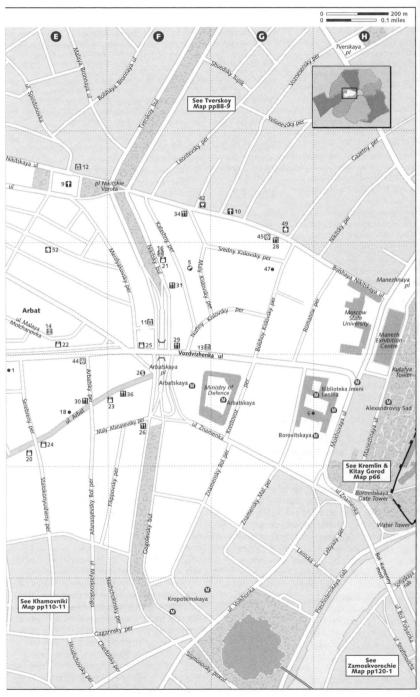

ARBAT (pp102-3)

MELNIKOV HOUSE
Krivoarbatsky per 10; Ⓜ Smolenskaya

On a side street near the Arbat, the home of Konstantin Melnikov still stands as testament to the innovation of the Russian avant-garde in the 1920s (see the boxed text, opposite). This plot of land was granted to the architect on the grounds that the house was a social experiment that would then be applied to mass housing. (It never was.) He created his unusual new home – the only private house built during the Soviet period – from two interlocking cylinders. It is an ingenious design that employs no internal load-bearing wall and has a self-reinforcing wooden grid floor. The house was also experimental in its designation of living space: the whole family slept in one room, painted a golden yellow and divided by narrow wall screens. Melnikov softened the corners in the room, even those on the

hexagonal windows, to create a soothing environment for peaceful sleep.

This house, an icon of the Russian avant-garde, is inhabited by the architect's granddaughter, Ekaterina Melnikova. Ekaterina is attempting to execute her father Victor's will, which states that the house should be turned into a state-run museum. Unfortunately, Ekaterina is not the sole owner of the house, and her colleague – a senator and business developer and patron of the arts – is at odds with her end goal.

When she is not in the courtroom, Ekaterina is at home. If you knock on the door, you may be lucky and be given a tour (in Russian only). The interior has largely been kept intact since the death of Victor, who tried to keep the house exactly as it was when his father lived there, down to the tubes of paint scattered across his desk. The place reeks of authenticity and artistry

CONSTRUCTIVISM: ARCHITECTURE FOR A NEW MAN *Clementine Cecil*

Constructivism was part of the Russian avant-garde movement that followed the revolution and lasted until Stalin's reactionary regime became entrenched in the early 1930s. The term first appeared in the early 1920s, originally in connection with the visual arts and then increasingly with architecture.

When first built, due to their simple forms, the buildings of the avant-garde looked like spaceships dropped among the Moscow sprawl, much of which was still wooden houses. Not only were the engineers and architects of the 1920s and early '30s creating much-needed factories, housing and administrative buildings, they were also providing an image of a bright, clean, technologically advanced future that broke with the past in every way imaginable.

The 1920s was a time of extreme poverty and the authorities saw the power of such futuristic structures. They were necessary to inspire a broken nation onwards to the creation of a new way of life. It was a time of great experimentation in form, building materials and technology. During this brief period, architects devised new forms of living for a 'new man': the Soviet citizen.

Some of the building technology utilised in constructivism came from the Bauhaus school. In the Depression following WWI, foreign architects came to Russia to practise. However, this very internationalism contributed to the official rejection of constructivism in 1932. Under Stalin, contact with the West was deemed antirevolutionary, thus discrediting the buildings.

The constructivists created functional buildings out of simple geometrical forms, making them light and open through quantities of glazing. They believed that form followed function. Stalin, with his iron fist, wanted a grander style proclaiming the might of the Soviet Empire as it entered a phase of economic prosperity. Architects were ordered to return to the classical model, so buildings were brought back down to earth from their pillar supports, and decoration became important for its own sake.

Russia's seminal contributions to international modernist architecture are sparse, elegant buildings that stand out among Moscow's grand Stalinist parades and colourful Orthodox churches. But many of these buildings have gone without even basic maintenance since they were constructed in the late 1920s and early 1930s; or they have been deformed by crude restoration and additions.

However, over the last two years the situation has changed dramatically and there are many indications that buildings of this period are becoming fashionable again. Narkomfin (p98) is to be converted into an Art Hotel; there are movements towards opening the Melnikov House (opposite) as a museum; and Dasha Zhukova has opened an art gallery in Melnikov's Bakhmetevsky Garage, now called Garazh Centre for Contemporary Culture (p130). This change in attitude will hopefully have positive repercussions for other buildings of the period that remain under threat.

Clementine Cecil is the cofounder of the Moscow Architecture Preservations Society (www.maps-moscow.com).

and it remains one of the most important architectural sites in the country.

HOUSE OF FRIENDSHIP WITH PEOPLES OF FOREIGN COUNTRIES Map pp102–3
Vozdvizhenka ul 16; Ⓜ Arbatskaya

The 'Moorish Castle' studded with seashells was built in 1899 for an eccentric merchant, Arseny Morozov, who was inspired by a real one in Spain. The inside is sumptuous and equally over the top. Morozov's mother, who lived next door, apparently declared of her son's home, 'Until now, only I knew you were mad; now everyone will'. This place is not normally open to the public, but sometimes exhibitions are held here; alternatively, Dom Patriarshy Tours (p252) occasionally brings groups here.

LERMONTOV HOUSE-MUSEUM
Map pp102–3

☎ 495-291 5298; ul Malaya Molchanovka 2; adult/student/child R50/30/20; ⏰ 2-5pm Wed & Fri, 11am-4pm Thu, Sat & Sun; Ⓜ Arbatskaya

'While I live I swear, dear friends, not to cease to love Moscow.' So wrote the 19th-century poet Mikhail Lermontov about his hometown. The celebrated author of *A Hero of Our Time* lived in this little pink house on a small lane off ul Novy Arbat. Here, he was raised by his grandmother, and wrote poetry and prose in the primitive office in the attic. Today, the cosy bungalow evokes the family's everyday life, displaying the poet's books, artwork and hobbies.

DOROGOMILOVO

Eating p173; Shopping p154; Sleeping p211

Back in the early centuries, the Romanovs and other aristocrats would build country estates on the outskirts of the city, spurring on the creation of roads and other infrastructure to cater to the travellers along the way. And so the routes of the rich influenced the development of the city. In the same way, the western Dorogomilovo district has grown up along the route that takes the president and other politicians and players out to 'Rouble Road' (p108), home of Moscow's millionaires.

The district occupies a sort of peninsula formed by a loop in the Moscow River. The eastern tip of the peninsula is almost an extension of Arbat, connected by two heavily trafficked bridges. The northern shore faces Presnya, and in fact gets some spillover from the development at Moskva-City (as it is connected by a pedestrian bridge). The south shore, dominated by Kievsky vokzal (Kyiv station), faces the outer reaches of Khamovniki (also connected by pedestrian bridge).

And running down the centre of the peninsula, shooting west all the way to MKAD, is Kutuzovsky pr. A wide highway lined with big cement blocks, it's not the most charming part of Moscow. But these behemoth buildings contain upscale boutiques and restaurants, catering to the big spenders who might be passing by on their way home from the city. Furthermore, a few more modern skyscrapers are springing up along the river. Several times a day the road is closed to traffic, as official motorcades race through at top speeds to and from the Kremlin.

Besides the route of the royals, this was also the route taken by armies attacking from (and retreating to) the west. Just outside the Third Ring Rd, the Borodino Panorama depicts the decisive battle that took place in the western village (p236), and the nearby Triumphal Arch celebrates the eventual defeat of Napoleon in 1812. The original arch was demolished at its original site in front of the Belorusskaya metro station during the 1930s and reconstructed here in a fit of post-WWII public spirit.

And speaking of WWII, this is the main draw for visitors to Dorogomilovo. Magnificent Park Pobedy (Victory Park) at Poklonnaya Hill contains a monument, museum, church and synagogue, all unveiled on the 50th anniversary of the Great Patriotic War.

From Kievskaya station, two metro lines run west across Dorogomilovo. The light-blue Filevskaya line goes to Studencheskaya and Kutuzovskaya stations before turning north to Fili and Bagrationovskaya. The newer dark-blue Arbatsko–Pokrovskaya line goes to Park Pobedy (at 84m the deepest metro station in Moscow) and beyond.

MUSEUM OF THE GREAT PATRIOTIC WAR Map p107

☎ 495-142 4185; ul Bratiev Fonchenko 10; adult/child R100/40; ☽ 10am-5pm Tue-Sun Nov-Mar, to 7pm Apr-Oct; Ⓜ Park Pobedy

To the west of the Borodino Panorama, Victory Park is a huge memorial complex celebrating the Great Patriotic War. The park includes endless fountains and monuments, the Memorial Synagogue (right) at Poklonnaya Hill and the memorial Church of St George. The dominant monument is a 142m obelisk (every 10cm represents a day of the war).

The Museum of the Great Patriotic War, located within the park, has a diorama of every major WWII battle the Russians fought in. Exhibits highlight the many heroes of the Soviet Union and also show weapons, photographs, documentary films, letters and many other authentic wartime memorabilia.

MEMORIAL SYNAGOGUE AT POKLONNAYA HILL Map p107

☎ 495-148 1907; Minskaya ul; admission free; ☽ 10am-6pm Tue-Thu, noon-7pm Sun; Ⓜ Park Pobedy

This synagogue opened in 1998 as a part of the complex at Park Pobedy. It is a memorial to Holocaust victims, as well as a museum of the Russian Jewry. Admission is with a guide only, so you must make arrangements in advance, especially if you want a tour in English. Otherwise, you might be able to join an existing group.

BORODINO PANORAMA Map p107

☎ 495-148 1967; Kutuzovsky pr 38; adult/student R150/50; ☽ 10am-5pm Sat-Thu; Ⓜ Park Pobedy

Following the vicious but inconclusive battle at Borodino (p236) in August 1812, Moscow's defenders retreated along what are now Kutuzovsky pr and ul Arbat, pursued

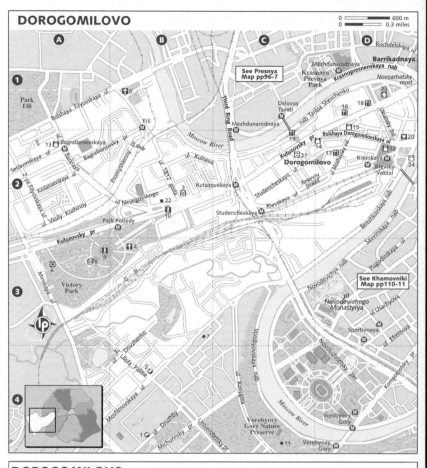

DOROGOMILOVO

ROUBLE ROAD

West of Moscow, just outside MKAD, the swanky street called Rublyovka is the residence of choice for the movers, the shakers, the big moneymakers...Moscow's megarich.

In Soviet times, high-level political officials and cultural figures were awarded modest cottages in this ecologically pure district. These days, the Moscow River provides a picturesque backdrop for multimillion-dollar mansions. The average cost of a house in this high-rolling 'hood is upwards of 100 million roubles, and prices are climbing. Home to Prime Minister Putin and President Medvedev, Rublyovka is the pinnacle of prestige in Moscow.

But it's not only Russians that are here: Armani, Dolce & Gabana, Ferrari, Gucci and Lamborghini all have outlets along this strip, as do Ralph Lauren and Harley Davidson. For a spot of shopping, stop in at Barvikha Luxury Village. This is where local folk might pop in to pick up a Prada handbag, an Armani suit or – why not – a Ferrari Testarossa. There is also a hotel in this swanky shopping centre (see the boxed text, p212).

There is not a whole lot to see along Rublyovka, as most of the mansions are hidden behind birch forests and high fences. But there is plenty to eat, especially in the village of Zhukovka, about 2km west of Barvikha (see the boxed text, p174). Multimillionaire restaurateur Arkady Novikov is right at home here, with his elaborate ethnic menus and matching, over-the-top decor.

About 15km further west from Zhukovka, the village of Nikolina Gora is Moscow's original *elitny* district, where you can actually see the Soviet-era dachas that were so sought after back in the day. It is no longer so exclusive, and you can wander down to the banks of the Moscow River, where you will find the beach that was prominently featured in the Oscar-winning film *Burnt by the Sun*. Apparently, director Nikita Mikhalkov has a place around here, and is sometimes spotted swimming in the river himself.

---

by Napoleon's Grand Army. Today, about 3km west of Novoarbatsky most and Hotel Ukraina (where Russian commander Mikhail Kutuzov stopped for a war council) is the Borodino Panorama, a pavilion with a giant 360-degree painting of the Borodino battle. Standing inside this tableau of bloodshed – complete with sound effects – is a powerful way to visualise the event.

MOSFILM Map p107

☎ 495-143 9599; www.mosfilm.ru; Mosfilmovskaya ul 1; adult/student R140/85; ☼ tours 10am, 1pm & 3pm Mon-Fri; Ⓜ Kievskaya

It's not exactly Universal Studios, but it is the oldest and most established film studio in Russia, responsible for films such as *Alexander Nevsky, War & Peace, White Sun of the Desert* and *Irony of Fate* (see the boxed text, p191). Make a reservation to book your spot on a 90-minute tour (some tours are in English, so be sure to inquire).

The highlight of the tour is the opportunity to stroll around some of the sets, including a quaint rendition of old Moscow and the desolate medieval village that was used in the fantasy thriller *Wolfhound* (said to be Russia's version of *Lord of the Rings*). There is also an impressive display of old cars, tanks, Rolls Royces and fire engines that are all in working order for use in the films. A costume exhibit features some of the outfits

from famous films such as *Ruslan & Ludmila* and *Andrei Rublyov*. Otherwise, the display of costumes, masks and make-up is rather half-hearted. Of course, it wouldn't be Russia without the obligatory exhibit of old equipment, which is mildly amusing. Film buffs should look out for the camera used by Eisenstein to shoot *The Battleship Potemkin*.

To reach Mosfilm take trolleybus 7, 17 or 34 from Kievskaya metro station.

CHURCH OF THE INTERCESSION AT FILI Map p107

Novozavodskaya ul 6; Ⓜ Fili

North of Kutuzovsky pr, Fili is a neighbourhood that was once the estate of Lev Naryshkin (brother-in-law to Tsar Alexei Mikhailovich and uncle to Peter the Great). The story goes that Naryshkin's brothers were killed in the Moscow uprising of 1682. In their honour, he constructed the Church of the Intercession at Fili in the 1690s. All church records were destroyed in a fire, so the name of the architect and exact date of construction are not known.

Fili is most famous for the events that unfolded here after the Battle of Borodino. While the Russian Army was camped nearby, a meeting took place in Fili. Here, General Kutuzov insisted that the army abandon Moscow without fighting, allowing the city to burn to the ground.

KHAMOVNIKI

Eating p173; Shopping p153; Sleeping p211

With the spectacular Cathedral of Christ the Saviour at its northern end and the historic Novodevichy Convent and Cemetery at the southern end, the Khamovniki district positively sparkles. Stretching between these two landmarks, ul Prechistenka and ul Ostozhenka are lined with graceful classical mansions, adding to the grandeur of the neighbourhood.

While the architecture is something to marvel at, it is not the highlight of this neighbourhood south-west of the Kremlin. These streets are also home to a slew of world-class museums and art galleries, making Khamovniki one of Moscow's most vibrant art districts. The Pushkin Fine Arts Museum and the neighbouring Museum of Private Collections are long-standing attractions for art lovers, housing unexpected but impressive collections. In recent years the area has also seen a flourishing of smaller galleries, mostly dedicated to contemporary artists. Indeed, grand cathedrals aside, Khamovniki is a veritable goldmine for art lovers, who could easily spend several days appreciating all of its riches.

Ul Volkhonka branches out from the southwest corner of the Kremlin to the Boulevard Ring (here, Gogolevsky bul). This intersection is dominated by the massive Cathedral of Christ the Saviour and the classical edifice of the Pushkin Fine Arts Museum. An incongruous Fredrick Engels oversees the activity from a corner of the square. To reach the sights in the vicinity, take the red Sokolnicheskaya metro line to Kropotkinskaya.

From here, ul Prechistenka continues southwest to the Garden Ring. The equally grand ul Ostozhenka heads more directly south, running somewhat parallel to the Moscow River. Ul Ostozhenka intersects with the Garden Ring (here, Zubovsky bul) as the latter heads east to cross the Moscow River. This corner contains the ring-line metro station Park Kultury.

Things quiet down south of the Garden Ring. The streets are not so clogged with cars; the pavements are nearly empty; there is not a crane or wrecking ball in sight. Peaceful parks – Maiden's Field and Mandelshtam Park – offer respite to passers-by, but they are not as busy as the parks closer to the centre. Even Tolstoy, whose statue adorns Maiden's Field, looks like he might be falling asleep.

The centrepiece of this southern part of Khamovniki is the Novodevichy Convent and Cemetery. A cluster of sparkling domes behind turreted walls on the river, the convent is rich in history. The name Novodevichy (New Maidens) probably originates from a market, once held in the locality, where Tatars bought Russian girls to sell to Muslim harems.

The huge Luzhniki sports complex (p200) occupies the area within the wide river bend southwest of Novodevichy. Luzhniki – meaning 'marshes', which is what this area used to be – was the main venue for the 1980 Olympics. Across the river is Vorobyovy Gory and the vibrant area surrounding the Moscow State University (p132).

Khamovniki is surrounded on three sides by the Moscow River, as it dips down south and loops back up to the north. In the north it borders the Arbat district, with a rough boundary at per Sitsev Vrazhek. The red Sokolnicheskaya metro line runs from the city centre at Aleksandrovsky Sad and Biblioteka imeni Lenina, via Kropotkinskaya, out to Khamovniki. The stops here are Park Kultury (also on the Ring line), Frunzenskaya and Sportivnaya. If you prefer to travel above ground, you might consider taking trolleybus 5 or 15, both of which run down ul Prechistenka and Bolshaya Pirogovskaya ul.

CATHEDRAL OF CHRIST THE SAVIOUR Map pp110–11

☎ 495-202 4734; www.xxc.ru; admission free; ☒ 10am-5pm; Ⓜ Kropotkinskaya

This gargantuan cathedral now dominates the skyline along the Moscow River. It sits on the site of an earlier and similar church of the same name, built between 1839 and 1860, and finally consecrated in 1883. The church commemorates Russia's victory over Napoleon. The original was destroyed during Stalin's orgy of explosive secularism. Stalin planned to replace the church with a 315m-high Palace of Soviets (including a 100m-high statue of Lenin), but the project never got off the ground – literally. Instead, for 50 years the site served an important purpose: the world's largest swimming pool.

This time around, the church was completed in a mere two years, in time for Moscow's 850th birthday in 1997, and at an estimated cost of US$350 million. It is

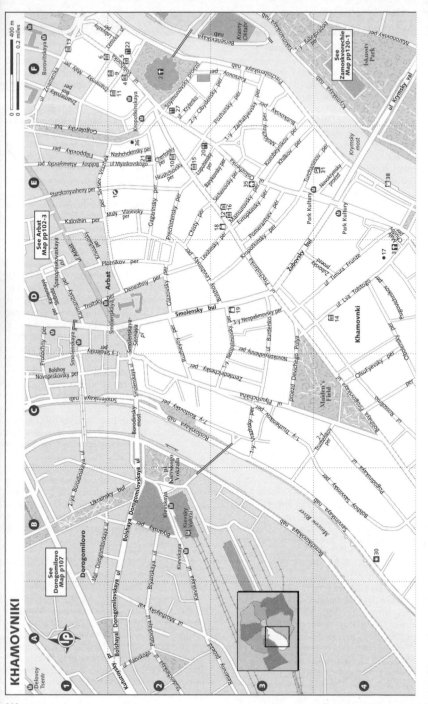

See Arbat
Map pp102-3

See Arbat
Map pp102-3

See Dorogomilovo
Map p107

See
Zamoskvorechie
Map pp120-1

Dorogomilovo

Arbat

Khamovniki

Maiden's
Field

Moskva River

Delovoy
Tsentr

400 m
0.2 miles

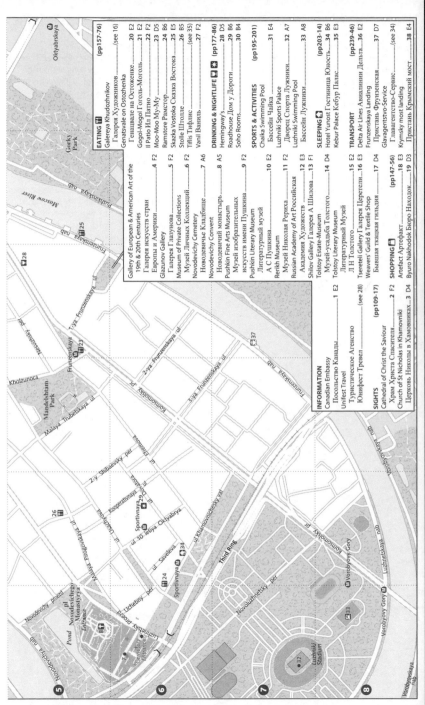

INFORMATION
Canadian Embassy
  Посольство Канады 1 E2
Unifest Travel
  Туристическое Агентство
  Юнифест Трэвел .... (see 28)

SIGHTS (pp109-17)
Cathedral of Christ the Saviour
  Храм Христа Спасителя 2 F2
Church of St Nicholas in Khamovniki
  Церковь Николы в Хамовниках 3 D4
Gallery of European & American Art of the
  19th & 20th Centuries
  Галерея искусства стран
  Европы и Америки 4 F2
Glazunov Gallery
  Галерея Глазунова 5 F2
Museum of Private Collections
  Музей Личных Коллекций 6 F2
Novodevichy Cemetery
  Новодевичье Кладбище 7 A6
Novodevichy Convent
  Новодевичий монастырь 8 A5
Pushkin Fine Arts Museum
  Музей изобразительных
  искусств имени Пушкина 9 F2
Pushkin Literary Museum
  Литературный музей
  А С Пушкина 10 E2
Rerikh Museum
  Музей Николая Рериха 11 F2
Russian Academy of Art Российская
  Академия Художеств 12 E3
Shilov Gallery Галерея А Шилова 13 F1
Tolstoy Estate-Museum
  Музей-усадьба Толстого 14 D4
Tolstoy Literary Museum
  Литературный Музей
  Л Н Толстого 15 E2
Tsereteli Gallery Галерея Церетели 16 E3
Weavers' Guild & Textile Shop
  Бывшая ткацкая гильдия 17 D4

SHOPPING (pp147-56)
Artefact Артефакт 18 E3
Byuro Nakhodok Бюро Находок 19 D3

EATING (pp157-76)
Galereya Khudozhnikov
  Галерея Художников 20 E2
Genatsvale on Ostozhenka .... (see 16)
  Генацвале на Остоженке
Gogol-Mogol Гоголь-Моголь 21 E2
Il Patio Ил Патио 22 F2
Moo-Moo Му-Му 23 D5
Ramstore Рамстор 24 B6
Skaza Vostoka Сказка Востока 25 E5
Stolle Штолле 26 B5
Tifis Tiflis Тифлис .... (see 35)
Vanil Ваниль 27 F2

DRINKING & NIGHTLIFE (pp177-86)
Hemingway's 28 D5
Roadhouse Дом у Дороги 29 B6
Soho Rooms 30 B4

SPORTS & ACTIVITIES (pp195-201)
Chaika Swimming Pool
  Бассейн Чайка 31 E4
Luzhniki Sports Palace
  Дворец Спорта Лужники 32 A7
Luzhniki Swimming Pool
  Бассейн Лужники 33 A8

SLEEPING (pp203-14)
Hotel Yunost Гостиница Юность 34 B6
Kebur Palace Кебур Палас 35 E3

TRANSPORT (pp239-46)
Delta Air Lines Авиалинии Дельта 36 E2
Frunzenskaya Landing
  Пристань Фрунзенская 37 D7
Glavagentstvo-Service
  Главагентство-Сервис .... (see 34)
Krymsky most landing
  Пристань Крымский мост 38 E4

111

amazingly opulent, garishly grandiose and truly historic. Much of the work was done by Mayor Luzhkov's favourite architect Zurab Tsereteli (see the boxed text, opposite) and it has aroused a range of reactions from Muscovites, from pious devotion to abject horror. Its sheer size and splendour guarantee its role as a love-it-or-hate-it landmark and spark of controversy. Muscovites should at least be grateful they can admire the shiny domes of a church instead of the shiny dome of Lenin's head.

NOVODEVICHY CONVENT Map p112

☎ 499-246 8526; adult/student R150/60; ☾ grounds 8am-8pm daily, museums 10am-5pm Wed-Mon; Ⓜ Sportivnaya

The Novodevichy Convent was founded in 1524 to celebrate the taking of Smo-

lensk from Lithuania, an important step in Moscow's conquest of the old Kyivan Rus lands. From early on, noblewomen would retire to the convent, some more willingly than others. Novodevichy was rebuilt by Peter the Great's half-sister Sofia, who used it as a second residence when she ruled Russia as regent in the 1680s. By this time the convent was a major landowner: it had 36 villages and about 10,000 serfs around Russia.

When Peter was 17, he deposed Sofia and confined her to Novodevichy; in 1698 she was imprisoned here for life after being implicated in the Streltsy rebellion. (Legend has it that Peter had some of her supporters hanged outside her window to remind her not to meddle.) Sofia was joined in her enforced retirement by Yevdokia Lop-

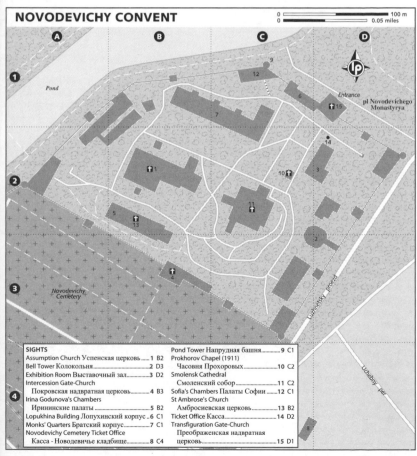

NOVODEVICHY CONVENT

0 ——————— 100 m
0 ——————— 0.05 miles

SIGHTS		
Assumption Church Успенская церковь	1	B2
Bell Tower Колокольня	2	D3
Exhibition Room Выставочный зал	3	D2
Intercession Gate-Church		
Покровская надвратная церковь	4	B3
Irina Godunova's Chambers		
Ирининские палаты	5	B2
Lopukhina Building Лопухинский корпус	6	C1
Monks' Quarters Братский корпус	7	C1
Novodevichy Cemetery Ticket Office		
Касса - Новодевичье кладбище	8	C4
Pond Tower Напрудная башня	9	C1
Prokhorov Chapel (1911)		
Часовня Прохоровых	10	C2
Smolensk Cathedral		
Смоленский собор	11	C2
Sofia's Chambers Палаты Софии	12	C1
St Ambrose's Church		
Амбросиевская церковь	13	B2
Ticket Office Касса	14	D2
Transfiguration Gate-Church		
Преображенская надвратная		
церковь	15	D1

top picks

KHAMOVNIKI

- **Novodevichy Convent & Cemetery** (opposite and right) Five centuries of artistry and history.
- **Gallery of European & American Art of the 19th & 20th Centuries** (p115) An incredible array of Impressionist and post-Impressionist art.
- **Pushkin Fine Arts Museum** (p115) Fabulous museum of foreign art from antiquity through to the Renaissance.
- **Rerikh Museum** (p116) The place for lovers of fantastical art.
- **Cathedral of Christ the Saviour** (p109) This massive creation evokes a range of reactions.

ukhina, Peter's first wife, whom he considered a nag.

You enter the convent through the red-and-white Moscow-baroque Transfiguration Gate-Church, built in the north wall between 1687 and 1689. The first building on the left, after the ticket office, contains a room for temporary exhibitions. Yevdokia Lopukhina lived in the Lopukhina Building against the north wall, while Sofia probably lived in the chambers adjoining the Pond Tower.

The oldest and most dominant building in the grounds is the white Smolensk Cathedral, modelled in 1524–25 on the Kremlin's As-

sumption Cathedral. It was closed at the time of research, but the sumptuous interior is covered in 16th-century frescoes. The huge iconostasis, donated by Sofia, has some more icons from the time of Boris Godunov. The tombs of Sofia, a couple of her sisters and Yevdokia Lopukhina are in the south nave.

The bell tower against the convent's east wall was completed in 1690 and is generally regarded as the finest in Moscow. Other churches on the grounds include the red-and-white Assumption Church, dating from 1685 to 1687, and the 16th-century St Ambrose's Church.

Boris Godunov's sister, Irina, lived in the building adjoining the latter church. Today, Irina's Chambers hold a permanent exhibit of 16th- and 17th-century religious artwork such as icons and embroidery.

NOVODEVICHY CEMETERY Map p114
Luzhnetsky proezd; admission free; ☉ **9am-6pm;** Ⓜ **Sportivnaya**

Adjacent to the Novodevichy Convent, the Novodevichy Cemetery is one of Moscow's most prestigious resting places – a veritable who's who of Russian politics and culture. Here you will find the tombs of Bulgakov, Chekhov, Gogol, Mayakovsky, Prokofiev, Stanislavsky and Eisenstein, among many other Russian and Soviet cultural notables.

In Soviet times Novodevichy Cemetery was used for eminent people the

LEAVING A MARK ON MOSCOW

Zurab Tsereteli is nothing if not controversial. As the chief architect of the Okhotny Ryad shopping mall (p149) and the massive Cathedral of Christ the Saviour (p109), he has been criticised for being too ostentatious, too gaudy, too overbearing and just plain too much.

The most despised of Tsereteli's masterpieces is the gargantuan statue of Peter the Great, which now stands in front of the Krasny Oktyabr chocolate factory on the Moscow River. At 94.5m (that's twice the size of the Statue of Liberty without her pedestal), Peter towers over the city. Questions of taste aside, Muscovites were sceptical of the whole idea: why pay tribute to Peter the Great, who loathed Moscow, and even moved the capital to St Petersburg? Some radicals even attempted – unsuccessfully – to blow the thing up. After that incident, a 24-hour guard had to stand watch.

Mixed reactions are nothing new to Zurab Tsereteli. An earlier sculpture of Christopher Columbus has been rejected by five North American cities for reasons of cost, size and aesthetics. Some believe the Peter the Great statue is actually a reincarnation of homeless Chris. Despite his critics, who launched a 'Stop Tsereteli' website, this favourite artist of Mayor Luzhkov does not stop.

He founded the Moscow Museum of Modern Art (MMOMA) and took over the Russian Academy of Art. He then opened the aptly named Tsereteli Gallery, which houses room after room of his primitive paintings and elaborate sculptures.

To see where all these whimsical creatures originate, stroll down Bolshaya Gruzinskaya ul, north of the zoo, to Gruzinskaya pl, where Mr Tsereteli has his studio (Map pp96–7). You can't miss the mint-green baroque facade, its front door flanked by crazy clowns, its front yard littered with leftovers – St George killing the dragon, and other historical figures.

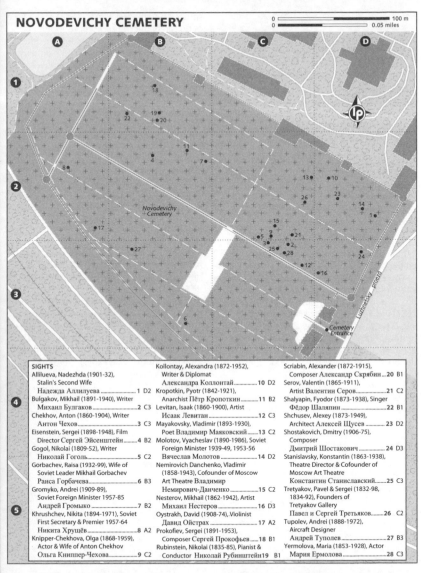

NOVODEVICHY CEMETERY

0 ▬▬▬▬▬▬ 100 m
0 ▬▬▬▬▬▬ 0.05 miles

Novodevichy Cemetery

Luzhnetsky proezd

Cemetery Entrance

SIGHTS

Allilueva, Nadezhda (1901-32), Stalin's Second Wife Надежда Аллилуева 1 D2

Bulgakov, Mikhail (1891-1940), Writer Михаил Булгаков 2 C3

Chekhov, Anton (1860-1904), Writer Антон Чехов 3 C3

Eisenstein, Sergei (1898-1948), Film Director Сергей Эйзенштейн 4 B2

Gogol, Nikolai (1809-52), Writer Николай Гоголь......5 C2

Gorbachev, Raisa (1932-99), Wife of Soviet Leader Mikhail Gorbachev Раиса Горбачева......6 B3

Gromyko, Andrei (1909-89), Soviet Foreign Minister 1957-85 Андрей Громыко 7 B2

Khrushchev, Nikita (1894-1971), Soviet First Secretary & Premier 1957-64 Никита Хрущёв......8 A2

Knipper-Chekhova, Olga (1868-1959), Actor & Wife of Anton Chekhov Ольга Книппер-Чехова......9 C2

Kollontay, Alexandra (1872-1952), Writer & Diplomat Александра Коллонтай......10 D2

Kropotkin, Pyotr (1842-1921), Anarchist Пётр Кропоткин......11 B2

Levitan, Isaak (1860-1900), Artist Исаак Левитан......12 C3

Mayakovsky, Vladimir (1893-1930), Poet Владимир Маяковский......13 C2

Molotov, Vyacheslav (1890-1986), Soviet Foreign Minister 1939-49, 1953-56 Вячеслав Молотов 14 D2

Nemirovich Danchenko, Vladimir (1858-1943), Cofounder of Moscow Art Theatre Владимир Немирович-Данченко......15 C2

Nesterov, Mikhail (1862-1942), Artist Михаил Нестеров 16 D3

Oystrakh, David (1908-74), Violinist Давид Ойстрах 17 A2

Prokofiev, Sergei (1891-1953), Composer Сергей Прокофьев......18 B1

Rubinstein, Nikolai (1835-85), Pianist & Conductor Николай Рубинштейн19 B1

Scriabin, Alexander (1872-1915), Composer Александр Скрябин...20 B1

Serov, Valentin (1865-1911), Artist Валентин Серов......21 C2

Shalyapin, Fyodor (1873-1938), Singer Фёдор Шаляпин......22 B1

Shchusev, Alexey (1873-1949), Architect Алексей Щусев 23 D2

Shostakovich, Dmitry (1906-75), Composer Дмитрий Шостакович 24 D3

Stanislavsky, Konstantin (1863-1938), Theatre Director & Cofounder of Moscow Art Theatre Константин Станиславский......25 C3

Tretyakov, Pavel & Sergei (1832-98, 1834-92), Founders of Tretyakov Gallery Павел и Сергей Третьяков......26 C2

Tupolev, Andrei (1888-1972), Aircraft Designer Андрей Туполев......27 B3

Yermolova, Maria (1853-1928), Actor Мария Ермолова......28 C3

authorities judged unsuitable for the Kremlin wall, most notably Khrushchev. The intertwined white-and-black blocks round Khrushchev's bust were intended by sculptor Ernst Neizvestny to represent Khrushchev's good and bad sides.

The tombstone of Nadezhda Alliluyeva, Stalin's second wife, is surrounded by unbreakable glass to prevent vandalism. The most recent notable addition to the cemetery is former President Boris Yeltsin, who died of congestive heart failure in 2007. His grave is marked by an enormous Russian flag, which is sculpted out of stone but gives the appearance that it is rippling in the wind.

If you want to investigate this place in depth, buy the Russian map (on sale at the kiosk), which pinpoints nearly 200 graves.

PUSHKIN FINE ARTS MUSEUM

Map pp110–11

☎ 495-203 7998; www.museum.ru/gmii; ul Volkhonka 12; adult/student R300/150, audio tour R200; ☺ 10am-6pm Tue-Sun; Ⓜ Kropotkinskaya

This is Moscow's premier foreign-art museum, showing off a broad selection of European works, mostly appropriated from private collections after the revolution. The Pushkin's collections are located not only in this main building, but also in the Museum of Private Collections (right) and the Gallery of European & American Art of the 19th & 20th Centuries (right). A collective ticket to all three museums is available for adults/students for R500/300. To see the incredible collection of Impressionist and post-Impressionist paintings, visit the Gallery of European & American Art.

What's left in the main building is still impressive, especially since the place has been revamped, with more modern museum lighting and improved layout. This is only the first phase of a multiyear project that will have the Pushkin expanding into a new complex designed by UK architect Norman Vincent Foster.

In the meantime, the museum has room to show off some of its paintings that have never been displayed before, including Renaissance masterpieces. Artists such as Botticelli, Tiepolo and Veronese are all represented.

The highlight is perhaps the Dutch masterpieces from the 17th century, the so-called Golden Age of Dutch art. Rembrandt is the star of the show, with many paintings on display, including his moving *Portrait of an Old Woman*. The rest of Europe is also well represented from this period.

The Ancient Civilisation exhibits contain a surprisingly excellent collection, complete with ancient Egyptian weaponry, jewellery, ritual items and tombstones. Most of the items were excavated from burial sites, including two haunting mummies. Another room houses the impressive exhibit 'Treasures of Troy', with excavated items dating to 2500 BC. A German archaeologist donated the collection to the city of Berlin, from where it was appropriated by the Soviets in 1945.

Keep an eye out for special exhibits at the Pushkin, which has mounted some ambitious temporary shows in recent years. The Pushkin Gallery also hosts the prestigious December Nights Festival (p23), which accompanies the artwork with musical performances.

GALLERY OF EUROPEAN & AMERICAN ART OF THE 19TH & 20TH CENTURIES Map pp110–11

☎ 495-203 1546; ul Volkhonka 14; adult/student R300/150; ☺ 10am-6pm Tue, Wed & Fri-Sun, 10am-8pm Thu; Ⓜ Kropotkinskaya

The Pushkin Fine Arts Museum is expanding (see left for more information) and the first step was to move its excellent collection of 19th- and 20th-century European art into its own gallery. A collective ticket to both museums, as well as the Museum of Private Collections (below), is available for adults/students for R500/300.

The new gallery contains a famed assemblage of French Impressionist works, based on the collection of two well-known Moscow art patrons, Sergei Shchukin and Ivan Morozov. It includes representative paintings by Degas, Manet, Renoir and Pisarro, with an entire room dedicated to Monet. Rodin's sculptures include pieces from the *Gates of Hell* and the *Monument to the Townspeople of Calais*.

The gallery displays many of the most famous paintings by Matisse, such as *Goldfish*; some lesser-known pieces by Picasso; a few exquisite primitive paintings by Rousseau; and works by Miro, Kandinsky and Chagall. The museum also contains several pieces by Van Gogh, including the scorching *Red Vineyards* and the tragic *Prison Courtyard*, painted in the last year of his life. There is an entire room devoted to works by Gauguin, representing his prime period. The rich collection of 20th-century art continues to grow, with recent additions by Arp and others.

MUSEUM OF PRIVATE COLLECTIONS

Map pp110–11

☎ 495-203 1546; ul Volkhonka 10; adult/student R50/25; ☺ 10am-6pm Wed-Sun; Ⓜ Kropotkinskaya

Next door to the Pushkin Fine Arts Museum, this smaller museum shows off art collections donated by private individuals, many of whom amassed the works during the Soviet era. Exhibits are organised around the collections, each as a whole, and the details of collectors and donors are displayed alongside the art. The centrepiece, perhaps, is the collection of the museum's founder, Ilya Silberstein, an accomplished historian of Russian literature and art. Other highlights include a collection of Old Believer icons from the 16th to

20th centuries, the Lemkul room exhibiting fantastic glassworks, and impressive exhibits of 20th-century artists such as Alexander Rodchenko and Barbara Stepanova.

RERIKH MUSEUM Map pp110–11

☎ 495-203 6419; Maly Znamensky per 3/5; adult/student R220/110; ⊗ 11am-5pm Wed-Sun; Ⓜ Kropotkinskaya

Nikolai Rerikh (known internationally as Nicholas Roerich) was a Russian artist from the late 19th and early 20th centuries, whose fantastical artwork is characterised by rich, bold colours, primitive style and mystical themes. This museum, founded by the artist's son Sergei, includes work by father and son, as well as family heirlooms and personal items. The artwork is intriguing: Rerikh spent a lot of time in the Altay Mountains of Siberia, Central Asia and India, so his paintings feature distinctive landscapes and mythological scenes. The building – the 17th-century Lopukhin manor – is a grand setting in which to admire the artwork.

GLAZUNOV GALLERY Map pp110–11

☎ 495-291 6949; www.glazunov.ru; ul Volkhonka 13; adult/student R160/80; ⊗ 11am-6pm Tue-Sun; Ⓜ Kropotkinskaya

This elaborate Russian empire–style mansion, opposite the Pushkin Fine Arts Museum, houses a new gallery dedicated to the work of Soviet and post-Soviet artist Ilya Glazunov. Apparently this gallery was a long time coming, due primarily to the artist's own insistence on moulded ceilings, marble staircases and crystal chandeliers. But it was worth the wait, as the interior is impressive: three floors filled with fanciful illustrations of historic events and biblical scenes.

Glazunov is famous for his huge, colourful paintings that depict hundreds of people, places and events from Russian history in one monumental scene. His most famous work is *Eternal Russia (Bechnaya Rossiya)*, while more recent examples are *Mystery of the 20th Century* and *Market of Our Democracy*. Such social commentary is a rather recent development, of course; the artist's earlier work tended to focus on medieval and fairytale themes.

SHILOV GALLERY Map pp110–11

☎ 495-203 4208; www.shilov.su; ul Znamenka 5; adult/student R160/80; ⊗ 11am-7pm Fri-Wed; Ⓜ Biblioteka imeni Lenina

'What is a portrait? You have to attain not only an absolute physical likeness…but you need to express the inner world of the particular person you are painting.' So Alexander Shilov described his life work as contemporary Russia's most celebrated portrait painter. Indeed, Shilov is known for his startling realism. His paintings are so close to the truth that he is sometimes criticised for producing little more than photographs on canvas. But others claim that the artist provides great insight into his subjects, with some high-level political figures among them. (Shilov denies the rumour that he painted all the members of the Politburo during the Soviet period.)

Among Shilov's fans is one Yury Luzhkov, who oversaw the opening of this gallery in 1997. At that time the artist donated 355 paintings to the museum, and he continues to make donations of new paintings – every year on the anniversary of the opening – so the collection continues to grow.

PUSHKIN LITERARY MUSEUM
Map pp110–11

☎ 495-637 5674; ul Prechistenka 12; admission R80; ⊗ 10am-5pm Tue-Sun; Ⓜ Kropotkinskaya

Housed in a beautiful empire-style mansion dating from 1816, this museum is devoted to Russia's favourite poet's life and work. Personal effects, family portraits, (mostly) reproductions of notes and handwritten poetry provide insight into the work of the beloved bard. Tours (adult/child costs R120/50) are held daily at 1pm and 3.30pm.

The elegant interior recreates a fancy 19th-century atmosphere, especially the grand ballroom, which is decorated with mirrors, sconces, chandeliers and heavy drapes. Several rooms are dedicated to Pushkin's specific works, demonstrating the links between his personal life and the poetry he produced. Perhaps the most interesting exhibit is 'Pushkin & His Time', which puts the poet in a historical context, demonstrating the influence of the Napoleonic Wars, the Decembrists' revolt and other historic events. This literary museum provides much more in-depth insights than the Pushkin House-Museum (p100) on ul Arbat.

TOLSTOY LITERARY MUSEUM
Map pp110–11

☎ 495-637 7410; www.tolstoymuseum.ru; ul Prechistenka 11; adult/student R200/100; ⊗ 11am-6pm Tue-Sun; Ⓜ Kropotkinskaya

Opposite the Pushkin Literary Museum is the Tolstoy Literary Museum, supposedly the oldest literary memorial museum in the world (founded in 1911). In addition to its impressive reference library, the museum contains exhibits of manuscripts, letters and artwork focusing on Leo Tolstoy's literary influences and output. Family photographs, personal correspondence and artwork from the author's era all provide insight into his work. This museum undoubtedly contains the largest collection of portraits of the great Russian novelist. Entire exhibits are dedicated to his major novels such as *Anna Karenina* and *War and Peace*. The museum does not contain so much memorabilia from Tolstoy's personal life, which is on display at the Tolstoy Estate-Museum (right).

RUSSIAN ACADEMY OF ART Map pp110–11
☎ 495-637 2569; www.rah.ru; ul Prechistenka 21; admission R80; 11am-8pm Tue-Sun; M Kropotkinskaya
Next door to the Tsereteli Gallery (below), the Russian Academy of Art hosts rotating exhibits in the historic 19th-century mansion of the Morozov estate. Despite the institutional-sounding name, this is part of the Tsereteli empire, but it still puts on inspired and varied shows featuring mostly contemporary Russian and foreign artists.

TSERETELI GALLERY Map pp110–11
☎ 495-637 4150; ul Prechistenka 19; admission R200; noon-7pm Tue-Sat; M Kropotkinskaya
Housed in the 18th-century Dolgoruky mansion, this is the latest endeavour of the tireless Zurab Tsereteli (see the boxed text, p113). The gallery shows how prolific this

guy is. The rooms are filled with his often-over-the-top sculptures and primitive paintings. If you don't want to spend the time or money exploring the gallery, just pop into the Galereya Khudozhnikov café (p174), which is an exhibit in itself.

TOLSTOY ESTATE-MUSEUM Map pp110–11
☎ 499-246 9444; www.tolstoymuseum.ru; ul Lva Tolstogo 21; adult/student R200/50; 10am-5pm Wed-Sun; M Park Kultury
Leo Tolstoy's winter home during the 1880s and 1890s now houses an interesting museum dedicated to the writer's home life. While it's not particularly opulent or large, the building is fitting for junior nobility – which Tolstoy was. Exhibits here demonstrate how Tolstoy lived, as opposed to his literary influences, which are explored at the Tolstoy Literary Museum (opposite). See the salon where Rachmaninov and Rimsky-Korsakov played piano, and the study where Tolstoy himself wove his epic tales.

CHURCH OF ST NICHOLAS IN KHAMOVNIKI Map pp110–11
ul Lva Tolstogo; M Park Kultury
This church, commissioned by the weavers' guild in 1676, vies with St Basil's Cathedral for the title of most colourful in Moscow. The ornate green-and-orange-tapestry exterior houses an equally exquisite interior, rich in frescoes and icons. Leo Tolstoy, who lived up the street, was a parishioner at St Nicholas, which is featured in his novel *Resurrection*. Look also for the old white stone house, built in 1689, which housed the office of the weavers' guild and textile shop (ul Lva Tolstogo 10).

ZAMOSKVORECHIE

Drinking p182; Eating p175; Shopping p155; Sleeping p212

The atmosphere of 19th-century Moscow lives on in the low buildings, old courtyards and clusters of onion domes in Zamoskvorechie. This district – its name meaning 'Beyond Moscow River' – stretches south from the bank opposite the Kremlin, inside a big loop in the river. The many churches located in the area make up a wonderful scrapbook of Muscovite architectural styles.

South was the direction from which Tatars used to attack, so Moscow's defensive forces were stationed in Zamoskvorechie (Donskoy and Danilovsky Monasteries), along with quarters devoted to servicing the royal court. In fact, the name of the main thoroughfare 'Ordynka' comes from *orda* (horde). Other sources maintain that the street received its name from the *ordyntsy*, who lived in this area in the 15th century. *Ordyntsy* were the people taken hostage by Tatars then bought by wealthy Russians to work as servants.

After the Tatar threat abated, more and more merchants moved to the area from the noisy and crowded Kitay Gorod. Most of the Zamoskvorechie churches date to this era, as they were built by merchants to secure luck in business. Only at the end of the 18th century were merchants joined by nobles, and later by factory owners and their workers. Playwright Alexander Ostrovsky, who lived here in the 19th century, often described the secluded life of Zamoskvorechie in his plays, including *Groza (The Storm)*.

Although this area was little damaged by Stalin, present-day critics claim it has suffered at the hands of unbridled real-estate development. Certainly, construction marks every corner. The most prominent project is the development of the island between the Moscow River and the Vodootvodny Canal, which includes the conversion of the Krasny Oktyabr factory into luxury condominiums. Preservationists are celebrating this particular project, which will retain the parts of the factory that are architecturally significant, converting some of the space into galleries and studios for artists.

Even before the opening of Art Strelka (p155), Zamoskvorechie was a thriving art district, thanks to the proliferation of galleries at TsDKh (p155), not to mention both branches of the Tretyakov Gallery. From almost any vantage point in Zamoskvorechie you can see the giant sculpture of Peter the Great, product of the tireless Zurab Tsereteli (see the boxed text, p113).

Directly south of the Kremlin, Zamoskvorechie is surrounded by the Moscow River on three sides. The Vodootvodny Canal slices across the top of the district, preventing spring floods in the city centre and creating a sliver of an island opposite the Kremlin. Tretyakovskaya and Novokuznetskaya metro stations serve the northern tip of Zamoskvorechie, near the Tretyakov Gallery. This northern part of the district is also accessible by walking over the Bolshoy Moskvoretsky most from the Kremlin or the smaller pedestrian bridge from the Cathedral of Christ the Saviour.

The main roads, ul Bolshaya Yakimanka, ul Bolshaya Ordynka and Pyatnitskaya ul run roughly parallel to each other, heading southward from the canal. The grey Serpukhovksko-Timiryazevskaya metro line also cuts through here heading south, with stops at Polyanka and Serpukhovskaya stations.

Ul Bolshaya Yakimanka terminates at busy Oktyabrskaya pl, site also of Oktyabrskaya metro station. West of Oktyabrskaya pl, along the Moscow River, is Gorky Park, the Art Muzeon Sculpture Park and the massive New Tretyakov Gallery. East of Oktyabrskaya pl, along the Garden Ring (here, ul Zatsepsky val), busy Paveletsky vokzal (Pavelets train station) dominates the square of the same name. It is served by the Paveletskaya metro station.

TRETYAKOV GALLERY Map pp120–1

☎ 495-951 1362; www.tretyakovgallery.ru, in Russian; Lavrushinsky per 10; adult/student R250/150, audio tour R300; ☼ 10am-5.30pm Tue-Sun; Ⓜ Tretyakovskaya; ♿

The exotic *boyar* castle on a little lane in Zamoskvorechie contains the main branch of the State Tretyakov Gallery, housing the world's best collection of Russian icons and an outstanding collection of other pre-revolutionary Russian art. Show up early to beat the queues.

The building was designed by Viktor Vasnetsov between 1900 and 1905. The gallery started as the private collection of the 19th-century industrialist brothers Pavel and Sergei Tretyakov. Pavel was a patron of the Peredvizhniki, or Wanderers, a group of 19th-century painters who broke away from the conservative Academy of Arts and started depicting common people and social problems. Nowadays, these are among Russia's most celebrated painters, and the Tretyakov boasts some of the most exquisite examples of their work.

Within the museum grounds is the Church of St Nicholas in Tolmachi (noon-4pm Tue-Sun), where Pavel Tretyakov regularly attended services. It was transferred to this site and restored in 1997, and now functions as an exhibit hall and working church. The exquisite five-tiered iconostasis dates back to the 17th century. The centrepiece is the revered 12th-century *Vladimir Icon of the Mother of God,* protector of all Russia, which was transferred here from the Assumption Cathedral in the Kremlin.

The Tretyakov's 62 rooms are numbered and progress in chronological order from rooms 1 to 54, followed by eight rooms containing icons and jewellery. In rooms 20 to 30, the art of the most prominent Peredvizhniki artists occupies its own space. Look for Repin's realist work, including the tragic *Ivan the Terrible and his Son Ivan,* in rooms 29 and 30. A selection of Levitan's landscapes is in room 37. Vrubel's masterpieces, including *Demon Seated* (1890), are in rooms 32 and 33.

Icons are found on the ground floor in rooms 56 to 62. Rublyov's *Holy Trinity* (1420s) from Sergiev Posad, widely regarded as Russia's greatest icon, is in room 60.

The entrance to the gallery is through a lovely courtyard; the Engineer's Building (Lavrushinsky per 12) next door is reserved for special exhibits.

NEW TRETYAKOV GALLERY Map pp120–1
☎ 499-238 1378; adult/student R225/150; ⏰ 10am-6.30pm Tue-Sun; Ⓜ Park Kultury or Oktyabrskaya

The premier venue for 20th-century Russian art is this branch of the State Tretyakov Gallery, better known as the New Tretyakov. This place has much more than the typical socialist realist images of muscle-bound men wielding scythes, and busty women milking cows (although there's that too).

The exhibits showcase avant-garde artists such as Malevich, Kandinsky, Chagall, Goncharova and Popova.

In the same building as the Tretyakov, TsDKh (Tsentralny Dom Khudozhnikov; ☎ 495-238 9843; admission R100, special exhibits R200; ⏰ 11am-7pm Tue-Sun), or Central House of Artists, is a huge exhibit space used for contemporary-art shows. A number of galleries are also housed here on a permanent basis (see p155). The surrounding grounds contain the Art Muzeon Sculpture Park (below).

ART MUZEON SCULPTURE PARK
Map pp120–1
☎ 499-238 3396; ul Krymsky val 10; admission R100; ⏰ 9am-9pm; Ⓜ Park Kultury or Oktyabrskaya

The wonderful, moody Sculpture Park, behind and beside the New Tretyakov, is Moscow's most atmospheric spot to indulge in some Soviet nostalgia. Formerly called the Park of the Fallen Heroes, it started as a collection of Soviet statues (Stalin, Dzerzhinsky, Sverdlov, a selection of Lenins and Brezhnevs) put out to pasture after they were ripped from their pedestals in the post-1991 wave of anti-Soviet feeling.

These discredited icons have now been joined by contemporary work, ranging from the playful to the provocative. Tsereteli's Peter the Great (p113) surveys the scene from his post on the embankment of the Moscow River.

GORKY PARK Map pp120–1
Park Kultury; ☎ 495-237 1266; ul Krymsky val; adult/child R80/20; ⏰ 10am-10pm; Ⓜ Park Kultury

top picks

ZAMOSKVORECHIE

- Tretyakov Gallery (opposite) Superb Russian icons and other prerevolutionary art.
- New Tretyakov Gallery (left) Showcase of 20th-century Russian art.
- Art Muzeon Sculpture Park (above) See the fallen heroes of the Soviet era.
- Danilovsky Monastery (p123) The Orthodox Church's spiritual and administrative centre.
- Gorky Park (above) Festive refuge from the hustle and bustle.

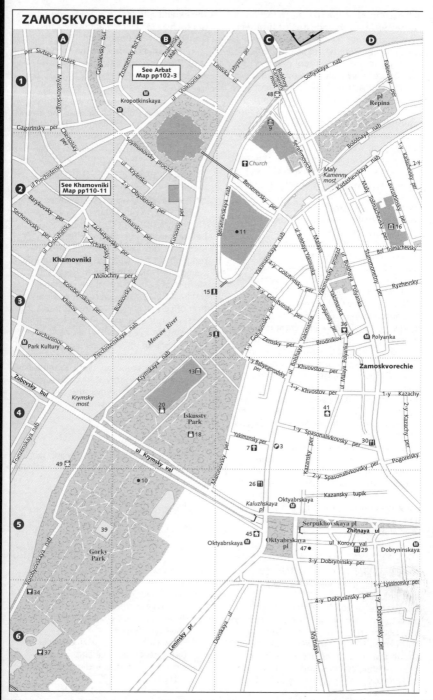

ZAMOSKVORECHIE

See Arbat
Map pp102-3

See Khamovniki
Map pp110-11

Khamovniki

Zamoskvorechie

Iskusstv
Park

Gorky
Park

Moscow River

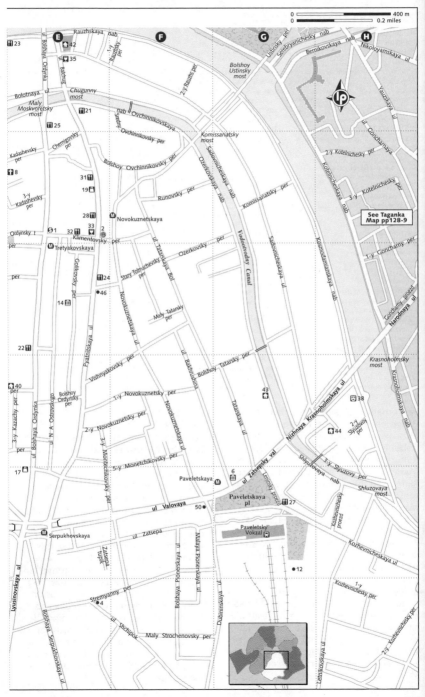

See Taganka
Map pp128-9

ZAMOSKVORECHIE (pp120-1)

Part ornamental park, part fun fair, Gorky Park is one of the most festive places in Moscow – a perfect way to escape the hubbub of the city. Officially the Park Kultury (Park of Culture), it's named after Maxim Gorky. The park stretches almost 3km along the river, upstream of Krymsky most. You can't miss the showy entrance, marked by colourful flags waving in the wind, and the happy sounds of an old-fashioned carousel.

Inside, Gorky Park has a small Western-style amusement park, which features two roller coasters and almost a dozen other terror-inducing attractions (that is, aside from the view of the Peter the Great statue). Most of the rides cost around R50 to R100. Space buffs can shed a tear for the *Buran*, the Soviet space shuttle that never carried anyone into space. In winter the ponds are flooded for skating (p198) and tracks are made for cross-country skiing.

KRASNY OKTYABR CHOCOLATE FACTORY & MUSEUM Map pp120–1

Red October; ☎ 499-255 5352; www.uniconf.ru, in Russian; Bersenevskaya nab 6; ⌚ tours 10am & 3pm; Ⓜ Kropotkinskaya

After more than a century of producing chocolates and other sweets, the famed Krasny Oktyabr factory, opposite the Church of Christ the Saviour, was finally forced to close. The closure happened as part of an effort to remove industry from the historic centre of the capital. This prime real estate, which boasts the best views of the Kremlin, is being converted into high-rent real estate. However, in a rare and enlightened move, the historic industrial building is being preserved. The garages and other outbuildings have already been taken over by artists for gallery and studio space, known as Art Strelka (p155). A small museum will remain open to document the history of the complex and the company.

DOM NA NABEREZHNOY Map pp120–1

House on the Embankment; ☎ 495-959 0317; www.museumdom.narod.ru, in Russian; ul Serafimovicha 2; admission free; ☿ 5-8pm Wed, 2-6pm Sat; Ⓜ Novokuznetskaya

It isn't much to look at, but this big apartment block on Bolotny Island is a historic building, once home to many old Bolsheviks and Civil War heroes, as well as artists, writers and scientists. The small museum on site recounts the life histories of its noteworthy residents, many of whom were eventually persecuted for their accomplishments. As such, the exhibit is sometimes called the Museum of Repression. Unfortunately, hours are sporadic and information is only in Russian.

BAKHRUSHIN THEATRE MUSEUM

Map pp120–1

☎ 495-953 4470; www.gctm.ru; ul Bakhrushina 31/12; admission R100; ☿ noon-6pm Wed-Sun; Ⓜ Paveletskaya

Russia's foremost stage museum, founded in 1894, is in the neo-Gothic mansion on the north side of Paveletskaya pl. The museum exhibits all things theatrical – stage sets, costumes, scripts and personal items belonging to some of Russia's stage greats. The exhibits are not limited only to drama, also tracing the development of opera, ballet and puppetry. Highlights include the costumes and stage set from *Boris Godunov* (starring the famous bass, Fyodor Shalyapin) and the ballet shoes worn by Vaslav Nijinsky.

CHURCH OF ST JOHN THE WARRIOR

Map pp120–1

ul Bolshaya Yakimanka 48; Ⓜ Oktyabrskaya

The finest of all Zamoskvorechie's churches mixes Moscow and European baroque styles, resulting in a melange of shapes and colours. It was commissioned by Peter the Great in thanks for his 1709 victory over Sweden at Poltava. Inside, the gilt, wood-carved iconostasis was originally installed in the nearby Church of the Resurrection at Kadashi (2-y Kadashevsky per 7). The iconostasis was moved when the latter church was closed (it now houses a restoration centre).

DANILOVSKY MONASTERY Map p124

☎ 495-955 6757; Danilovsky val; admission free; ☿ 7am-7pm; Ⓜ Tulskaya

The headquarters of the Russian Orthodox Church stand behind white fortress walls. The Danilovsky Monastery was built in the late 13th century by Daniil, the first Prince of Moscow, as an outer city defence. It was repeatedly altered over the next several hundred years, and served as a factory and a detention centre during the Soviet period.

It was restored in time to replace Sergiev Posad as the Church's spiritual and administrative centre, and became the official residence of the Patriarch during the Russian Orthodoxy's millennium celebrations in 1988. Today, it radiates an air of purpose befitting the Church's role in modern Russia. On holy days this place seethes with worshippers murmuring prayers, lighting candles and ladling holy water into jugs at the tiny chapel inside the gates.

Enter beneath the pink St Simeon Stylite Gate-Church on the north wall. The monastery's oldest and busiest church is the Church of the Holy Fathers of the Seven Ecumenical Councils, where worship is held continuously from 10am to 5pm daily. Founded in the 17th century and rebuilt repeatedly, the church contains several chapels on two floors: the main one upstairs is flanked by side chapels to St Daniil (on the northern side) and SS Boris and Gleb (south). On the ground level, the small main chapel is dedicated to the Protecting Veil, and the northern one to the prophet Daniil. The yellow and neoclassical Trinity Cathedral, built in the 1830s, is an austere counterpart to the other buildings.

West of the cathedral are the patriarchate's External Affairs Department and, at the far end of the grounds, the Patriarch's Official Residence. Against the north wall, to the east of the residence, there's a 13th-century Armenian carved-stone cross, or *khachkar*, a gift from the Armenian Church. The church guest house, in the southern part of the monastery grounds, has been turned into the elegant Danilovskaya Hotel (p213).

DONSKOY MONASTERY Map pp60–1

☎ 495-952 1646; Donskaya ul; Ⓜ Shabolovskaya

The youngest of Moscow's fortified monasteries, Donskoy was founded in 1591 and built to house the *Virgin of the Don* icon (now in the Tretyakov Gallery). This revered icon is credited with the victory in the 1380

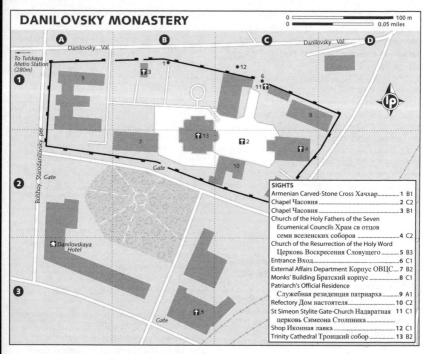

DANILOVSKY MONASTERY

battle of Kulikovo; it's also said that in 1591, the Tatar Khan Giri retreated without a fight after the icon showered him with burning arrows in a dream.

Most of the monastery, surrounded by a brick wall with 12 towers, was built between 1684 and 1733 under Regent Sofia and Peter the Great. From 1918 to 1927 it was the Russian Orthodox Church headquarters; later it was closed as a monastery, falling into neglect despite being used as an architecture museum. Restored in 1990 and 1991, it's now back in Church hands.

The Virgin of Tikhvin Church over the north gate, built in 1713 and 1714, is one of the last examples of Moscow baroque. In the centre of the grounds is the large brick New Cathedral, built between 1684 and 1693. Just to its south is the smaller Old Cathedral, dating from 1591 to 1593.

When burials in central Moscow were banned after the 1771 plague, the Donskoy Monastery became a graveyard for the nobility, and it is littered with elaborate tombs and chapels.

The Donskoy Monastery is a five-minute walk from Shabolovskaya metro. Go south along ul Shabolovka, then take the first street west, 1-y Donskoy proezd.

LENIN FUNERAL TRAIN Map pp120–1
Traurny proezd V I Lenina; Paveletsky vokzal;
Ⓜ **Paveletskaya**
Paveletsky vokzal is a hive of activity, with shiny trains chugging to and fro at all hours. The finest loco in the neighbourhood, however, stands idle in an air-conditioned pavilion just east of the station. It is the funeral train that brought Lenin's body to Moscow from Gorki Leninskie, where he died, in January 1924. The old steam engine is in beautiful condition, but does not attract many visitors these days. In fact, it is technically closed to visitors but the security guard might let you in for a small fee, especially if you show up after hours. From Kozhevnicheskaya ul, cut behind the row of kiosks and through the overgrown park to the pavilion in the back.

OSTROVSKY ESTATE-MUSEUM
Map pp120–1
☎ 495-231 1140; ul Malaya Ordynka 9; admission R50; ☻ noon-5.30pm Wed-Sun; Ⓜ **Tretyakovskaya**

Alexander Ostrovsky is the 19th-century playwright who is often considered to be Russia's greatest realist writer. This museum is devoted to his life and work. It is a tribute to Ostrovsky's work for the Maly Theatre, which he founded, and also covers the area of Zamoskvorechie, where he lived and loved. Some of the writer's personal effects are on display here. More intriguing are the paintings and engravings of old Moscow, which featured so prominently in Ostrovsky's work.

Eating p175

Taganskaya pl, on the Garden Ring, is the monster intersection – loud, dusty and crowded – that is the hub of the Taganka district. The district, south of the little Yauza River, was originally developed in the 16th and 17th centuries as the territory of the blacksmith guild. Very few remains of this early period can be found around the square, which was built up in the 1970s and 1980s. However, traces of the past are still visible in the streets that radiate from it.

Wandering north on Goncharnaya ul reveals a few unexpected architectural gems: several impressive classical mansions and some charming little merchants' churches, including the Potters' Church of the Assumption and the Church of St Nikita Beyond the Yauza. The Taganka Gates Church of St Nicholas used to serve as the neighbourhood's landmark but today the whole area is dwarfed by the Kotelnicheskaya Apartment, one of Stalin's 'Seven Sisters' (p51).

Taganka is dotted with 16th-century monasteries that also served as the outer ring of Moscow's defence system, including Novospassky and Andronikov. An Old Believers' Community still thrives east of here, as it has for hundreds of years. These historic monasteries somehow seem out of place amid the wide highways and mammoth apartment blocks that dominate the area. The flashing lights and traffic jams on Taganskaya pl certainly represent another world.

This chaotic square is something of an entertainment district, boasting the renowned Taganka Theatre (p193), a jazz club (p185) and a huge new casino. The impressive new Moscow International House of Music (p188) is just across the Moscow River.

Taganka is a triangle-shaped area and sits south-east of the Kremlin. It is defined in the north by the little Yauza River, and in the west by the Moscow River. The heart of the district is Taganskaya pl, which forms at the intersection of the Garden Ring (Narodnaya ul and Zemlyanoy val meet here) and several major roads. From the square, Taganskaya ul shoots off to the east, Marksistskaya ul heads on a diagonal to the south-east, and Bolshoy Komenshchiki ul – which becomes Novospassky proezd – heads south towards the monastery of the same name. The Andronikov Monastery towers over the Yauza River to the northeast.

The metro stations in this area are Marksistskaya on the yellow Kalininskaya line, Taganskaya on the ring line and the purple Tagansko-Krasnopresnskaya line. The latter metro line continues south to Proletarskaya, which is the closest access point to the Novospassky Monastery.

About 4km east of Taganskaya pl is another busy square, pl Ilycha, which is formed at the intersection of Rogozsky val and sh Entusiastov. Ilycha is accessible via the yellow Kalininskaya metro line (Ploshchad Ilycha station) or the light-green Lyublinskaya line (Rimskaya station).

ZKP TAGANSKY COLD WAR MUSEUM
Map pp128–9

☎ 495-500 0554; www.zkp42.ru; 5-y Kotelnichesky per 11; admission R1000-2000; ⓨ by appointment; Ⓜ Taganskaya

On a quiet side street near Taganskaya pl sits a nondescript neoclassical building. This is the gateway to the secret Cold War–era communications centre, ZKP Tagansky. Operated during the Cold War by Central Telephone and Telegraph, the facility was meant to serve as the communications headquarters in the event of a nuclear attack. As such, the building was just a shell and served as entry into the 7000-sq-metre space that is 60m underground.

Now managed by private interests, the facility is being converted into a sort of museum dedicated to the Cold War. Unfortunately, not much remains from that era. The vast place is nearly empty, except for a few exhibits set up for the benefit of visitors, such as a scale model of the facility.

Visitors are herded into a small elevator and whisked downwards for 18 stories to the museum. A 20-minute film about the history of the Cold War is followed by a guided tour of the four underground 'blocks', which are dark, dank and more than a little bit creepy. Through a locked door, visitors can hear the rumble of trains ploughing by – this facility is at the same depth underground as the Taganskaya metro station.

This new museum is a work in progress. Research about the activities that took place here in the past is ongoing, so it has the potential to provide a unique perspective on a secret and sexy subject. At the time of research, however, there was not much to see, especially considering the admission price, which varies according to the size of your group. That said, this may be your only opportunity to explore a secret underground Cold War command centre.

RUBLYOV MUSEUM OF EARLY RUSSIAN CULTURE & ART Map pp128–9
☎ 495-678 1467; Andronevskaya pl 10; adult/student R150/75; 🕙 11am-5.30pm Thu-Tue; Ⓜ Ploshchad Ilycha
On the grounds of the former Andronikov Monastery, the Rublyov Museum exhibits icons from days of yore and from the present. Unfortunately, it does not include any work by its acclaimed namesake artist. It is still worth visiting though, not least for its romantic location. Andrei Rublyov, the master of icon painting, was a monk here in the 15th century. He is buried in the grounds, but no one knows quite where.

In the centre of the monastery grounds is the compact Saviour's Cathedral, built in 1427, the oldest stone building in Moscow. The cluster of *kokoshniki,* or gables of colourful tiles and brick patterns, is typical of Russian architecture from the era. To the left is the combined rectory and 17th-century Moscow-baroque Church of the Archangel Michael; to the right, the old monks' quarters house the museum.

NOVOSPASSKY MONASTERY Map pp128–9
New Monastery of the Saviour; ☎ 495-676 9570; Verkhny Novospassky pro; admission free; 🕙 7am-7pm Mon-Sat, 8am-7pm Sun; Ⓜ Proletarskaya
Novospassky Monastery is a 15th-century fort-monastery, which is located about 1km south of Taganskaya pl. The centrepiece of the monastery, the Transfiguration Cathedral, was built by the imperial Romanov family in the 1640s in imitation of the Kremlin's Assumption Cathedral. Frescoes depict the history of Christianity in Russia, while the Romanov family tree, which goes as far back as the Viking Prince Rurik, climbs one

wall. The other church is the 1675 Intercession Church.

Under the river bank, beneath one of the towers of the monastery, is the site of a mass grave for thousands of Stalin's victims. At the northern end of the monastery's grounds are the brick Assumption Cathedral and an extraordinary Moscow-baroque gate tower.

Across the road that runs south of Novospassky Monastery is the sumptuous Ecclesiastic Residence (Krutitskoe Podvorye; 1-y Krutitsky per; admission free; 🕙 10am-6pm Wed-Mon; Ⓜ Proletarskaya). It was the home of the Moscow metropolitans after the founding of the Russian patriarchate in the 16th century, when they lost their place in the Kremlin.

OLD BELIEVERS' COMMUNITY Map pp60–1
Staroobryadcheskaya Obshchina; admission free; 🕙 9am-6pm Tue-Sun; Ⓜ Ploshchad Ilycha
One of Russia's most atmospheric religious centres is the Old Believers' Community, located at Rogozhskoe, 3km east of Taganskaya pl. The Old Believers split from the main Russian Orthodox Church in 1653, when they refused to accept certain reforms. They have maintained the old forms of worship and customs ever since. In the late 18th century, during a brief period free of persecution, rich Old Believer merchants founded this community, which is among the most important in the country.

The yellow, classical-style Intercession Church contains one of Moscow's finest collections of icons, all dating from before 1653, with the oldest being the 14th-century *Saviour with the Angry Eye (Spas yaroe oko),* protected under glass near the south door. The icons in the deesis row (the biggest row) of the iconostasis are supposedly by the Rublyov school, while the seventh, *The Saviour,* is attributed to Rublyov himself. North of the church is the Rogozhskoe Cemetery.

Visitors are welcome at the church, but women should take care to wear long skirts (no trousers) and headscarves. The community is a 30-minute walk from pl Ilycha. Otherwise, take trolleybus 16 or 26, or bus 51, east from Taganskaya pl and get off after crossing a railway. Rogozhskoe's tall, green-domed 20th-century bell tower is clearly visible to the north.

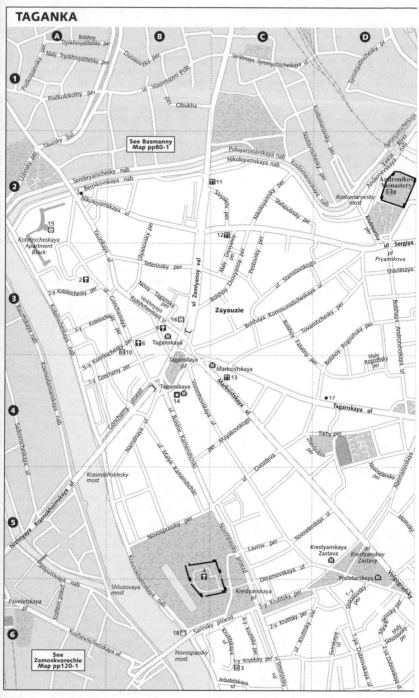

See Basmanny
Map pp80-1

Kotelnicheskaya
Apartment
Block

Zayauzie

Andronikov
Monastery

Taganskaya

Taganskaya
pl

Taganskaya

Krestyanskaya
Zastava

pl
Krestyanskoy
Zastavy

Proletarskaya

See
Zamoskvorechie
Map pp120-1

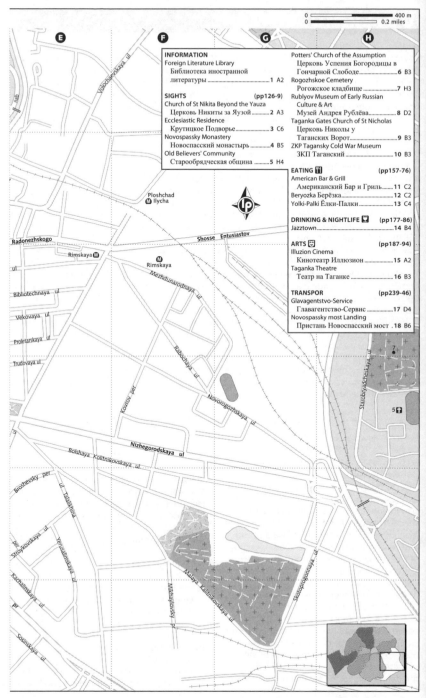

0 ————————— 400 m
0 ————————— 0.2 miles

INFORMATION
Foreign Literature Library
  Библиотека иностранной
  литературы 1 A2

SIGHTS (pp126-9)
Church of St Nikita Beyond the Yauza
  Церковь Никиты за Яузой 2 A3
Ecclesiastic Residence
  Крутицкое Подворье.....................3 C6
Novospassky Monastery
  Новоспасский монастырь 4 B5
Old Believers' Community
  Старообрядческая община 5 H4

Potters' Church of the Assumption
  Церковь Успения Богородицы в
  Гончарной Слободе......................6 B3
Rogozhskoe Cemetery
  Рогожское кладбище 7 H3
Rublyov Museum of Early Russian
  Culture & Art
  Музей Андрея Рублёва.................8 D2
Taganka Gates Church of St Nicholas
  Церковь Николы у
  Таганских Ворот...........................9 B3
ZKP Tagansky Cold War Museum
  ЗКП Таганский 10 B3

EATING (pp157-76)
American Bar & Grill
  Американский Бар и Гриль.......11 C2
Beryozka Берёзка...........................12 C2
Yolki-Palki Ёлки-Палки 13 C4

DRINKING & NIGHTLIFE (pp177-86)
Jazztown...14 B4

ARTS (pp187-94)
Illuzion Cinema
  Кинотеатр Иллюзион 15 A2
Taganka Theatre
  Театр на Таганке 16 B3

TRANSPOR (pp239-46)
Glavagentstvo-Service
  Главагентство-Сервис 17 D4
Novospassky most Landing
  Пристань Новоспасский мост .18 B6

Ploshchad
Ilycha

Radonezhskogo
Rimskaya
ul
Rimskaya
Mezhdunarodnaya ul
Shosse Entusiastov
Bibliotechnaya ul
Vekovaya ul
Proletarskaya ul
Trudovaya ul
Kovrov per
Rabochaya ul
Novorogozhskaya ul
Nizhegorodskaya ul
Bolshaya Kolitnikovskaya ul
Brochevsky per
ul Talalikhina
Strokovskaya ul
Yerusalimskaya ul
Kachalinskaya ul
pr
Sosinskaya ul
Malaya Kolitnikovskaya ul
Mikhaylovsky pr
Skotoprogonnaya ul
Starobryadcheskaya ul
Volochaevskaya ul
nab

OUTER MOSCOW

Shopping p156; Sleeping p213

Moscow extends all the way to the Outer Ring Rd, a multilane highway known as MKAD. And the city continues to sprawl, especially as large international stores, shopping centres and movie theatres spring up on the outskirts. Retailers are realising that Muscovites, who now own cars, are willing to drive to places that offer lower prices and larger selections. Furthermore, there are few space constraints on the outskirts, meaning cheaper real estate and bigger stores.

By the same token, people are moving to the outskirts. The Russian version of suburban sprawl comes in two forms: gated communities containing the mansions of Moscow's nouveaux riches, who choose not to live in the busy centre; and massive Soviet-style blocks housing Muscovites who can't afford to live any closer to the centre.

Outer Moscow offers a few sights to lure the traveller away from the centre, not to mention a vast array of accommodation options that are more affordable than those in the centre.

The main roads heading north out of the centre are Leningradsky pr (also called Leningradskoe sh further north), which is the continuation of Tverskaya and Tverskaya-Yamskaya ul; and pr Mira, which is the continuation of ul Sretenka and Bolshaya Lubyanka ul. The former heads toward Sheremetyevo airport, while the latter is where you will find Rizhsky Market and the All-Russia Exhibition Centre.

West of the centre, Kutuzovsky pr leads through Dorogomilovo and beyond. In the southwest, Moscow State University dominates the neighbourhoods around Vorobyovy Gory (Sparrow Hills). Both pr Vernadskogo and Leninsky pr head out of the centre through the neighbourhood known as Yugo-Zapadnaya, or 'south-west'. Varshavskoe sh comes directly south out of the centre through Zamoskvorechie to the Donskoy and Danilovsky Monasteries and beyond. Pr Andropova leads from Taganskaya pl to the Kolomenskoe Museum-Reserve.

Heading east, Shchyolkovskoe sh leads to the long-distance bus station, passing just north of Izmaylovsky Park. Sh Entuziastov passes just south of Izmaylovsky Park. Ryazansky pr runs further south, passing Kuskovo Park.

No less than 14 branches of the metro extend out from central Moscow. More often than not, there is a stop near your destination, which is specified in the listings that follow. If additional transport is required, such as a bus or trolley from the metro stop, this information is provided in the review.

NORTH OF THE CENTRE

GARAZH CENTRE FOR CONTEMPORARY CULTURE Map pp60–1
GCCC; ☎ 499-503 1038; ul Obratsova 19a;
Ⓜ Savyolovskaya

Dasha Zhukova has so many claims to fame. She is the gorgeous girlfriend of Russian billionaire Roman Abramovich, she is a successful fashion designer and she has her own inheritance. Now she is also a proud patron of the arts, with the 2008 opening of the Garazh Centre for Contemporary Culture. Known affectionately as Dashkin Garazh, or Dasha's Garage, it is an old bus depot that has been converted into Moscow's largest exhibition hall. It's an incredible space, originally designed in 1926 by constructivist architect Konstantin Melnikov (p105). It is not clear if the space will be used to show off pieces from the private collection of Abramovich and Zhukova. In the meantime, GCCC has opened to much

fanfare with an exhibit from husband-and-wife team Ilya and Emilia Kabakov.

ALL-RUSSIA EXHIBITION CENTRE
Map pp60–1
Vserossiysky Vystavochny Tsentr (VVTs); ☎ 495-544 3400; www.vvcentre.ru, in Russian; ☼ pavilions 10am-7pm, grounds 8am-10pm; Ⓜ VDNKh

No other place sums up the rise and fall of the great Soviet dream quite as well as the All-Russia Exhibition Centre. The old initials by which it's still commonly known, VDNKh, tell half the story – they stand for Vystavka Dostizheny Narodnogo Khozyaystva SSSR (USSR Economic Achievements Exhibition).

Originally created in the 1930s, the VDNKh was expanded in the 1950s and '60s to impress upon one and all the success of the Soviet economic system. Two kilometres long and 1km wide, it is composed of wide pedestrian avenues and grandiose pavilions, glorifying every aspect of socialist construction from education and health to agriculture, technology and science. The pavilions represent a huge variety of architectural styles, symbolic of the contributions from diverse ethnic and artistic movements to the common goal. Here you will find the kitschiest socialist realism, the most inspiring of socialist optimism and, now, the tackiest of capitalist consumerism.

VDNKh was an early casualty when those in power finally admitted that the Soviet economy was in dire straits – funds were cut off by 1990. Today, as the VVTs, it's a commercial centre, with its pavilions given over to sales of the very imported goods that were supposed to be inferior. The domed Kosmos (Space) pavilion towards the far end became a wholesaler for TV sets and VCRs, and Lenin's slogan 'Socialism is Soviet power plus electrification' still adorns the electrification pavilion to its right. Although you may not want to do your shopping here, VVTs does host international trade exhibitions.

The grounds of VVTs are huge, so you may wish to catch a ride on the tourist train (R30) that leaves from the front gate. Otherwise, you can rent bicycles and in-line skates (R100/300 per hour/day) just outside.

COSMONAUTICS MUSEUM Map pp60–1
☎ 495-683 8197; ☽ 10am-7pm Tue-Sun; Ⓜ VDNKh

The soaring 100m titanium obelisk outside the All-Russia Exhibition Centre is a monument 'To the Conquerors of Space', built in 1964 to commemorate the launch of Sputnik. In its base is the Cosmonautics Museum, a high-concept series of displays from the glory days of the Soviet space program. Exhibits rely heavily on cool space paraphernalia – Yury Gagarin's space suit, the first Soviet rocket engine and lots of charts and diagrams of various expeditions. The highlight is the awe-inspiring video footage from various orbit missions. Sadly there is no gift shop selling freeze-dried astronaut food. The museum was closed for renovations at the time of research, so who knows what new wonders will be on display upon reopening?

OSTANKINO PALACE & TV TOWER
Map pp60–1
☎ 495-683 4645; www.museum.ru/museum /ostankino; admission R80, excursion R150; ☽ 10am-6pm Wed-Sun mid-May–Sep; Ⓜ VDNKh

The pink-and-white Ostankino Palace, a wooden mansion with a stucco exterior made to resemble stone, was built in the 1790s as the summer pad of Count Nikolai Sheremetev, probably Russia's richest aristocrat of the time and son of Count Pyotr Sheremetev. Note that the palace is closed on days when it rains or when humidity is high.

The lavish interior, with hand-painted wallpaper and intricate parquet floors, houses the count's art treasures. The ornate rooms include the Italian Pavilion and the Egyptian Hall. The centrepiece is the oval theatre-ballroom built for the Sheremetev troupe of 250 serf actors. In 1801 Count Nikolai married one of the troupe, Praskovia Zhemchugova, and the two retired to Ostankino to avoid court gossip. These days, the theatre hosts a summer music festival (tickets R200-750), featuring intimate concerts.

After a fire in the late 1990s, the 540m Ostankino TV Tower is no longer open to the public, although it still provides a distinctive landmark for the area.

To reach the Ostankino Palace, walk west from VDNKh metro, across the car parks, to pick up tram 7 or 11 or trolleybus 13, 36, 69 or 73 west along ul Akademika Korolyova.

EAST OF THE CENTRE
IZMAYLOVSKY PARK & ROYAL ESTATE Map pp60–1
☎ 499-166 5881; Izmaylovskoe sh; admission free; ☽ 11.30am-5pm Wed-Sun; Ⓜ Partizanskaya

Izmaylovo is best known for its extensive arts and crafts market (p156), held every weekend beside the royal estate. After shopping, Izmaylovsky Park and the crumbling royal estate are nice for a picnic or more serious outdoor activity.

A former royal hunting reserve 10km east of the Kremlin, Izmaylovsky Park is the nearest large tract of undeveloped land to central Moscow. Its 15 sq km contain a recreation park at the western end and a much larger expanse of woodland (Izmaylovsky Lesopark) east of Glavnaya alleya, the road that cuts north–south across the park. Trails wind around this park, making it a good place to escape the city for hiking or biking. From Partizanskaya metro station, take bus 7 or 131 and get off at the third stop.

The royal estate is on a small, moated island to the north-west of the park. Tsar

Alexey had an experimental farm here in the 17th century, where Western farming methods and cottage industries were sampled. It was on the farm ponds that his son Peter learned to sail in a little boat; he came to be called the 'Grandfather of the Russian Navy'.

Past an extensive 18th-century barracks (now partly occupied by the police) is the beautiful five-domed 1679 Intercession Cathedral, an early example of Moscow baroque. The nearby triple-arched, tent-roofed Ceremonial Gates (1682) and the squat brick bridge tower (1671) are the only other original buildings remaining.

KUSKOVO PARK & MANSION
off Map pp60–1

☎ 495-370 0160; ul Yunosti 2; per exhibit R30-100; ☽ 10am-4pm Wed-Sun Nov-Mar, 10am-6pm Wed-Sun Apr-Oct; Ⓜ Ryazansky Prospekt

When Count Pyotr Sheremetev married Varvara Cherkassakava in 1743, their joint property amounted to 1200 villages and 200,000 serfs. They turned their country estate at Kuskovo, 12km east of the Kremlin, into a mini-Versailles, with elegant buildings scattered around formal gardens, as well as an informal park. It's a pleasant trip out from central Moscow.

The main wooden mansion, Kuskovo Mansion, overlooks a lake where the count staged mock sea battles to entertain Moscow society. Across the lake to the south is the informal park. North of the mansion, in the formal grounds, are an orangery, now housing an exhibition of 18th- to 20th-century Russian ceramics; an open-air theatre, where the Sheremetev troupe of serf actors performed twice weekly; a pondside grotto with exotic 'sea caverns'; a Dutch house, glazed inside with Delft tiles; an Italian villa; a hermitage for private parties; and a church with a wooden bell tower. The buildings are closed when humidity exceeds 80% or when it's very cold, counting out much of the winter.

Bus 133 and 208 go from Ryazansky Prospekt metro to the park.

SOUTH OF THE CENTRE

MOSCOW STATE UNIVERSITY (MGU)
Map pp60–1

Moskovsky Gosudarstvenny Universitet; Universitetskaya pl; Ⓜ Universitet

The best view over Moscow is from Universitetskaya pl, at the top of the hill. From here, most of the city spreads out before you. It is also an excellent vantage point to see Luzhniki, the huge stadium complex built across the river for the 1980 Olympics, as well as Novodevichy Convent and the Cathedral of Christ the Saviour.

Behind Universitetskaya pl is the Stalinist spire of Moscow State University, one of the 'Seven Sisters' (see the boxed text, p51). The building is the result of four years of hard labour by convicts between 1949 and 1953. It boasts an amazing 36 stories and 33km of corridors. The shining star that sits atop the spire is supposed to weigh 12 tonnes. Among other socialist realist frills on the facade, look for the eager students looking forward to communism. The building is not open to the public, which is a shame, because the lobby is equally elaborate, featuring bronze statues of distinguished Soviet scientists.

VOROBYOVY GORY NATURE PRESERVE Map pp60–1

☎ 499-739 2708; www.vorobyovy-gory.ru, in Russian; admission free; Ⓜ Vorobyovy Gory

Vorobyovy Gory, or Sparrow Hills, is the green hilly area south of the Moscow River, opposite the tip of the Khamovniki peninsula. This wooded hillside is a pleasant surprise, especially since it has been recently converted into an ecological park. Following the south shore of the Moscow River, the narrow strip of land contains a network of wooded trails and a sandy beach. An ecotrain runs along the bank of the river; otherwise you can rent bicycles or in-line skates at the south-eastern entrance. From the river bank, the walking trails lead up to Universitetskaya pl, as does the ski lift (R100).

KOLOMENSKOE MUSEUM-RESERVE
Map pp60–1

☎ 499-615 2768; www.mgomz.ru, in Russian; grounds admission free; ☽ grounds 8am-9pm; Ⓜ Kolomenskaya

Set amid 4 sq km of parkland, on a bluff above a bend in the Moscow River, this Museum-Reserve is an ancient royal country seat and Unesco World Heritage Site. Many festivals are held here, so check if anything is happening during your visit.

From Bolshaya ul, enter at the rear of the grounds through the 17th-century Saviour

Gate to the whitewashed Our Lady of Kazan Church, both built in the time of Tsar Alexey.

The church faces the site of his great wooden palace, which was demolished in 1768 by Catherine the Great. Ahead, the white, tent-roofed 17th-century front gate and clock tower mark the edge of the old inner-palace precinct. The golden double-headed eagle that tops the gate is the symbol of the Romanov dynasty.

The adjacent buildings house an interesting museum (adult/child R300/100; 🕙 10am-5pm) with a bit of everything: a model of Alexey's wooden palace, material on rebellions associated with Kolomenskoe, and Russian handcrafts from clocks and tiles to woodcarving and metalwork.

Outside the front gate, overlooking the river, rises Kolomenskoe's loveliest structure, the quintessentially Russian Ascension Church. Built between 1530 and 1532 for Grand Prince Vasily III, it probably celebrated the birth of his heir, Ivan the Terrible. It is actually an important development in Russian architecture, reproducing the shapes of wooden churches in brick for the first time, and paving the way for St Basil's Cathedral 25 years later. Immediately west of it are the round 16th-century St George's Bell Tower and another 17th-century tower.

About 300m further south-west, across a gully, the white St John the Baptist Church was built for Ivan the Terrible in the 1540s or 1550s. It has four corner chapels that make it a stylistic 'quarter-way house' between the Ascension Church and St Basil's. Among the old wooden buildings on the grounds is Peter the Great's cabin, where he lived while supervising ship- and fort-building at Arkhangelsk.

TSARITSYNO PALACE off Map pp60–1

☎ 495-355 4844; www.tsaritsyno-museum .ru; grounds admission free; 🕙 dawn-dusk; Ⓜ Tsaritsino

On a wooded hill in far south-east Moscow, Tsaritsyno Palace is a modern-day manifestation of the exotic summer home that Catherine the Great began in 1775 but never finished. Architect Vasily Bazhenov worked on the project for 10 years before he was sacked. She hired another architect, Matvey Kazakov, but the project was eventually forgotten as she ran out of money. For hundreds of years, the palace was little more than a shell, until the government finally decided to finish it in 2007.

Nowadays, the Great Palace (admission R150) is a fantastical building that combines old Russian, Gothic, classical and Arabic styles. Inside, exhibits are dedicated to the history of Tsaritsyno, as well as the life of Catherine the Great. The nearby kitchen building, or khlebny dom (admission R100), also hosts rotating exhibits, sometimes culinary and sometimes on less-tantalising topics such as icons and art. The *khlebny dom* is a pleasant place to hear classical concerts (☎ 499-725 7291; tickets R150-300; 🕙 5pm Sat & Sun) in summer.

The extensive grounds include some other lovely buildings, including the Small Palace, the working Church of Our Lady Lifegiving Spring, the cavalier buildings and some interesting bridges. A pond is bedecked by a fantastic fountain set to music.

The English-style wooded park stretches all the way south to the Upper Tsaritsynsky Pond, which has rowing boats available for hire in summer, and west to the Tsaritsyno Palace complex.

WALKING TOURS

Moscow is a city for walking, which is evident from the hordes crowding the footpaths. Of course, it is too huge to walk everywhere, which is why there is the metro. Much of the city was built when cars were a rarity (or nonexistent for that matter), so despite the proliferation of road traffic on the streets today, most of the city is accessible by public transport and a strong pair of legs.

The following walking tours suggest some routes by which to see the city under your own steam. The Underground Odyssey (p143) is a tour of the artistic highlights of Moscow's metro system.

KREMLIN & KITAY GOROD

WALK FACTS

Start Red Square (Ⓜ Ploshchad Revolyutsii)
End Staraya pl (Ⓜ Kitay-Gorod)
Distance 3km
Duration Three hours
Fuel Stops Loft Café (p162); Drova (p164)

Walking Tour

1 Red Square With St Basil's Cathedral before you, the Kremlin on one side and GUM on the other, Red Square (p73) is an awe-inspiring introduction to Moscow.

2 Manezhnaya ploshchad Walk through Resurrection Gate to this triumphant square (p75), centred on the heroic statue of Marshall

KREMLIN & KITAY GOROD WALKING TOUR

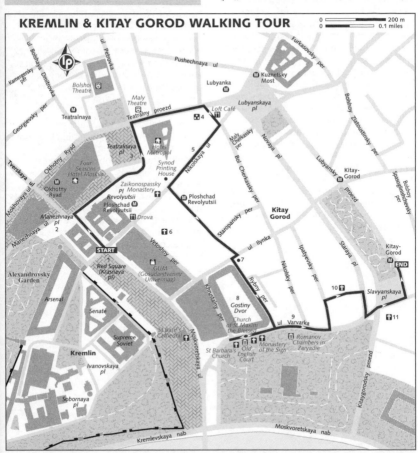

Zhukov and dominated by the new Four Seasons Hotel Moskva.

3 Teatralnaya ploshchad The third majestic square (p76) on the tour, this one is aptly named for the ring of theatres at its northern flank.

4 Starye Polya This historical and architectural complex (p76) includes excavations of the 16th-century fortified wall that surrounded Kitay Gorod. Beside the church is a statue of Ivan Fyodorov, reputedly responsible for Russia's first book in 1563. The gated walkway of Tretyakovsky proezd leads into Kitay Gorod.

5 Nikolskaya Ulitsa Kitay Gorod's busiest street was the main road to Vladimir and used to be the centre of a busy icons trade. Admire the former Slavyansky Bazaar at No 17, the Synod Printing House (p77) at No 15 and the ancient Zaikonospassky Monastery (p77) at Nos 7 to 9.

6 Monastery of the Epiphany The baroque Epiphany Cathedral was built in the 1690s, but the monastery (p77) dates to the 13th century. If you are lucky, you might catch a concert (or rehearsal) performed in the bell tower.

7 Stock Exchange On the corner of ul Ilyinka, notice the exquisite details on the street's south-side buildings. This was Moscow's financial heart in the 18th and 19th centuries. The old Stock Exchange is on the corner at No 6.

8 Gostiny Dvor The Old Merchants' Court, or Gostiny Dvor (p148), occupies the block between ul Ilyinka and ul Varvarka. It is now partially renovated and filled with shops, including some excellent stops for souvenir hunters.

9 Ulitsa Varvarka This little street has Kitay Gorod's greatest concentration of interesting buildings. They were long dwarfed by the gargantuan Hotel Rossiya, which was demolished in 2006. At the time of research, it was still a mystery what would be built in its place. Walking from west to east, pass the pink-and-white St Barbara's Church, dating to 1804; the peak-roofed Old English Court (p77), dating to the 16th century; the 1698 Church of St Maxim the Blessed, now housing folk-art; the monks' building and golden-domed cathedral of the Monastery of the Sign; the Romanov Chambers in Zaryadie (p77); and the colourful St George's Church, which dates to 1658.

10 Church of the Trinity in Nikitniki This enchanting 1630s church (p77), hidden amid overbearing facades of surrounding buildings, is an exquisite example of Russian baroque.

11 Slavyanskaya ploshchad Head east from Ipatevsky per out to Staraya pl. At the southern end of this square is All Saints Cathedral on the Kulishka, which was built in 1687. Some remains of the old city wall can be seen in the underground passage at the corner of ul Varvarka and Staraya pl. This *perekhod* (cross walk) is also the entrance to the Kitay-Gorod metro stop.

TVERSKOY
Walking Tour

1 Teatralnaya Ploshchad This stately square (p76) straddles ul Okhotny Ryad, but the

WALK FACTS

Start Teatralnaya pl (Ⓜ Teatralnaya)
End Hermitage Gardens (Ⓜ Mayakovskaya)
Distance 2.5km
Duration Three hours
Fuel stops Akademiya (p168), Gogol (p183), Chaikhona No 1 (p180)

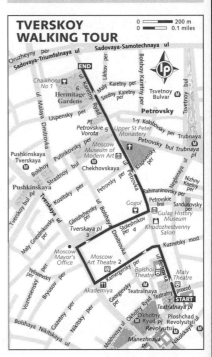

namesake Bolshoi Theatre (p87) is the centrepiece. The Maly Theatre (p192) and the National Youth Theatre frame it on either side.

2 Kamergersky pereulok Lined with restaurants and cafés with outdoor seating, this pleasant pedestrian strip is Moscow's prime people-watching spot. Look out for the Moscow Art Theatre (p192), founded by Konstantin Stanislavsky in 1898.

3 Tverskaya Ploshchad This prominent square (p92) is home to two Moscow heroes named Yury: the centre statue is Yury Dolgoruky, founder of Moscow; across in city hall sits Yury Luzhkov, mayor of Moscow.

4 Stoleshnikov Pereulok East of Tverskaya pl, Stoleshnikov per is another quaint cobblestone strip, lined with fancy boutiques and trendy cafés. The lane terminates at ul Petrovka, where you will find the thought-provoking Gulag History Museum (p87) and the fun-filled Khudozhestvenny Salon (p151).

5 Ploshchad Petrovskie Vorota Named for the gates that used to guard the city, the square at the top of ul Petrovka is home to the

ancient Upper St Peter Monastery (p91) and the fresh Moscow Museum of Modern Art (p90).

6 Hermitage Gardens Cross the Boulevard Ring and walk up ul Karenty Ryad to finish your tour amid the shady greenery of Hermitage Gardens. Stop for a drink at Chaikhona No 1 (p180), then stroll west on the Boulevard Ring to reach Mayakovskaya metro station.

PRESNYA
Walking Tour

1 Patriarch's Ponds Start your tour with a stroll around Patriarshy Prudy (p95), or Patriarch's Ponds. (Despite the name, there is only one pond.) Literature fans can shed a tear for Berlioz, who met his bloody end here, in *The Mas-*

WALK FACTS

Start Patriarch's Ponds (Ⓜ Mayakovskaya)
End Moskva-City (Ⓜ Delovoy Tsentr)
Distance 5km
Duration Three hours (plus zoo time)
Fuel stop Coffee Mania (p172), Pinocchio Pasticceria (p173)

PRESNYA WALKING TOUR

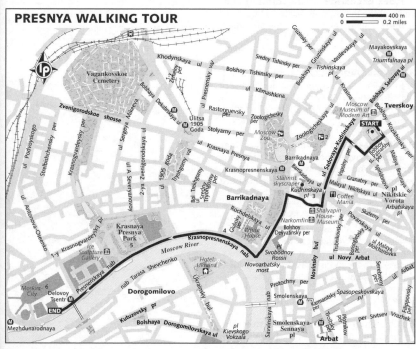

ter and Margarita. Art fans can consider the branch of the Moscow Museum of Modern Art (p95).

2 Moscow Zoo The big Moscow Zoo (p95) is a walking tour in and of itself. But it's worth the detour for animal lovers. Look for the secondary entrance on ul Sadovaya-Kudrinskaya.

3 Kudrinskaya Ploshchad Dominated by the massive skyscraper that is one of Stalin's Seven Sisters (see the boxed text, p51), this is a loud, busy square. Just south of here is one of Moscow's last and best examples of modernist architecture, Narkomfin (p98). The Shalyapin House-Museum (p99) is nearby.

4 Krasnopresnenskaya Naberezhnaya On the banks of the Moscow River, the massive white facade is the White House (p98) – home not of the Russian president, but the Russian parliament. The Stalinist Hotel Ukraina (p211), another of the Seven Sisters, stands on the opposite side of the river, almost a tribute to times gone by.

5 Krasnaya Presnya Park The fountains, flowers and cafés make this park a pleasant place for a pause. But the Ice Sculpture Gallery (p98) makes it a really unique experience.

6 Moskva-City See the latest and greatest developments in the capital's skyline, as these steel and glass structures sprout up along the Moscow River. A massive construction project at the time of research, Moskva-City will soon be home to legions of bureaucrats, business people and perhaps a few billionaires.

ARBAT
Walking Tour

1 Arbatskaya Ploshchad Your stroll down *stary* Arbat, or 'old' Arbat, starts at traffic-filled Arbatskaya pl, dominated by the massive Ministry of Defence building. Across the street, the whimsical House of Friendship with Peoples of Foreign Countries (p105) shows off its incongruous Moorish style.

WALK FACTS

Start Arbatskaya pl (Ⓜ Arbatskaya)
End Smolenskaya-Sennaya pl (Ⓜ Smolenskaya)
Distance 3km
Duration Two hours
Fuel stops Prime Star (p164), Vostochny Kvartal (p172)

ARBAT WALKING TOUR

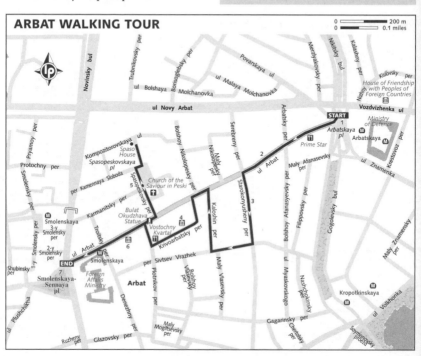

2 Stary Arbat Things quiet down at the cobblestones of ul Arbat. Besides the souvenir stalls and street performers, look for the Wall of Peace (p100), composed of individually painted tiles.

3 Starokonyusheny Pereulok The quiet lanes off ul Arbat offer some exemplary Art Nouveau architecture: the fine tile work at No 41; the sculptures supporting the balconies at No 39; the rough stone at No 37; and the new-empire style of No 35. These *dokhodnye doma* contained flats, built for rich professionals who could not afford their own homes.

4 Melnikov House This strange cylindrical house (p104) was the only privately owned home built during the Soviet period. It is still owned by the architect's granddaughter, though it is not usually open to the public.

5 Spasopeskovsky pereulok This little lane contains architectural gems. Right at the intersection with ul Arbat, you can't miss the statue of the bard Bulat Okudzhava (see the boxed text, p101), who lived on the Arbat. Heading north, you will come to the lovely Church of the Saviour in Peski, built in the 17th century, and the elegant Spaso House, home of the US ambassador.

6 Pushkin House-Museum Alexander Pushkin and Natalya Goncharova moved to this house (p100) on the Arbat after they wed (see the happy couple featured in a statue across the street). Next door, the flat where Silver Age writer Andrei Bely lived is now the Memorial Apartment of Andrei Bely (p101).

7 Smolenskaya-Sennaya Ploshchad The towering Stalinist skyscraper, one of the Seven Sisters, is the Ministry of Foreign Affairs (see the boxed text, p51).

KHAMOVNIKI
Walking Tour
1 Borovitskaya Ploshchad From Borovitskaya pl, stroll along ul Volkhonka, which

WALK FACTS

Start Borovitskaya Ploshchad (Ⓜ Borovitskaya)
End Novodevichy Cemetery (Ⓜ Sportivnaya)
Distance 4km
Duration Three hours
Fuel stops Il Patio (p174), Galereya Khudozhnikov (p174), Stolle (p174)

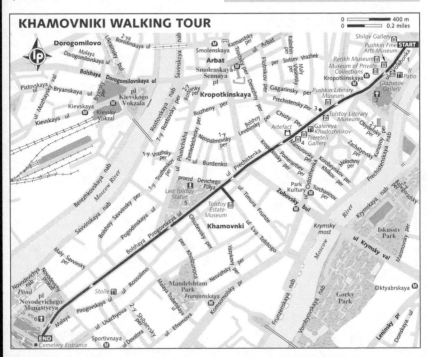

KHAMOVNIKI WALKING TOUR

is packed with galleries and art museums. In addition to the Pushkin Fine Arts Museum (p115), the premier gallery of European art in the capital, you will also find smaller art collections including the Gallery of European & American Art of the 19th & 20th Centuries (p115), the Shilov Gallery (p116), the Rerikh Museum (p116), the Museum of Private Collections (p115) and the Glazunov Gallery (p116).

2 Cathedral of Christ the Saviour The landmark church (p109) was built in 1997 but has a long and sordid history – this masterpiece by Zurab Tsereteli is a re-creation of a similar church that stood on this spot in the 19th century.

3 Ulitsa Prechistenka This street has some of Moscow's most exquisite architecture from the 17th to early 20th centuries. The beautiful empire-style mansion houses the Pushkin Literary Museum (p116), while the former Lopukhin mansion is now the Tolstoy Literary Museum (p116). Keep your eyes peeled for many other gems.

4 Russian Academy of Art Two side-by-side mansions house the Russian Academy and Art (p117) and the Tsereteli Gallery (p117). If you are inspired to invest in some Russian artwork, head across the street to Artefact (p153).

5 Maiden's Field Across the Garden Ring, a brooding Tolstoy surveys this small park. The great novelist's estate, now the Tolstoy Estate-Museum (p117), is down a side street.

6 Novodevichy Convent & Cemetery Although it is located in the outer reaches, Novodevichy is really the centrepiece of Khamovniki. The convent (p112) contains centuries of art and history, while the cemetery (p113) is a veritable who's who of 20th-century Russian culture.

ZAMOSKVORECHIE
Walking Tour
1 Cathedral of Christ the Saviour It's not in Zamoskvorechie, but from this church (p109)

WALK FACTS

Start Chistye Prudy (Ⓜ Chistye Prudy)
End Christ the Saviour Cathedral (Ⓜ Kropotkinskaya)
Distance 8km
Duration Four hours
Fuel stops Shatyor (p180); Avocado (p163); Gallery (p166); Il Patio (p174)

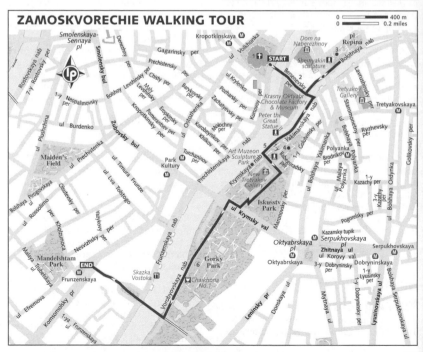

ZAMOSKVORECHIE WALKING TOUR

a pedestrian bridge leads across the Moscow River to Bolotny Island, the small slice of land south of the Kremlin. The bridge offers a fantastic panorama of the Kremlin towers and of the cathedral itself.

2 Bolotny Island South of the bridge is the old Krasny Oktyabr chocolate factory, (p122), now being refurbished into luxury lofts. The cluster of galleries known as Art Strelka (p155) is immediately below the bridge. Make a detour north along Sofiyskaya nab to the Dom na Naberezhnoy (p123), which was a prestigious residential building during Soviet times.

3 Bolotnaya Ploshchad The centrepiece of this little park is an intriguing sculpture by Mikhail Shemyakin, *Children are Victims of Adults' Vices* (with all the vices depicted in delightful detail).

4 Yakimanka In this former industrial neighbourhood, many 19th-century factories have been converted to office buildings and banks. The Tretyakov Gallery (p118) is a few blocks to the east, but if you don't want to be sidelined for the rest of the day, head south along Yakimanskaya nab, passing Zurab Tsereteli's unmistakeable sculpture of Peter the Great (see the boxed text, p113), or 'Peter the Ugly' according to some sources.

5 Krymskaya Naberezhnaya From the embankment, enter the Art Muzeon Sculpture Park (p119), an art museum and history lesson all in one. From here, you can enter the New Tretyakov (p119), the branch dedicated to 20th-century art, and TsDKh (p155), or the Central House of Artists, which is filled with galleries and exhibitions. On weekends, artists' stalls line the embankment.

6 Gorky Park Cross ul Krymsky val using the underground passageway. You will reappear at ground level at the entrance to Gorky Park (p119), marked by colourful flags and an old-fashioned carousel. Stroll across the fun-filled theme park, stopping to eat ice cream or ride the Ferris wheel. At the southern end, you can stroll across the pedestrian bridge to Frunzenskaya metro station.

AROUND THE RING
Walking Tour
The Boulevard Ring was created in the late 18th and early 19th centuries, replacing Mos-

cow's old defensive walls with a dual-carriage ring road. The new boulevard circling the city centre was lined with stately mansions and theatres, and the shady path between the two carriageways became the place for Moscow residents to promenade.

Today the Boulevard Ring has more cars than carriages. But the strip of green down the middle is still a pleasant place to walk and is Moscow's oddest-shaped park. Eight kilometres long by 20m wide, it forms a near-complete circle around the centre, from the banks of the Yauza River south-east of the Kremlin, to the banks of the Moscow River in the south-west. This walking tour takes you most of the way around the ring, traversing Basmanny, Krasnoselsky and Meshchansky, Tverskoy, Arbat and Khamovniki.

The Boulevard Ring changes its name at every major intersection, but it is usually 'something bulvar', and it is always recognisable by the green strip down the centre. If you are not up for the walk, you can do part of this tour by trolleybus 15 or 31, which run both ways along the ring between Trubnaya pl and ul Prechistenka.

1 Chistye Prudy The area surrounding Chistye Prudy, or 'Clean Ponds' was largely developed by the merchant Alexander Menshikov in the 18th century. As you head north, you will see the golden cross that tops Menshikov Tower (p79). Near the metro stands a statue in honour of Alexander Griboyedov, a 19th-century playwright and diplomat. His comedy *Woe from Wit*, a brilliant satire on Moscow aristocratic life, is one of Russia's most-often-staged plays.

2 Sretensky Bulvar At the opposite end of Sretensky bul stands a monument to Nadezhda Krupskaya – revolutionary, writer and wife of Vladimir Ilych Lenin. Krupskaya is widely recognised as Lenin's top adviser and confidante, and an active Bolshevik in her own right.

3 Rozhdestvenny Bulvar The pretty, whitewashed Church of the Assumption of the Virgin is usually open for a look around its candle-lit interior. At the end of the block, duck into the Nativity Monastery (Rozhdestvensky monastir), for which this section of the boulevard is named. Founded in 1380, it is one of Moscow's oldest monasteries, and it looks it. The walled grounds contain a 16th-century church and a grand bell tower, both of which retain an air of dilapidated grace.

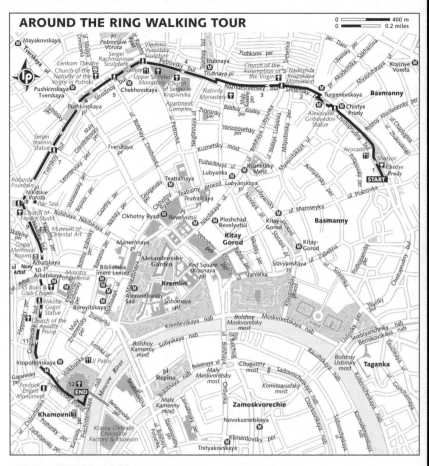

AROUND THE RING WALKING TOUR

WALK FACTS

Start Cathedral of Christ the Saviour
(Ⓜ Kropotkinskaya)
End Gorky Park (Ⓜ Frunzenskaya)
Distance 4km
Duration Three hours
Fuel stops Chaikhona No 1 (p180), Skazka Vostoka (p174)

4 Petrovsky Bulvar The left-hand side of this strip is dotted with architectural and religious landmarks. Look for the Art Nouveau apartment complex (ansambl zhilikh domov) at No 4 Krapivensky per and the equally decorative Church of Sergei in Krapivnika, visible from the side street. The corner of ul Petrovka is dominated by its namesake, Upper St Peter Monastery (p91).

5 Strastnoy Bulvar In season, this section of the Boulevard Ring is dotted with summer cafés (letny kafe). Sculptures along the way commemorate two celebrated musicians: Vladimir Vyssotsky, bard and social revolutionary from the 1960s; and Sergei Rachmaninov, the celebrated turn-of-the-century pianist and composer.

6 Pushkinskaya Ploshchad This busy square is named for the gallant poet whose statue commands the square. Cross Bolshoy Putinkovsky per so you can admire the tent roofs on the Church of the Nativity of the Virgin in Putinki (p92) and the impressive facade of the Lenkom Theatre (p192).

7 Tverskoy Bulvar Lined with lovely mansions and theatres and dotted with statues, this is one of the loveliest stretches of the Boulevard Ring. In the middle of the boulevard is a statue of Sergei Yesenin, an early-20th-century poet who wrote about love and landscapes, earning him the nickname 'the peasant poet'.

8 Ploshchad Nikitskie Vorota This beautiful square takes its name from the gates that stood here from the 15th to the 18th centuries. The Rotunda Fountain, by Zurab Tsereteli, hides a statue of Pushkin and Goncharova, erected in 1999 to celebrate the poet's birthday. On the eastern side, there are fantastic photos of the week's events on display in the window of the Russian news agency Itar-Tass. South of the square, the beautiful Church of Fyodor Studit is all that remains of a 17th-century monastery.

9 Nikitsky Bulvar The classical building at No 12A now houses the Museum of Oriental Art (p100), but it was built for the musical Lunin family (as evidenced by the moulded lyre on the front). The quiet courtyard at No 7 contains the Gogol Memorial Rooms (p101), where the writer spent his final, tortured months.

10 Arbatskaya Ploshchad South of the square, the hulking Ministry of Defence occupies much of the block. It leaves just a corner of space for the sweet SS Boris & Gleb Chapel, which commemorates a 1483 church of the same name that was destroyed in the 1930s.

11 Gogolevsky Bulvar The statue of Nikolai Gogol marks the start of Gogolevsky bul, another peaceful stretch of the Boulevard Ring. The golden domes of the 17th-century Church of the Apostle Philip rise above the baroque buildings on the west side of the street.

12 Cathedral of Christ the Saviour The boulevard ends at its intersection with ul Prechistenka, at the base of the mammoth Cathedral of Christ the Saviour (p109). Fredrick Engels surveys the square from its western side. The bridge at the back leads to the Krasny Oktyabr Chocolate Factory & Museum (p122), yielding unimpeded Kremlin views along the way.

LITERARY SOJOURN
Walking Tour

A walk around Moscow offers a chance to see some original settings from Russian literature, as well as the environs where various authors and poets lived and worked. Start at

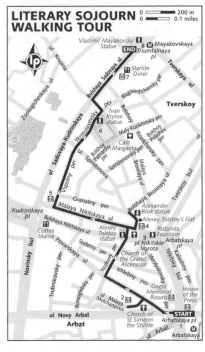

busy Arbatskaya pl, at the southern end of Nikitsky bul.

1 Arbatskaya Ploshchad The quiet courtyard at No 7 contains the Gogol Memorial Rooms (p101), where the writer threw his manuscript for *Dead Souls* into the fireplace. Across the street, the mansion at No 8A was the House of the Press during the Soviet period and writers such as Yesenin, Blok and Mayakovsky all presented their work here.

2 Lermontov House-Museum Turn right off ul Novy Arbat at the Church of St Simeon the Stylite, which was Gogol's parish church. Taking a detour on ul Malaya Molchanovka, you'll arrive at the home of Mikhail Lermontov (p105), author of *A Hero of Our Time.*

3 Ploshchad Nikitskie Vorota The graceful Church of the Grand Ascension (p101) was the site where Alexander Pushkin married Natalya Goncharova in 1831; the happy couple grace the Rotunda Fountain, east of the church. A statue of the lesser-known Tolstoy (and distant relative of Leo) Alexey Tolstoy stands in the small park across the lane from the church. Also a writer, Alexey Tolstoy is known primarily for his 20th-century novels about the civil war and the revolution, the most famous being the trilogy *The Ordeal*.

4 Gorky House-Museum Designed by Fyodor Shekhtel, with mosaics by Mikhail Vrubel, the house (p101) was later gifted to writer Maxim Gorky, who often complained about the extravagant decor. Behind the Gorky House-Museum is Alexey Tolstoy's flat. The statue of another early-20th-century poet, Alexander Blok, stands a bit further up this street.

5 Chekhov House-Museum Anton Chekhov lived and wrote such masterpieces as *Three Sisters* and *The Seagull* in this house (p98). Chekhov described his style: 'All I wanted was to say honestly to people: have a look at yourselves and see how bad and dreary your lives are! The important thing is that people should realise that, for when they do, they will most certainly create another and better life for themselves.'

6 Patriarch's Ponds This little park (p95) is infamous as the opening scene of *The Master and Margarita,* by Mikhail Bulgakov. The huge statue west of the pond is of the 19th-century Russian writer Ivan Krylov, known to every Russian child for his didactic tales. Scenes from his stories are depicted around the statue.

7 Bulgakov House-Museum Bulgakov lived in a flat at No 10 (p91), where he wrote *The Master and Margarita*. A black cat lives in the courtyard.

8 Triumfalnaya ploshchad This square was previously named for the poet and playwright Vladimir Mayakovsky, whose statue is in its centre. A Bolshevik regime favourite, Mayakovsky sought to demystify poetry, adopting crude language and ignoring traditional poetic techniques.

UNDERGROUND ODYSSEY
Walking Tour
The Moscow metro is a marvel of urban design. Every day, as many as nine million people use the metro system – that's more than in New York and London combined. What's more, this transport system combines function and form. Many of Moscow's metro stations are marble-faced, frescoed, gilded works of art. So while you are waiting for that train, stroll around and admire the frescoed ceilings, mosaic tiles and crystal chandeliers. Note that diversity of theme is not a strength here: it does not go too far beyond revolutionary heroism, unity between the workers and peasants, and friendship between the Soviet peoples. But the craft is nonetheless extraordinary. Not exactly a walking tour, this odyssey is an opportunity to explore the most magnificent of Moscow's metro stations.

These days, the metro has implemented a sort of public-relations campaign. You will notice posters decorated with pretty, smiling young ladies in uniform promising, 'Good weather, any time of year'. These *devushky* (young women) bear little resemblance to the babushky sitting at the bottom of the escalators, but let's not mull over a technicality.

When Stalin announced plans for *metrostroy* (construction of the metro), loyal communists turned out in droves to contribute their time and energy to this project. Thousands of people toiled around the clock in dire conditions, but it was all worth it when the first metro line opened in 1935, travelling from Park Kultury in the south to Sokolniki in the north (known as the Sokolnicheskaya, or Sokolniki line). Apparently, the first stations are very deep because they were designed to double as bomb shelters.

1 Komsomolskaya Start at Komsomolskaya, the station where the Sokolnicheskaya line intersects with the Koltsevaya line, or Ring line. Both stations have the same name: they are named for the youth workers who helped construct the first stations. At the Komsomolskaya (Sokolnicheskaya line) station, you will see the Komsomol emblem at the top of the limestone pillars. The Komsomolskaya (Koltsevaya line) station has a huge stuccoed hall, the ceiling featuring mosaics of past Russian military heroes, including Peter the Great, Dmitry Donskoy and Alexander Suvorov. From Komsomolskaya, proceed around the Ring line, getting off at each stop along the way. When you are through admiring the underground artwork, hop back on the train (heading in the same direction) and go to the next station.

2 Prospekt Mira Prospekt Mira is decorated in elegant, gold-trimmed white porcelain. The bas-reliefs feature productive farmers picking fruit, children reading books and other happy socialists.

3 Novoslobodskaya The stained-glass panels at Novoslobodskaya envelop this station in Art Nouveau artistry. Besides the usual cast of workers and farmers, you might recognise Vladimir Ilych Lenin.

4 Belorusskaya The ceilings at Belorusskaya station are festooned with mosaics. Once again, the models were joyful, productive workers and farmers – this time from Belarus, as you can tell from the traditional dress.

WALK FACTS

Start Komsomolskaya metro station
End Mayakovskaya metro station
Distance 10km
Duration Three hours
Fuel stops Shesh-Besh (p173), Drova (p164), Mon Café (p181)

5 Krasnopresnenskaya Done in dramatic red-and-white marble, Krasnopresnenskaya has bas-reliefs depicting the fateful events of 1905 and 1917. This neighbourhood was the scene of some of the terrible battles from those years, not to mention the fateful events of 1991 and 1993 (see p33), which also took place nearby.

6 Kievskaya At Kievskaya you don't have to break your neck looking at the ceiling, as the mosaics adorn the walls. The themes are predictably Ukrainian, or more accurately, Russo-Ukrainian. Look for Pushkin among the Ukrainian folk singers and also the friendship between Russian and Ukrainian farmers. Other scenes are from Ukrainian history, such as the *Battle of Poltava,* 1709. At Kievskaya, switch over to the Arbatsko–Pokrovskaya line, which is dark blue. The hall of this station (also called Kievskaya) continues the theme, with panels depicting 300 years of Russian-Ukrainian cooperation. The colourful frescoes stand out against the elegant marble columns and granite floor.

7 Ploshchad Revolyutsii From here, take the train to Ploshchad Revolyutsii, one of the

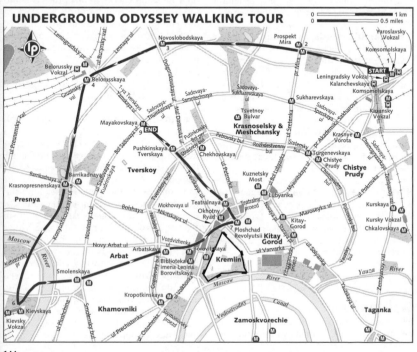

UNDERGROUND ODYSSEY WALKING TOUR

most dramatic stations. The life-size bronze statues in the main hall and beside the escalators illustrate the idealised roles of ordinary Russians. Heading up the escalators, the themes are: carrying out and protecting the revolution, industry, agriculture, hunting, education, sport and child rearing.

8 Teatralnaya Switch to Teatralnaya, on the Zamoskvoretskaya line (green). This station was formerly called Ploshchad Sverdlova in honour of Lenin's right-hand man, whose bust is in the hall. The labradorite and marble that adorn this hall are apparently from the original Church of Christ the Saviour.

9 Mayakovskaya Take the Zamoskvoretskaya line to Mayakovskaya, the pièce de résistance of the Moscow metro. This grand-prize winner at the 1938 World's Fair in New York has an art deco central hall that's all stainless steel and pink rhodonite, with inspiring, upward-looking mosaics on the ceiling. This is also one of the deepest stations (33m), which allowed it to serve as an air-raid shelter during WWII.

top picks

- **Khudozhezestvenny Salon** (p151)
- **Atman** (p149)
- **Yekaterina** (p152)
- **Transylvania** (p153)
- **Ministerstvo Podarkov** (p151)
- **Bukle** (p153)
- **Russkie Chasovye Traditsii** (p154)
- **Izmaylovo Market** (p156)

SHOPPING

Back in the old days, the only place to buy a tin of caviar or a painted box was at an elite Beriozka store. Entry was restricted to foreigners and people with foreign currency, every store carried the same dull stuff and prices were high. The only other options were the sad selections at the State Department Store (GUM) or the notorious black market. Russia has come a long way since then – basic toiletries are no longer luxuries and one no longer need defy the law to bring home a decent souvenir.

That said, shopping is not among Russia's main attractions. Foreign goods, especially clothing, jewellery and anything with a designer label, are ridiculously expensive. High-quality Russian goods are priced to compete (meaning they are equally expensive).

Which is not to say that Muscovites are not shoppers. On the contrary. They are the reason that prices are so high. In the centre, eager consumers are packing into clothing boutiques, shoe stores, art galleries and bookshops. High-end shopping malls are opening on every corner – most recently, the Evropeysky Shopping Centre (p155), the world's biggest urban mall. On the outskirts, more cost-conscious shoppers are flocking to megamalls in search of cheaper goods. After eight years of record-breaking economic growth, Muscovites have money and they are ready to spend!

A small but enterprising fashion industry is up and coming in Moscow. A few local designers are blazing this trail, selling classy and creative designs. Moscow's vibrant art scene means that the capital's galleries are filled with paintings, sculpture and photographs. The selection of souvenir-type items is always changing and growing, as craftspeople unleash long-dormant creativity and collectors uncover long-hidden treasures.

See p248 for details on export restrictions concerning antiques and anything else more than 25 years old. For details on shopping for food items, see p161.

OPENING HOURS

Most shops are open from 9am or 10am until 8pm or 9pm. Large shopping centres stay open until 10pm or later. Hours are usually shorter on Sunday, from about noon to 8pm. Hours of operation are indicated in this chapter only when they differ from this norm.

KREMLIN & KITAY GOROD

The streets around the Kremlin are home to some of the capital's largest and most prominent shopping venues. The most historic occupies a prime locale on Red Square – GUM is now among the capital's snazziest shopping malls. Within a 500m radius around Red Square, you will find two other shopping centres, Okhotny Ryad and Nautilus. Meanwhile, Kitay Gorod is home to the capital's oldest marketplace and its swankiest shopping strip. The ancient trading arcades known as Gostiny Dvor are now a minimall, filled with small shops and souvenir stalls. And the ancient entryway into the city, Tretyakovsky proezd, might as

well be called 'Designer Way', as it is lined with boutiques and showrooms by Europe's hottest names.

GUS-KHRUSTALNY FACTORY STORE

Map p66   Antiques & Souvenirs
☎ 495-232 5658; www.ghz.ru; Gostiny Dvor;
Ⓜ Ploshchad Revolyutsii
Since the glass production factory was founded there in 1756, the town of Gus-Khrustalny (east of Moscow) has been known for its high-quality glassware. This factory store carries an excellent selection of beautiful and reasonably priced crystal and glassware, especially coloured glass.

VOLOGDA LINEN

Map p66   Antiques & Souvenirs
☎ 495-604 5915; www.linens.ru, in Russian;
Gostiny Dvor; Ⓜ Ploshchad Revolyutsii
Russia's cool, moist summers are ideal for producing flax, the fibre used to manufacture linen. This elegant, durable fabric is respectfully known in Russia as 'His Majesty Linen'. High-quality linen products such as tablecloths, napkins, bed covers and even clothing are still manufactured in Russia.

VASSA & CO Map p66 Clothing & Accessories

☎ 495-698 1812; www.vassatrend.com; Nikolskaya ul 5/1; Ⓜ Ploshchad Revolyutsii
Vassa is a Russian designer but was trained in New York City and her designs reflect a classical and classy sense of style. Catering to modern Moscow women since 2000, Vassa offers suits, skirts, dresses and other professional clothing that stylish women might wear at the office or out on the town.

GUM Map p66 Shopping Mall

Gosudarstvenny Universalny Magazin; ☎ 495-788 4343; www.gum.ru, in Russian; Krasnaya pl 3; Ⓜ Ploshchad Revolyutsii
In the elaborate 19th-century building on Red Square, the State Department Store – better known as GUM – is a bright and bustling centre filled with shops and cafés.

OKHOTNY RYAD Map p66 Shopping Mall

☎ 495-737 7393; www.oxotniy.ru, in Russian; Manezhnaya pl; Ⓜ Okhotny Ryad
The best part about this underground mall is the fanciful fountain that splashes the shoppers as they enter and exit from Alexandrovsky Garden. Aside from the clothing and electronic stores, there is a big, crowded food court and a 24-hour internet café (p250) on the ground floor.

BASMANNY

The streets east of Kitay Gorod are lined with shops and boutiques, making the inner part of Basmanny a busy, bustling shopping district. You'll find one of Moscow's biggest bookshops, a slew of small boutiques (some featuring local designers) and a few art galleries.

BIBLIO-GLOBUS Map pp80–1 Books

☎ 495-781 1900; www.biblio-globus.ru; Myasnitskaya ul 6; Ⓜ Lubyanka
Moscow's favourite bookshop is huge, with lots of reference and souvenir books on language, art and history, and a good selection of maps and travel guides. Just to prove that Russia's consumer culture can keep up with the best of them, this old-school bookshop now has a coffee shop on the ground floor.

ATMAN Map pp80–1 Clothing & Accessories

☎ 495-917 4640; ul Pokrovka 31; Ⓜ Kurskaya
This boutique of Siberian designer Veronika Samborskaya features free-flowing, rough-

top picks

SHOPPING STRIPS

- Tretyakovsky proezd (opposite) A veritable who's who of luxury goods, whether it's clothes (Prada, Gucci etc), cars (Ferrari, Maserati) or couches (Armani Casa).
- Ulitsa Petrovka (p151) A large department store, a fancy shopping centre and a bounty of boutiques. This shopping strip culminates in Stoleshnikov per, a pedestrian strip given over to the most exclusive shops.
- Ulitsa Arbat (p153) A long-standing tourist attraction, littered with souvenir stalls and antique shops.
- Izmaylovo Market (p156) Still the number-one spot for souvenir shopping.

hewn styles, often made from Russian linen. Samborskaya's unique designs somehow manage to combine rusticity and elegance.

MASHA TSIGAL

Map pp80–1 Clothing & Accessories
☎ 495-915 8464; www.mashatsigal.com; ul Pokrovka 11; Ⓜ Kitay-Gorod
Masha Tsigal's boutique sells mostly casual clothes in skimpy styles, bright colours and bold designs – very playful and a little trampy. Masha has outfitted Russian pop stars tATu, among others.

MON AMOUR Map pp80–1 Clothing & Accessories

☎ 495-544 3900; Myasnitskaya ul 18; Ⓜ Lubyanka
By clothing we mean lingerie. And by accessories we mean Pherone candles, tease toys, masks and whips, as well as a whole line of rings and chains that you won't find at your more mainstream jeweller.

MAGAZIN CHAI-KOFE

Map pp80–1 Food & Drink
Tea-Coffee Store; ☎ 495-625 4656; Myasnitskaya ul 19; Ⓜ Turgenevskaya
In 1894 the old Perlov Tea House was redecorated in the style of a Chinese pagoda. Today this fantastical facade contains the Tea-Coffee Store – a simple name for a place that is filled with coffee beans from Italy, Brazil, Costa Rica and Kenya, and tea leaves from China, India and South Africa.

KRASNOSELSKY & MESHCHANSKY

The crowded streets around Kuznetsky most are crammed with souvenir shops, bookstores and fashion boutiques. Outside of this area, Krasnoselsky and Meshchansky is an unlikely shopping destination.

IKONY-PODARKY

Map pp84–5   Antiques & Souvenirs

Icons-Gifts; ☎ 495-623 8046; ul Bolshaya Lubyanka 17; M Lubyanka
Not much remains of the 14th-century Sretensky Monastery, only the main church, Vladimirsky Cathedral, and, as it turns out, the gift shop. Get your icons – hanging icons, tabletop icons, triptych icons – and other souvenirs to soothe the spirit.

K FABERGE Map pp84–5   Antiques & Souvenirs

☎ 495-624 4969; www.moonstone.ru, in Russian; Kuznetsky most 20; M Kuznetsky Most
Owned by the granddaughter of the famed jeweller to the tsars, this little boutique contains everything that glitters. Besides jewellery, the glass cases are stuffed with crystal and fine china, ornately carved weapons, old-fashioned watches and – of course – the namesake ceramic Easter eggs.

M'ARS CONTEMPORARY ART CENTRE

Map pp84–5   Art Gallery

☎ 495-623 6690; www.marsgallery.ru; Pushkarev per 5; ☽ gallery noon-8pm Tue-Sun, café noon-11pm daily; M Tsvetnoy Bulvar or Sukarevskaya
Founded by artists who were banned during the Soviet era, this gallery space in-

top picks

RUSSIAN DESIGNERS

- Veronika Samborskaya (p149) A unique Siberian style.
- Vereteno (p153) Clothing for the free spirit.
- Valentin Yudashkin (p154) Is it fashion or is it art?
- Denis Simachyov (p152) Take a walk on the wild side.
- Igor Chapurin (p152) Fashionable men, fashionable women, fashionable children, fashionable home.
- Vassa & Co (p149) Clothing for the working woman.

cludes 10 exhibit halls showing the work of top contemporary artists, as well as a cool club and café in the basement.

DOM INOSTRANNIKH KNIG

Map pp84–5   Books

House of Foreign Books; ☎ 495-628 2021; Kuznetsky most 18/7; M Kuznetsky Most
The House of Foreign Books is a small place with a wide selection of literature in foreign languages. Most books are in English, though there are smaller selections of German, French and other European languages.

MANTRAM Map pp84–5   Clothing & Accessories

☎ 495-625 4264; www.mantram.ru; Kuznetsky most 11; ☽ 11am-9pm; M Kuznetsky Most
This small boutique features Russian designs influenced by the mystic East. Richly coloured fabrics and exotic patterns characterise the clothes for men and women. Slippers, tapestries, pillows and other imported interior-design elements are also on sale.

PODIUM Map pp84–5   Clothing & Accessories

☎ 495-540 1535; Kuznetsky most 14; ☽ 11:30am-midnight; M Kuznetsky Most
This gorgeous 'concept store' offers six storeys of high fashion and fun design. Huge windows framed with heavy drapes, an embossed tin ceiling and plush furniture provide an exquisite setting for edgy and exotic (and expensive) clothing.

DETSKY MIR Map pp84–5   Department Store

Children's World; Teatralny proezd 5; M Lubyanka
As of 2008, Children's World is closed for a complex and highly controversial renovation project. Developers have promised not to alter the building's art deco exterior, which is considered a Moscow landmark. But the interior will be completely revamped, with the addition of underground parking, an internal atrium, a multiplex cinema and a family-focused entertainment zone. Stay tuned.

A KORKUNOV Map pp84–5   Food & Drink

☎ 495-625 6411; www.korkunov.ru; ul Bolshaya Lubyanka 13/16; M Lubyanka
That this candy company was founded in 1997 may come as a surprise, as the shop's interior feels like an old-fashioned confectioner. The seductive line of handmade

chocolates – 15 kinds of filled candies and two types of bars – are lined up in a glass case, defying your will power. There are also a few tables, in case you care to indulge in a hot chocolate (R75 to R120).

top picks

ART GALLERIES

- Winzavod (p78) Contemporary art in an old wine factory.
- Art Strelka (p155) Contemporary art in an old chocolate factory.
- Artefact (p153) Dozens of galleries under one roof.
- Khudozhezestvenny Salon (left) Three rooms packed with paintings, crafts and jewellery.

TVERSKOY

Tverskoy is among Moscow's busiest commercial districts, as evidenced by the traffic jams and crowded footpaths along its namesake street. This busy thoroughfare is lined with shoes, clothing and jewellery shops, most of which you might find in London, Paris or New York. But Moscow's premier shopping district centres on posh ul Petrovka. Trendy little boutiques and big, fancy shopping centres line this centuries-old street. Nearby, the pedestrian-friendly Stoleshnikov per contains more exclusive boutiques.

KHUDOZHEZESTVENNY SALON
Map pp88–9   Art Gallery
Art Salon; ☎ 495-628 4593; ul Petrovka 12; Ⓜ Chekhovskaya
Although it has a rather innocuous name, this art gallery is packed with paintings, sculpture, ceramics, jewellery and handicrafts by local artists. This place is owned by the artists, so you won't have the high gallery mark-ups you might find at some other art centres. There is another outlet in Basmanny (☎ 495-625 3064; ul Maroseyka 4; Ⓜ Kitay-Gorod).

MINISTERSTVO PODARKOV
Map pp88–9   Art Gallery
Ministry of Gifts; ☎ 495-629 9732; Maly Gnezdnikovsky per 12/27; Ⓜ Pushkinskaya
For quirky, clever souvenirs, stop by this network of artists' cooperatives. Each outlet has a different name, but the goods are more or less the same: uniquely Russian gifts such as artist-designed *tapki* (slippers) and hand-woven linens. Most intriguingly, artist Yuri Movchan has invented a line of funky, functional fixtures (lights, clocks, etc) made from old appliances and other industrial discards. There is another outlet – Podarky, Dekor & Podarky (☎ 495-203 0417; Malaya Bronnaya ul 28/2; ⏰ 11am-9pm Mon-Fri, noon-9pm Sat, noon-8pm Sun; Ⓜ Mayakovskaya) – near Patriarch's Ponds.

MOSTOK Map pp88–9   Art Gallery
☎ 495-650 7022; www.mostok-salon.ru, in Russian; Bolshaya Sadovaya 3; Ⓜ Mayakovskaya

Shelves are stacked with trade books and counters are piled high with postcards. The walls are crammed with posters, prints and original artwork, some portraying unusual panoramas and historic Moscow scenes. Part frame store, part graphic-design service, part print shop, you never know what treasures you might find.

ROOM ARTERIUM Map pp88–9   Art Gallery
☎ 495-783 0505; www.room.su, in Russian; 1-ya Tverskaya-Yamskaya ul 7; Ⓜ Mayakovskaya
Room is really an interior-design service and showroom, its 1st floor displaying modern furniture and accessories, as well as some on-topic coffee-table books (in English). Downstairs, the 'Arterium' is a sort of gallery with an ever-changing exhibit of contemporary art.

ANGLIA Map pp88–9   Books
☎ 495-299 7766; Vorotnikovsky per 6/11; ⏰ 10am-7pm Mon-Fri, 10am-6pm Sat, 10am-5pm Sun; Ⓜ Tverskaya
This is one of Moscow's oldest English-language bookshops, carrying an impressive selection of contemporary literature and reference books. If you are not up for *Anna Karenina* in Russian, this is also a good place to pick up your English translation. The sale of used books benefits a local children's charity.

ADRESS Map pp88–9   Clothing & Accessories
☎ 495-629 0253; Kamergersky per 5; Ⓜ Teatralnaya
The tagline is 'unusual clothing', which means playful, romantic European fashions with labels such as Noa Noa, Just in Case and Kookaï. Besides women's wear, this sweet boutique also carries children's styles for the bohemian baby.

BUSTIER Map pp88–9 Clothing & Accessories
☎ 495-787 5976; Tverskaya ul 6; ⏰ 10am-11pm;
Ⓜ Okhotny Ryad

Underwear is yet another measure of Russia's amazing transition to capitalism. Gone are the days of one-size-fits-all, baggy cotton briefs; sensational, sexy lingerie is now on sale all over Moscow. Several top-of-the-line stores stock European designer lingerie that is devastatingly sensual and devastatingly expensive. Bustier is more moderately priced, but also features classy French and Italian styles. One of many outlets around town.

CHAPURINBAR Map pp88–9 Clothing & Accessories
Kuznetsky most 6/3; Ⓜ Kuznetsky Most

Fashion maven Igor Chapurin got his start designing theatre costumes, but his creativity knows no bounds: in addition to men's and women's clothing, he has a line of children's clothing and sportswear. Following in the footsteps of Denis Simachyov (right), he has opened a boutique with a hip club to accompany it. Set on two storeys, the place was designed by Chapurin himself and furnished with elements of the Chapurincasa line.

SIMACHYOV BOUTIQUE & BAR
Map pp88–9 Clothing & Accessories
☎ 495-629 5701; www.denissimachev.com;
Stoleshnikov per 12/2; Ⓜ Chekhovskaya

The wild child of Russian fashion, Denis Simachyov has become a household name in Moscow, thanks to his popular nightclub and irreverent clothing. His collections have been inspired by themes as diverse as Russian sailors, Chechen war victims, Siberian peasants, hip hop gangsters and gypsy nomads.

YEKATERINA Map pp88–9 Clothing & Accessories
☎ 495-692 4843; ul Bolshaya Dmitrovka 11;
Ⓜ Teatralnaya

One of Russia's oldest furriers, this place has been manufacturing *shapky* (fur hats)

HOW MATRYOSHKA GOT HER START

Rare is the tourist who leaves Russia without a *matryoshka*. The hand-painted wooden nesting doll that so symbolises Russia is not, as you might imagine, an ancient handicraft developed and perfected by generations of peasant families. Rather, the concept was adapted from a traditional Japanese toy.

In the 19th century, Russian artists were eager to embrace cultural styles that would unite traditional and modern elements and contribute to the growing sense of national identity at that time. Savva Mamontov, a celebrated patron of the arts, established art studios at his Abramtsevo estate (see the boxed text, p221) where artists could do just that. Toys were considered a particularly creative form of folk art, and Savva's brother, Anatoly, set up a workshop to revive and develop folk-peasant toys. In this workshop, Mamontov had a collection of toys from around the world, including a Japanese nesting doll depicting the Buddhist sage Fukuruma. Inspired by this prototype, the toy maker Vassily Zviozdochkin and the artist Sergei Maliutin created the earliest Russian nesting dolls, identifiable by their Slavic features and peasant dress.

During this time, Matryona and Matryosha were popular female names. Derived from the word for 'mother', the names conjured up images of a healthy, plump woman with plenty of children. Thus the diminutive of the name was applied to the nesting dolls, symbolic of motherhood, fertility and Mother Russia.

At the beginning of the 20th century, large-scale production of the Russian *matryoshka* began at the toy centre at Sergiev Posad. Here, artists developed a unique, realistic style of painting the dolls, depicting colourful scenes of village life, patriotic historical figures and beloved literary characters.

The Bolshevik regime began cracking down on this creative outlet as early as 1923. The exhibition and sale of any *matryoshki* not consistent with the regime's artistic or ideological goals were banned. The ban included the depiction of such controversial figures as tailors, bakers and any entrepreneurial types; gypsies (Roma), Jews and other ethnic groups; and fantastical figures such as mermaids and goblins. Eventually, the *matryoshka's* diversity and creativity diminished, and she adopted one standard female image. Factory production began in the 1930s, and this 'art' was nearly lost.

The 1990s saw a revival of the more original *matryoshki*, designed and painted by individuals. Production returned to artists and craftspeople, who are free to paint whom and how they wish. As a result, modern-day *matryoshki* take on every imaginable character and style.

Once again (this time due to market forces) artists often get inspiration for this Russian handcraft from foreign sources. From Warner Brothers to the Bush brothers, from the Red Sox to the Red Wings, from the *Simpsons* to *Star Wars*, many Western pop-culture images are depicted on the dolls these days.

and *shuby* (fur coats) since 1912. While Yekaterina has always maintained a reputation for high-quality furs and leather, its designs are constantly changing and updating to stay on top of fashion trends. There is another outlet in Dorogomilovo (☎ 499-243 1196; Bolshaya Dorogomilovskaya ul 14; Ⓜ Kievskaya).

TSUM Map pp88–9   Department Store
☎ 495-933 7300; www.tsum.ru, in Russian; ul Petrovka 2; Ⓜ Teatralnaya
TsUM stands for Tsentralny Universalny Magazin (Central Department Store). Built in 1909 as the Scottish-owned Muir & Merrilees, it was the first department store aimed at middle-class shoppers. But it doesn't do this any more, as it is now filled with designer labels and luxury items.

YELISEEV GROCERY Map pp88–9 Food & Drink
Tverskaya ul 14; ☽ 8am-9pm Mon-Sat, 10am-6pm Sun; Ⓜ Pushkinskaya
Peek in here for a glimpse of prerevolutionary grandeur, as the store is set in the former mansion of the successful merchant Yeliseev. It now houses an upscale market selling caviar and other delicacies.

TIME AVENUE Map pp88–9 Jewellery & Watches
☎ 495-621 9633; ul Petrovka 17; Ⓜ Chekhovskaya
These days Russians are obsessed with foreign brands, so this store carries mainly Swiss watches, but you will also find some top-quality Russian names such as Aviator, Burano and Poljot (most of which use Swiss technology anyway).

TRANSYLVANIA Map pp88–9   Music
☎ 495-629 8786; www.transylvania.ru, in Russian; Tverskaya ul 6/1, Bldg 5; ☽ 11am-10pm; Ⓜ Okhotny Ryad
From the courtyard, look for the black metal door that leads down into this dungeon of a shop, which houses room after room of CDs, in every genre imaginable. If you are curious about the *russky* rock scene, this is where you can sample some songs.

ARBAT & KHAMOVNIKI

The Arbat has always been popular among shoppers in the capital. Ul Novy Arbat is lined with huge shopping centres on both sides (including the classic bookshop, Dom Knigi); while the pedestrian-friendly Stary (Old) Arbat is perfect for scoping out antiques and other souvenirs.

Khamovniki, by contrast, caters more to the culture vulture than to the consumer. Nonetheless, this vibrant art district has a number of galleries where you can mix those two pursuits.

ARTEFACT Map pp110–11   Art Gallery
☎ 495-933 5178; ul Prechistenka 30; Ⓜ Kropotkinskaya
Near the Russian Academy of Art, this is a sort of art mall, housing a few dozen galleries under one roof. Look for paintings, sculptures, dolls, pottery and other kinds of art that people actually buy, as opposed to the more avant-garde exhibits at other art centres.

BYURO NAKHODOK Map pp110–11 Art Gallery
☎ 495-244 7697; www.buro-nakhodok.ru, in Russian; Smolensky bul 7/9; Ⓜ Park Kultury
In 2003 three Moscow artists opened this shop to sell their fun and funky gifts and souvenirs. It was the first of what would become a network of artists' cooperatives around the city. See Ministerstvo Podarkov, p151, for a full review.

DOM KNIGI Map pp102–3   Books
☎ 495-789 3591; www.mosdomknigi.ru, in Russian; ul Novy Arbat 8; ☽ 9am-11pm Mon-Fri, 10am-11pm Sat & Sun; Ⓜ Arbatskaya
The old Soviet bookshop is changing with the times, with a selection of foreign-language books to rival any other shop in the city. This huge, crowded place holds regularly scheduled readings, children's programs and other bibliophilic activities.

BUKLE Map pp102–3 Clothing & Accessories
☎ 495-291 6624; www.vereteno.com, in Russian; ul Arbat 27/47; Ⓜ Arbatskaya
The collection of Lyudmila Mezentsevaya, called Vereteno, is on display at this little café-cum-boutique. It's not so outrageous – but no less creative – as some other Russian fashion. On sale is mostly casual wear, including T-shirts, skirts, sweaters, scarves, handbags and watches, all with an innovative twist. For shoppers who are not worried about squeezing into a miniskirt, there is an outlet of Gogol-Mogol (p175) on site.

VASSA & CO Map pp102–3   Clothing & Accessories
☎ 495-290 5220; www.vassatrend.com; ul Novy Arbat 2/5; Ⓜ Arbatskaya
The largest outlet of this Russian designer is at the corner of ul Novy Arbat. See p149 for a full review.

CONFAEL CHOCOLATE
Map pp102–3   Food & Drink
☎ 495-202 2937; Nikitsky bul 12; Ⓜ Arbatskaya
This upmarket boutique and café is chock-full of mouth-watering chocolates, in every shape and size imaginable. Besides the boxes of truffles and chocolate-covered cherries, Confael also stocks themed chocolates relating to holidays, hobbies and national events. Sample the goods in the attached café.

RUSSKIE CHASOVYE TRADITSII
Map pp102–3   Jewellery & Watches
Russian Watch Traditions; ☎ 495-940 4149; ul Arbat 11 & 25; Ⓜ Arbatskaya
If you are in the market for a fancy time-piece, pop into one of these outlets on the Arbat. On this touristy drag, these small shops cater primarily to tourists, meaning they carry exclusively Russian brands, including Aviator, Buran, Vostok, Poljot, Romanoff and Denissov.

BEL POSTEL Map pp102–3   Homewares
☎ 495-241 4241; ul Arbat 43; Ⓜ Smolenskaya
This lovely linens store carries a sumptuous selection of bathrobes, blankets, sheets and towels. For a unique souvenir, take home a set of richly coloured tablecloths and napkins made from Russian linen. You will find some international designers, but most of the product line is soft Russian fabrics and unique Eastern prints.

DOROGOMILOVO
With its wide avenues and whizzing cars, Dorogomilovo does not seem like an ideal place to stroll and shop. But its location, midway between the city centre and swanky Rublyovka (see the boxed text, p108), makes it a convenient place for megarich Muscovites to stop and shop. So Kutuzovsky pr is home to some of Moscow's most exclusive stores. Besides these individual shops, Dorogomilovo also contains the world's largest urban shopping mall, the new Evropeysky Shopping Centre, so add that to Moscow's list of superlatives.

top picks

MOSCOW SOUVENIRS

- **Chocolate chess set** Perhaps you don't play chess, but there's no reason you can't indulge in Russia's most popular pastime. Get the sweet-tooth version at Confael Chocolate (left).
- **Fur Hat** If you venture out in winter without covering your head, you're bound to get a scolding from some local babushka. Find a fashionable *shapka* at Yekaterina (p152).
- **Swan Lake Palekh box** The quintessential Russian souvenir is a painted lacquer box depicting one of the classics. Take your pick from the enormous selection at Izmaylovo Market (p156).
- **Poljot watch** This acclaimed brand of watch was worn by Yury Gagarin when he blasted into space. The famed First Moscow Watch Factory now produces a slew of different Poljot styles, some of which are pretty slick. Check out options at Russkie Chasovye Traditsii (left).
- **Yuri Dolgoruki vodka** This ultrasmooth vodka, produced by Moscow's Kristall factory, comes in a smooth bottle featuring an artistic rendition of St Basil's. Get it at Yeliseev Grocery (p153).

VALENTIN YUDASHKIN BOUTIQUE
Map p107   Clothing & Accessories
☎ 495-240 1189; www.yudashkin.com; Kutuzovsky pr 19; Ⓜ Kievskaya
The best-known Russian fashion designer is Valentin Yudashkin, whose classy clothes are on display at the Louvre and the Met, as well as the State History Museum (p75) in Moscow (look but don't touch!). If you wish to try something on, head to this swanky boutique, which seems like a museum but has many things that you can, in fact, buy.

GORBUSHKA MARKET Map p107   Electronics
☎ 495-730 0006; www.gorbushka.ru, in Russian; ul Barklaya; Ⓜ Bagrationovskaya
Located in the former Rubin furniture factory, the Gorbushka market has electronics on the 1st floor, and music and movies on the 2nd floor. Mayor Luzhkov has been working hand in hand with the landlord of the Rubin building to crack down on sales of pirated goods, so Gorbushka is no longer the emporium of illegal CDs and DVDs that it used to be.

EVROPEYSKY SHOPPING CENTRE
Map p107   Shopping Mall

☎ 495-229 6187; Kievskaya pl 1; Ⓜ Kievskaya

At the time of construction this was the largest urban shopping centre in the world. It does not compare to the mega-malls on the city outskirts, but it is big. It contains many of the stores that are reviewed in this chapter, including Bustier (p152), Bel Postel (opposite) and Vassa & Co (p149). Besides the hundreds of shops and restaurants, highlights include an ice-skating rink, a movie theatre and a supermarket.

ZAMOSKVORECHIE

Between the slew of galleries at TsDKh and the smaller art houses littering the streets of Zamoskvorechie, this district is one of the top spots for shoppers interested in Moscow's contemporary art scene. The newest gallery addition is Art Strelka, on Bolotny Island, where artists have started to convert the old empty warehouses into studios and galleries.

APTEKA PODARKOV & ZAYTSY
Map pp120–1   Art Gallery

Pharmacy of Gifts; ☎ 495-238 9374; ul Bolshaya Ordynka 68; ☽ 11am-9pm Mon-Sat, 11am-8pm Sun; Ⓜ Dobryninskaya

Perhaps a little creative whimsy is just what the doctor ordered. If so, this is the place for you. It calls itself an *apteka* (pharmacy), but it's really a boutique of creative gifts

and souvenirs – one in a network of artists' cooperatives around Moscow. See Ministerstvo Podarkov, p151, for full details.

ART STRELKA
Map pp120–1   Art Gallery

☎ 8-916-112-7180; Bersenevskaya nab 14/5; ☽ 4-8pm; Ⓜ Novokuznetskaya

The garages and warehouses at the old Krasny Oktyabr Factory (p122) now serve as studio and gallery space for up-and-coming artists.

MOSKOVSKY FOND KULTURY
Map pp120–1   Art Gallery

Moscow Culture Fund; ☎ 495-951 3302; Pyatnitskaya ul 16; ☽ 10am-7.30pm Mon-Fri, 11am-7pm Sat & Sun; Ⓜ Novokuznetskaya

Packed with books, art, jewellery, ceramics and figurines, the Fond Kultury is a treasure trove for antiquers, art lovers and other collectors. The place is tiny but somehow they manage to squeeze in centuries worth of stuff.

TSDKH
Map pp120–1   Art Gallery

Central House of Artists; ☎ 499-238 9843; admission R100, special exhibits R200; ☽ 11am-7pm Tue-Sun; Ⓜ Park Kultury

The initials stand for Tsentralny Dom Khudozhnikov (Central House of Artists). This huge building attached to the New Tretyakov contains studios and galleries, as well as exhibition space for rotating collections. Artists also set up a more informal art market on ul Krymsky val, opposite the entrance to Gorky Park.

CLEAN THE WORLD OF CAPITALIST DEBRIS!

The most intriguing Soviet paraphernalia, both historically and artistically, are the old propaganda posters that touted the goals of the Soviet Union and denounced the enemies of the day. The bold colours of the posters, and even bolder messages, provide a fascinating insight into Soviet culture.

Although printed in vast quantities, original Soviet posters are rare today. Most of them were posted, as they were meant to be, and eventually destroyed from wear and tear. The rarest posters feature political characters such as Trotsky or Kirov, who fell out of favour with the regime. In true Soviet style, evidence of these people was systematically destroyed.

Work by the most celebrated poster artists, such as Rodchenko, Lissitsky and Klutsis, might sell for as much as US$100,000. More recent posters, especially post-WWII, are available for a few hundred dollars or less, depending on their size and condition. Pick your favourite cause – abstinence, literacy, feminism, the military, anticapitalism etc – and soak up the propaganda. A few vendors with incredible collections hang out in the northwest corner of the Izmaylovo Market (p156).

The old propaganda posters are also now being reproduced and sold in bookshops. Interestingly, these are being marketed not to tourists, as they are all in Russian, but to curious (younger) and nostalgic (older) Russians. Contemporary Moscow society regards public campaigns to stamp out capitalism and build communism a peculiar novelty. These reproductions are available for a few hundred roubles.

KRASNY OKTYABR STORE
Map pp120–1   Food & Drink

Red October; ☎ 495-230 0049; Bersenevskaya nab 16; Ⓜ Kropotkinskaya

For more than 100 years, the sweet aroma of chocolate permeated every corner of Bolotny Island and beyond. Alas, the factory is no longer functioning and the air has cleared, much to the dismay of local chocolate lovers, who had come to savour the mouth-watering scents. The good news is that the Krasny Oktyabr Store still operates on site and it sure smells sweet.

OUTER MOSCOW

Real estate is relatively cheap outside the city centre. As a result, huge new hypermarkets are springing up on Moscow's outskirts, where Muscovites go in droves to take advantage of low prices and huge selections. Travellers are also drawn to the city's fringes for other kinds of markets. Besides the farmers markets (p161),

Gorbushka (p154) and Izmaylovo markets are among the capital's top shopping spots.

IZMAYLOVO MARKET
Map pp60–1   Art & Craft Market

🕑 9am-6pm Sat & Sun; Ⓜ Partizanskaya

This sprawling area, also known as Vernisazh market, is packed with art, handmade crafts, antiques, Soviet paraphernalia and just about anything you might want for a souvenir. You'll find Moscow's biggest original range of *matryoshki, palekh* and *khokhloma* ware, as well as less traditional woodworking crafts. There are also rugs from the Caucasus and Central Asia, pottery, linens, jewellery, fur hats, chess sets, toys, Soviet posters and much more.

Feel free to negotiate, but don't expect vendors to come down more than 10%. This place is technically open every day, but many vendors come out only on weekends, when your selection is greater.

top picks

- Loft Café (p162)
- Simple Pleasures (p163)
- Café Pushkin (p167)
- Botanika (p170)
- Akademiya (p168)
- Volkonsky Keyser (p169)
- Correa's (p170)
- Mayak (p172)
- Suliko (p175)

EATING

In the past decade Moscow has blossomed into a culinary capital. Foodies will be thrilled by the plethora of dining options, from old-fashioned *haute russe* to contemporary fusion. Young chefs are breaking down Soviet stereotypes and showing the world how creative they can be. They're importing exotic ingredients, rediscovering ancient cooking techniques and inventing new ones. And Moscow diners are eating it up. Literally. Restaurants are packed with patrons eager to sample world cuisines, sip expensive wines, share small plates, eat raw fish, taste exotic fruits and smoke hookahs.

When you tire of borsch (beetroot soup) and beef stroganoff, you'll be able to find excellent European, American and Asian cuisine. Many of these restaurants have foreign-trained chefs, foreign management and standards, and foreign prices to match. Cuisine from former Soviet republics such as Georgia, Armenia, Uzbekistan and Ukraine is also ubiquitous and delicious.

Because of the explosion of eateries in Moscow, restaurateurs are desperate to entice diners. Themed restaurants are all the rage, so your dinner experience might include picking out produce at an Asian market (p165), sharing company with farm animals (p170) or watching a belly dancer shake her thang (p166). The effect is sometimes classy, sometimes comical, but always interesting. The good news is that the best restaurants still manage to keep their focus on the food, producing ever more innovative cuisine for an ever more informed clientele.

HISTORY

Russian cuisine is strongly influenced by climate and class. Long winters and short growing seasons mean the cuisine is dependent on root vegetables such as potatoes and beets. Fresh produce has always been a rarity, so vegetables are often served pickled; fruit is frequently served in the form of compote. According to an old Russian proverb, '*shchi* (cabbage soup) and *kasha* (porridge) is our nourishment'. This saying emphasises the important role played by soups and grains in sustaining generations of peasants through cold, dark winters.

Most formal Russian meals commence with an elaborate spread of *zakuski,* or appetisers, often leaving little room for the main course. This tradition dates to the earliest days of Rus. Due to unpredictable weather and poor roads, a host never knew when to expect his guests, so he always kept a table set with *zakuski* to accommodate the tired and hungry travellers when they arrived.

During the tsarist period, the Russian upper classes took their cues from Europe, for example, speaking French and English among themselves. France, especially, was considered the epitome of high culture, an estimation reflected in Russian food. Grilled fish and meats, usually topped with rich sauces, are the essence of *haute russe* cuisine.

Options for dining out during the Soviet period were so limited that Russians hardly ever did it. They might have taken lunch at the local *stolovaya* (cafeteria), but otherwise they cooked, ate and drank at home; home-cooked meals tasted far better than the slab of meat and lump of potatoes served in most restaurants.

Indeed, the 70 years of mistreatment by the Soviets gave Russian cuisine a bad rap. Now, many restaurants in Moscow allow the diner to experience Russian food as it is meant to be – exquisite *haute russe* masterpieces once served at banquets and balls, as well as tasty and filling meals that have for centuries been prepared in peasant kitchens with garden ingredients.

ETIQUETTE

Russian hospitality has deep roots. If you visit a Muscovite at home, you can expect to be regaled with stories and drowned in vodka, to receive many toasts and to offer a few yourself. You can also expect to eat an enormous amount of food off a tiny plate. Once the festivities begin, it is difficult to refuse any food or drink – you will go home stuffed, drunk and happy.

Should you be lucky enough to be invited to a Muscovite's home, bring a gift. Wine, confectionery and cake are all appropriate. Keep in mind that food items are a matter of national pride, so unless you bring something really exotic (eg all the way from home), a Russian brand will be appreciated more. Flow-

ROE TO RUIN

Caviar: the very word evokes glamorous lifestyles, exotic travel and glittering festivities. But the sturgeon, the source of this luxury item, is in grave danger. Although they have survived since dinosaurs roamed the Earth, the question now is whether these 'living fossils' can withstand the relentless fishing pressure, pollution and habitat destruction that have brought many sturgeon species to the brink of extinction. Surveys show that the population of osetra sturgeon is less than half the size it was in 1978, while the beluga sturgeon population has declined by 45% since 2004.

Sturgeon today face several major obstacles to survival. Primarily, the global caviar market has placed a premium on sturgeon, prompting overfishing and poaching. Political turmoil in sturgeon-producing countries, including Russia, has resulted in a flourishing black-market trade. Many sturgeon migrate through the waters of different states and countries, resulting in a lack of effective management of their populations. Coupled with an ongoing loss of habitat and a slow pace of reproduction, the sturgeon are facing an upstream swim.

Contrary to many conservationist recommendations, a 2007 international conference on endangered species (CITES) declined to pass emergency measures to protect the Russian sturgeon population. But it did take important steps to improve monitoring of the caviar trade. Most importantly for travellers, governments are encouraged to reduce the amount that individuals are allowed to carry across borders, from 250g to 125g of caviar per person. Fish-friendly travellers might consider sticking to red caviar (salmon) until the sturgeon is in a better place.

For more information on the plight of the sturgeon, see www.caviaremptor.org.

---

ers are also popular, but make certain there's an odd number because even numbers are for funerals.

SPECIALITIES

Traditional Russian breakfast favourites include bliny (crêpes) and *kasha* (porridge). Sunday brunch is an institution for many expats and wealthy Russians (see the boxed text, p170, for some of the best brunch options).

Russia is famous for its caviar *(ikra)*, the snack of tsars and New Russians. Caviar is no longer the bargain it once was due to declining sturgeon populations and the good old market economy. The best caviar is black (sturgeon) caviar *(ikra chyornaya* or *zirnistaya)*, from osetra or beluga sturgeon. Unfortunately, due to overfishing, sturgeon populations have declined drastically in recently years (see the boxed text, above), driving up prices and threatening the fish with extinction. The much cheaper and saltier option is red (salmon) caviar *(ikra krasnaya* or *ketovaya)*. Russians spread it on buttered bread or bliny and wash it down with a slug of vodka or a toast of champagne. Vegetarians can try ersatz caviar made entirely from eggplant or other vegetables.

Most restaurant menus offer a truly mind-boggling array of salads *(salat)*, including standards such as *ovoshnoy salat* (vegetable salad, which contains tomatoes and cucumbers) and *stolichny salat* (capital salad, which contains beef, potatoes and eggs in mayonnaise). Even if you read Russian, the salads are usually not identifiable by their often nonsensical names.

Rich soups, offered as a first course, may well be the pinnacle of Russian cooking. There are dozens of varieties, often served with a dollop of sour cream. Most are made using meat stock. The most common soups include borsch, *shchi* (cabbage soup), *okroshka* (cucumber soup with a *kvas* – a beerlike drink – base) and *solyanka* (a tasty meat soup with salty vegetables and hint of lemon).

The second course can be poultry *(ptitsa)*, meat *(myaso)* or fish *(ryba)*. Russian dumplings *(pelmeni)* are usually filled with meat. However, they may also come with potatoes, cabbage or mushrooms. Often you must order a *garnir* (side dish) or you will just get a hunk of meat on your plate. Options here are usually potatoes *(kartoshki)*, rice *(ris)* or undefined vegetables *(ovoshchi)*. Bread is served with every meal. Black bread (a vitamin-rich sour rye) is delicious and uniquely Russian.

Perhaps most Russians are exhausted or drunk by dessert time, because this is the least imaginative course. The most common options are ice cream *(morozhenoye)*, supersweet cake *(tort)* or chocolate *(shokolat)*.

Most restaurants in Moscow offer English-language menus so it's unlikely you'll have to decode a Russian menu. Interpreting the translated menu often presents its own challenges.

VEGETARIANS & VEGANS

Russian is a heavy, meat-dependent cuisine. Soups are usually made with beef or chicken stock, all traditional meals revolve around a meaty main course, and even salads usually have dead animals mixed in with a few vegies. Most frustrating is the lack of fresh fruit and vegetables. Until recently, vegetarians in Moscow had a pretty tough time of it.

Fortunately, the culinary revolution has opened up some new options for vegetarians and vegans. Most restaurants now recognise the need to offer at least one vegetarian choice on their menu. Additionally, there is no shortage of Indian and Italian restaurants, which offer plenty of meat-free options. For more suggestions, see the boxed text, below.

When dining at traditional Russian restaurants, vegies should keep in mind the following tips. Fresh vegetables are rare, but pickled vegetables are not: learn to love sauerkraut, beets and salty cucumbers. Most importantly, there is no shortage of starch in Russia. Bread, bliny and potatoes are always on the menu, and they are filling. During the 40 days before Orthodox Easter (*post,* in Russian), many restaurants offer a Lenten menu that is happily animal-free. If you are serious about your vegetarianism, timing your trip with this period will give you some extra options when eating out.

COOKING COURSES
Russian cooking classes are hard to come by, but Dom Patriarshy Tours (p252) does offer an occasional half-day course. Learn to whip up some bliny, then eat them for lunch.

PRACTICALITIES
Opening Hours
Many eateries are open from noon to midnight daily, often with later hours on Friday and Saturday. In this book, hours are listed only when they vary from this standard.

top picks
VEG-FRIENDLY RESTAURANTS
- **Avocado** (p163) The menu features avocados and other meat-free specialities.
- **Jagannath** (p165) Restaurant, cafeteria and health-food store all in one.
- **Maharaja** (p163) Moscow's oldest Indian restaurant.
- **Botanika** (p170) A garden-themed café featuring many treats from the garden.
- **Prime Star** (p164) Fresh sandwiches and salads to go.

UNDERRATED RUSSIAN FOODS
- **Seld pod shuby** Try the classic Russian salad, the so-called 'herring in a fur coat', a colourful conglomeration of herring, beets and carrots.
- **Kasha** There are dozens of kinds of *kasha* (porridge), but they are all delicious when drowned in butter and brown sugar.
- **Kefir** A sour yogurt drink, often served for breakfast. To adapt the wise words of Mary Poppins – just a spoonful of sugar helps the *kefir* go down.
- **Pelmeni** Russian comfort food: dumplings stuffed with ground beef and topped with a dollop of sour cream.
- **Soup** Hot and hearty, nothing beats a steaming bowl of goodness on a cold winter day.

Discounts of up to 25% are sometimes available for dining before 4pm or 5pm. Alternatively, many places offer a fixed price 'business lunch' during this time. This is a great way to sample some of the pricier restaurants around town.

How Much?
Sudden wallet-thinning shock is common at many Moscow restaurants, where prices are geared to free-spending New Russians and flush expats rather than the average person. The situation is improving, though. Muscovites are eating out in droves, and restaurants, cafés and kiosks are opening up left and right to cater to them.

While diners with deep pockets might spend upwards of R2000 at upmarket Moscow restaurants, most visitors can expect to pay about R600 to R1000 per person for a meal in the capital. 'Business lunch' specials are usually R200 to R500, offering excellent value for a midday meal (usually three courses). Frequent the places listed in the Quick Cheap Eats boxed text (p164) for meals that cost R200 or less.

Some restaurants set their menu prices in *uslovie yedenitsiy* (often abbreviated as y.e.), or standard units, which is equivalent to euros or US dollars (although you will have to pay in roubles calculated at the exchange rate of the day). Prices in this chapter are quoted in roubles, regardless of the currency quoted on the menu. Credit cards are widely accepted, especially at upmarket restaurants.

PRICE GUIDE

$$$	over R1500 per person
$$	R600-1500 per person
$	under R600

Booking Tables

Most of the fancier places require booking in advance for dinner, as well as for lunch or brunch on weekends.

Tipping

The standard for tipping in Moscow is 10%, while a slightly smaller percentage is acceptable at more casual restaurants. The service charge is occasionally included in the bill, in which case an additional tip isn't necessary.

Self-Catering

FARMERS MARKETS

The Russian market *(rinok)* is a busy, bustling place, full of activity and colour. Even if you're not shopping, it's entertaining to peruse the tables piled high with multicoloured produce: homemade cheese and jam; golden honey straight from the hive; vibrantly coloured spices pouring out of plastic bags; slippery silver fish posing on beds of ice; and huge slabs of meat hanging from the ceiling. Many vendors bring their products up from the Caucasus to sell them in the capital. Prices are lower and the quality of product is often higher than in the supermarkets. Bring your own bag and don't be afraid to haggle.

Farmers markets include the following:

Danilovsky Market (Map pp60–1; Mytnaya ul 74, Zamoskvorechie; ⏰ 8am-6pm; Ⓜ Tulskaya)

Dorogomilovsky market (Map p107; ul Mozhaysky val 10, Dorogomilovo; ⏰ 10am-8pm; Ⓜ Kievskaya) One of Moscow's largest markets, with overflow spreading along Kievskaya ul to Kievsky vokzal (Kyiv station).

Rizhsky Market (Map pp60–1; pr Mira 94-96; ⏰ 7am-7pm; Ⓜ Rizhskaya)

SUPERMARKETS

Gone are the days when shopping for food required waiting in a different line for each item. These days, Moscow boasts many Western-style supermarkets, complete with prepackaged foods, Western brands and shopping carts. Unless you stick to Russian brands, prices tend to be as high as, if not higher than, prices in the West.

Azbuka Vkusa (www.azbukavkusa.ru; ⏰ 24hr) is a Russian chain of deluxe markets, selling premium quality (mostly imported) goods at premium prices. It has stores at **Basmanny** (Map pp80–1; Sadovaya-Chyornogryazskaya ul 13; Ⓜ Chistye Prudy), **Tverskoy** (Map pp88–9; Sadovaya-Triumfalnaya ul 22/31; Ⓜ Mayakovskaya), **Meshchansky** (Map pp84–5; Trubnaya pl 2; Ⓜ Trubnaya) and **Dorogomilovo** (Map p107; Kutuzovsky pr 8; Ⓜ Kievskaya)

The well-stocked **Seventh Continent** (☎ 495-777 7779; ⏰ 24hr) supermarkets are convenient and reasonable places to stock up on food. There are outlets at **Basmanny** (Map pp80–1; ul Bolshaya Lubyanka 12/1; Ⓜ Lubyanka), though it was closed for renovation at the time of research; **Arbat** (Map pp102–3; ul Arbat 54/2; Ⓜ Smolenskaya); and **Zamoskvorechie** (Map pp120–1; ul Serafimovicha 2; Ⓜ Kropotkinskaya).

The more affordable, Turkish-owned Ramstore includes three shopping malls, as well as a number of self-standing supermarkets in and around Moscow. 'Club card' holders (R25) are eligible for discounts of 20% to 30% on some products. The selection is impressive,

---

DO TRY THIS AT HOME

If you love Russian cooking, you may want to try to make bliny or borsch at home. Here are a few recipe books that will guide you through the process.

- Please, To the Table (Anya Von Bremzen) A tried-and-true authority on Russian cooking. Learn to make bliny (and just about every other Russian dish) like the babushky.
- Tastes and Tales from Russia (Alla Danishevsky) Presents each recipe accompanied by a folktale – a great way to introduce children to Russian cooking.
- The Georgian Feast (Darra Goldstein) One of the few English-language cookbooks focusing on this spicy Caucasian cuisine.
- A Year of Russian Feasts (Catherine Cheremeteff Jones) Part cookbook and part travelogue, describing the author's experiences with Russian traditions and customs, culinary celebrations and day-to-day life.
- Classic Russian Cooking: A Gift to Young Housewives (Elena Molokhovets) More of a history lesson than a recipe book, this tome is based on the most popular cookbook from the 19th century.

but these places can be overwhelming due to their size and the number of shoppers they attract. There are stores at Krasnoselsky (Map pp84–5; ☎ 495-207 0241; Komsomolskaya pl 6, Moskovsky Univermag; 🕐 24hr; Ⓜ Komsomolskaya), Presnya (Map pp96–7; ☎ 495-255 5412; ul Krasnaya Presnya 23; 🕐 24hr; Ⓜ Ulitsa 1905 Goda) and Khamovniki (Map pp110–11; ☎ 495-771 7092; ul Usachyova 35; 🕐 8am-11pm; Ⓜ Sportivnaya).

KREMLIN & KITAY GOROD

Moscow has come a long way in developing a consumer culture, but the dining options in the city centre suggest the capital still has a way to go. The area where the majority of tourists spend their time is markedly void of eateries. Pack a picnic on the day you visit the Kremlin – otherwise, you can check out the few places in Kitay Gorod.

RED SQUARE, 1 Map p66   Russian $$
☎ 495-692 1196; www.redsquare.ru; State History Museum, Krasnaya pl 1; business lunch R350, meals R1000-1500; Ⓜ Ploshchad Revolyutsii
Appropriately for a place located in the State History Museum, the chefs are real historians, successfully re-creating the cuisine that was enjoyed in the days of yore, complete with old-fashioned ingredients and recipes. For real culinary history buffs, check out the schedule of historic dinners, re-creating specific meals in history, such as Nicholas II's Easter dinner in 1900. The only drawback is the dark basement setting, a drab venue for an otherwise exciting eating experience.

LOFT CAFÉ Map p66   Fusion $$
☎ 495-933 7713; Nikolskaya ul 25; meals R1000-1500; 🕐 9am-midnight; Ⓜ Lubyanka
On the top floor of the Nautilus shopping centre, next door to the luxury spa, you'll find this tiny, trendy café. An even smaller terrace gives a fantastic view of Lubyanka pl. Innovative, modern dishes fuse the best of Russian cuisine with Western and Asian influences – for example, grilled salmon with spinach, pine nuts and caviar sauce.

BOSCO CAFE Map p66   International $$
☎ 495-620 3182; GUM, Krasnaya pl 3; meals R600-1000; 🕐 10am-11pm; Ⓜ Ploshchad Revolyutsii
Sip a cappuccino in view of the Kremlin. Munch on lunch while the crowds line up

top picks

KIDS' MEALS

- **American Bar & Grill** (p175). The playroom is open daily, while a clown engages kids with games on Sunday afternoons.
- **Chaikhona No 1** (p180) Almost like a picnic in the park.
- **Il Patio** (p174) Have fun with crayons, cartoons and pizza cut into crazy shapes. Kids can also learn how to make their own pizza.
- **Tinkoff** (p181) Offers a children's menu and cartoons. A clown supervises a kids' playroom on weekends.

at Lenin's Mausoleum. Enjoy an afternoon aperitif while admiring St Basil's domes. This café on the 1st floor of GUM is the only place to sit right on Red Square and marvel at its magnificence. Service can be slightly harried, but overall its a pleasant – and not outrageously overpriced – experience.

SUSHI VYOSLA Map p66   Japanese $$
☎ 495-937 0521; ul Nikolskaya 25; meals R600-800; 🕐 noon-1am Sun-Thu, to 3am Fri & Sat; Ⓜ Lubyanka
Sushi is all the rage in Moscow these days. To get in on it, head to this hip Japanese café in the basement of the Nautilus shopping centre (enter from Teatralnaya proezd). Dishes are colour coded to specify price; at the end of the meal the server clears the empty plates and uses them to calculate the bill.

BASMANNY

The underexplored streets to the east of Staraya pl contain their fair share of culinary choices. It is a refined residential area with dining to match the clientele, plus a few extravagant themed restaurants just for fun. Choose the aromatic Armenian grill to get your meats, or the cosy Swiss hole in the wall. Other options in the area are diverse, including one of the capital's few vegetarian-only restaurants.

EXPEDITION Map pp80–1   Russian $$$
☎ 495-775 6075; www.expedicia.ru; Pevchesky per 6; meals R1500-2000; Ⓜ Kitay-Gorod

This outrageous themed restaurant takes diners on an expedition to the great white north, capturing the adventure and excitement of Siberia. You can imagine you arrived by helicopter, as the vehicle is the centrepiece of the dining room. Feast on typical 'northern cuisine' – famous Baikal fish soup *(ukha)*; *pelmeni* (Russian-style ravioli stuffed with meat) stuffed with wild boar or Kamchatka crab; and venison stroganoff. There is also an expensive but authentic Siberian *banya* (hot bath) on the premises.

KOVCHYOG NOYEV Map pp80–1 Armenian $$
Noah's Ark; ☎ 495-621 5885; Maly Ivanovsky per 9; meals R1000-1500; Ⓜ Kitay-Gorod
This Armenian grill features many varieties of shashlyk, many more varieties of *konyak* (brandy) and an Armenian orchestra every night. The vast dining hall is aromatic and atmospheric, thanks to the meat roasting over charcoal in the central brazier.

SYRNAYA DYRKA Map pp80–1 European $$
Cheese Hole; ☎ 495-917 1676; Pokrovsky bul 6/20; meals R800-1200; Ⓜ Kitay-Gorod
Fondue, *fromage* plates and other cheesy specialities are the highlights of the menu at this hole in the wall. Besides the warm basement with windows looking on to the Boulevard Ring, there is also a summer terrace out the back. Both are perfectly delightful settings for a romantic date or even a solo meal. The place is Swiss-owned, which means French, Italian and German fare all show up on the menu.

MAHARAJA Map pp80–1 Indian $$
☎ 495-621 7758; Starosadsky per 1; meals R600-1000; Ⓥ 11am-11pm; Ⓜ Kitay-Gorod; Ⓥ
Moscow's oldest Indian restaurant features lots of spicy tandoori specialities, including several variations of kebabs and roti hot from the tandoor. The decor of the lower-level restaurant is understated – a welcome change from the over-the-top theme restaurants that dominate Moscow's dining scene.

AVOCADO Map pp80–1 Vegetarian $
☎ 495-621 7719; Chistoprudny bul 12/2; breakfast R80-100, business lunch R180, meals R200-400; Ⓥ 10am-11pm; Ⓜ Chistye Prudy; ⊠ ▯ Ⓥ
Less atmospheric than Jagannath (p165), Avocado has a more diverse menu, drawing on dishes from cuisines from around

top picks

MEALS WITH A VIEW

- Loft Café (opposite) Lofty views of Lubyanskaya pl (Lubyanka Square).
- Pavilion (p170) Picture windows facing Patriarch's Ponds.
- Shatyor (p180) Watch the sun set over the Chistye Prudy.
- Bosco Cafe (opposite) Outdoor café on Red Square.

the world. Meatless versions of soups and salads, pasta and *pelmeni* are all featured (although there is no English-language menu, so bring your phrasebook). Grab a seat near the window to watch the passers-by on the boulevard, because the place is otherwise rather austere.

KRASNOSELSKY & MESHCHANSKY

There is an infinite number of eating options in the crowded streets around Kuznetsky most. For some of the more refined restaurants head up Bolshaya Lubyanka ul and ul Sretenka.

SIMPLE PLEASURES
Map pp84–5 International $$
☎ 495-607 1521; ul Sretenka 22; meals R1000-1500; Ⓥ noon-midnight Mon-Fri, 2pm-midnight Sat & Sun; Ⓜ Sukharevskaya
For a place called Simple Pleasures this is unexpectedly chic, with plush couches and low tables taking the café scene up a level. The menu is varied, featuring the chef's selection of speciality cheeses and wines, as well as grilled fish and meats, pastas and salads. The common denominator is fresh ingredients and simple cooking techniques, an ideal match for this uncluttered space.

KAVKAZSKAYA PLENNITSA
Map pp84–5 Caucasian $$
Prisoner of the Caucasus; ☎ 495-280 5111; pr Mira 36; meals R800-1200; Ⓜ Prospekt Mira
Moscow's favourite Georgian restaurant is named after a popular Soviet film (and a Pushkin poem). Feast on *lavash* (flat bread) straight from the oven, cheeses from the

restaurant's own dairy, and shashlyk from seemingly every animal. Come with a group and enjoy the classically cheesy Georgian music and the over-the-mountaintop decor.

GLAVPIVTORG Map pp84–5 Russian $$

☎ 8-901-564 5955; ul Bolshaya Lubyanka 5; business lunch R125-195, meals R600-1000; ⏰ noon-midnight, music 9pm; Ⓜ Lubyanka
At the 'central beer restaurant No 5' every effort is made to re-create an upscale apparatchik drinking and dining experience. The Soviet fare is authentic, as is the *russky* crooner music (maybe too authentic for some tastes). But the three varieties of beer brewed on site are decidedly New Russia.

SKROMNOE OBAYANIE BURZHUAZI

Map pp84–5 International $$
Modest Charms of the Bourgeoisie; ☎ 495-623 0848; ul Bolshaya Lubyanka 24; meals R600-1000; ⏰ 24hr; Ⓜ Lubyanka; Ⓥ
The main draw of the 'Bourgeoisie' is the cool, casual setting. It's an attractive space, with its arched ceiling, tiled floor and sun motif – ideal for settling into the comfy couches and reading the newspapers that are left lying about. The menu is reasonably priced and wide-ranging, from pizza to sushi and nice, fresh salads, but don't expect gourmet fare.

COURVOISIER CAFE Map pp84–5 European $$

☎ 495-632 995; Malaya Sukharevskaya pl 8; meals R400-800; ⏰ 24hr; Ⓜ Sukharevskaya

This informal, French-themed café is furnished with picnic tables and park benches, evoking an idyllic outdoor setting. (There is outdoor seating too but, fronting the Garden Ring, it is not so peaceful.) Serving breakfast, soups, pasta and grills, it's a popular spot for happy hour (4pm to 7pm), lunch or a late-night snack.

SHERBET Map pp84–5 Uzbek $$

☎ 495-607 3318; ul Sretenka 32; business lunch R300, meals R400-800; ⏰ 24hr; Ⓜ Sukharevskaya
Sitting amid plush pillows and woven tapestries, you'll feel like a sheik in this extravagantly decorated eatery. Feast on *plov* (rice mixed with lamb and vegetables), shashlyk and other Uzbek specialities. And of course, it wouldn't be Moscow if they didn't also offer hookahs and an evening belly-dance show. There is another outlet of Sherbet in Tverskoy (☎ 495-628 1597; ul Petrovka 15; ⏰ Chekhovskaya).

SHCHIT I MECH Map pp84–5 Russian $

Shield & Sword; ☎ 495-667 4446; ul Bolshaya Lubyanka 13/16; meals R400-600; Ⓜ Lubyanka
In an all-too-appropriate location opposite the former Lubyanka prison, this novelty place is also known as the 'KGB bar'. You can't miss it, with the emblem of the former security service hanging prominently in the windows. Inside, the Soviet paraphernalia continues: the centrepiece in the dining room is a replica of the Felix Dzerzhinsky statue that once graced Lubyanskaya pl.

QUICK CHEAP EATS

A few chain restaurants have brought the Soviet concept of *stolovaya* (cafeteria) into the 21st century.

Prime Star (meals R200-300; ⏰ 7am-11pm; Ⓥ) is a novel concept: a sandwich shop. And not only that, a *healthy* sandwich shop, also serving soups, salads, sushi and other 'natural food'. Everything is pre-prepared and neatly packaged, so you can eat in or carry out. There are restaurants in Basmanny (Map pp80–1; ☎ 495-781 8080; ul Maroseyka 6/8; Ⓜ Kitay-Gorod), Tverskoy (Map pp88–9; ☎ 495-692 1276; Kamergersky per; Ⓜ Teatralnaya) and Arbat (Map pp102–3; ☎ 495-290 4481; ul Arbat 9; Ⓜ Arbatskaya).

You will recognise Moo-Moo (meals R200-300; ⏰ 9am-11pm) by its black-and-white Holstein-print decor. The cafeteria-style service offers an easy approach to all the Russian favourites. You'll find outlets in Basmanny (Map pp80–1; ☎ 495-623 4503; Myasnitskaya ul 14; Ⓜ Lubyanka), Khamovniki (Map pp110–11; ☎ 495-245 7820; Komsomolsky pr 26; Ⓜ Frunzenskaya) and Arbat (Map pp102–3; ☎ 495-241 1364; ul Arbat 45/24; Ⓜ Smolenskaya).

The self-serve buffet at Drova (meals R200-400, all-you-can-eat buffet R350; ⏰ 24hr) features offerings ranging from *solyanka* (a salty vegetable and meat soup) to sushi to sweet-and-sour pork. It's not the best place to sample any of these items, but the price is right. Hungry student types really take advantage of the all-you-can-eat option: it's not always pretty. There are Drova restaurants in Kitay Gorod (Map p66; ☎ 8-901-532 8252; Nikolskaya ul 5; Ⓜ Ploshchad Revolyutsii), Basmanny (Map pp80–1; ☎ 495-916 0445; ul Pokrovka 17; Ⓜ Chistye Prudy) and Arbat (Map pp102–3; ☎ 495-202 7570; Nikitsky bul 8A; Ⓜ Arbatskaya)

RHYMIN' IVAN

Perhaps Pushkin is to blame. Just when you think the Russians have become sophisticated capitalists, they surprise you with a primitive publicity campaign such as rhyming restaurant names. With the unchecked success of Yolki-Palki (below), at least three other chains and a number of individual restaurants are trying their hand at poetry. If you are interested in exploring the relationship between poetry and food, check out these rhyme-time restaurants: Pasta & Basta (below); Kishmish (p172); Shashlyk Mashlyk (p173); Shesh Besh (p173); and Gogol-Mogol (p175).

The menu features Soviet specials – mains such as chicken Kiev and *pelmeni*, served more often than not with 100g of vodka.

PASTA & BASTA Map pp84–5   Italian $
☎ 495-624 5252; Sretensky bul 4; meals R400-600; Ⓜ Turgenevskaya
The faux classical facade on Sretensky bul hides a popular little pasta house that really capitalises on a theme. With funky spaghetti-shaped lamps hanging from the high ceiling and noodle art on the walls, it's no secret what this place is all about. When they say 'Basta pasta', they mean it.

JAGANNATH Map pp84–5   Vegetarian $
☎ 495-628 3580; Kuznetsky most 11; meals R400-600; ⊙ 10am-11pm; Ⓜ Kuznetsky Most; ⊠ ▢ Ⓥ
If you are in need of vitamins, this is a funky, vegetarian café, restaurant and shop. Its Indian-themed decor is more New Agey than ethnic. Service is slow but sublime, and the food is worth the wait.

YOLKI-PALKI Map pp84–5   Russian $
☎ 495-628 5525; Neglinnaya ul 8/10; meals R200-400; ⊙ 10am-midnight Mon-Fri, 11am-midnight Sat & Sun; Ⓜ Kuznetsky Most
This excellent Russian chain is beloved for its country-cottage decor and its well-stocked salad bar. Outlets all over the city specialise in traditional dishes and cheap beer. Other Yolki-Palki locations include Arbat (☎ 495-291 7654; ul Novy Arbat 11; ⊙ 11am-midnight; Ⓜ Arbatskaya), Zamoskvorechie (☎ 495-953 9130; Klimentovsky per 14; ⊙ 10am-9pm; Ⓜ Tretyakovskaya) and Taganka (☎ 495-912 9187; Taganskaya pl 2; ⊙ 9am-11pm Mon-Fri, 10am-11am Sat & Sun; Ⓜ Taganskaya).

TVERSKOY

Who could be surprised by the plethora of dining options in this smart shopping district? The range of prices, cuisines and themes is vast. Food in Moscow does not come much simpler or cheaper than at the unnamed cafeteria, while Gallery represents the other end of the scale. Happily, Tverskoy includes just about everything in between, as well as some interesting and innovative themed restaurants. We have divided the district into smaller geographic units: ul Petrovka; Tverskaya ul and Tverskoy bul; and Outer Tverskoy.

ULITSA PETROVKA

If window shopping and people-watching works up your appetite, you'll find a restaurant to sate it. This section includes all the streets between ul Bolshaya Dmitrovka and ul Malaya Dmitrovka in the west, and Neglinnaya ul and Tsvetnoy bul in the east.

VARVARY Map pp88–9   Russian $$$
Barbarians; ☎ 495-229 2800; Strastnoy bul 8A; meals from R2000; Ⓜ Chekhovskaya
Touted as 'the first Russian haute cuisine restaurant', this is the latest venue of molecular chef Anatoly Komm. Komm – Russia's only chef who employs scientific process to break ingredients down to their most basic component and present the flavours in new forms. As you might expect, Vavary is an elegant affair, offering a sophisticated new take on familiar flavours, eg black bread and beet salad in the form of foams and gels.

MARKET Map pp88–9   Seafood $$$
☎ 495-650 3770; Sadovaya-Samotechnaya ul 18; meals R1200-2000; Ⓜ Tsvetnoy Bulvar

top picks

EAT STREETS

- **Kamergersky pereulok** (p167) Trendy and pedestrian-friendly.
- **Spiridonevsky pereulok** (p167) Exceptional eating on a tiny strip near Patriarch's Ponds.
- **Ulitsa Petrovka** (above) Shopping and lunch. Lunch and shopping.

This innovative restaurant evokes a market in Southeast Asia – you're invited to take your wicker basket and shop among the displays of colourful produce and fresh fish, choosing the ingredients for your meal. The chef will then cook it up according to your instructions. Or, if you don't trust your culinary instincts, choose from the à la carte menu, which fuses contemporary European and Asian elements to show off the same ingredients. The brains behind this unique place is Arkady Novikov, a restaurant mogul in Moscow.

SYR Map pp88–9 Italian $$$
Cheese; ☎ 495-650 7770; Sadovaya-Samotechnaya ul 16; meals R1200-2000; Ⓜ Tsvetnoy Bulvar
Not to be confused with its French neighbour, Syrnaya Dyrka (right), this place also has an interior resembling a block of cheese. The decor might seem silly, but the pizzas, pastas and other Italian dishes are expertly prepared. The salad buffet is hard to resist, overflowing with vegetables, olives, cured meats and cheeses – all the elements of antipasto. If the mouse's perspective doesn't sound atmospheric, request a table on the patio, shaded by umbrellas (yellow, of course) and flanked by potted plants.

UZBEKISTAN Map pp88–9 Uzbek $$
☎ 495-623 0585; Neglinnaya ul 29/14; meals R1000-1500; ⓧ noon-3am; Ⓜ Tsvetnoy Bulvar
One of the city's oldest restaurants, this place serves Central Asian fare in exotic environs, reminiscent of an Oriental palace. Make yourself comfortable on the plush cushions, order some spicy *plov* or delicious fried kebabs and enjoy the bellydancing show.

GALLERY Map pp88–9 International $$
☎ 495-790 1596; ul Petrovka 27; meals R800-1500; ⓧ 24hr; Ⓜ Chekhovskaya
At the end of the night, the best of Moscow socialites find themselves at another Novikov hot spot. This place is popular around the clock, but it's most crowded in the wee hours, when the beautiful people come to refuel after a night out on the town. And they are beautiful…by the looks of things, high heels and short skirts are part of the dress code. Art on the walls and sushi on the menu complete the trendy picture.

SYRNAYA DYRKA Map pp88–9 French $$
Cheese Hole; ☎ 495-650 1007; ul Bolshaya Dmitrovka 32; meals R800-1200; Ⓜ Chekhovskaya
Where the original Syrnaya Dyrka in Basmanny (p163) is quintessentially quaint, this second location is self-consciously stylish. The avocado-and-indigo colour scheme is bold, contrasting with the pale-yellow walls and arched ceilings that manage to evoke the inside of a cheese hole. This outlet is meant to be French, as opposed to Swiss at the Basmanny restaurant, but that does not result in a dramatically different menu. It still features deliciously aromatic *fromage* in all its forms, including fondue, quiche, sandwiches and cheese plates.

KITEZH Map pp88–9 Russian $$
☎ 495-650 6685; ul Petrovka 23/10; meals R600-800; Ⓜ Chekhovskaya
Kitezh is named after a legendary town that, as a defence mechanism, could magically disappear from the sight of an enemy at the sound of a bell. This welcoming eatery re-creates a 17th-century interior in the basement of a building near the Upper St Peter Monastery. The Russian standards are tasty and reasonably priced.

TARAS BULBA Map pp88–9 Ukrainian $
☎ 495-694 6082; ul Petrovka 30/7; meals R400-600; Ⓜ Chekhovskaya
Servers at Taras Bulba dress up in traditional embroidered outfits, complemented by Ukrainian tapestries and wood floors, which provide a homey atmosphere. Specialities include black bread with *salo* (lard), and *vareniki* (dumplings) filled with potatoes, cabbage or meat. Other branches include one in Zamoskvorechie (Map pp120–1; ☎ 495-953 7153; Pyatnitskaya ul 14; ⓧ noon-2am; Ⓜ Tretyakovskaya).

CAFETERIA Map pp88–9 Cafeteria $
☎ 495-694 0061; Tsvetnoy bul; meals R200; ⓧ 8am-9pm; Ⓜ Tsvetnoy Bulvar
If you are feeling nostalgic for the simplicity of Soviet life, this unnamed cafeteria will be a welcome reminder of the olden days. Students frequent this throwback, which offers only one main dish, one soup and a few salads each day. The food is fresh and cheap and made with care by babushky in hairnets.

TVERSKAYA ULITSA & TVERSKOY BULVAR

The Tverskoy district, like the hustling, bustling street for which it is named, offers something for everyone. This section covers Tverskaya ul and Tverskoy bul, as well as ul Bolshaya Dmitrovka and ul Malaya Dmitrovka.

This area contains two prime eat streets – the trendy, car-free Kamergersky per, at the foot of Tverskaya ul, and the hidden-gem Spiridonevsky per, near Patriarch's Ponds.

CAFÉ PUSHKIN Map pp88–9　　　Russian $$$
☎ 495-739 0033; Tverskoy bul 26a; business lunch R750, meals R1500-2000; ◷ 24hr; Ⓜ Pushkinskaya

The tsarina of *haute-russe* dining, with an exquisite blend of Russian and French cuisines – service and food are done to perfection. The lovely 19th-century building has a different atmosphere on each floor, including a richly decorated library and a pleasant rooftop café.

TURANDOT Map pp88–9　　　Asian $$$
☎ 495-739 0011; Tverskoy bul 26/5; meals R1500-2000; Ⓜ Pushkinskaya

If you wanted to go to Disney World, but somehow ended up in Moscow, Turandot should be at the top of your dining wish list. Completely costumed in wigs and gowns, musicians play chamber music and servers scuttle to and fro. The decor is unbelievably extravagant, with hand-painted furniture, gilded light fixtures and frescoed cupola ceiling. It is certainly every bit as elaborate as Cinderella's castle. Turandot is named for a Puccini opera set in old Peking, which is as good a reason as any to serve Chinese and Japanese food in this baroque interior.

SCANDINAVIA Map pp88–9　　　European $$$
☎ 495-937 5630; Maly Palashevsky per 7; lunch R600-800, meals R1500-1800; Ⓜ Pushkinskaya

In most parts of the world, Swedish cuisine is not really celebrated; in Moscow, it is. Much beloved of Moscow expats, Scandinavia offers an enticing interpretation of what happens 'when Sweden meets Russia'. A delightful summer café features sandwiches, salads and treats from the grill (including the best burgers in Moscow, by

some accounts). Inside, the dining room offers a sophisticated menu of modern European delights.

CAFÉ DES ARTISTES Map pp88–9　European $$
☎ 495-292 4042; www.artistico.ru; Kamergersky per 5/6; business lunch R600, meals R1000-1500; ◷ 11am-1am; Ⓜ Teatralnaya

A restaurant and art gallery in one, this gay-friendly, Swiss-owned establishment is an interesting and elegant place to enjoy a meal. The glitzy interior has rich red tapestries, marble walls and a frescoed ceiling. The menu is full of delicious options, but the specialities of the house include cream of spinach soup and fresh oysters. Come for the 'Hungry Sunday' special, which offers an excellent, alternating three-course meal for R600.

FILIMONOVA & YANKEL FISH HOUSE
Map pp88–9　　　　　　　　　Seafood $$
☎ 495-223 0707; Tverskaya ul 23; business lunch R390, meals R1000-1200; Ⓜ Pushkinskaya

Head to this fish house when you can't stand the sight of another grilled salmon. At Filimonova & Yankel, you can take your pick from 10 varieties of fish – baked, grilled or fried – not to mention other seasonal specialities such as lobster and Kamchatka crab. The fruits of the sea are expertly prepared and efficiently served in an upscale, stylish setting. There is another outlet in Basmanny (☎ 495-223 0707; ul Zemlyanoy val 11-19; Ⓜ Kurskaya).

MARI VANNA Map pp88–9　　　Russian $$
☎ 495-650 6500; Spiridonyevsky per 10; meals R800-1200; ◷ 9am-11pm; Ⓜ Pushkinskaya

top picks

RUSSIAN CUISINE

- Varvary (p165) As interpreted by a molecular chef.
- Café Pushkin (left) As interpreted by the old aristocrats.
- Mari Vanna (above) Like being invited into someone's home.
- Yolki-Palki (p165) A long-time favourite with an enormous salad bar.
- Beryozka (p176) Sample the Siberian speciality, *pelmeni* (dumplings).

Remember when the best Russian food was served in somebody's crowded living room, on tiny mismatched plates, on a table cluttered with dried flowers in vases and framed photographs? Mari Vanna invites you to recall these days – don't look for the sign (there is none), just ring the doorbell at No 10. You will be ushered into these homey environs, complete with overstuffed bookcases and B&W TV showing old Soviet shows. You will be served delicious Russian home cooking and, just when you begin to think it is 1962, you will be handed your bill with the prices of modern-day Moscow. Ouch.

SHAFRAN Map pp88–9 Lebanese $$
Saffron; ☎ 495-737 9500; Spiridonyevsky per 12/9; meze R200-600, meals R800-1200; Ⓜ Pushkinskaya

While ethnic restaurants in Moscow tend to be overdone, Shafran is understated and sophisticated. Strewn with colourful pillows, it is otherwise simply decorated. Arabic music wafts through the air, but does not obstruct conversation. The menu includes a wide range of hot and cold meze (small plates), as well as a selection of kebabs, all expertly prepared and perfect for sharing.

AKADEMIYA Map pp88–9 Italian $$
☎ 495-692 9649; Kamergersky per 2; business lunch R280, meals R600-1000; Ⓨ 9am-midnight Mon-Fri, 11am-midnight Sat & Sun; Ⓜ Teatralnaya; Ⓥ

Somebody at Akademiya knows real estate. That's the only way to explain how this upscale pizzeria is able to find all the sweetest spots. The obvious example is this outlet on Kamergersky per, the pedestrian strip that is prime for people-watching. Not surprisingly, you'll also find Akademiya near the Arbat (☎ 495-662 1442; Gogolevsky bul 33/1; Ⓜ Arbatskaya).

STARLITE DINER Map pp88–9 American $$
☎ 495-690 9638; Bolshaya Sadovaya ul 16; meals R500-700; Ⓨ 24hr; Ⓜ Mayakovskaya; Ⓥ

Outdoor seating and classic diner decor make this a long-time favourite of Moscow expats. The extensive breakfast menu includes all kinds of omelettes, French toast and freshly squeezed juice. Otherwise, you can't go wrong with burgers and milkshakes, any time of day or night. A second,

less atmospheric outlet is in Zamoskvorechie (☎ 495-959 8919; ul Korovy val 9; Ⓜ Oktyabrskaya).

BAVARIUS Map pp88–9 German $
☎ 495-699 4189; Sadovaya-Triumfalnaya ul 2/30; meals R400-600; Ⓜ Mayakovskaya

German-style brew pubs are popping up all over Moscow, confirming the Russian penchant for salty sausages and thirst-quenching beer. Bavarius competes with the best of them, offering pork chops, sauerkraut and plenty of cold, delicious draughts. It's particularly inviting in summer, when there is seating in the shady courtyard.

MAKI CAFÉ Map pp88–9 International $
☎ 495-692 9731; Glinishchevsky per 3; meals R400-600; Ⓜ Pushkinskaya or Tverskaya

With a menu ranging from its namesake maki rolls to fresh green salads to Italian soft drinks, the theme at the Maki Café is diverse. The café is complemented by its minimalist, industrial decor – clunky light fixtures, lots of brick and metal. It appeals to a hip, urban audience, including a regular crowd of gay and lesbian patrons.

HOMEMADE CAFÉ Map pp88–9 International $
☎ 495-629 6656; Bolshoy Gnezdnikovsky per 10; business lunch R280, meals R400-600; Ⓨ 9am-11pm Mon-Fri, 11am-11pm Sat & Sun; Ⓜ Pushkinskaya; ▣

Hidden away on a side street, this café is unassuming, affordable and appetising. The staff go out of their way to make you feel welcome, from the friendly guy behind the bar to the newspapers scattered about for perusal. The menu changes daily, but it always features several different kinds of kasha for breakfast and at least half-a-dozen hearty soups for lunch. Main courses range from the simple (homemade pelmeni) to the sublime (pork loin with aubergine caviar), including at least one recipe supplied by a guest.

PUSHKIN KONDITERSKAYA
Map pp88–9 Café $
☎ 495-739 0033; Tverskoy bul 26; desserts R100-300; Ⓜ Pushkinskaya

If you want to impress your date, but you can't afford the Café Pushkin for dinner, head next door to the konditerskaya (confectioner) for dessert. It's every bit as opulent as the restaurant, from the crystal chandeliers down to the marble floors, with plenty of embellishments in between (not the least of which is the glass case displaying the sweets).

COFFEE BEAN Map pp88–9 Café $
☎ 495-788 6357; Tverskaya ul 10; 🕙 8am-11pm Mon-Sat, 9am-10pm Sun; coffees R100-200, desserts & sandwiches R100-200; Ⓜ Pushkinskaya; ☒ 🖵

One could claim that Coffee Bean started the coffee thing in Moscow, as the original outlet on Tverskaya ul has been around for years. It's still one of the coolest cafés in the city, with high ceilings, fantastic architectural details and large windows looking out onto the main drag. There are additional outlets in Basmanny (☎ 495-623 9793; ul Pokrovka 18; 🕙 Chistye Prudy) and Zamoskvorechie (☎ 495-953 6726; Pyatnitskaya ul 5; Ⓜ Tretyakovskaya).

VOLKONSKY KEYSER Map pp88–9 Bakery $
☎ 495-699 4620; Bolshaya Sadovaya ul 2/46; meals R200-400; Ⓜ Mayakovskaya

The queue often runs out the door, as loyal patrons wait their turn for the city's best fresh-baked breads, pastries and pies. It's worth the wait, especially if you decide on a fruit-filled croissant or to-die-for olive bread. Choose something sweet or savoury from the glass case, then head next door to the big wooden tables for large bowls of coffee or tea. There is another outlet in Basmanny (☎ 495-741 1442; ul Maroseyka 4/2; Ⓜ Kitay-Gorod).

BALTISKY KHLEB Map pp88–9 Bakery $
Baltic Bread; ☎ 495-699 4873; ul Malaya Dmitrovka 3/10; meals R200-300, desserts R100-200; 🕙 9am-11pm; Ⓜ Pushkinskaya; ☒

St Petersburg's favourite bakery has made its way to the capital, bringing along its secret recipes for delectable pastries and desserts. This outlet near Pushkinskaya pl, resembling an old-fashioned confectioner, is an excellent place to stop for breakfast, lunch or a late-afternoon coffee.

OUTER TVERSKOY

Outer Tverskoy includes the restaurants that are located outside the Garden Ring.

GORKY Map pp88–9 European $$$
☎ 495-775 2456; 1-ya Tverskaya-Yamskaya 3; meals R2000-3000; Ⓜ Mayakovskaya

Gorky, which was the former name of Tverskaya ul, is a grandiose space, filled with heavy wooden furniture, plush chairs and marble columns. The stylish setting is perfect for the even-more-stylish guests, who look nothing less than fabulous while nibbling fresh pasta and other contemporary cuisine. The menu is primarily Italian, but the clientele is all-Russian.

MI PIACE Map pp88–9 European $$
☎ 495-970 1129; 1-ya Tverskaya-Yamskaya 7; meals R600-1000; Ⓜ Mayakovskaya

We can't explain who those kids are, or why they are making funny faces, but we can vouch for this cool, contemporary pizzeria. Big windows allow loads of light into the dining room, and diamond-shaped wine racks are filled with bottles and books. You can sit at a table if you like, but it's much more appealing to hunker down on one of the couches with your pizza pie. There is another outlet near Pushkinskaya pl (☎ 495-650 7575; Tverskaya ul 20; Ⓜ Pushkinskaya) with outdoor seating.

SHYOLK Map pp88–9 Chinese $$
Silk; ☎ 495-250 5389; 1-ya Tverskaya-Yamskaya ul 29/1; meals R600-800; 🕙 11am-5am; Ⓜ Belorusskaya

Not too expensive, but still stylish, Shyolk is popular for authentic northern Chinese fare. Connoisseurs credit this to fresh ingredients and bold spices, not to mention the chefs hired straight from China. 'Bamboo Fire' comes highly recommended for those with a tough palate.

DRUZHBA Map pp88–9 Chinese $$
☎ 495-973 1234; Novoslobodskaya ul 4; meals R600-800; 🕙 11am-11pm; Ⓜ Novoslobodskaya

Druzhba earns high marks for authenticity, and as far as Sichuan cuisine goes, that means spicy. Chinese restaurants in Moscow are notorious for turning down their seasoning to appeal to Russian taste buds, but Druzhba is the exception, which goes a long way towards explaining why this place is often packed with Chinese patrons. The chicken with peppers gets red-hot reviews.

BABAY Map pp88–9 Uzbek $$
☎ 495-258 8279; 1-ya Tverskaya-Yamskaya ul 5; meals R600-800; Ⓜ Mayakovskaya

The big-screen TVs do not exactly add to the authenticity of this place, but the spicy *plov* and accommodating service do. Televisions aside, the decor is not as interesting as some of the other ethnic restaurants in Moscow, but that may be because the focus is on preparing excellent, filling food.

BOTANIKA Map pp88–9   Fusion $$
☎ 495-254 0064; Bolshaya Gruzinskaya ul 61; meals R500-700; ◷ 11am-10pm;
Ⓜ Belorusskaya; Ⓥ
Rare is it to find a restaurant in Moscow that is both fashionable and affordable. Somehow Botanika manages to be both. It offers light, modern fare, with plenty of soups, salads and grills. Wood furniture and subtle floral prints complement the garden-themed decor, all of which makes for an enjoyable, all-natural eating experience.

PRESNYA

Loud, crowded Kudrinskaya pl might seem an unlikely spot for a pleasant dining experience, but you will be surprised. The area around Patriarch's Ponds boasts one of Moscow's most exciting eat streets; elegant houses on the quiet streets east of the Garden Ring offer an exquisite atmosphere for sharing a meal; and the World Trade Centre, further south, has its own strip of extravagant themed restaurants featuring excellent cooking. All this, plus it has one of Moscow's favourite expat hang-outs.

PAVILION Map pp96–7   Fusion $$$
☎ 495-203 5110; Bolshoy Patriarshy per; meals R1200-1800; ◷ 24hr; Ⓜ Mayakovskaya
Occupying the old boathouse overlooking Patriarch's Ponds, it's hard to beat this place for atmosphere. While the pavilion dates from the 19th century, the interior is chic and contemporary – a good match for the menu, which attempts to update the Russian classics. Go for one of the rich, creamy soups served with dark peasant bread baked on the premises.

GANDHARA Map pp96–7   Pakistani $$
☎ 495-255 9959; Rochdelskaya ul 15/7; meals R1000-1500; Ⓜ Ulitsa 1905 Goda; Ⓥ
Named for an ancient city in present-day Pakistan, Gandhara promises to return its

top picks

SUNDAY BRUNCH

- Hotel Baltschug Kempinski (p212) Splurge on a buffet breakfast.
- Correa's (below) Think fresh fruit and homemade omelettes.
- Scandinavia (p167) The name says it all.
- Starlite Diner (p168) Classic Amerikansky breakfast fare.

guests to the 1st century BC. The dining room is decorated with replicas of ancient Gandhara sculptures. Guests feast on charcoal-grilled Peshawar *chanp* (lamb chops), spicy curries and traditional *daal* (lentil) and *biryani* (rice) dishes.

SHINOK Map pp96–7   Ukrainian $$
☎ 495-255 0204; ul 1905 goda 2; meals R1000-1200; Ⓜ Ulitsa 1905 Goda; Ⓥ
In case you didn't think Moscow's themed dining was over the top, this restaurant has re-created a Ukrainian peasant farm in central Moscow. Servers wear colourfully embroidered shirts and speak with Ukrainian accents (probably lost on most tourists). The house speciality is *vareniki* (the Ukrainian version of *pelmeni*). As you dine, you can look out the window at a cheerful *babushka* while she tends the farmyard animals (very well taken care of, we're assured).

CORREA'S Map pp96–7   European $$
☎ 495-605 9100; Bolshaya Gruzinskaya ul 32; brunch R400-600, sandwiches R200-300, meals R600-1000; ◷ 8am-midnight; Ⓜ Belorusskaya; Ⓥ
It's hard to characterise a place that is so simple. Correa's occupies a tiny space and there are only seven tables. But the existence of large windows and an open kitchen guarantee that it does not feel cramped, just cosy. The menu – sandwiches, pizza and grills – features nothing too fancy, but everything is prepared with the freshest ingredients and the utmost care. The outlet in Zamoskvorechie (☎ 495-725 6035; ul Bolshaya Ordynka 40/2; Ⓜ Tretyakovskaya) is roomier, but reservations are still

TALKING WITH YOUR MOUTH FULL

Laura Bridge is an executive chef and consultant who develops menus and provides training for start-up restaurants. In Moscow she has consulted with Prime Star (p164) and Correa's (opposite), among others. We chatted with Laura about the dining scene in the Russian capital.

How did you find yourself working as a chef in Moscow? I was bored working in London, and was offered the exciting opportunity to work as executive chef for Arkady Novikov's new business called Prime Star, similar to the British Pret a Manger chain. I had never been to Russia before, could not speak the language, did not know anyone and had nowhere to live, so it seemed a big adventure and challenge.

Russian food is not well known or appreciated in other parts of the world. What should inexperienced eaters try to sample from this under-appreciated cuisine? Try delicious dishes such as beluga caviar with homemade bliny; borsch, the traditional beetroot soup; and shashlyk, which is grilled barbecued meat. These dishes shatter the myth that Russian cuisine is bland, heavy and tasteless.

What makes the Moscow dining scene unique? I would say it is unique because it is so very new. It has only been the past 10 years that entrepreneurs such as Arkady Novikov really changed the face of the restaurant scene and introduced such an international choice and standard. Before that, you had to go to a hotel to try international cuisine.

What trends and changes can diners look for in the future? The current trend is for fusion and Asian menus, but I believe that classical Italian and French cuisine will develop a bigger following. Also, international hotels will become increasingly competitive and play a much larger part in the restaurant and bar scene.

recommended for Sunday brunch. Enter from the courtyard.

DYMOV NO 1 Map pp96–7 European $$
☎ 492-641 3222; ul 1905 goda 11; meals R600-1000; Ⓜ Ulitsa 1905 Goda

Restaurant-ruler Arkady Novikov teamed up with meat-mogul Vadim Dymov to create this pub and grill. Universally described as 'democratic', the menu is relatively affordable for a Novikov affair, and features an endless array of sausages. Dymov brews only two beers (one light and one red), but there are plenty of other interesting options on draught. Other outlets are in Zamoskvorechie (☎ 495-951 7571; Sofiyskaya nab 34; Ⓜ Borovitskaya) and Tverskoy (☎ 495-699 0770; ul Malaya Dmitrovka 6; Ⓜ Tverskaya).

SANTA FE Map pp96–7 Mexican $$
☎ 495-256 2126; ul Mantulinskaya 5/1; meals R600-800; Ⓜ Ulitsa 1905 Goda

If the Moscow winter is getting you down, head south of the border at Krasnaya Presnya park. The long-standing expat favourite Santa Fe has a big atrium that lets in the sunlight, even when temperatures outside are subzero. Exotic fruit juices add to the tropical ambience. Big plates of nachos, burritos and other Tex-Mex specialities will tantalise the taste buds and warm your soul.

IL CUCININO Map pp96–7 Italian $$
☎ 495-291 9398; ul Spiridonova 24/1; meals R600-1000; Ⓜ Barrikadnaya

Sweet and simple, this tiny trattoria is a refreshing change from the elaborate eateries that are the norm in Moscow. There are two big windows, five tables and an open kitchen. You'll receive a hand-written menu, but it's hard to resist the spread of sandwiches and antipasti that are on display. Beware: the restaurant charges by weight and it adds up quickly.

ARBAT

Ul Arbat practically introduced the pavement café to Moscow. Considering that, the selection of restaurants in the Arbat today is mildly disappointing (although there is no shortage of cafés). That said, strollers and shoppers have options to ease their hunger, whether on ul Arbat itself or tucked into the surrounding streets. Ul Novy Arbat, to the north, is lined with decent Russian chain restaurants that offer dependably tasty and hearty food.

VESNA CAFE Map pp102–3 Fusion $$$
☎ 495-783 6966; ul Novy Arbat 19; meals R1500-2000; Ⓜ Arbatskaya

Spring is in the air! Fashion designer Igor Chapurin (p152) is responsible for the fresh,

EATING ARBAT

fertile decor at this excellent fusion restaurant. The menu brings together all corners of the world, offering Asian-style noodles, handmade pasta and risotto, seafood and grills. Save room for one of the delightful, delectable desserts. The chef is Sicilian, and you won't get cannoli like this anywhere else in Moscow.

GENATSVALE ON ARBAT

Map pp102–3   Caucasian $$

☎ 495-203 9453; ul Novy Arbat 11; meals R600-1000; Ⓜ Arbatskaya

Subtle, it is not. Bedecked with fake trees and flowing fountains, it conjures up the Caucasian countryside, leaving little to the imagination. But what better setting to feast on favourites such as *khachipuri* (cheesy bread) and lamb dishes. If you prefer a more intimate atmosphere, head to the original location in Khamovniki (☎ 495-202 0445; ul Ostozhenka 12/1; Ⓜ Kropotkinskaya).

KARETNY DVOR Map pp102–3   Caucasian $$

☎ 495-291 6376; Povarskaya ul 52; meals R600-1000; ⏱ 24hr; Ⓜ Barrikadnaya

A classic Azeri place with private rooms, so your party can enjoy its dolmas and lamb kebabs in complete privacy. Otherwise, select a table in the leafy courtyard and imagine yourself in the foothills of the Caucasus.

MAYAK Map pp102–3   European $$

☎ 495-291 7503; Bolshaya Nikitskaya ul 19; meals R600-800; Ⓜ Okhotny Ryad

Named for the Mayakovsky Theatre downstairs, this is a remake of a much beloved club that operated in this spot throughout the 1990s. The reincarnated version is more café than club, exuding the air of a welcoming, old-fashioned inn. But it still attracts actors, artists and writers, who come to see friendly faces and to eat filling European fare.

COFFEE MANIA Map pp102–3   Café $$

☎ 495-775 4310; Bolshaya Nikitskaya ul 13, Moscow Conservatory; meals R600-800; ⏱ 24hr; Ⓜ Alexandrovsky Sad; ✗ ▢

With all of Moscow's opportunities for high stepping, fine dining and big spending, where is the most popular place for the rich and famous to congregate? Can you believe it's somewhere called Cof-

fee Mania? The friendly, informal café is beloved for its homemade soups, freshly squeezed juices and steaming cappuccinos, not to mention its summer terrace overlooking the leafy courtyard of the conservatory. There are additional outlets near Kuznetsky Most (☎ 495-924 0075; Pushechnaya ul; ⏱ 8am-11pm; Ⓜ Kuznetsky Most) and Kudrinskaya pl (☎ 495-290 0141; Kudrinskaya pl 46/54; ⏱ 8am-midnight; Ⓜ Barrikadnaya).

JEAN-JACQUES Map pp102–3   French $$

☎ 495-290 3886; Nikitsky bul 12; breakfast R100, meals R400-800; ⏱ 7am-midnight Sun-Thu, 7am-1am Fri & Sat; Ⓜ Arbatskaya

In a prime location on the Boulevard Ring, this friendly wine bar welcomes everybody wanting a glass of wine, a bite to eat, a few songs and a few smiles. The basement setting is cosy but not dark, making it an ideal spot to share a bottle of Bordeaux and nibble on brie. Bottles of wine start at R350, although most are priced around R1000 – still refreshingly reasonable in this town where wine is usually ridiculously overpriced.

VOSTOCHNY KVARTAL Map pp102–3 Uzbek $$

☎ 499-241 3803; ul Arbat 45/24; meals R400-800; Ⓜ Smolenskaya; Ⓥ

Vostochny Kvartal used to live up to its name, acting as the 'Eastern Quarter' of the Arbat. Uzbek cooks and Uzbek patrons assured that this was the real-deal place to get your *plov*. The place has since gone the way of the Arbat itself, drawing in more English speakers than anything else. Nonetheless, it still serves some of the best food on the block.

KISHMISH Map pp102–3   Uzbek $$

☎ 495-290 0670; ul Novy Arbat 28; meals R400-800; ⏱ 11am-1am; Ⓜ Smolenskaya

Besides being a word that rhymes with itself, *kishmish* is a kind of a grape – often a dried grape or raisin – that is often used in Central Asian cuisine. This place is decked out like an Uzbek *chaikhona* (teahouse), complete with plush Oriental carpets, staff in national costume and painted ceramic place settings. Everything was imported from Tashkent (except the staff, presumably). It serves simple spicy standards such as shashlyk and *plov* at the cheapest prices you will find. The *dastarkhan,* or salad bar, is chock-full of vegies and salads and *kishmish* to fill up the herbivores.

SHESH-BESH Map pp102–3   Caucasian $$
☎ 495-290 1922; ul Novy Arbat 24; meals R400-800; M Smolenskaya

Following the rhyming restaurant trend, Shesh-Besh is a chain offering hearty Azeri fare. The thick soup is easily a meal in itself, as is the extensive salad bar. The place is not overly atmospheric – this being the TGI Friday's of Azeri cuisine – but the food is still spicy and prices are affordable. There are more rhyming restaurants in Presnya (☎ 495-255 1883; ul Krasnaya Presnya 1; M Krasnopresnenskaya) and Zamoskvorechie (☎ 495-959 6270; Pyatnitskaya ul 24/1; M Novokuznetskaya).

SHASHLYK MASHLYK
Map pp102–3   Caucasian $$
☎ 495-241 2107; ul Arbat 38/1; meals R400-800; ⏱ 11am-11pm; M Smolenskaya

Can you think of a word that rhymes with shashlyk? Neither can we…but we'll allow a little poetic license when the result is spicy, delicious, affordable grilled meats and vegies. This is a pretty simple place, but the beer is cold and the open-air terrace gives a sweet view of the passers-by on the Arbat.

BAGUETTERIA Map pp102–3   Fast Food $
☎ 495-518 9925; ul Arbat 1; sandwiches R100-130; ⏱ 8am-11pm; M Arbatskaya

Fast food. Fresh food. Cheap food. What more do you need to know? This is one of the few places in Moscow where somebody will make you a sandwich. Not an open-face *buterbrod* but a real sandwich on a fresh-baked baguette. The interior has all the charm of your local McD's so you may want to order your sandwich to go and sit on the Arbat.

DOROGOMILOVO

The Evropeysky Shopping Centre (p155) is filled with restaurants of every shape and size, including branches of some of Moscow's most popular chain restaurants. Heading out along Kutuzovsky pr, the dining scene goes upscale, catering to the wealthy residents of the western suburbs (see the boxed text, p174).

PINOCCHIO Map p107   Italian $$$
☎ 495-545 0171; Kutuzovsky pr 4/2; meals R1000-2000; M Kievskaya

This classy trattoria evokes 1930s Italy, with its black-and-white tiled floors, comfy leather armchairs and sky-high ceilings. Music from the era imbues the neoclassical dining room, creating a luxury setting to sip wine and feast on pasta and grills.

PINOCCHIO PASTICCERIA
Map p107   Italian $
☎ 495-730 0818; nab Tarasa Shevchenko 23a; meals R300-500, desserts R100-200; M Delovoy Tsentr

Strolling across the pedestrian bridge over the Moscow River, you'll run smack into this little bakery and café, which is in the tall tower on the embankment. It's not just for sweets and snacks, as it also serves soups, salads and pastas. Snag a table on the balcony for a windy view of Moskva-City.

KHAMOVNIKI

This neighbourhood, crowded with art galleries and dominated by the massive cathedral, has an eclectic array of eateries. The restaurants in this area complement their surroundings: the whimsical Artist's Gallery inside the Tsereteli Gallery; extravagant Vanil, opposite the Cathedral of Christ the Saviour, which fits the same description; and Tiflis, one of Moscow's top Georgian restaurants, housed in a gorgeous Georgian manor house.

VANIL Map pp110–11   Asian $$$
Vanilla; ☎ 495-637 1082; ul Ostozhenka 1; meals R1200-3000; M Kropotinskaya

It's hard to say which sight is more grandiose: the glitzy interior of this ultrafancy eating establishment or the Cathedral of Christ the Saviour that looms across the street. Actually, the views of the cathedral through the restaurant's picture windows are a perfect complement to the crystal chandelier and giant gold-framed mirror that hang in the dining room. The modern Asian menu features sushi and other seafood dishes, which are all prepared with delightful innovations. And the service is top notch. Don't be put off by the row of Mercedes parked out the front; you will be

RESTAURANT TSAR

Arkady Novikov's name is a household word in Moscow. He was originally employed at an innocuous establishment called Universitetsky, where he was apparently fired for too much experimentation and innovation. Now this multimillionaire restaurateur oversees 45 venerated venues around the capital, including several restaurants along the swanky Rublyovo-Uspenskoe sh (see the boxed text, p108).

Novikov is known for his theme restaurants, featuring elaborate ethnic menus and matching over-the-top decor. But in recent years he has turned his creative energy to creating slick, stylish sites that are more about class than kitsch.

In the first category, Tsarskaya Okhota (Tsar's Hunt; ☎ 495-635 7982; Rublyovo-Uspenskoe sh 186, Zhukovka; meals R1500-2000) is a much-loved Russian restaurant, located on the ritzy Rublyovka. A favourite destination of former presidents Yeltsin and Putin, the rustic restaurant is reminiscent of a hunting lodge, with animal pelts on the walls and game on the menu.

Nearby, Novikov's unassuming Veranda u Dachi (Terrace at the Dacha; ☎ 495-635-3394; Rublovo-Uspenskoe sh 70, Zhukovka; meals R1500-2000) has been dubbed 'a love letter to one's home'. The well-worn rugs and slightly shabby furniture do not exactly jive with the fusion menu, which features Asian and Italian specialities at soaring prices. Nonetheless the cosy café and the adjoining art gallery are eternally popular spots among local residents.

Meanwhile, back in the city, Novikov forgoes tradition for trendiness. See Gallery (p166) and GQ (p182).

treated well here – even if you show up on foot.

TIFLIS Map pp110–11 Caucasian $$
☎ 499-766 9728; ul Ostozhenka 32; meals R800-1200; Ⓜ Kropotinskaya

'Guests are a gift from God.' So goes the Georgian saying, and Tiflis will make you believe it. The name of this restaurant comes from the Russian word for the Georgian capital, Tbilisi, and when you enter this restaurant you might think you are there. Its airy balconies and interior courtyards recall a 19th-century Georgian mansion – a romantic and atmospheric setting.

GALEREYA KHUDOZHNIKOV
Map pp110–11 European $$
Artists' Gallery; ☎ 495-687 2866; ul Prechistenka 19; meals R600-1000; Ⓜ Kropotkinskaya

This fantastical restaurant inside the Tsereteli Gallery is everything that you would expect from this over-the-top artist. The gallery's five rooms follow different themes, all of which are equally elaborate and which culminate in a huge, light-filled atrium that is wallpapered with stained glass and primitive paintings. The place certainly lives up to its name, which means Artists' Gallery. The menu is a fusion of European and Asian influences. Though it is secondary to the art, the food is well prepared and, appropriately enough, artistically presented.

SKAZKA VOSTOKA
Map pp110–11 Caucasian $$
Legend of the East; ☎ 499-766 8343; Frunzenskaya nab; meals R400-800; Ⓨ 24hr; Ⓜ Frunzenskaya

This boat moored on the Moscow River provides the romantic setting for exotic Eastern fare. Tables are laden with fruits, nuts and salads, while mystical sounding music drifts through the air. Skazka Vostoka has a huge menu, specialising in spicy Georgian and Azeri delights.

IL PATIO Map pp110–11 Italian $$
☎ 495-201 5626; ul Volkhonka 13a; meals R400-800; Ⓜ Kropotkinskaya; Ⓥ

This ubiquitous chain has a slew of outlets, each representing a different Italian city. The most inviting one, near the Cathedral of Christ the Saviour, has a large glass-enclosed seating area, making a perfectly pleasant setting for feasting on wood-oven pizzas and fresh salads.

STOLLE Map pp110–11 Caucasian $
☎ 499-246 0589; Malaya Pirogovskaya ul 16; meals R200-500; Ⓨ 9am-9pm; Ⓜ Sportivnaya; Ⓧ Ⓥ

This is one of Moscow's coolest places to come for coffee, although you'd be a fool to leave without sampling one of its magnificent *pirogi* (pies). In fact, the entire menu is excellent, but the pies are irresistible. A 'stolle' is a traditional Saxon Christmas cake: the selection of sweets and savouries sits on the counter, fresh from the oven. It may be difficult to decide (mushroom or meat, apricot or apple?) but you really can't go wrong.

GOGOL-MOGOL Map pp110–11 — Cafe $

☎ 495-203 5506; Gagarinsky per 6; desserts R100-200; ⏰ 10am-11pm; Ⓜ Kropotkinskaya

The front door is painted with a cake recipe in French, which should give you a pretty good idea of what you are getting into. There are a few lunch items on the menu, but this is really a place to come to indulge in rich French pastries and sweet drinks such as the namesake Gogol-Mogol (which is like egg-nog but it rhymes).

ZAMOSKVORECHIE

The cafés and restaurants in this charming area are outnumbered only by the churches. While Zamoskvorechie is less developed and offers fewer eating options than the districts north of the Kremlin, this situation is rapidly changing, with new eateries opening on a regular basis (which is not the case with the churches).

LOS BANDIDOS Map pp120–1 — Spanish $$$

☎ 495-953 0466; ul Bolshaya Ordynka 7; tapas R350-800, meals R1200-2000; Ⓜ Tretyakovskaya

Widely planked floors and dark-stained wood, not to mention the *jamon* (ham) suspended from the ceiling, create the romantic atmosphere associated with Andalusía. The menu does not disappoint, offering a wide array of Spanish red wines and lots of traditional tapas. The paella (R800), chock-full of spicy shellfish, can feed two.

SULIKO Map pp120–1 — Caucasian $$

☎ 495-238 2888; ul Bolshaya Polyanka 42/2; meals R600-1000; Ⓜ Polyanka

Often cited as the city's most authentic Georgian restaurant, this place has fantastic Caucasian dishes, especially the *khachapuri* (cheesy bread) topped with a fried egg. Of course you can't eat such food in a plain old dining room. Here, the interior evokes the Caucasian countryside, with grape vines hanging from the ceiling and a huge stone fireplace.

PANCHO VILLA Map pp120–1 — Mexican $

☎ 495-238 7913; ul Bolshaya Yakimanka 52; business lunch R120, meals R300-600; ⏰ 24hr; Ⓜ Oktyabrskaya

Near Oktyabrskaya pl, this is still Moscow's top choice for 'Meksikansky' food. If the *fajitas* and margaritas aren't enough of a draw, come for breakfast burritos, happy-hour specials (before 7pm Monday to Thursday) or live Latin music nightly (from 9pm).

GRABLY Map pp120–1 — Cafeteria $

☎ 495-545 0830; Pyatnitskaya ul 27; meals R200-300; ⏰ 10am-11pm; Ⓜ Novokuznetskaya

The big buffet features an amazing array of fish, poultry and meat, plus salads, soups and desserts. After you run the gauntlet and pay the bill, take a seat in the elaborate winter-garden seating area. This Zamoskvorechie outlet is particularly impressive, with two levels of tiled floors, vines draped over wrought-iron rails, and chandeliers suspended from the high ceilings. Beer and wine are available at the bar upstairs.

PELMESHKA Map pp120–1 — Cafeteria $

Kozhevnicheskaya ul 1; meals R150-200; ⏰ 10am-7pm Mon-Fri; Ⓜ Paveletskaya; 🚇

Pelmeshka is a clean, post-Soviet *stolovaya*, serving many different kinds of *pelmeni*, the most filling of Russian favourites. This place is packed with patrons at lunchtime, a sign that the food is tasty as well as cheap.

TAGANKA

Taganskaya pl is filled with chain restaurants, including Il Patio (opposite), Yolki-Palki (p165) and some others that have been reviewed earlier in the chapter. Otherwise, your dining choices are fairly limited in Taganka, although it is still home to one of the oldest and dearest expatriate institutions in Moscow.

AMERICAN BAR & GRILL

Map pp128–9 — American $$

☎ 495-912 3615; ul Zemlyanoy val 59; ⏰ noon-2am; meals R600-800; ⏰ 24hr; Ⓜ Taganskaya

One of Moscow's oldest expat hang-outs, this place still attracts a regular crowd to its outdoor terrace and its Wild West interior at all hours of day and night. With classic fare such as big burgers and spicy chicken wings, it's always a pleasant place for cold beers. You're bound to meet some other *innostrantsy* (foreigners) who are quaffing them, too.

BERYOZKA Map pp128–9 Russian $

Birch; ☎ 495-915 5467; Nikoloyamskaya ul 29; meals R400-600; Ⓜ Taganskaya; 🖵

At first glance this little place appears to be your typical kitschy *pelmeny* bar, decorated with faux birch trees and serving up the Siberian speciality. Indeed, you'll find more kinds of *pelmeny* on the menu than in any other restaurant. But you'll also find freshly brewed beer, sometimes available for self-service from the table-side taps. Each table is also equipped with a mini-TV, often showing cartoons, old movies and other nostalgia. *Pelmeny, pivo* and moving pictures: what more can you ask for?

top picks

- Art Garbage (p183)
- Krizis Zhanra (p183)
- Roadhouse (p186)
- Petrovich (p180)
- Kvartira 44 (p182)
- GQ Bar (p182)
- Soho Rooms (p184)
- The Most (p184)
- Ikra (p185)

What's your recommendation? www.lonelyplanet.com/russia/moscow

DRINKING & NIGHTLIFE

These days, Moscow nightlife is much about being elite. The trendiest spots are guarded by bouncers who take their job a little too seriously. They use 'face control' to keep out potential patrons who won't enhance the atmosphere at their establishment by looking fabulous and spending money. For tips on easing past face control, see the boxed text, p182.

Fortunately, plenty of night-time establishments offer a more welcoming ambience, even for those of us who are not blessed with a pretty face or a padded pocketbook (see the boxed text, p181). Most clubs and bars offer food as well as drinks. Indeed, the newest thing in Moscow nightlife is the club-café (see the boxed text, p183), which is often restaurant, bar, music club and art gallery all in one.

DRINKING

'Drinking is the joy of the Rus. We cannot live without it.' With these words Vladimir of Kiev, father of the Russian state, is said to have rejected abstinent Islam on his people's behalf in the 10th century. And the grateful Russian people have confirmed old Vlad's assessment, as drinking remains an integral part of Russian culture and society.

ETIQUETTE

Few traditions in Russia are as sacrosanct as the drinking of vodka, the national drink. Forget any foreign notions of drinking vodka mixed with tonic or orange juice – this is anathema to your average Russian. If you need something to wash it down, you can chase with a lemon, a pickle or, perhaps, a mixer in a separate glass.

Vodka is served chilled. One person makes a toast, then everyone clinks glasses and knocks it back. Women can usually get away with sipping, but men will be scoffed at if they don't drink up – at least the first round. Back in the day, vodka bottles rarely had resealable caps, which meant that once opened it must be finished. Times have changed, however;

these days, finishing off the bottle is not technically required.

It is bad luck to place an empty bottle on the table; it must be placed on the floor. Most importantly of all, snack between shots; Russians swear that by doing this you'll *never* get drunk…

Many visitors are surprised by the ubiquity of drinking, with people cracking open a beer anywhere. It is not illegal to drink in public places, so it's not unusual to see young people sipping beers on the sidewalk or in the park. It was only recently that consuming alcohol on the metro was prohibited. (It is now illegal to consume alcohol at or around national and historic monuments, however, so you might want to forgo that beer at Park Pobedy.)

SPECIALITIES

The word 'vodka' is the diminutive of the Russian word for water, *voda*, so it means something like 'a wee drop'. Russians sometimes drink vodka in moderation, but more often it's tipped down in swift shots, often followed by a pickle. Russky Standard and Stolichnaya are two good brands of vodka that are commonly available. It's very rare to get bad vodka in a restaurant, so do not fear if

---

NA ZDAROVYE!

'To your health!' is what Russians say when they throw back a shot of vodka. But this pronouncement hardly suffices as a proper toast in a public forum or an intimate drinking session among friends. A proper toast requires thoughtfulness and sincerity.

A few themes prevail. The first toast of the night often acknowledges the generosity of the host, while the second usually recognises the beauty of the ladies present. In mixed company you can't go wrong raising your glass to international friendship or world peace. But in all cases, the toast requires a personal anecdote or a profound insight, as well as a bit of rambling preamble to make it meaningful.

In Russia, drinking vodka is a celebration of life in all its complexity – the triumph, the tragedy and the triviality. A toast is a vocalisation of that celebration, so say it like you mean it. And drink it in the same way – *zalpom* – bottoms up!

you don't recognise the brand name, as there are many. In shops it's a different story: always buy vodka from a respectable-looking store (avoid street kiosks if possible) and always check for an unbroken seal.

Many visitors to Russia are surprised to learn that *pivo* (beer) is actually Russia's most popular alcoholic drink. The market leader is Baltika, a Scandinavian joint venture with Russian management, based in St Petersburg. It makes no less than 12 excellent brews. No 3 and 7 are the most popular standard lagers, but there is also a wheat beer (No 8), dark beers (No 4 and No 6) and 'strong beer' (No 9), which, at 8% proof, is extremely popular. Tinkoff (p181) is a national chain of micro-breweries that has begun bottling its potent brews for retail sale. Other leading Russian beers are Bochkaryov, Nevskoye, Stepan Razin and Tri Medvedi.

Russians drink sparkling wine, or *Sovietskoe shampanskoe,* to toast special occasions and to sip during intermission at the theatre. It tends to be sickeningly sweet: look for the label that says *sukhoe,* or dry.

Kvas is a mildly alcoholic, fermented, ryebread water. Cool and refreshing, it is a popular summer drink that tastes something like ginger beer. In the olden days it was dispensed on the street from big, wheeled tanks. Patrons would bring their own bottles or plastic bags and fill up. The *kvas* truck is a rare sight these days, but this cool, tasty treat is still available from Russian restaurants.

WHERE TO DRINK

Back in the day, the equivalent of the local pub was a *ryumochnaya,* which comes from the word *ryumka,* or 'shot'; or a *pivny bar,* meaning 'beer bar'. These were pretty grim places, serving up *sto gramov* (100g) but not much else.

In recent years Moscow's drinking possibilities have expanded exponentially (although there are still a few old-school *ryumochnye* and *pivnye bary* around town, such as Zhiguli, p181). Now, drinkers can take their pick from wine bars, whisky bars, Irish pubs, sports bars, microbreweries and more.

There is not one area of Moscow where bars and pubs are clustered; indeed, the whole city is now littered with such establishments, with more opening every day. Ul Arbat is traditionally a prime spot for the café scene, especially as it is closed to automobile traffic. Likewise, the newer and trendier Kamergersky

per is pedestrian-only, which makes it a hot spot for strollers and drinkers. Also popular in summer months is the *letnoe kafe,* or summer café, which opens in parks such as Hermitage Gardens and Gorky Park (see the boxed text, p180).

PRACTICALITIES
Opening Hours
Most Russians prefer to drink with meals, so almost all bars and pubs double as restaurants. As such, they generally have the same opening hours as eating venues (from noon to midnight). Popular drinking venues are more likely to stay open later – usually until 2am – though the kitchen may close. Some hot spots stay open for drinking until 5am or 6am.

How Much?
Prices for alcohol vary widely, depending on where you are drinking. Expect to pay anywhere from R100 to R300 for a pint of beer or for 50g of vodka.

KITAY GOROD & BASMANNY

TEMA BAR Map pp80–1   Cocktail Bar
☎ 495-624 2720; www.temabar.ru; Potapovsky per 5; ⏰ 24hr; Ⓜ Chistye Prudy
There are too many cocktails to count…but we know that Tema serves more than 20 different martinis, so that should give you an idea of the extent of the drinks menu. The talented bar staff are sure to serve up something that you like. Popular among both expats and locals, Tema has a fun, friendly and sometimes raucous vibe.

SOLYANKA Map pp80–1   DJ Bar
☎ 495-221 7557; http://s-11.ru; ul Solyanka 11; cover R300-500; ⏰ noon-midnight Sun-Wed, noon-5am Thu-Sat; Ⓜ Kitay-Gorod; ▣
Solyanka No 11 is a historic 18th-century merchant's mansion that has been revamped into an edgy, post-industrial club. Wide plank-wood floors, exposed brick walls, leather furniture and funky light fixtures transform the space. By day it's an excellent restaurant, serving contemporary, creative Russian and European food. On Thursday, Friday and Saturday nights, the big bar room gets cleared of tables and the DJ spins hip hop, techno and rave. The music

HOT TOWN, SUMMER IN THE CITY

Summer doesn't last very long in Moscow, so locals know they need to take advantage of the warm weather. That's why every restaurant worth going to opens a *letnoe kafe*, or summer café. They take over the courtyard, or the sidewalk, or the rooftop – because they know that people want to be outside. Gone are the days when *letnoe kafe* referred to a tent in the park with a few tables and a lot of beer. Of course, these still are the crucial parts of the definition of *letnoe kafe* – tent, tables, beer – but Muscovites have really refined the concept. Here are a few of our favourites (open from May to September):

Shatyor (Map pp80–1; ☎ 495-916 9486; Chistoprudny bul 12A; 🕑 24hr; M Chistye Prudy) Step into this 'Tent' and step inside a Bedouin camp, right on the shores of Chistye Prudy. Lounge on comfy cushions and feast on grilled meats, à la the *Thousand and One Nights*.

Chaikhona No 1 (www.chaihona.com) Hermitage Gardens (Map pp88–9; ☎ 495-971 6842; 🕑 2pm-last guest; M Chekhovskaya); Gorky Park (Map pp120–1; ☎ 495-778 1756; M Frunzenskaya) Housed in an inviting, exotic tent, laid with oriental rugs and plush pillows, this cool Uzbek lounge and café is one of the best chill-out spots in the city. Enjoy fruity drinks and spicy hookahs. If you are hungry, there is *plov* (meat and rice) and shashlyk on the menu. There are other outlets around the city but the setting can't compare to these park cafés.

Lebedinoe Ozero (Map pp120–1; ☎ 495-782 5813; http://s-11.ru/lebedinoe-ozero; Gorky Park; 🕑 noon-2am; M Frunzenskaya) The name means 'Swan Lake' and, yes, it overlooks a little pond where resident swans float contentedly. Aside from the idyllic setting at the southern end of Gorky Park, this place is a happening summertime haunt thanks to lounge chairs in the sun, (expensive) fruity cocktails and a small swimming pool for cooling dips or late-night aquatic dancing. To really cure the summertime blues, book some time in the massage hut (per hour R1400 to R1600).

---

usually starts at 11pm (and so does the face control).

CLUB CHE Map p66 · Latin Bar
☎ 495-621 7477; www.clubche.ru; Nikolskaya ul 10/2; meals R800-1000; 🕑 24hr; M Lubyanka; 🖵
The revolution lives on at this popular, divey bar. The walls are covered with revolutionary graffiti and photos of the iconic namesake hero. Patrons get their groove on the dance floor to salsa and merengue music. The cuisine is more Tex-Mex than Cuban, but nobody is complaining about the huge plates of nachos and the spicy chilli. Bartenders also mix a mean *mojito* (rum drink with lime, sugar and mint) with Havana Club rum.

PETROVICH Map pp80–1 · Retro Bar
☎ 495-923 0082; Myasnitskaya ul 24/1; meals R800-1000; M Chistye Prudy
The Soviet Union is gone but not forgotten. Remember simpler times at this popular retro restaurant, which reminisces with propaganda posters, hammer-and-sickle cutlery and Soviet pop music. The menu is riddled with inside jokes about the good ol' days. This doesn't seem like the kind of place that would have face control, but it is, so book a table in advance to play it safe. Enter through an unmarked door in the courtyard.

KRASNOSELSKY & MESHCHANSKY

LIGA PAP Map pp84–5 · Sports Bar
☎ 495-624 3636; www.ligapap.ru; ul Bolshaya Lubyanka 24; meals R500-1000; M Lubyanka
It's a sports bar, but it sure is a snazzy one. The gorgeous interior features big windows, tiled floors and Gothic arched ceilings, in addition to the 20-plus flat-screen TVs. The centrepiece of the main hall is the huge screen, complete with projector and dramatic auditorium-style seating.

TVERSKOY

VREMYA YEST Map pp88–9 · Beer Pub
☎ 495-251 6873; Lesnaya ul 1/2; business lunch R200-300, meals R400-800; 🕑 noon-5am; M Belorusskaya
Instead of Vremya Yest ('Time to Eat'), this place should be called Vremya Pit ('Time to Drink'). It specialises in cold beer and unusual cocktails. If you can't decide, try the *pivovar*, which mixes vodka with beer. This place is deservedly popular, considering the free-flowing drinks and reasonably priced food. During dinner hours, expect to wait for a table – an excellent excuse to sidle up to the bar and check out that cocktail menu.

12 VOLTS Map pp88–9   Café
☎ 495-933 2815; www.12voltclub.ru, in Russian; Tverskaya ul 12; meals R400-600; ☽ 6pm-6am; Ⓜ Mayakovskaya
The founders of Moscow's lesbian movement opened this welcoming café-cum-social club, tucked in a courtyard off Tverskaya ul.

CAFE MARGARITA Map pp88–9   Café
☎ 495-699 6534; Malaya Bronnaya ul 28; meals R400-600; ☽ noon-2am; Ⓜ Mayakovskaya
With walls lined with bookshelves, and a location opposite Patriarch's Ponds, this offbeat café is popular with a well-read, young crowd. These bookworms are pretty quiet during the day, but the place livens up in the evening, when it often hosts live acoustic, folk and jazz music.

MON CAFÉ Map pp88–9   Café
☎ 495-250 8800; 1-ya Tverskaya-Yamskaya ul 4; meals R800-1200; ☽ 24hr; Ⓜ Mayakovskaya
The hot-to-trot clientele is the decor at this otherwise minimalist French café north of the Mayakovskaya metro. The vaguely European fare is tasty, if overpriced. Don a short skirt or black shirt and take a seat on the upper level for the best view of the activity below.

TSIFRI Map pp88–9   Gay
Digits; ☎ 495-692 2911; Glinishchevsky per 3; ☽ noon-2am; Ⓜ Pushkinskaya or Tverskaya
Formerly known as 911, this used to be a straight bar with a gay night, but it has grown into a gay bar with some straight guests – 'gay expansion' as described by one local-in-the-know. Although the place has a small dance floor and a drag show on Saturday night, it is more of a café scene.

ARBAT

TINKOFF Map pp102–3   Beer Pub
☎ 495-777 3300; www.tinkoff.ru; Protochny per 11; 500ml beer R180, meals R600-800; ☽ noon-2am; Ⓜ Smolenskaya
Moscow's branch of this now-nationwide microbrewery features sport on the big screen, lagers and pilsners on draught, and a 1m-long sausage on the menu (yikes). This hip-and-happening venue is a great place to watch your favourite footballers and sample seven different brews.

ZHIGULI Map pp102–3   Beer Pub & Cafeteria
☎ 495-691 4144; www.zhiguli.net, in Russian; ul Novy Arbat 11; 500ml beer R100-150; ☽ 10am-2am Sun-Thu, 10am-4am Fri & Sat; Ⓜ Arbatskaya

---

FACE FRIENDLY *Micha Rinkus*

Visitors to Moscow are confronted with an unpleasant surprise when they try to enter nightclubs – 'face control', the practice of denying entry to people based on their appearance. It's not uncommon for nightlife hot spots around the world to strive to create the illusion of exclusivity, but the Russian capital takes it to a new level, arbitrarily, aggravatingly barring access to half-full, midrange clubs and bars. The Western egalitarian spirit is easily bruised by the blatancy of face control – the naked appraisal of your jeans, your watch and, yes, your face when you step up to the door – so a couple of rejections can really take the wind out of your sail for the night. In that case, you may want you may want to head straight for a safety zone, where even your ugliest friends can get in.

The following places can be considered 'face-control friendly'.

- Boho bar Gogol (p183) is an anomaly on Stoleshnikov per, the city centre's haute-couture pedestrian lane. Come here to drink and dance with a shaggy-haired student crowd.
- Silver's (Map pp88–9; ☎ 495-690 4222; Tverskaya ul 5/6; Ⓜ Okhotny Ryad) is a pocket-sized Irish pub a short jig from the Kremlin, typically filled to the hilt with smoke and all variety of English-speaking expat.
- Hate techno music? Try Krizis Zhanra (p183), a Mancunian-style rock club also known for welcoming ugly faces with open arms.
- Tema Bar (p179) has a relaxed face-control policy, and its reasonably priced cocktails make it the place to go to get trashed and dance on, say, a Tuesday night.
- A classy, retro-style restaurant by day, Mayak (p172) turns into quite the party on weekend nights, offering live music and no trouble at the door.
- Expat-owned sports bar Hemingway's (Map pp110–11; ☎ 495-246 5726; Komsomolsky pr 13; Ⓜ Park Kultury) was opened specifically for people to have a place to drink a beer and watch the game without worrying about their outfit.

Micha Rinkus is a nightlife and entertainment reviewer who lives in Moscow.

It's hard to classify this old-style *stolovaya* (cafeteria) that happens to brew great beer. The place harks back to the Soviet years, when a popular *pivny* bar by the same name was a Novy Arbat institution. The minimalist decor and cafeteria-style service recalls the heyday, although this place has been updated with big-screen TVs and a separate table-service dining room. The overall effect is a nostalgic place without the Soviet memorabilia and other retro kitsch. The namesake Zhiguli beer (not to be confused with the original Zhiguli beer that comes from Samara) is brewed on site. Enter from Arbatsky per.

KVARTIRA 44 Map pp102–3   Restaurant
Apartment 44; ☎ 495-291 7503; www.kv44.ru, in Russian; Bolshaya Nikitskaya ul 22/2; ⏱ noon-2am Sun-Thu, noon-6am Fri & Sat; Ⓜ Okhotny Ryad
Somebody had the brilliant idea to convert an old Moscow apartment into a crowded, cosy bar, with tables and chairs tucked into every nook and cranny. It may be a little too close to home for many Muscovites, but it's wildly popular with expats. There's jazz and piano music on Friday nights at 10pm, and there is another apartment in Zamoskvorechie (☎ 495-238 8234; ul Malaya Yakimanka 24/8; Ⓜ Polyanka).

DOROGOMILOVO
PROBKA Map p107   Brew Pub
☎ 499-243 3336; Ukrainsky bul 15; beer R185-290, meals R500-800; Ⓜ Kievskaya
With exposed brick walls, copper ceiling and dark stained-wood bar, this is a classy brew pub. Join the crowds who come to quench their thirst on one of 15 beers on tap. Whether you want to watch sports on the big screen or enjoy the Russian version of pub grub, this is one of the more atmospheric places in the neighbourhood.

ZAMOSKVORECHIE
APSHU Map pp120–1   Café
☎ 495-953 9944; www.apshu.ru, in Russian; Klimentovsky per 10; ⏱ 24hr; Ⓜ Tretyakovskaya; 🖳
It was a little fishing village on the Baltic coast that inspired this trendy place. Once discovered by worldly Muscovites, the village was transformed into a bohemian beacon – a magnet for artists and other creative types. This so-called club-café tries to do the same

in Moscow, offering inexpensive food and drinks, board games, art exhibitions, concerts…basically something for everyone.

GQ BAR Map pp120–1   Restaurant
☎ 495-956 7775; http://bar.gq.ru; ul Balchug 5; ⏱ 24hr; Ⓜ Novokuznetskaya
Anything that Arkady Novikov touches seems to turn to gold. Which may explain why this joint project with Condé Nast is currently Moscow's hippest destination for drinks, dinner and other early evening socialising. The contemporary decor features an open kitchen and a subtle Asian theme, which is echoed in the menu. If you actually intend to sit down and eat, be sure to reserve a table and bring a bucket of money.

NIGHTLIFE
Moscow nightlife is notorious for its decadence and debauchery, not to mention its *devushki* (young women). Indeed, this reputation is not unfounded. A wild night in Moscow is guaranteed for anyone who knows where to look (and *how* to look). But this is a big city and there is something for everyone, including down-and-out dives, up-and-coming art cafés, blues bars, dance clubs and good-old-fashioned *russky* rock.

Dance and music clubs might open at 10pm or 11pm, but they don't get hopping until after midnight. On weekends, Moscow clubs stay open until the very early hours – usually 6am or 7am. Most operate every night of the week, although some are open only on weekends (specified in the listings).

The key to finding out what's on in Moscow is the entertainment weekly element (www

---

TOP TIPS TO GET PAST FACE CONTROL
- If possible, book a table.
- Dress up: think short skirts and tall heels for women, black for men.
- Arrive by car. The bigger the better.
- Arrive in a small group, preferably with more men than women. If you're alone, imply that you're meeting somebody, even if you're not.
- Speak English. Foreigners are not as special as they used to be, but they're still pretty special. And they still (supposedly) have money.
- If all else fails, hire the 'nightlife concierge' that the Ritz-Carlton (p209) has on staff.

CLUB-CAFÉ

Some places are hard to categorise. The full menu would indicate that it's a restaurant, yet many people just come for drinks. There is live music in one hall and some people are dancing, but elsewhere people are playing board games or (gasp!) reading. Such diverse offerings under one roof have sparked a new concept in entertainment: the club-café. Here are a few of our favourites:

bilingua (Map pp80–1; ☎ 495-623 6683; www.bilinguaclub.ru, in Russian; Krivokolenny per 10/5; meals R400-600; ☯ noon-midnight, concerts 9pm or 10pm Tue & Fri-Sun; Ⓜ Chistye Prudy) Crowded with grungy, artsy, student types, this café also sells books and funky clothing. If you can stand the smoke, it's a cool place to grab a bite to eat and listen to some music or peruse the literary offerings. Despite the name, there's not much in the way of foreign-language literature.

Art Garbage (Map pp80–1; ☎ 495-628 8745; www.art-garbage.ru; Starosadsky per 5; ☯ noon-6am; Ⓜ Kitay-Gorod) Enter this funky club-café through the courtyard littered with sculpture. Inside, the walls are crammed with paintings of all genres, and there are DJs spinning or live music playing every night. The restaurant is relatively minimalist in terms of decor, but the menu is creative. Is it art or is it garbage? We'll let you decide.

ArteFAQ (Map pp88–9; ☎ 495-650 3971; www.artefaq.ru, in Russian; ul Bolshaya Dmitrovka 32; cover R400-600; ☯ 24hr, concerts Fri-Sun; Ⓜ Chekhovskaya) It's a club! It's a restaurant! It's a gallery! Set on four levels, ArteFAQ makes use of every inch of space, with music in the basement, a bar and outdoor terrace at ground level and dining upstairs. If you choose to check out the underground, be ready to get your groove on, as the music is heavy on the disco.

Gogol (Map pp88–9; ☎ 495-514 0944; www.gogolclubs.ru, in Russian; Stoleshnikov per 11; cover R350; ☯ 24hr, concerts 9pm or 10pm Thu-Sat; Ⓜ Chekhovskaya) Fun, informal and affordable (so surprising on swanky Stoleshnikov), Gogol is great for food, drinks and music. The underground club takes the bunker theme seriously, notifying customers that their food is ready with an air-raid siren. In summer the action moves out to the courtyard, where the gigantic tent is styled like an old-fashioned street scene.

.elementmoscow.ru), as well as the Moscow Times (www.themoscowtimes.com) weekly entertainment supplement. Both of these English-language publications are distributed (free!) throughout the city – check at centrally located hotels and popular expat eating and drinking establishments.

CLUBBING

DYKE CAFE off Map pp60–1
☎ +7-903-759 5944; www.dyke-cafe.ru, in Russian; Pokhodny proezd 4; cover R600 (men); Ⓜ Tushkinskaya
More of a club than a café, this place is way out on the northwest edge of town. Dancing, games and erotic performances…it's all about the women.

KARMA BAR Map pp84–5
☎ 495-624 5633; Pushechnaya ul 3; cover R100-200; ☯ 9pm-6am Thu-Sat, 11pm-6am Sun; Ⓜ Kuznetsky Most
The Karma Bar is home to a worldly mix of Asian food, Latin music and Russian fun. Thursday night usually features live music, while the other nights are for DJs and

dancing – there are free lessons from 9pm to 11pm on Friday and Saturday. Sunday night is dedicated to hip hop and R 'n' B. Add to this mix happy hours and hookah pipes, and you've got one of Moscow's top expat clubs.

KRIZIS ZHANRA Map pp80–1
☎ 495-623 2594; www.kriziszhanra.ru; ul Pokrovka 16/16; ☯ concerts 9pm Sun-Thu, 11pm Fri & Sat; Ⓜ Chistye Prudy
Everybody has something good to say about Krizis: expats and locals, old timers and newcomers, young and old. What's not to love? Good cheap food, copious drinks and rockin' music every night, all of which inspires the gathered to get their groove on.

KULT Map pp80–1
☎ 495-917 5706; Yauzskaya ul 5; admission free; ☯ noon-midnight Sun-Wed, noon-6am Thu-Sat; Ⓜ Kitay-Gorod
This hang out for arty types comes complete with a big screen showing avant-garde films (9pm Sunday through Thursday) and a gallery featuring local

artists. DJs spin all kinds of music, especially hip hop, funk, reggae and jazz. Board games, hookah pipes and cool vibes make this one of Moscow's most chilled locations.

PROPAGANDA Map pp80–1

☎ 495-624 5732; www.propagandamoscow.com; Bolshoy Zlatoustinsky per 7; meals R500-700; ☼ noon-6am; Ⓜ Kitay-Gorod

This long-time favourite looks to be straight from the warehouse district, with exposed brick walls and pipe ceilings. It's a café by day, but at night they clear the dance floor and let the DJ do his stuff. This is a gay-friendly place, especially on Sunday nights.

REAL MCCOY Map pp102–3

☎ 495-255 4144; www.mccoy.ru, in Russian; Kudrinskaya pl 1; meals R500-1000; ☼ 24hr; Ⓜ Barrikadnaya

This 'bootlegger's bar' has walls plastered in old newspapers, two-for-one happy-hour specials (5pm to 8pm) and a dance floor crowded with expats. There is live jazz and rock music in the evenings (9pm Wednesday to Sunday) then, after 11pm, the serious drinking begins. The later it gets, the more they drink. The Real McCoy is considered to be the last of Moscow's old-fashioned debauched and depraved dive bars, where women are invited to dance on the bar (preferably without a shirt on) and men are practically guaranteed to take home a new friend, if they are not too picky.

SIMACHYOV Map pp88–9

☎ 495-629 8085; www.denissimachev.com; Stoleshnikov per 12/2; ☼ 11am-last guest; Ⓜ Chekhovskaya

By day it's a boutique and café, owned and operated by the famed fashion designer of the same name. By night, this place becomes a hip-hop-happening nightclub that combines glamour and humour. The eclectic decor includes leopard-skin rugs tossed over tile floors, toilet stools pulled up to a wash-basin bar, Catholic confessionals for private dining, and more. You still have to look sharp to get in here, but at least you can be bohemian about it.

SOHO ROOMS Map pp110–11

☎ 495-988 7474; www.sohorooms.ru; Savinskaya nab 12; ☼ club 11pm-last guest, restaurant 24hr; Ⓜ Sportivnaya

At the time of research, the coolest club in Moscow is this uberexclusive nightclub with scantily clad women, cool music and expensive cocktails. Of course, many clubs in Moscow can boast such things, but only Soho Rooms has a swimming pool and a poolside terrace too.

THE MOST Map pp88–9

☎ 495-660 0706; ul Kuznetsky Most 6/3; ☼ 11pm-last guest; Ⓜ Kuznetsky Most

If you want to party like the *novy russky* (New Russians) this is the place for you. It is certainly among the most expensive, the most exclusive and the most extravagant clubs in Moscow. Located in the basement of a fancy French restaurant, its post-industrial space is decorated with baroque architectural elements (think gold-framed mirrors bedecking red brick walls, and crystal chandeliers suspended alongside black iron pipes). Girls in gowns groove along the catwalk overlooking the dance floor. The place is co-owned by Roman Abramovich, *the most* rich and famous of all New Russians. PS – face control; the most.

TRI OBEZYANI NEW AGE Map pp80–1

☎ 495-916 3555; www.gaycentral.ru, in Russian; Nastavnichesky per 11/1; ☼ 10pm-7am Thu-Sun; Ⓜ Chkalovskaya; ▣

The biggest and best club on the gay scene. Besides the dance floor, which is hopping, the club has drag queens and go-go boys, an internet café and a cinema. The clientele comes dressed to kill. Go in a group or take a taxi from the metro: there have been reports of attacks on the surrounding streets.

LIVE MUSIC

Live bands and DJs travel from other parts of Russia and all over Europe to play in this metropolis. For more information about Moscow's music scene, see p46. Tickets are usually available at the venue's box office in the hours leading up to the show. For big names, look for advertisements in *element* or in the *Moscow Times;* tickets for these events can be bought in advance.

B1 MAXIMUM Map pp60–1

☎ 495-648 6777; www.b1club.ru; ul Ordzhonikidze 11; tickets R1000-2000; ☼ 6pm-6am; ☼ Leninsky Prospekt

top picks

GAY & LESBIAN

- **Café des Artistes** (p167) Artist-friendly and queer-friendly restaurant and gallery.
- **Maki Café** (p168) A popular place for the gay and lesbian community to congregate and eat sushi.
- **Propaganda** (opposite) Super Sunday-night gay party.
- **Tsifri** (p180) Intimate and atmospheric club and cabaret.
- **Tri Obezyani New Age** (opposite) Boys gone wild: Moscow's biggest, baddest gay club.
- **12 Volts** (p181) An electrifying night out for queers.
- **Dyke Cafe** (p183) Moscow's only lesbian club.

When the big names come to Moscow, this is where they perform. Russia's most popular groups, from old-timers such as Mashina Vremeni to modern-day heroes such as Leningrad, all make appearances on this stage on a regular basis. Occasional acts from the USA and Europe also appear here. If they are well-known artists, you will see posters around town advertising the show.

BB KING Map pp88–9
☎ 495-699 8206; www.blues.ru; Sadovaya-Samotechnaya ul 4/2; cover R350; ☾ noon-midnight, music from 8.30pm; Ⓜ Tsvetnoy Bulvar
This old-style blues club hosts an open jam session on Wednesday night, acoustic blues on Sunday and live performances other nights. The restaurant is open for lunch and dinner, when you can listen to jazz and blues on the old-fashioned jukebox. Enter from the courtyard.

CLUB FORTE Map pp88–9
☎ 495-694 0881; www.forteclub.com, in Russian; Bolshaya Bronnaya ul 18; cover R300-500; ☾ 2pm-midnight, concerts 9pm; Ⓜ Tverskaya
Here the nightly concerts range from swing jazz to Latin jazz to golden oldies. The atmosphere is more formal than at some of the other places, attracting a pseudo-intellectual crowd. Thursday and Friday are reserved for local band Arsenal, which plays rather uninspired big band. Be sure to book.

IKRA Map pp80–1
☎ 495-505 5351; http://nobullshit.ru; ul Kazakova 8a; admission R350-3000; ☾ concerts from 8pm Wed-Sun; Ⓜ Kurskaya
Its unexpected industrial location and its trendy trash-glam decor give Ikra an edge. But it's the music that makes this quirky club so excellent. Others must agree, as Ikra was awarded the prestigious National Nightlife Award for live music in 2007. National and international acts range from Sean Lennon to Gogol Bordello.

JAZZTOWN Map pp128–9
☎ 495-912 5726; www.jazztown.ru; Taganskaya pl 12; cover R500-1000; ☾ 6pm-last guest, concerts 9pm; Ⓜ Taganskaya
In the same building as the casino, this flashy place hosts Russian and international acts on most nights. The gigantic complex includes a restaurant. Starting at 11pm on Thursday, Friday and Saturday, Lounge Jazz Night makes for a fun night out, if you don't mind the Las Vegas–style atmosphere.

KITAYSKY LYOTCHIK DZHAO-DA
Map pp80–1
Chinese Pilot; ☎ 495-623 2896; www.jao-da.ru, in Russian; Lubyansky proezd 25; cover R300-500; ☾ concerts 10pm Thu, 11pm Fri & Sat; Ⓜ Kitay-Gorod
A relaxed and relatively inexpensive place to hear live music. This divey basement place hosts lots of different kinds of bands – from around Europe and Russia – so check out the website in advance. Look out for free concerts on Monday nights.

MUSIC TOWN Map pp88–9
☎ 495-937 5419; www.musictownclub.ru, in Russian; ul Bolshaya Dmitrovka 11; cover R300-400; ☾ 24hr, concerts 9pm; Ⓜ Okhotny Ryad
True to its name, Music Town books live acts seven nights a week. The bands run the gamut, from true blues to exotic ethno-jazz to raw rock and roll. You never know what you're getting, but you're sure to get your groove on. On Friday and Saturday there is often a second concert at midnight.

PIROGI Map p66
☎ 495-621 5827; Nikolskaya ul 19/21; cover R100-500; ☾ 24hr; Ⓜ Lubyanka
This vaguely hippie (but definitely hip) place is definitely out of place in posh Tretyakovsky

proezd. Enter through the unmarked door in the corner of the courtyard and descend into the underground – literally and figuratively. Live music plays most nights.

ROADHOUSE Map pp110–11
☎ 499-245 5543; www.roadhouse.ru, in Russian; ul Dovatora 8; 🕑 noon-midnight, concerts 9pm; Ⓜ Sportivnaya
If your dog got run over by a pick-up truck, you could find some comfort at the Roadhouse Blues Bar, with down-and-out live music every night, plus cold beer and a

whole menu of salty cured meats. Great fun and a friendly vibe, with people actually listening to the music. Book a table if you want to sit down.

SIXTEEN TONS Map pp96–7
☎ 495-253 1550; www.16tons.ru; ul Presnensky val 6; cover R300-800; 🕑 11am-6am, concerts 10pm or 11pm Thu-Sat; Ⓜ Ulitsa 1905 Goda
Downstairs, the brassy English pub-restaurant has an excellent house-brewed bitter. Upstairs, the club gets some of the best local and foreign bands that play in Moscow.

top picks

- Bolshoi Theatre (p189)
- Moscow International House of Music (p188)
- New Ballet (p189)
- Russian Ball at Yar (p190)
- Nikulin Circus on Tsvetnoy Bulvar (p194)
- Moscow Art Theatre (p192)
- Kuklachev Cat Theatre (p193)

THE ARTS

The classical performing arts are one of Moscow's biggest draws. Highly acclaimed, professional artists stage productions in elegant theatres around the city, most of which have been recently revamped and look marvellous. Seeing a Russian opera or ballet in a magnificent baroque theatre makes for a magical night out, and Russian symphonic music is among the world's most moving.

Such shows remain an incredible bargain in Moscow, especially if you go anywhere other than the Bolshoi Theatre. Generally speaking, only the most expensive tickets, in front of the orchestra, can compare to what you would pay in the West for a similar performance.

Nearly all the drama is in Russian, which makes it more difficult for non–Russian speakers to appreciate. However, the incredible 19th-century interiors and the sense of occasion surrounding the performances mean that seeing a play is an interesting night out, even if you only stay for the first half (and tickets are generally cheap enough to make this perfectly feasible).

The standard way to buy tickets is from a *teatralnaya kassa* (theatre kiosk), several of which are scattered about the city. Or you can get tickets directly from the theatre box offices. You can also make arrangements for tickets through most hotels, but be prepared to pay a significant mark-up. Unfortunately for summer visitors, most venues are closed between late June and early September.

CLASSICAL MUSIC

It's not unusual to see highly talented musicians working the crowds inside the metro stations, often violinists single-handedly performing Vivaldi's *Four Seasons* and flautists whistling away at Mozart or Bach. That such talented musicians are busking in the streets (or under the streets, as the case may be) is testament to the incredible talent and training of Russian music students – and to the lack of resources of their cultural institutions. While it's possible to hear a good show in the metro station, a visit to one of the local orchestra halls is highly recommended.

MOSCOW INTERNATIONAL HOUSE OF MUSIC Map pp120–1
☎ 495-730 1011; www.mmdm.ru; Kosmodamianskaya nab 52/8; tickets R200-2000; Ⓜ Paveletskaya

This newish venue opened in 2003 in a graceful, modern, glass building. It has three halls, including Svetlanov Hall, which holds the largest organ in Russia. Needless to say, organ concerts held here are impressive. This is the usual venue for performances by the National Philharmonic of Russia (☎ 495-730 3778; www.nfor.ru, in Russian), a privately financed and highly lauded classical-music organisation. Founded in 1991, the symphony is directed and conducted by the esteemed Vladimir Spivakov.

MOSCOW TCHAIKOVSKY CONSERVATORY Map pp102–3
☎ 495-629 9410, box office 495-629 8183; www.mosconsv.ru; Bolshaya Nikitskaya ul 13; Ⓜ Okhotny Ryad or Arbatskaya

The country's largest music school, named for Tchaikovsky of course, has two venues, both of which – the Great Hall (Bolshoy Zal) and the Small Hall (Maly Zal) – are in Moscow. Once every four years, hundreds of musicians gather at the conservatory to compete for the titles of top pianist, singer, cellist and violinist at the prestigious International Tchaikovsky Competition. A competition will take place here in summer 2010.

TCHAIKOVSKY CONCERT HALL
Map pp88–9
☎ 495-232 5353, box office 495-699 0658; www.classicalmusic.ru; Triumfalnaya pl 4/31; tickets R100-1000; Ⓜ Mayakovskaya

Home to the famous State Philharmonic (Moskovsky Gosudarstvenny Akademichesky Filharmonia), the capital's oldest symphony orchestra, the concert hall was established in 1921. It's a huge auditorium, with seating for 1600 people. This is where you can expect to hear the Russian classics such as Stravinsky, Rachmaninov and Shostakovich, as well as other European favourites.

TICKETS FOR THE BOLSHOI

Unlike other theatres around Moscow, it is not possible to buy tickets to the Bolshoi at the *teatralnaya kassa* (theatre kiosk). In theory, tickets can be reserved by phone or over the internet, or (depending on the season) it is often possible to purchase tickets at the Bolshoi's box office (⏱ Main Stage 11am-3pm & 4-8pm, New Stage 11am-2pm & 3-7pm), especially if you go several days in advance. Otherwise, you can show up shortly before the show and try to buy tickets from a scalper. Scalpers are easy to find (they will find you); the trick is negotiating a price that is not several times the ticket's face value. Expect to pay upwards of R1000. Most importantly, make sure you examine the ticket and the date of the show (even the year) before money changes hands.

A limited number of reduced-price student tickets (R20) go on sale at the box office one hour before the performance. Go to window No 3 and bring your student ID.

OPERA & BALLET

Nobody has ever complained about a shortage of Russian classics at the opera and ballet. Take your pick from Tchaikovsky, Prokofiev, Rimsky-Korsakov or one of the other great Russian composers, and you are guaranteed to find him or her on the playbill at one of the theatres listed in the following columns. The choreography and staging of these classics is usually pretty traditional (some might even say uninventive), but then again, that's why they're classics.

Critics complain that the Russian renditions of well-known Western works often seem naïve and overly stylised, so steer clear of Mozart. If you tire of Russian classics, keep your eye out for more modern productions and premieres that are also staged at the Bolshoi and the Gelikon. The New Ballet is especially original, and perhaps even extreme, in its exploration of dance and movement.

BOLSHOI THEATRE Map pp88–9

☎ 495-250 7317, hot line 8-800-333 1333; www .bolshoi.ru; Teatralnaya pl 1; tickets R200-2000; Ⓜ Teatralnaya

An evening at the Bolshoi is still one of Moscow's most romantic and entertaining options, with an electric atmosphere in the glittering six-tier auditorium. Both the ballet and opera companies perform a range of Russian and foreign works here. After the collapse of the Soviet Union the Bolshoi was marred by politics, scandal and frequent turnover (see p47). Yet the show must go on – and it will.

At the time of research, the Bolshoi had just completed a long-needed renovation. The theatre was preparing to reopen the doors of its main stage after several years of work. In the meantime, the smaller

New Stage (Novaya Stsena), remodelled in 2003, continues to host performances as well.

See the boxed text above for details on how to purchase tickets.

GELIKON OPERA Map pp102–3

☎ 495-202 6584; www.helikon.ru; ul Novy Arbat 11; tickets R200-2000; Ⓨ box office noon-2pm & 2.30-7pm; Ⓜ Arbatskaya

Named after famous Mt Helicon, home to the muses and inspiration for musicians, this early-1990s opera company is unique in Moscow for its innovative, even experimental, opera performances. Director Dmitry Bertman is known for 'combining musical excellence with artistic risk', according to one local dramaturge. The Gelikon's 250-seat theatre provides an intimate setting that allows for some interaction between the performers and the audience.

KREMLIN BALLET THEATRE Map p66

☎ 495-620 7729, 495-928 5232; www.kremlin -gkd.ru; ul Vozdvizhenka 1; Ⓨ box office noon-8pm; Ⓜ Alexandrovsky Sad

The Bolshoi Theatre doesn't have a monopoly on ballet in Moscow. Leading dancers also appear with the Kremlin Ballet and the Moscow Classical Ballet Theatre, and both companies perform here. The Bolshoi is magical, but seeing a show inside the Kremlin is something special too, and the repertoire is similarly classical. The box office is in the underground passageway, near the entrance to the metro station.

NEW BALLET Map pp80–1

☎ 495-632 2911; www.newballet.ru, in Russian; Novaya Basmannaya ul 25/2; Ⓨ box office 11am-7pm; Ⓜ Krasnye Vorota

If you can't stand to see another *Swan Lake*, you will be pleased to know that the New Ballet performs innovative contemporary dance. This performance art, called 'plastic ballet', incorporates elements of classical and modern dance, as well as pantomime and drama. The theatre is tiny, providing an up-close look at original, cutting-edge choreography.

NOVAYA OPERA Map pp88–9
☎ 495-200 0868; www.novayaopera.ru; ul Karetny Ryad 3; M Tsvetnoy Bulvar

This theatre company was founded in 1991 by Mayor Luzhkov and artistic director Evgeny Kolobov. Maestro Kolobov himself stated, 'we do not pretend to be innovators in this beautiful and complicated genre of opera'. As such, the 'New Opera' stages the old classics, and does it well. The gorgeous, modern opera house is set amid the lovely Hermitage Gardens.

STANISLAVSKY & NEMIROVICH-DANCHENKO MUSICAL THEATRE
Map pp88–9
☎ 495-629 2835; www.stanislavskymusic.ru, in Russian; ul Bolshaya Dmitrovka 17; ✆ box office 11.30am-7pm; M Chekhovskaya

This is a opera and ballet company with a similar classical repertoire to the Novaya Opera and high-quality performances. This historic company was founded when two legends of the Moscow theatre scene – Konstantin Stanislavsky and Vladimir Nemirovich-Danchenko – joined forces in 1941. Their newly created theatre became a workshop for applying the innovative dramatic methods of the Moscow Art Theatre to opera and ballet (see the boxed text, p192).

FILM

Russia – as well as the Soviet Union before it – boasts a rich cinematic culture, and Moscow is its capital (see p48). These days, most theatres show the latest blockbusters from Hollywood, usually dubbed in Russian, as well as the hottest releases from Mosfilm (opposite). A few cinemas show more interesting Russian and foreign films, especially during Moscow's film festivals (p22), while the Dome Cinema (right) shows films almost exclusively in English. Show times vary, so stop by the cinemas (or call) for the schedule.

DOME CINEMA Map pp84–5
☎ 495-931 9873; www.domecinema.ru; Renaissance Moscow Hotel, Olympiysky pr 18/1; tickets R250; M Prospekt Mira

This is one of Moscow's first deluxe American-style theatres. These days films are shown in the original language – usually English – with dubs in Russian on the headphones.

ILLUZION CINEMA Map pp128–9
☎ 495-915 4353; Kotelnicheskaya nab 1/15; tickets R20-60; M Taganskaya

The location inside one of Stalin's Seven Sisters (see the boxed text, p51) is appropriate for the repertoire, which focuses on old-school Soviet films, including some that were stolen by the Nazis.

NESCAFÉ IMAX CINEMA Off Map pp60–1
☎ 495-775 7779; www.nescafe-imaxcinema .ru, in Russian; Ramstore City, Leningradskoe sh; adult R350-580, child R250-350; M Rechnoy Vokzal

Moscow's first Imax theatre is just inside the MKAD ring. The theatre surrounds viewers with fantastic 3-D images of sharks, butterflies, astronauts, dinosaurs or whatever happens to be the subject of the day. The advantage here is that it doesn't matter what language the movie is in, as the dialogue isn't really the point. A free shuttle runs from Rechnoy Vokzal metro station.

ROLAN CINEMA Map pp80–1
☎ 495-916 9190; Chistoprudny bul 12; tickets R100-500; M Chistye Prudy

The two theatres – one large and one small – show art-house films and host interesting festivals, usually featuring contemporary Russian cinema. This place is popular with Moscow's bohemian crowd.

FOLK SHOWS

While opera and ballet dominate the playbills at the top venues in Moscow, there are also elaborate folk shows performed, featuring Cossack dancing, gypsy music and traditional costumes.

RUSSIAN BALL AT YAR Map pp60–1
☎ 495-960 2004; Leningradsky pr 32/2, Sovietsky Hotel; tickets R1000, dinner R800-1200; M Dinamo

MOSFILM

In the Hollywood Hills they have Leo the MGM lion, and in Sparrow Hills they have the iconic socialist sculpture *Worker and Peasant Woman,* the instantly recognisable Mosfilm corporate logo.

In Russia, politics and cinema were always closely connected. Russia's nascent film industry received a big boost from the Bolshevik Revolution, as the proletarian culture needed a different kind of canvas. Comrade Lenin recognised that motion pictures would become the new mass medium for the new mass politics. By government decree, Mosfilm was officially founded in 1923, under the leadership of Alexander Khanzhokov, the pioneer of Russian cinema.

In this golden age, the studio soon earned an international reputation for its artistic experimentation and propaganda techniques. Legendary director Sergei Eisenstein, a socialist true believer, popularised a series of innovations, such as fast-paced montage editing and mounted tracking cameras. These techiques were designed to arouse an emotional response in the audience that could be used to shape political views. His *Battleship Potemkin* (1925), which depicted a 1905 uprising by the crew of a Russian battleship who rebelled against the oppressive Tsarist regime, remains one of film history's most admired and most studied silent classics.

During Josef Stalin's regime, the Mosfilm avant-garde was kept on a tight leash. Stylistic experimentation was repressed and, in its place, socialist realism was promoted. There was no mistaking the preferred social values of the Stalinist political regime – characters and plot lines were simple and the future looked bright. In the typical commie-kitsch film ending, a collective-farm peasant woman would reluctantly give up her true love and ride off into the sunset atop a new modern tractor. For his own private screenings, Stalin preferred forbidden American Westerns and gangster films, but these were not allowed to be distributed for mass consumption.

When Stalin departed the scene, Mosfilm directors such as Andrei Tarkovsky and Elem Klimov quickly responded with more honest depictions of Soviet daily life and more creative styles. Mosfilm productions again began to receive serious international acclaim, earning top honours at Cannes, Venice and the Academy Awards. However, getting past the censors at home in Russia still posed challenges, especially during the gerontocratic Brezhnev administration. Then Gorbachev loosened up the ideological constraints on culture, and some of the studio's most politically daring and artistically innovative works finally made it off the shelf and onto the big screen. Audiences could now see these films for the first time. At the end of the Soviet regime, Mosfilm was one of the largest film studios in Europe, and was among the most prolific, with over 2500 films having been created under its banner.

In the early 1990s the studio fell on hard times. It was finally reorganised into a quasi-private concern, although it still receives significant state patronage; and politics still influences cinema. Under Putin's rule, Mosfilm has contributed to the search for Russia's lost national identity, which was concealed and distorted by Soviet communism. While doing this it has continued to produce world-class cinema, as presented in the work of popular actor and director Nikita Mikhailkov in such films as the Cannes Grand Prize and Academy Award–winning *Burnt by the Sun* (1994).

Everything about Yar is over the top, from the vast, gilded interior to the traditional Russian menu to the Moulin Rouge–style dancing girls. The thematic show is infamous for its elaborate costumes. The old-fashioned Russian food is pretty elaborate, too.

RUSSIAN NATIONAL DANCE SHOW

Map pp60–1

☎ 495-234 6373; www.nationalrussianshow.ru; pr Mira 150, Hotel Cosmos; tickets R1400; ⏰ 7.30pm Jun-Sep; Ⓜ VDNKh

The Kostroma Dance Company puts on quite a show, with 50 performers, dozens of ensembles and 300 costumes. It amounts to a history of Russian song and dance. Summer months only.

THEATRE

Due to the language barrier, drama and comedy are less alluring prospects for non–Russian speakers than are music and dance. Nonetheless, Moscow has a long tradition in theatre, which remains vibrant today. The capital has around 40 professional, and countless amateur, theatres, staging a wide range of plays – contemporary and classic, Russian and foreign. Most performances are in Russian.

Tickets are available at the theatre box offices, which are open from 11am or noon daily until showtime (normally about 7pm), usually with a break for lunch. The cheapest seats are usually around R100, but even prime seats are usually less than R500. For more on Russian theatre, see p50.

STANISLAVSKY'S METHODS

In 1898, over an 18-hour restaurant lunch, actor-director Konstantin Stanislavsky and playwright-director Vladimir Nemirovich-Danchenko founded the Moscow Art Theatre as the forum for method acting. The theatre is known by its Russian initials, MKhT, short for Moskovsky Khudozhestvenny Teatr.

More than just providing another stage, the Art Theatre adopted a 'realist' approach, which stressed truthful portrayal of characters and society, teamwork by the cast (not relying on stars) and respect for the writer. 'We declared war on all the conventionalities of the theatre…in the acting, the properties, the scenery, or the interpretation of the play,' Stanislavsky later wrote.

This treatment of *The Seagull* rescued playwright Anton Chekhov from despair after the play had flopped in St Petersburg. *Uncle Vanya*, *Three Sisters* and *The Cherry Orchard* all premiered in the MKhT. Gorky's *The Lower Depths* was another success. In short, the theatre revolutionised Russian drama.

Method acting's influence in Western theatre has been enormous. In the USA Stanislavsky's theories are, and have been, the primary source of study for many actors, including such greats as Stella Adler, Marlon Brando, Sanford Meisner, Lee Strasberg, Harold Clurman and Gregory Peck.

MKhT (below), now technically called the Chekhov Moscow Art Theatre, still stages regular performances of Chekhov's work, among other plays.

FOMENKO STUDIO THEATRE Map p107

☎ 499-249 1136; www.fomenko.theatre.ru; Kutuzovsky prosp 30/32; M Kutuzovskaya

The theatre world is talking about Pyotr Fomenko. Ever since the founding of his theatre in 1988, he has been known for his experimental productions, which used to take place in a run-down old cinema house. In 2008, Fomenko moved his troupe into fancy new digs overlooking the Moscow River – a marble and glass beauty built by architect Sergei Gnedovsky.

LENKOM THEATRE Map pp88–9

☎ 495-699 9668, box office 495-699 0708; www.lenkom.ru, in Russian; ul Malaya Dmitrovka 6; tickets R200-2000; box office noon-3pm & 4-7pm; M Pushkinskaya

The Lenkom isn't the most glamorous theatre, but it's widely considered to have the strongest acting troupe in the country. The flashy productions and lots of musicals that are performed here keep non-Russian speakers entertained.

MALY THEATRE Map pp88–9

☎ 495-623 2621; Teatralnaya pl 1/6; M Teatralnaya

'Maly' means small, meaning smaller than the Bolshoi across the street. Actually, these names date back to the time when there were only two theatres in town: the opera theatre was always called the 'Bolshoi' while the drama theatre was the 'Maly'. This elegant theatre, founded in 1824, mainly features performances of 19th-century works by Ostrovsky and the like, many of which premiered here back in the day.

MOSCOW ART THEATRE Map pp88–9

MKhT; ☎ 495-629 8760; http://art.theatre.ru, in Russian; Kamergersky per 3; box office noon-7pm; M Teatralnaya

Often called the most influential theatre in Europe, this is where method acting was founded over 100 years ago, by Stanislavsky and Nemirovich-Danchenko (see the boxed text, above). Besides the theatre itself and an acting studio-school, a small museum about the theatre's history is also on site. Watch for English-language versions of Russian classics performed by Studio Six (www.studiosix.nyc.org), an American offspring of MKhT.

PUSHKIN DRAMA THEATRE Map pp88–9

☎ 495-694 1289; www.pushkin.theatre.ru, in Russian; Tverskoy bul 23; box office noon-3pm & 4-7pm; M Pushkinskaya

This 18th-century theatre sits at the heart of romantic Tverskoy bul. The strategy employed by the theatre's artistic director Roman Kozak is to attract established directors to the large stage, while using the small stage to showcase young, up-and-coming names. The result is a diverse repertoire.

SATIRIKON THEATRE Map pp60–1

☎ 495-602 6583; www.satirikon.ru, in Russian; Sheremetyevskaya ul 8; tickets R100-1500; box office 11am-8pm; M Rizhskaya

Boasting one of Moscow's most talented theatre producers, Konstantin Raikin, as well as a host of big-name directors, the Satirikon earned a reputation in the early 1990s with its outrageously expensive production of the *Threepenny Opera*. It has since broken its own record for expenditure with *Chantecler,* which featured ducks, cockerels and hens dancing on stage. From Rizhskaya metro take any trolleybus to the Kinoteatr Gavana stop and follow the crowds.

TAGANKA THEATRE Map pp128–9
☎ 495-915 1217; www.taganka.org, in Russian; ul Zemlyanoy val 76; Ⓜ Taganskaya
This legendary theatre is famous for its rebellious director, Yury Lyubimov, and the unruly actor Vladimir Vysotsky. During the 1980s, in response to his provocative plays, Lyubimov was exiled to London and had his citizenship revoked. These days he's back in Moscow and continues to stage top-notch contemporary productions.

CHILDREN'S THEATRE
Cultural instruction starts at a young age in Moscow, with many companies and performances geared specifically towards young kids. Performances are almost always in Russian, but at that age the language of fun is universal. Performances are usually in the afternoons.

DUROV ANIMAL THEATRE Map pp84–5
☎ 495-631 3047; www.ugolokdurova.ru; ul Durova 4; tickets R150-600; ☯ show times vary, 11am-5pm Wed-Sun; Ⓜ Prospekt Mira
Dedushka Durov (Grandpa Durov) founded this zany theatre for kids as a humane alternative to the horrible treatment of animals he saw at the circus. His shows feature mostly domestic animals, including cats and dogs, farm animals and the occasional bear. His most popular show is *Railway for Mice,* and guided tours of the museum give kids a closer look at the railway.

KUKLACHEV CAT THEATRE Map p107
☎ 499-249 2907; Kutuzovsky pr 25; tickets R200-700; ☯ noon, 2pm or 4pm Thu-Sun; Ⓜ Kutuzovskaya
At this unusual theatre, acrobatic cats do all kinds of stunts for the audience's

delight. Director Yury Kuklachev says: 'We do not use the word "train" here because it implies forcing an animal to do something, and you cannot force cats to do anything they don't want to. We *play* with the cats.'

MOSCOW CHILDREN'S MUSICAL THEATRE Map pp60–1
☎ 495-930 5240; www.teatr-sats.ru; pr Vernadskogo 5; tickets R50-500; ☯ times vary Wed, Fri & Sun; Ⓜ Universitet
Founded by theatre legend Natalya Sats (the official name of the theatre is the Natalya Sats Moscow Children's Theatre) in 1965, this was the country's first children's theatre. Sats, apparently, was the inspiration for Prokofiev's famous rendition of *Peter and the Wolf,* which is still among the best and most popular performances at the children's theatre. All performances staged here are highly entertaining and educational, as actors appear in costume before the show and talk with the children.

OBRAZTSOV PUPPET THEATRE & MUSEUM Map pp88–9
☎ 495-699 7972; www.puppet.ru; Sadovaya-Samotechnaya ul 3; adult R300-1000, child R200-600; ☯ box office 11am-2.30pm & 3.30-7pm; Ⓜ Tsvetnoy Bulvar
The country's largest puppet theatre performs colourful Russian folk tales and adapted classical plays. Kids can get up close and personal with the incredible puppets at the museum, which holds a collection of over 3000.

CIRCUS
The circus has long been a favourite form of entertainment for Russians young and old (see p50 for more information). Moscow has two separate circuses, putting on glittering shows for Muscovites of all ages. The shows performed by both companies usually mix dance, cabaret and rock music with animals and acrobats. Performance schedules are subject to change.

BOLSHOI CIRCUS ON VERNADSKOGO Map pp60–1
☎ 495-930 0300; www.bolshoicircus.ru; pr Vernadskogo 7; tickets R100-1000; ☯ shows 7pm Wed, Fri & Sun, 3pm Sat & Sun; Ⓜ Universitet

This huge circus has five rings and holds 3400 spectators. The company includes hundreds of performers, from acrobats to animals. It is a great spectacle that is certain to entertain and amaze.

NIKULIN CIRCUS ON TSVETNOY BULVAR Map pp88–9

☎ 495-625 8970; www.circusnikulin.ru; Tsvetnoy bul 13; tickets R250-2000; ⊙ shows 7pm Thu-Mon & 2.30pm Sat; Ⓜ Tsvetnoy Bulvar

Founded in 1880, this smaller circus is now named after beloved actor and clown Yury Nikulin (1921–97), who performed at the studio here for many years. Unlike performances seen at most traditional circuses, Nikulin's shows centre on a given theme, which serves to add some cohesion to the productions. But the gist is the same – there are lots of trapeze artists, tightrope walkers and performing animals.

top picks

- *Banya* at **Sanduny Baths** (p196)
- Bike riding at **Vorobyovy Gory Nature Preserve** (p199)
- Ice skating at **Gorky Park** (p198)
- Frolicking at **Kva-kva Park** (p199)
- Watching Spartak at **Luzhinki Sports Palace** (p200)
- Sunbathing and socialising at **Beach Club** (p198)

SPORTS & ACTIVITIES

Traditionally, physical fitness is not exactly a priority in Russia. Exercise was always reserved for sportspeople and soldiers, while somebody running on the street was invariably trying to catch a bus.

As in all areas of life, however, times are changing in this workout underworld. Russians – some of them, at least – are discovering the joys of health and wellness, not to mention the fun of an active lifestyle.

HEALTH & FITNESS

The number of gyms and fitness centres in Moscow is growing, but these private clubs are generally out of the price range of everyday middle-class Russians. Whether for reasons financial or cultural, attendance at such facilities is much lower than in the West. The same is not true of the Russian *banya*, or bathhouse, which is still a popular way for Russians to relax and socialise. It is a uniquely Russian activity that all visitors should experience.

BANYA

What better way to cope with Moscow than to have it steamed, washed and beaten out of you? And nothing beats winter like the *banya*. Less hot but more humid than a sauna, the Russian bath sweats out all impurity, cleansing body and soul.

Enter the steam room, or *parilka*, stark naked (yes, the *banya* is normally segregated by gender). Bathers can control the temperature – or at least increase it – by ladling water onto the hot rocks. You might add a few drops of eucalyptus to infuse the steam with scent. Then sit back and watch the mercury rise. To eliminate toxins and improve circulation, bathers beat each other with a bundle of birch branches, known as *veniki*.

When you can't take the heat, retreat. A public *banya* allows access to a plunge pool, usually filled with ice-cold water. The contrast in temperature is invigorating, energising and purifying.

A *banya* is not complete without a table spread with snacks, or at least a thermos of tea. And just when you think you have recovered, it's time to repeat the process. As they say in Russia, '*s lyokum parom*' (easy steaming).

A few old-fashioned *bani* are recommended below. Some also have private *bani*, which can be rented for a small group. See also Day Spas (opposite) for facilities that may have a sauna or *banya* on site.

BANYA ON PRESNYA Map pp96–7
☎ men 495-255 5306, women 495-253 8690; Stolyarny per 7; general admission R700-800; ☻ 8am-8pm Wed-Mon, noon-8pm Tue; Ⓜ Ulitsa 1905 Goda
Lacking the old-fashioned, decadent atmosphere of the Sanduny Baths (below), this new, clean, efficient place nonetheless provides a first-rate *banya* experience.

SANDUNY BATHS Map pp84–5
☎ private 495-628 4633, general 495-625 4631; www.sanduny.ru; Neglinnaya ul 14; private room per hr from R1300, general admission per 2hr R600-800; ☻ 8am-10pm; Ⓜ Chekhovskaya

---

EASY STEAMING

The dos and don'ts of the *banya*:

- Do take advantage of the plunge pool (or at least the cold shower, if there is no pool on site). It's important to bring your body temperature back down after being in the *banya*.
- Don't bother with a bathing suit. Most public *bani* are segregated by gender, in which case bathers steam naked. In mixed company, it is customary to wrap yourself in a sheet (provided at the *banya*).
- Do rehydrate in between steams. While it is customary to drink tea, or even beer, it is also important to drink water or juice.
- Don't stop at one! Most bathers will return to the *parilka* anywhere from three to eight times over the course of an hour or two.

Sanduny is the oldest and most luxurious *banya* in the city. The Gothic Room is like a work of art with its rich wood carving, and the main shower room has an aristocratic Roman feel to it. Recommended.

GYMS & POOLS

With the exception of gyms that are affiliated with hotels, most private health clubs do not allow for casual memberships. However, many swimming pools are open to the public, charging a one-time admission fee. Most require bathers to obtain a health certificate prior to going in the water. There is usually an on-site doctor who can provide the necessary paperwork for a small fee (and sometimes without any sort of examination), as long as you look healthy.

CHAIKA SWIMMING POOL Map pp110–11

☎ 499-246 1344; Turchaninov per 1/3; 1hr R400-600, 2hr R600-700, unlimited R1000; ☽ 7am-10pm Mon-Sat, 8.30am-8pm Sun; Ⓜ Park Kultury

Boasting eight lanes and heated to a pleasant 29°C, this 50m open-air pool is an ideal place for swimming laps year-round. It is attached to a training room, so the price of admission also allows access to cardiovascular equipment and weights on site. Kids under 16 are only welcome at designated times, so phone before bringing the little ones along.

HOTEL COSMOS FITNESS CENTRE

Map pp60–1

☎ 495-234 1411; www.hotelcosmos.ru; pr Mira 150; admission R290; ☽ 7am-11pm; Ⓜ VDNKh

The state-of-the-art fitness centre is open to anyone who is willing to pay. The fee gives you access to a 240-sq-metre indoor swimming pool, complete with waterslides, geysers and cascades. The gym is fully equipped with cardio equipment and an aerobics centre with a whole range of courses. This is a fantastic place to drop your kids after an exhausting day of sightseeing.

LUZHNIKI SWIMMING POOL Map pp110–11

☎ 495-637 0764; www.luzhniki.ru; Luzhnetskya nab 24; ☽ 8.30am-8pm; Ⓜ Vorobyovy Gory

The vast complex built for the 1980 Olympic Games includes five swimming pools: two outdoor, two indoor and a kiddie pool. The pools are open year-round and the

water is heated to between 27°C and 29°C. The complex also includes a training room, sauna and tennis courts.

PLANET FITNESS Map pp88–9

☎ 495-933 1124; www.fitness.ru, in Russian; ul Malaya Dmitrovka 6; 8 classes R3000; Ⓜ Chekhovskaya

This chain of private gyms offers a range of fitness classes, including yoga, step-aerobics, Pilates and dance classes. There are six different classes a day, most of them in the evening. There is also cardio equipment and weights on site, although you have to upgrade your membership to take advantage of it. There is another outlet in Arbat (☎ 495-933 7100; Bolshoy Kislovsky per 9; Ⓜ Arbatskaya).

DAY SPAS

An upscale spa might have a Russian *banya* on site; however, a visit to such a facility is a completely different experience – with all of the delicious decadence of indulgence, but none of the democratic charm of the traditional *banya*.

EXPAT SALON Map pp96–7

☎ 495-650 3749; www.expatsalon.ru; Maly Patriarshy per 3; ☽ 9am-9pm; Ⓜ Mayakovskaya

Since this place caters to the expat community, the English-speaking staff is used to dealing with people like you. It offers all kinds of beauty treatments and massage, including hot rocks. There is another location near the Arbat (☎ 495-291 6467; Skartertny per 23; Ⓜ Arbatskaya).

FIRST SPA Map p107

☎ 495-148 9922; www.firstspa.ru; Pobedy pl 2; Ⓜ Park Pobedy

Besides the standard beauty treatments, First Spa has an impressive selection of exfoliation, wraps and massage – most exotically, the honey massage. Sweet! Hydro treatments are also a popular option, ranging from your traditional Turkish *hammam* to the slightly scary looking steam couch.

ACTIVITIES

Ice skating, sledding and skiing are forms of entertainment that date back to the pre-revolutionary period, as the aristocrats found plenty of fun to entertain themselves during

EXTREME MOSCOW

It can be extremely cold in winter; it's extremely expensive at all times. The nightlife is famous for its extreme debauchery. But when it comes to extreme sports, most Muscovites get enough adventure from dodging the Beamers that are trying to park on the footpath. Nonetheless, there are a few hearty souls who are pioneering daredevil sports in Moscow. Here are a few options for the *extreme*-ly adventurous.

Skydiving

If you have an unquenchable desire to jump out of an airplane, head to Kubinka Aerodrom (☎ 8-906-652 5830; www .kubinka.aero, in Russian; tandem jump R5000), about 60km southwest of Moscow. Instructors are members of the eight-time-world-champion Russian skydiving team. Unfortunately they do not speak English so bring a translator.

Ski Jumping

Another option for high flyers is to join Team Vorobey (☎ 8-903-778 2752; www.ski-jumping.ru, in Russian), which offers lessons and other events. Participants take off from the ski jump at Vorobyovy Gory (p132).

Shooting

Think you're a good shot? Hone your skills at the Central Sport Shooting Club (off Map pp60–1; ☎ 495-491 0290; http://cssk.ru, in Russian; Volokolamskoe sh 86; per shot R30-50, per 30min R1200; Ⓜ Tushkinskaya). This shooting range offers an arsenal of five different kinds of revolvers and just as many rifles, all of which look pretty deadly to the untrained eye. Besides the standard 25m and 50m target practice, there is also an interactive computerised training complex (the proverbial 'moving target').

---

the cold winter days. The capital is still a great place to engage in such traditional activities. The younger generation has also discovered the appeals of other more Western activities, such as cycling and in-line skating. It is perhaps not as widespread as in European and American cities, but it is not unusual to see active types speeding along Moscow's sidewalks and streets.

WINTER SPORTS

There's no shortage of winter in Moscow, so take advantage of it. Several indoor and outdoor venues offer the opportunity to rent ice skates and see where all those great Russian figure skaters come from. In addition to the venues listed below, you can also rent ice skates at Chistye Prudy (p78) and in Izmaylovsky Park (p131).

EVROPEYSKY SKATING RINK Map p107

☎ 495-229 6187; Evropeysky Shopping Centre, Kievskaya pl 1; adult/child per hr R360/240; 🕙 10am-1.30pm Sun-Thu, 11.30pm-6am Fri & Sat; Ⓜ Kievskaya

The top floor of the Evropeysky Shopping Centre contains an indoor ice rink, with big windows looking out at the Moscow city skyline. You'll often see young figure-skaters-in-training, practicing their spins and twirls. On weekends, come late at night for a party on the ice.

GORKY PARK SKATING RINK Map pp120–1

Park Kultury; ☎ 495-237 1266; ul Krymsky val; admission adult/child R80/20; 🕙 10am-10pm; Ⓜ Park Kultury

When the temperatures drop, Gorky Park turns into a winter wonderland. The ponds are flooded, turning the park into the city's biggest ice-skating rink. Tracks are created for cross-country skiers to circumnavigate the park. Ice skates and cross-country skis are available to rent (R100 to R200 per hour). Bring your passport.

SWIMMING & SUNBATHING

If you are interested in swimming laps – as in exercising – see Gyms & Pools (p197). If you're interested in frolicking in the waves and perhaps soaking up some sun, Moscow offers a few surprises.

BEACH CLUB Map pp60–1

☎ 495-979 9090; http://beach-club.ru; Leningradskoe sh 39; Ⓜ Vodny Stadion

When New Russians go to the beach, they might go to the Costa del Sol or the French Riviera, or they might go to the Beach Club at Vodny Stadion. A surprisingly beautiful white-sand beach flanks the Moscow River, furnished with lounge chairs, beach umbrellas and a well-stocked bar. Active types can rent jet skis, play volleyball and even swim. Of course there is a place to dock your yacht.

KVA-KVA PARK off Map pp60–1

☎ 495-258 0683; www.kva-kva.ru, in Russian; XL Shopping Centre, Yaroslavskoe sh; 2hr admission adult R710-1040, child R380-550; ⏰ 10am-10pm; Ⓜ VDNKh

Calling all kids! This huge complex features seven long and winding water slides, a terrific tsunami water ride, waterfalls and wave pools. There is something for everyone here: special pools for younger children have shallow waters and warmer temperatures, while adults can relax and feel the soothing pulse of 150 hydromassage jets. Note: children under the age of 18 must be accompanied by an adult. From VDNKh metro station, take any outward-bound bus to Furazhnaya, which is about 1km past MKAD.

SEREBRYANY BOR off Map pp60–1

While the beautiful people are at the Beach Club, the masses head to Serebryany bor, or 'Silver Forest'. This is a series of lakes and channels on the Moscow River, 20km north of the city centre. This is truly the people's beach. There are areas that are unofficially dedicated to families, gay people, nudists and even disco dancers. Take the metro to Sokol and then ride trolleybus 65 to the end of the line.

CYCLING & IN-LINE SKATING

Moscow is not exactly ideal for bikers. That said, there are a few places in the capital where bikers (and bladers) can go off road.

NESKUCHNY SAD Map pp60–1

Pushkinskaya nab; Ⓜ Leninsky Prospekt

A wide, flat, paved path follows the Moscow River all the way from Gorky Park to Vorobyovy Gory Nature Preserve (right). In the 19th century, this wooded area, which translates as 'not-so-boring garden', contained three country estates, but only a few dilapidated buildings remain. It's a pleasant, peaceful setting for a ride or a roll.

OSTANKINO PARK Map pp60–1

1-ya Ostankinskaya ul; ⏰ 10am-sunset Tue-Sun; Ⓜ VDNKh

The park behind Ostankino Palace is a lovely, car-free space to roll around on your own two wheels. You can also make your way around the vast grounds of the All-Russia Exhibition Centre (p130), which backs

up to the same park. Both bikes and skates are available for rent, either at the entrance to the All-Russia Exhibition Centre or on the grounds of Ostankino Park.

VOROBYOVY GORY NATURE PRESERVE Map p107

☎ 499-739 2708; www.vorobyovy-gory.ru, in Russian; Ⓜ Vorobyovy Gory

Bikes and skates are available to rent at the eastern entrance of this ecopark. The paved path that originates in Neskuchny Sad (left) continues along the river for several kilometres. Brave souls can try riding inland from the river, where the trails are not paved, nor are they flat.

KRYLATSKOYE VELOTREK off Map pp60–1

☎ 495-141 2224; Krylatskaya ul 10; Ⓜ Krylatskoye

If you have access to a car to transport your bicycle, head out to this challenging Olympic course on the Moscow fringe. It's closed to traffic, which is a good thing, as it will require your complete concentration to navigate these hills.

BOWLING & BILLIARDS

Ten-pin bowling has become a popular entertainment option, with vast complexes offering bowling and billiards, as well as bars, video games and, in some cases, dancing.

CHAMPION BOWLING Map pp60–1

☎ 495-747 5000; www.champion.ru, in Russian; Leningradskoe sh 16; bowling per hr R500-1200, billiards per hr R200-500; ⏰ 3pm-6am Mon-Fri, noon-6am Sat & Sun; Ⓜ Voykovskaya; ▣

Champion is a huge complex featuring 10-pin bowling, billiards, karaoke, sushi, big-screen TVs and more. It's easy to suffer from sensory overload, especially with the lights and whistles of nonstop slot machines and a dance floor packed with dooted-up *devushky* (young women).

SPECTATOR SPORTS

Russia's international reputation in sport is well founded, with athletes earning international fame and glory for their success in ice hockey, gymnastics and figure skating. In 2008 football fans watched the Russian national team upset the Netherlands in the European Cup quarter finals, then get knocked out after a hard loss to Spain. Now the country is

MOSKOVSKY FUTBOL *Marc Bennetts*

Moscow sides, and in particular perennial 1990s champion Spartak Moscow, have largely dominated Russian football since the break up of the Soviet Union.

Spartak, managed in their glory years by the wayward football genius of Oleg Romanstev, won the league title nine times between 1992 and 2001, and made a name for itself in Europe with some fine performances in the Champions League and the UEFA Cup. The side's success was largely down to a lucrative sponsorship deal with oil company LUKoil. However, in the New Russia, other clubs have caught up with, and even overtaken, Spartak in both financial and sporting terms. Of the other Moscow sides, CSKA and Lokomotiv are the most successful, the former becoming the first Russian side to win a major European trophy when it lifted the UEFA Cup in 2005. It was sponsored at the time by Roman Abramovich's Sibneft. Cross-town rival Lokomotiv has two league titles to its name since the turn of the decade.

The remaining Moscow teams in the top flight, Dynamo Moscow and FC Moskva, have had less success, although Dynamo are currently challenging for top spot for the first time in years.

Moscow's domination of the national sport was broken in 2007 when Zenit St Petersburg, controlled by state-run energy giant Gazprom, won the championship for the first time. It then followed up on its domestic success by lifting the UEFA Cup and the Super Cup in 2008.

Football in Russia is experiencing a boom at all levels, and the national side, managed by Dutch coach Guus Hiddink, unexpectedly reached the semifinals of Euro 2008. The team's memorable 3-1 victory over Holland in the last eight saw the largest spontaneous celebration in the capital since the conclusion of WWII.

Of the Moscow stadiums, Cherkizovo, home to Lokomotiv and the national team, is the most modern and, thanks to the lack of a running track, also the most traditional. The Luzhniki, which hosted the Champions League final in 2008, is an 80,000-capacity Soviet folly – great when full but depressing and soul-destroying when the crowd is less than 30,000. Dynamo Moscow's crumbling Petrovsky Park is the world's only constructivist-designed stadium. Reconstruction work on the stadium begins in 2009.

Marc Bennetts is the author of Football Dynamo: Modern Russia & the People's Game.

looking forward to the 2014 Winter Olympics, which will take place in Sochi, in southern Russia.

FOOTBALL

The most popular spectator sport in Russia is football (soccer), and five Moscow teams play in Russia's premier league (Vysshaya Liga). Currently, football is enjoying a boom, pumped up by large sponsorship deals with Russian big business. Lukoil has thrown its considerable financial weight behind FC Spartak (www.spartak.com), Moscow's most successful team. The team's nickname is Myaso, or 'Meat', because the team was sponsored by the collective farm association during the Soviet era. Since the start of the Russian League in 1990, Spartak has been the Champion of Russia nine times and runner up three times (2005 to 2007).

Other Moscow teams in the league are two-time winner FC Lokomotiv (www.fclm.ru), three-time winner Central Sports Club of the Army (CSKA; www.pfc-cska.com), FC Dynamo (www.fcdynamo.ru) and FC Moskva (www.fcmoscow.ru). These days, though, Russia's most famous football club is 'Chel-sky', billionaire Roman Abramovich's highly successful entry in the English premier league.

Despite (or maybe because of) the sport's popularity, running a soccer club in Russia has become a risky business – in the post-Soviet era, seven soccer officials have been the targets of assassination attempts. Corruption is believed to be rife, with match fixing a particular problem.

LUZHNIKI SPORTS PALACE Map pp110–11

☎ 495-785 9717; www.luzhniki.ru; Luzhnetskaya nab 24; Ⓜ Sportivnaya

Moscow's largest stadium seats up to 80,000 people and gleams from its recent reconstruction. Luzhniki is home to Torpedo and Spartak, both of which are teams in Russia's premier football league. This stadium is part of a larger complex that was the main venue for the 1980 Olympics. Besides the giant stadium, Luzhniki includes a collection of swimming pools (p197), ice-hockey rink, tennis courts and other facilities, which are used by casual and professional athletes alike.

DYNAMO STADIUM Map pp60–1

☎ 495-612 7172; Leningradsky pr 36; Ⓜ Dinamo

Of the five Moscow teams that play in Russia's premier football league, both CSKA and Dynamo play at Dynamo stadium. However, at the time of research, a new state-of-the-art stadium was being constructed for the Army team.

LOKOMOTIV STADIUM Map pp60–1
☎ 499-161 4283; Bolshaya Cherkizovskaya ul 125; Ⓜ Cherkizovskaya
Reconstructed in 2002, this smaller stadium hosts its namesake team, Lokomotiv, which plays in the premier football league.

ICE HOCKEY
After the 2007–08 season, the Russian Super League was disbanded and replaced by the Continental Hockey League (KHL). Three non-Russian teams (from Belarus, Latvia and Kazakhstan) joined the league during this first year, with more international teams expected in the future. Moscow's main entrant in the KHL is HC CSKA (www.cska-hockey.ru), or the Army team. HC CSKA has won more Soviet championships and European cups than any other team in history. In the 1990s, many players from CSKA made their way to the National Hockey League in the USA and led the Detroit Red Wings to two Stanley Cup victories.

HC Dinamo (www.dynamo.ru) plays at Luzhniki Sports Palace (opposite). As recently as 2006, Dinamo won the European Champions Cup.

HC Spartak (www.spartak.ru) has suffered from a debilitating lack of finances. In the past decade, Spartak has fluctuated between the Russian Super League and the lower-level *vyshaya liga* (Premier League). In 2006–07 the team was even temporary disbanded, but it is back for the inaugural KHL season. Spartak normally plays at Sokolniki Sports Palace (below).

CSKA ARENA Map pp60–1
☎ 495-225 2600; Leningradsky pr 39A; Ⓜ Aeroport
This 5500-person arena was built in the lead up to the 1980 Olympics, when it hosted the basketball tournament. These days it is home to Moscow's most successful basketball team and the city's most successful ice-hockey team.

SOKOLNIKI SPORTS PALACE Map pp60–1
☎ 495-645 2065; www.sokolniki.info, in Russian; ul Sokolnichesky val 1B; Ⓜ Sokolniki
In the midst of Sokolniki Park, this ice rink is the home of HC Spartak. Until 1973, it was an outdoor arena. These days the 5000-person indoor area fills up for Spartak games and other ice-skating events.

BASKETBALL
Men's basketball has dropped in popularity since its days of Olympic glory in the 1980s. But Moscow's top basketball team, CSKA (www.cskabasket.com), still does well in European league play. Often called 'Red Army', CSKA made it to the final four of Euroleague in 2004 and 2005 (undefeated in the regular season), before winning it all in 2006 and again in 2008. Only Real Madrid has won more European titles than CKSA. CKSA plays at the arena of the same name (left).

The other Moscow team is MBC Dinamo (http://dynamobasket.com), which has a fairly spotty history in terms of performance. But in recent years the team has made an impressive commitment to recruit some of the league's top players.

DINAMO SPORTS PALACE IN KRYLATSKY off Map pp60–1
☎ 499-726 4615; www.baskethall.ru; Ostrovnaya ul 7; Ⓜ Krylatskoye
This brand new, 5000-person sports centre was built in 2006 for MBC Dinamo. Resembling a giant spaceship, the state-of-the-art facility gives spectators two humungous screens to watch and a magnificent central cube-shaped scoreboard. Take bus 832 from the Krylatskoye metro station.

TENNIS
Anna Kournikova attracted the world's attention to Russian tennis, even though she became better known for her photogenic legs than her ripping backhand. More recently, Wimbledon champion Maria Sharapova has led a cohort of young Russian women who figure highly in the game. Moscow native Elena Dementieva is a world-ranked player who brought home a gold medal from the Beijing Olympics in 2008. US Open champ Marat Safin remains one of the most explosive stars on the men's circuit.

The Kremlin Cup (www.kremlincup.ru) is an international tennis tournament held in Moscow every year (see p23). In recent years, home-grown heroes Elena Dementieva, Marat Safin, Igor Andreev and Anastasia Myskina have taken home prizes from this prestigious event.

lonely planet Hotels & Hostels

Want more sleeping recommendations than we could ever pack into this little ol' book? Craving more detail – including extended reviews and photographs? Want to read reviews by other travellers and be able to post your own? Just make your way over to **lonelyplanet.com/hotels** and check out our thorough list of independent reviews, then reserve your room simply and securely.

SLEEPING

top picks

- Golden Apple (p209)
- East-West Hotel (p209)
- Assambleya Nikitskaya Hotel (p210)
- Ozerkovskaya Hotel (p212)
- Danilovskaya Hotel (p213)
- Sokol Exclusive Hostel (p214)
- Home from Home Hostel (p211)
- Nova House (p207)

Moscow is not a cheap place to stay. In fact, at the time of research, it was the world's most expensive place to stay. While many international luxury hotels have rushed to fill the void in accommodation, smaller, simpler and more affordable hotels are few and far between. Fortunately, a slew of hostels have opened around the city in recent years, so budget travellers have plenty of options. It is only midrange travellers who are left high and dry, stranded in old Soviet-era properties that have weathered the transition to a market economy with varying degrees of grace.

Staying within the Garden Ring guarantees easy access to major sights and plenty of dining and entertainment options. Tverskoy and Arbat are particularly lively districts, but Basmanny and Zamoskvorechie are also lovely. If you do find yourself far from the centre (which may be the case if you are on a tighter budget), look for easy access to the metro. An underground ride will whisk you from almost any stop into the centre in 20 minutes or less.

ACCOMMODATION STYLES

The most visible type of accommodation in Moscow is the palatial four- or five-star hotel that has proliferated in the past few years. Priced for the business market, they may be prohibitively expensive for some travellers (although many offer far better deals through travel agents and hotel websites).

At the other end of the spectrum is the Soviet *gostinitsa* (hotel). Some of these old-style institutions are now slowly adapting to the needs of the modern traveller. Many of these hotels have undertaken some degree of renovation. As a result, the quality of rooms can vary widely, and prices usually do, too (even within the same hotel).

In recent years, some smaller private hotels have opened in Moscow. Many are housed in historic buildings, and the smaller size means they offer more intimacy than the larger chain hotels. The level of comfort and service at these smaller hotels is not guaranteed. The high price – and it is higher than you expect – does not translate to five-star quality.

In recent years, dozens of hostels have opened in Moscow, much to the delight of budget travellers. Many have been converted from flats or *communalky* (communal apartments), so they are often located in innocuous, unmarked buildings on residential streets. All hostels offer English-speaking staff, internet access, linens, kitchens and laundry facilities. Hostel prices do not usually include breakfast.

CHECK-IN & CHECK-OUT TIMES

Most hotels will allow you to check in as early as you arrive, as long as the room is available. Check out is usually at noon, un-less you pay for a *sutki* (24-hour period), in which case you can check out at the same time that you checked in, whether at 6am or at 6pm.

LONGER-TERM RENTALS

Moscow real estate is among the most expensive in the world, which means you'll pay the price if you want to rent a flat in Moscow. Finding a flat usually requires working with an agency, which normally charges the renter a fee of one month's rent. The best source of information about apartments is the expat internet forums (p24). Another option is Flatmates.ru (www.flatmates.ru/eng), a site for travellers looking for somebody to share short- or long-term accommodation in Russia.

RESERVATIONS

Reservations are highly recommended. Although Moscow has plenty of hotel rooms, there is a definite shortage of affordable rooms, and a veritable dearth of affordable, comfortable rooms. Unfortunately, some old-style hotels still charge a reservation fee, usually 20% but sometimes as much as 50% of the first night's tariff.

BOOK YOUR STAY ONLINE

For more accommodation reviews and recommendations by Lonely Planet authors, check out the online booking service at www.lonelyplanet.com. You'll find the true, insider low down on the best places to stay. Reviews are thorough and independent. Best of all, you can book online.

PRICE GUIDE

$$$	over R10,000 per night
$$	R3000-10,000 per night
$	under R3000

ROOM RATES

Moscow doesn't provide much value for money when it comes to the hospitality industry. Luxury hotels are indeed top notch, but they have prices to match. Expect to pay upwards of R10,000 for a night at one of Moscow's top-end hotels. If you can forgo a degree of luxury, you can stay in a classy, comfortable and centrally located hotel for R8000 to R10,000 for a double. Midrange travellers can also choose from a range of hotels outside the centre, which offer decent rooms and amenities for R4000 to R8000 a double. This wide-ranging category includes a variety of Soviet-era properties that have not come completely into the 21st century, though many are very atmospheric (as reflected in the price). Budget accommodation is usually dorm-style, although there are a few private rooms available for less than R3000.

The hotel market in Moscow caters primarily to business travellers, as you can tell by the ridiculously high prices. It also means that accommodation is harder to find during the week than on weekends, and prices may be lower on Friday and Saturday nights. Prices do not generally fluctuate seasonally, although there are certainly exceptions. All prices listed in this chapter include breakfast, unless otherwise indicated.

Most hotels accept credit cards, but most hostels do not. Many hotels set their prices in *uslovie yedenitsiy* (often abbreviated as 'y.e.'), or standard units, which is usually equivalent to euros. Prices in this chapter are quoted in roubles, as you will always be required to pay in roubles. Prices listed here include the 18% value-added tax (VAT), but not the 5% sales tax, which is charged mainly at luxury hotels.

KREMLIN & KITAY GOROD

Within walking distance from Moscow's most famous sights, this central part of the city is certainly prime real estate. Unfortunately, with the reconstruction of the Hotel Moskva and the demolition of the Hotel Rossiya, only top-end options remain in the area. And 'top end' in Moscow's means the tippety top – prepare for prices to rival anything in the world.

FOUR SEASONS HOTEL MOSKVA

Map p66   Hotel $$$
www.fourseasons.com; Manezhnaya pl;
Ⓜ Okhotny Ryad

The story goes that Stalin was shown two possible designs for the Hotel Moskva on Manezhnaya pl. Not realising they were alternatives, he approved both. The builders

FIND A FLAT

Hotels in Moscow could easily break your bank. In response to the shortage of affordable accommodation, some entrepreneurial Muscovites have begun renting out flats on a short-term basis. Flats are equipped with kitchens and sometimes other useful amenities such as internet access. Often, a good-sized flat is available for the price of a hotel room, or less. It is an ideal solution for travellers in a group, who can split the cost.

Apartments are around €80 to €100 per night. Expect to pay more for fully renovated, Western-style apartments. Although there are usually discounts for longer stays, they are not significant, so these services are not ideal for long-term renters.

- www.cheap-moscow.com Heed the disclaimers, but this site has loads of listings for apartments to rent directly from the owner.
- www.enjoymoscow.com Rick's apartments are off the Garden Ring between Sukharevskaya and Tsvetnoy Bulvar metro stations. Studios start at US$135, with two-bedroom apartments about US$215.
- www.evans.ru Caters mainly to long-term renters, but also offers some apartments for US$150 to US$250 per night.
- www.hofa.ru Apartments from €62 per night and a variety of home-stay programs.
- www.moscow4rent.com Most flats are centrally located, with internet access, satellite TV and unlimited international phone calls. Prices start at US$150 per night.
- www.moscowapartments.net Not-too-fancy but fully furnished apartments for €85 to €100.

did not dare point out his error, and so built half the hotel in constructivist style and half in Stalinist style. The incongruous result became a familiar and beloved feature of the Moscow landscape, even gracing the label of Stolichnaya vodka bottles. After years of rumours, the infamous Hotel Moskva was finally demolished in 2003, one in a long list of Soviet-era institutions to bite the dust. At the time of research, Moscow was anticipating the opening of a new Four Seasons Hotel on this site. Happily, the new, high-class hotel is expected to re-create its predecessor's architectural quirks. The more things change…

HOTEL METROPOL Map p66 Historic Hotel $$$
☎ 499-501 7800; www.metmos.ru; Teatralny proezd 1/4; s/d from R12,744/14,868; Ⓜ Teatralnaya; ⊗ ⊠ ▯ ▣
Nothing short of an Art Nouveau masterpiece, the historic Metropol brings an artistic touch to every nook and cranny, from the spectacular exterior (see the boxed text, below) to the grand lobby to the individually decorated rooms. The place dates to 1907, so rooms are small by today's standards; if you need space, upgrade to a suite.

BASMANNY

The serene residential area surrounding Chistye Prudy is one of Moscow's most attractive neighbourhoods. Here you will find a handful of affordable accommodation options within walking distance of the city's main attractions, with the old streets of Kitay Gorod at your doorstep. But this area offers its own pleasant ambience, as well as some worthy dining and entertainment options, that make it enticing in its own right.

top picks

ROOMS WITH A VIEW

- **Hotel Baltschug Kempinski** (p212) Awake to sunlight glinting off the Kremlin domes.
- **Le Royal Meridien National** (p209) Watch the goings-on in Red Square from your hotel room.
- **Swissôtel Krasnye Holmy** (p212) Admire the ever-changing Moscow skyline.
- **Ritz-Carlton Moscow** (p209) Wraparound views of the Kremlin and the Cathedral of Christ the Saviour.
- **Hotel Ukraina** (p211) Once the tallest building in Moscow.
- **Korston Hotel** (p214) See the city from atop Sparrow Hills.

KAZAKH EMBASSY HOTEL
Map pp80–1 Hotel $$
☎ 495-608 0994; hotel@kazembassy.ru; Chistoprudny bul 3; s/d R5500/7400; Ⓜ Chistye Prudy; ▯
Caters – as you might guess – to guests and workers of the nearby Kazakh embassy. But anyone can stay in this grand, modern building that fronts the prestigious Boulevard Ring. The recent revamp has brought rooms into line with a generic international style.

HOTEL SVERCHKOV Map pp80–1 Minihotel $$
☎ 495-625 4978; Sverchkov per 8; sverchkov8@mail.ru; s/d from R3800/4400; Ⓜ Chistye Prudy
On a quiet residential lane, this is a tiny 11-room hotel in a graceful 18th-century building. The hallways are lined with green-leafed plants, and paintings by local artists adorn the walls. Though rooms have old-style bathrooms and faded furniture,

---

MAMONTOV'S METROPOL

The Hotel Metropol, among Moscow's finest examples of Art Nouveau architecture, is another contribution by famed philanthropist and patron of the arts, Savva Mamontov. The decorative panel on the hotel's central facade, facing Teatralny proezd, is based on a sketch by the artist Vrubel. It depicts the legend of the Princess of Dreams, in which a troubadour falls in love with a kind and beautiful princess and travels across the seas to find her. He falls ill during the voyage and is near death when he finds his love. The princess embraces him, but he dies in her arms. Naturally, the princess reacts to his death by renouncing her worldly life. The ceramic panels were made at the pottery workshop at Mamontov's Abramtsevo estate (p221).

The ceramic work on the side of the hotel facing Teatralnaya pl is by the artist Golovin. The script is a quote from Nietzsche: 'Again the same story: when you build a house you notice that you have learned something'. During the Soviet era, these wise words were replaced with something more appropriate for the time: 'Only the dictatorship of the proletariat can liberate mankind from the oppression of capitalism'. Lenin, of course.

this place is a rarity for its intimacy and homey feel.

NAPOLEON HOSTEL Map pp80–1   Hostel $
☎ 495-628 6695; www.napoleonhostel.com; Maly Zlatoustinsky per 2, 4th fl; dm R800-1000; Ⓜ Kitay-Gorod; 🖥 ✂

Ignore the decrepit entryway and climb to the 4th floor, where you'll find a fully renovated hostel. The light-filled rooms have six to 10 wooden bunks, for a total of 47 beds (but only two toilets and two showers – do the maths), plus a clean kitchen and a comfy common room that is well stocked with board games and a plasma TV. Helpful staff are on hand all the time (which is not the case in some of the smaller hostels).

COMRADE HOSTEL Map pp80–1   Hostel $
☎ 495-628 3126; www.comradehostel.com; ul Maroseyka 11; dm R840; Ⓜ Kitay-Gorod; 🖥 ✂

It's hard to find this tiny place – go into the courtyard and look for entrance No 3, where you might spot a computer-printed sign in the 3rd-floor window. Inside, there is a great, welcoming atmosphere, although the place is packed. Ten to 12 beds are squeezed into the dorm rooms, plus mattresses on the floor if need be. There is not really any common space, except the small foyer and kitchen, but everybody seems to get along like comrades.

NOVA HOUSE Map pp80–1   Hostel $
☎ 495-623 4659; novahostel@nm.ru; Devyatkin per 4, apt 6; dm R680, d R2600-2800; Ⓜ Kitay-Gorod; 🖥 ✂

It's hard to say who at Nova House is friendlier: Oleg, the owner; or Vasya, the loveable resident cat. Both ensure a homey atmosphere, enhanced by the funky contemporary decor, mural-painted ceilings and walls, and a beautiful upright piano in the common living room. Rooms are in two adjacent flats (one is cat free), each with its own kitchen, bathroom and laundry facilities. Bonus: bikes!

TRANS-SIBERIAN HOSTEL
Map pp80–1   Hostel $
☎ 495-916 2030; www.transsiberianhostel .com; Barashevsky per 12; dm R630-700, d R1750; Ⓜ Kitay-Gorod; 🖥 ✂

If you can snag one of the two double rooms in this tiny hostel, you're getting one of the capital's best bargains: you won't find a private room at this price anywhere else in central Moscow. There are also two dorm rooms, one with four heavy wooden bunks and one with eight. The only common space is the kitchen, but it's spacious and modern. A train-themed decor brightens the place up, starting from the moment you step off the street.

KRASNOSELSKY & MESHCHANSKY

The small streets around Kuznetsky most are home to some of Moscow's swankiest hotels, but even out near Komsomolskaya pl, guests can live a life of luxury at the new Hilton Leningradskaya.

ARARAT PARK HYATT Map pp84–5   Hotel $$$
☎ 495-783 1234; www.moscow.park.hyatt.com; Neglinnaya ul 4; r from R33,000; Ⓜ Teatralnaya; ✂ 🖥 ✂ 📶

This deluxe hotel is an archetype of contemporary design: its glass-and-marble facade is sleek and stunning, yet blends effortlessly with the classical and baroque buildings in the surrounding area. The graceful, modern appearance extends inside to the atrium-style lobby and the luxurious rooms. Guests enjoy every imaginable amenity, not the least of which are the Italian marble bathrooms, each with a separate shower and tub. The service in the Ararat Park is top-notch (twice-daily housekeeping!). Of the hotel's many restaurants, don't miss the Conservatory Lounge, which offers panoramic views of Teatralnaya pl.

HOTEL SAVOY Map pp84–5   Historic Hotel $$$
☎ 495-620 8500; www.savoy.ru; ul Rozhdestvenka 3; r from R21,000; Ⓜ Lubyanka; ✂ 🖥 ✂ 📶

Built in 1912, the Savoy maintains an atmosphere of prerevolutionary privilege for its guests. It is more intimate than the other luxury hotels, with just 70 elegant rooms. After a recent renovation, all rooms are equipped with marble bathrooms, king-sized beds and wi-fi access. The state-of-the-art health club includes a glass-domed 20m swimming pool, complete with geysers and cascades to refresh tired bodies. Look for significant discounts during holiday periods and in summer months.

HILTON LENINGRADSKAYA HOTEL

Map pp84–5   Historic Hotel $$$

☎ 495-627 5550; www.hilton.com; Kalanchevskaya ul 21/40; d from R19,000; Ⓜ Komsomolskaya; ⊠ 🖵 ✕ 🐾 ♿

Occupying one of the iconic Stalinist skyscrapers (see the boxed text, p51), the old Leningradskaya Hotel has a new life, thanks to Hilton and its multiyear upgrade (finally completed in 2008). Hilton has maintained the Soviet grandiosity in the lobby, but updated the rooms with contemporary design and state-of-the-art amenities. This is the most convenient option if you are arriving or departing by train, due to its proximity to three stations. This beauty overlooks Komsomolskaya pl, in all its chaotic, commotion-filled glory.

SRETENSKAYA HOTEL Map pp84–5   Hotel $$$

☎ 495-933 5544; www.hotel-sretenskaya.ru; ul Sretenka 15; s/d R11,220/11,880; Ⓜ Sukharevskaya; ⊠ 🖵 ✕

Special for its relatively small size and friendly atmosphere, the Sretenka boasts a romantic, Russian atmosphere. Rooms have high ceilings and tasteful, traditional decor. This place is particularly welcoming in winter, when you can warm your bones in the sauna, or soak up some sun in the tropical 'winter garden'. Discounts are available on weekends.

HOTEL VOLGA Map pp84–5   Hotel $$

☎ 495-783 9109; www.hotel-volga.ru; Bolshaya Spasskaya ul 4; s/d R5950/6475; Ⓜ Sukharevskaya; ⊠ 🖵 ✕

This characterless but comfortable hotel complex, run by Moscow's city government, is on a quiet corner northeast of the centre. The location is just outside the Garden Ring and not far from the metro. Most of the rooms are actually suites with several rooms or a kitchen, making the Volga ideal for small groups or families.

SUHAREVKA MINI-HOTEL

Map pp84–5   Minihotel & Hostel $

☎ +7-910-420 3446; www.suharevkahotel.ru; Bolshaya Sukharevskaya pl 16/18; dm R650-850, d R2500; Ⓜ Sukharevskaya; 🖵 ✕

Making the transition from hostel to minihotel, this place occupies two side-by-side flats in a big block on the Garden Ring. The 'hostel side' is cramped and cluttered, with no real common space. Some travellers will

appreciate the relative spaciousness and serenity across the hall on the 'hotel side'. Although the private rooms are also small, they evoke an atmosphere of old Moscow with high ceilings, heavy drapes and rich fabrics.

TVERSKOY

Busy, bustling Tverskaya ul, and the smaller streets around it, are home to a slew of places to stay, from elegant prerevolutionary palaces to Soviet-style skyscrapers and cool and contemporary boutique hotels. This neighbourhood also offers Moscow's best selection of eating and entertainment options, as well as easy access to the city centre.

ULITSA PETROVKA

AKVAREL Map pp88–9   Boutique Hotel $$$

Watercolour; ☎ 495-502 9430; www.hotelakvarel .ru; Stoleshnikov per 12; s/d R10,500/12,250; Ⓜ Chekhovskaya; ⊠ 🖵 ✕

Stoleshnikov per is one of Moscow's most prestigious lanes, home to exclusive boutiques, upmarket restaurants and the grand Marriott Royal Aurora Hotel. Set amid all this grandeur is this intimate business-class hotel, offering 23 simple but sophisticated rooms, adorned with watercolour paintings. The friendly Akvarel is tucked in behind Simachyov Boutique & Bar (p152). Reduced rates on weekends.

HOTEL BUDAPEST Map pp88–9   Hotel $$

☎ 495-925 3050; www.hotel-budapest.ru; Petrovskie linii 2/18; s R7400-8400, d R9900; Ⓜ Kuznetsky Most; ⊠ 🖵

This 19th-century neoclassical edifice is a perfect retreat after strolling in the surrounding swanky shopping district. Have a drink in the plush bar or dine under the crystal chandelier in the Grand Opera restaurant. Unfortunately, the grandeur does not extend to the rooms, unless you dish out some extra cash for a suite (from R10,800).

GODZILLAS HOSTEL Map pp88–9   Hostel $

☎ 495-699 4223; www.godzillashostel.com; Bolshoy Karetny per 6; dm/d/tr R725/1740/2175; Ⓜ Tsvetnoy Bulvar; 🖵 ✕

Godzillas is the biggest and most professionally run hostel in Moscow, with 90 beds spread out over four floors. The rooms come in various sizes, but they are all spacious and light-filled and painted in different colours. To cater to the many guests, there are bathroom facilities on each floor, three kitchens and a big living room with satellite TV.

TVERSKAYA ULITSA & TVERSKOY BULVAR

RITZ-CARLTON MOSCOW
Map pp88–9   Hotel $$$

☎ 495-225 8400; www.ritzcarlton.com; Tverskaya ul 3; r from R39,500; Ⓜ Okhotny Ryad; 🚫 💻 ✖ 🅿 ♿

The city is still buzzing about the new Ritz-Carlton, which opened in 2007 on the site of the much-maligned Soviet-era Intourist Hotel. The Ritz is everything that the Intourist wasn't: the guestrooms are spacious and sumptuous; service is impeccable; and amenities are virtually unlimited. Note that the Ritz is a few floors taller than its next-door neighbour, the National. That means that rooms on the upper floors enjoy spectacular views, as does the cool rooftop lounge, O2.

LE ROYAL MERIDIEN NATIONAL
Map pp88–9   Historic Hotel $$$

☎ 495-258 7000; www.national.ru; Okhotny ryad 14/1; s/d from R12,744/17,700; Ⓜ Okhotny Ryad; 🚫 💻 ✖ 🅿

For over a century, the National has occupied this choice location at the foot of Tverskaya ul, opposite the Kremlin. The handsome building is something of a museum from the early 20th century, displaying frescoed ceilings and antique furniture. The rooms are decorated and laid out uniquely – the singles are tiny, but the pricier rooms have spectacular views into the Kremlin. While the place reeks of history, the service and amenities are up to modern five-star standards.

GOLDEN APPLE Map pp88–9 Boutique Hotel $$$

☎ 495-980 7000; www.goldenapple.ru; ul Malaya Dmitrovka 11; s/d from R12,000/12,500; Ⓜ Pushkinskaya; 🚫 💻 ✖

'Moscow's first boutique hotel'. A classical edifice fronts the street, but the interior is sleek and sophisticated. The rooms are decorated in a minimalist, modern style – subdued whites and greys punctuated by contrasting coloured drapes and funky light fixtures. Comfort is also paramount, with no skimping on luxuries such as heated bath-room floors and down-filled duvets. This is the best of New Russia: contemporary, creative and classy.

EAST-WEST HOTEL
Map pp88–9   Boutique Hotel $$

☎ 495-232 2857; www.eastwesthotel.ru; Tverskoy bul 14/4; s/d R9000/10,000; Ⓜ Pushkinskaya; 🚫 💻 ✖

Located on the loveliest stretch of the Boulevard Ring, this small hotel evokes the atmosphere of the 19th-century mansion it once was. It is a kitschy but charming place with 24 individually decorated rooms and a lovely fountain-filled courtyard. The price comes down significantly on weekends; it goes up if you do not pay in advance.

OUTER TVERSKOY

SOVIETSKY HOTEL
Map pp60–1   Historic Hotel $$

☎ 495-960 2000; www.sovietsky.ru; Leningradsky pr 32/2; r from R7200; Ⓜ Dinamo; 🚫 💻 ✖ 🅿

Built in 1952, this historic hotel shows Stalin's tastes in all of its architectural details, starting from the gilded hammer and sickle and the enormous Corinthian columns flanking the front door. The sumptuous lobby is graced with grand, sweeping staircases, crystal chandeliers and plush carpets, and even the simplest rooms have ceiling medallions and other ornamentation. The legendary restaurant Yar (p190), complete with old-fashioned dancing girls, is truly over the top. The location is not super-convenient, but this throwback is still fun for a Soviet-style splurge.

PEKING HOTEL Map pp88–9   Hotel $$

☎ 495-234 2467, 650 2442; www.hotelpekin.ru; Bolshaya Sadovaya ul 5/1; s R5400-6400, d R7950; Ⓜ Mayakovskaya; 🚫 💻

This Stalinist building boasts a prime location towering over Triumfalnaya pl. It's hard to see past the flashing lights and raucousness of the casino, but this place is blessed with high ceilings, parquet floors and a marble staircase. All rooms have been renovated in attractive jewel tones with modern furniture. Discount available on weekends.

KITA INN Map pp88–9   Minihotel $$

☎ 8-926-664 4118, 8-919-772 4002; www.kitainn .com; 2-ya Tverskaya-Yamskaya ul 6/7, apt 9-10; r R3325; Ⓜ Mayakovskaya; 💻 ✖

Finally, somebody opened a proper pension in Moscow. It's a modest place, offering private rooms that are simple and sweet – Ikea beds, posters on the wall and windows overlooking a shady courtyard. Three rooms share access to a small, remodelled kitchen and a brand new bathroom. The owner has a few flats in the neighbourhood all offering similar facilities – see also www.flamingobed.com.

YELLOW BLUE BUS

Map pp88–9   Minihotel & Hostel $

☎ 495-250 1364; ybb@list.ru; 4-ya Tverskaya-Yamskaya ul 5, apt 8; dm R850-1000, d/tr/q R3250/4125/4500; Ⓜ Mayakovskaya; 🖳 ✕

Yellow Blue Bus is all about the love (*Ya lyublyu vas* means 'I love you' in Russian). It's a fun and friendly place, though the informal atmosphere may be a bit lackadaisical for some. (Staff are not necessarily on site at all times – make sure you know your code or you may not be able to get in.) Dorm rooms have four or eight wooden bunks, lockers, fresh paint and cool light fixtures. The spacious private rooms are in a separate nearby flat, which is much more grown-up, with real, plush purple furniture and oriental rugs.

PRESNYA

Mayor Luzhkov has big plans for this part of town: skyscrapers are going up at lightning speed, and a new metro line now branches off from Kievskaya station to Moskva-City. Besides the budget options listed here, there are several international chain hotels that are part of the Moskva-City development. The Grand Hyatt Moscow, the world's tallest hotel, is expected to open in 2010.

ALEXANDER BLOK Map pp96–7   Boat Hotel $

☎ 499-255 9278; www.nakorable.ru, in Russian; Krasnopresnenskaya nab 12A; r from R2840; Ⓜ Delovoy Tsentr; ▨

You wanted to go on a cruise, but somehow you ended up on vacation in Moscow instead. If this is you, consider staying on board the good ship *Alexander Blok,* named after the esteemed Soviet poet. Restaurant, bar, nightclub, casino and hotel – all are housed within this cruise ship moored on the Moscow River. The cabins are clean but cramped – unless you spring for the captain's quarters (R6000).

KREMLIN HOSTEL Map pp96–7   Hostel $

☎ 495-253 5038; www.hostel-kremlin.com; Malaya Gruzinskaya ul 38; dm R770, d R2200; Ⓜ Krasnopresnenskaya; 🖳 ✕

Just behind the zoo, this little hostel offers two six-bed dorm rooms and a private double. The rooms are pretty standard, with the welcome addition of big closets. Look for parquet floors, sheer curtains and whitewashed walls. The only common hang-out area is a spacious kitchen, which looks like something out of suburban America.

ARBAT

This historic district offers a wide variety of accommodation, including some surprisingly affordable options. There are a few hostels on the 'old' Arbat itself, and some excellent midrange hotels in the quiet residential streets surrounding it.

ARBAT HOTEL Map pp102–3   Hotel $$

☎ 499-271 2801; www.president-hotel.net/arbat; Plotnikov per 12; s/d from R8500/10,000; Ⓜ Smolenskaya; ▨ 🖳 ✕

One of the few hotels that manages to preserve some appealing Soviet camp – from the greenery-filled lobby to the mirrors behind the bar. For better or worse, the guest rooms are decorated tastefully and comfortably. But the whole place has an anachronistic charm. Its location is also very appealing – on a quiet residential street, just steps from the Arbat. Reserve online for the best rates.

ASSAMBLEYA NIKITSKAYA HOTEL

Map pp102–3   Boutique Hotel $$

☎ 495-933 5001; www.assambleya-hotels.ru; Bolshaya Nikitskaya ul 12; s R7110-7900, d R9450-10,500; Ⓜ Okhotny Ryad; ▨ 🖳 ✕

Nikitskaya offers a rare combination: superb location, reasonable prices and Russian charm (is that last one an oxymoron?). While the building and rooms are freshly renovated, it preserves an old-fashioned atmosphere, with heavy floral drapes and linens. But it's all very cosy and comfortable. And with Coffee Mania (p172) across the street and Kvartira 44 (p182) around the corner, you can't beat the location.

MELODY HOTEL Map pp102–3 Boutique Hotel $$

☎ 495-723 5246; www.melody-hotel.ru, in Russian; Skaterny per 13; s/d R5500/6900; Ⓜ Arbatskaya

Unique in size, Melody has only 46 small but comfortable rooms. It also has a fantastic location on a residential street just off the Arbat.

HOTEL BELGRAD Map pp102–3 Hotel $$
☎ 495-248 9500; www.hotel-belgrad.ru; Smolenskaya ul 8; s/d/ste R4300/5900/6600, breakfast R580; Ⓜ Smolenskaya; 🌐 🖥
This big block on Smolenskaya-Sennaya pl has no sign and a stark lobby, giving it a ghost-town aura. Rooms are similar – poky but functional – unless you upgrade to 'tourist' or 'business-class' accommodation, costing R7500 to R9300. The advantage is the location, which can be noisy but is convenient to the western end of ul Arbat.

HOME FROM HOME HOSTEL
Map pp102–3 Hostel $
☎ 495-229 8018; www.home-fromhome.com; ul Arbat 49, apt 9; dm R700-800, d R2000; Ⓜ Smolenskaya; 🖥 ✖
In an attempt to make this your home away from home, the owners have spruced up the entryway, putting comfy couches and potted plants on the landing and creating a pleasant first impression – a rare thing indeed in Moscow! Once inside, original art and mural-painted walls create a bohemian atmosphere, which is enhanced by ceiling medallions and exposed brick. The dorm rooms have three to six beds, and there are two double rooms and a comfy, cosy common area with kitchen facilities. The building is opposite the Hard Rock Café but you must enter the courtyard from Plotnikov per and look for entrance No 2.

HM HOSTEL Map pp102–3 Hostel $
☎ 495-291 8390; www.hostel-moscow.com; Maly Afanasevsky per 1/33, apt 14; dm R875; Ⓜ Arbatskaya; 🖥 ✖
Staff are friendly, though not exactly fluent (in English). A+ for location.

SWEET HOSTEL Map pp102–3 Hostel $
☎ 8-910-420 3446; www.sweetmoscow.com; ul Arbat 51, apt 31; dm R750; Ⓜ Smolenskaya; 🖥 ✖
Standard hostel facilities (bunk beds, lockers, etc). The only thing that sets it apart is the fantastic location on the Arbat.

DOROGOMILOVO
Dorogomilovo has only one hotel, but it's a biggy.

HOTEL UKRAINA Map p107 Historic Hotel $$$
☎ 495-221 5555; www.ukraina-hotel.ru; Kutuzovsky pr 2/1; Ⓜ Kievskaya
This bombastic beauty sits majestically on the banks of the Moscow River facing the White House, meaning superb vistas from some rooms. The hotel used to boast that it had preserved the atmosphere of the 1950s, which was no empty assertion. Besides crystal chandeliers and wide staircases, the lobby featured a fantastic ceiling fresco depicting the joyous communist-Ukrainian countryside. It remains to be seen whether these quirky details will survive the ongoing renovations when the Ukraina reopens as a five-star property.

KHAMOVNIKI
Stretching southwest of the Kremlin, along the Moscow River, Khamovniki is packed with Orthodox monuments and art museums, but not hotels. Choose from one of two options.

KEBUR PALACE Map pp110–11 Hotel $$$
☎ 495-733 9070; www.hoteltiflis.com; ul Ostozhenka 32; s R5175-9660, d R12,040; Ⓜ Park Kultury or Kropotkinskaya; 🌐 🖥 ✖ 🛁
Georgians know hospitality. The proof is in the fine restaurants, such as the landmark Tiflis (p174), and in this refined, four-star hotel under the same management (formerly Hotel Tiflis). With 80 rooms, the hotel offers an intimate atmosphere and personalised service. The small singles are excellent value – ask for one with a balcony overlooking the fountain-filled patio.

HOTEL YUNOST Map pp110–11 Hotel $$
☎ 499-242 4860; ynkom@comtv.ru; ul Khamovnichesky val 34; s/d from R3350/3600; Ⓜ Sportivnaya
Yunost – meaning 'youth' – looks decidedly middle aged (it was built in 1961, after all). The humourless security guard at the front and the slow-moving staff at reception also hark back to these times. The Soviet-style rooms are clean and comfortable, but won't win any design awards; some have been upgraded (single/double R5200/5800). In any case, this place is a decent option for

NEW RUSSIAN HOLIDAY

To get a taste of the New Russians' New Russia, book a room at the Barvikha Hotel & Spa (off Map pp60–1; ☎ 495-225 8880; www.barvikhahotel.com; Rublyovskoe sh; Ⓜ Molodyozhnaya). Scheduled to open at the end of 2008, this modern, minimalist hotel and spa is in the ritzy suburbs on Rublyovka (p108). The hotel is amazingly understated, offering sophisticated suites with private terraces (for summer) and fireplaces (for winter). A project of Italian designer Antonio Citterio, the place utilises custom-designed furniture, natural materials such as marble and oak, and rich earthy colours to create an exquisitely soothing ambience. Some of the 65 rooms, known as Spa Suites, are equipped with massage tables, guaranteeing complete relaxation. The on-site restaurant is by Anatoly Komm, Russia's only chef with a Michelin star. Take *marshrutka* 101 from Molodyozhnaya metro station.

the money. It's just around the corner from Novodevichy Convent.

ZAMOSKVORECHIE

The charming, old, narrow streets of Zamoskvorechie are lined with art galleries, old churches, trendy restaurants and more than a few places to stay. The area around Paveletskaya pl, especially, is a target of development, with many new hotels – small and large – opening in the vicinity.

HOTEL BALTSCHUG KEMPINSKI

Map pp120–1   Historic Hotel $$$

☎ 495-287 2000; www.kempinski-moscow.com; ul Balchug 1; r from R36,600, Fri & Sat R14,400; Ⓜ Kitay-Gorod or Ploshchad Revolyutsii; 🔀 🖳 🔀 🔄 🕭

If you want to wake up to views of the sun glinting off the Kremlin's golden domes, this luxurious property on the Moscow River is the place for you. It is a historic hotel, built in 1898, with 230 high-ceilinged rooms that are sophisticated and sumptuous in design. The on-site restaurant is famous for its Sunday brunch, or 'linner' if you prefer, as it's served from 12.30pm to 4.30pm. Russian champagne and live jazz accompany an extravagant buffet. The room prices on Friday and Saturday nights make this a great place for a weekend splurge.

SWISSÔTEL KRASNYE HOLMY

Map pp120–1   Hotel $$$

☎ 495-787 9800; www.moscow.swissotel.com; Kosmodamianskaya nab 52; s/d R30,700/32,800; Ⓜ Paveletskaya; 🔀 🖳 🔀 🔄 🕭

The metallic skyscraper towering over the Moscow River is the swish Swissôtel Krasnye Holmy, named for this little-known neighbourhood of Moscow. Rooms are sumptuous, subtle and spacious. The decor is minimalist: rich, dark hardwood floors

and a few modernist paintings, but nothing to detract from the striking city skyline. If you don't want to dish out the cash to spend the night, you can still enjoy the views by heading up to the City Space Bar on the 32nd floor. If you snag a table on the west side of the building, you will witness a spectacular sunset over Moscow's golden domes. Reduced rate on weekends.

ALROSA ON KAZACHY

Map pp120–1   Boutique Hotel $$$

☎ 495-745 2190; www.alrosa-hotels.ru; 1-y Kazachy per 4; s/tw/d/ste R10,500/12,600/14,200/16,100; Ⓜ Polyanka; 🔀 🖳 🔀 🔄

Set in the heart of Zamoskvorechie, one of the oldest and most evocative parts of Moscow, the Alrosa re-creates the atmosphere of an 18th-century estate. The light-filled atrium, bedecked with a crystal chandelier, and 15 classically decorated rooms provide a perfect setting for old-fashioned Russian hospitality. Reduced rates on weekends.

OZERKOVSKAYA HOTEL

Map pp120–1   Boutique Hotel $$

☎ 495-951 7644; www.cct.ru; Ozerkovskaya nab 50; s/d from R5400/6300; Ⓜ Paveletskaya; 🖳 🔀

top picks

SLEEPS THAT WON'T BUST YOUR BUDGET

- Danilovskaya Hotel (opposite) Moscow's holiest hotel.
- Hotel Sverchkov (p206) A hidden gem of a hotel.
- Ozerkovskaya Hotel (above) A small, homey hotel near Paveletsky vokzal.
- Melody Hotel (p210) A sweet, small-scale retreat.

This comfy, cosy hotel has only 25 rooms, including three that are tucked up under the mansard roof. The rooms are simply decorated, but parquet floors and comfortable queen-sized beds rank it above the standard post-Soviet fare. Add in attentive service and a central location (convenient for the express train to Domodedovo airport), and you've got an excellent-value accommodation option.

DANILOVSKAYA HOTEL

Map pp60–1   Hotel $$

☎ 495-954 0503; www.danilovsky.ru; Bul Staro-danilovsky per; s/d/ste R5500/6000/9000; M Tulskaya; 🖭 🖵 🗙

Moscow's holiest hotel is on the grounds of the 12th-century monastery of the same name – the exquisite setting comes complete with 18th-century churches and well-maintained gardens. The modern five-storey hotel was built so that nearly all the rooms have a view of the grounds. The recently renovated rooms are simple but clean, and breakfast is modest: no greed, gluttony or sloth to be found here.

WARSAW HOTEL Map pp120–1   Hotel $$

☎ 495-238 7701; warsaw@sovintel.ru; Leninsky pr 2/1; s R3600-4100, d R4750-5000; M Oktyabrskaya; 🖭 🖵 🗙

The Warsaw sits at the centre of Oktyabrskaya pl, voted by Muscovites as the ugliest square in the city. Nonetheless, the location is the main drawcard here: it offers lots of restaurants, easy access to the metro and a short walk into the heart of Zamoskvorechie. The hotel itself does not exactly add to the aesthetics of the square. However, the interior has recently undergone extensive renovations, as evidenced by the sparkling, space-age lobby, adorned with lots of chrome, blue leather furniture and spiderlike light fixtures. The new rooms are surprisingly good value for the location.

CAMELOT HOSTEL Map pp120–1   Hostel $

☎ 495-238 8652; www.hostel-camelot.com; ul Malaya Polyanka 10, apt 5; dm R770-800; M Polyanka; 🖵 🗙

Although this flat has been updated, it still retains a slightly Soviet feel, thanks to the papered walls and linoleum floors. Three rooms (16 beds in total) share access to the fully equipped and modern kitchen, which is the only common space in the little flat.

AIRPORT ACCOMMODATION

Recommended for transit travellers who need to crash between flights, both hotels listed here operate free shuttle buses from their respective airports.

- Aerotel Domodedovo (☎ 495-795 3868; www .airhotel.ru; Domodedovo airport; s/d R6500/7000; 🖭 🖵) Bog-standard but satisfactory rooms, plus a fitness centre and billiards room.

- Atlanta Sheremetyevo Hotel (☎ 498-720 5785; www.atlantahotel.ru; 36/7 Tsentralnaya ul, Sheremetyevsky; s/d from R5450/5675; 🖵 🗙) Friendly, small and convenient, the Atlanta is an anomaly in the airport world. Reduced rates available for six- and 12-hour layovers.

OUTER MOSCOW

Many midrange accommodation options are located on the outskirts of the city. Moscow is vast, but the places listed here are all within walking distance of the metro, which will whisk you into the centre in 15 to 20 minutes. And even outer Moscow has its charms, including the lovely grounds of old country estates, a few museums, the city's best markets and the vast exhibition centre at VDNKh.

NORTH OF THE CENTRE

OKSANA HOTEL Map pp60–1   Hotel $$

☎ 495-980 6100; www.dinaoda.ru; Yaroslavskaya ul 15, Bldg 2; s R5100-5950, d R7550; M VDNKh; 🖭 🖵 🗙 ♿

In a classical, six-storey building near the All-Russia Exhibition Centre, Oksana caters mostly to business travellers, but this place offers good value for anyone. Its 63 rooms benefit from natural sunlight and spacious interiors. The well-manicured miniature golf course is perhaps out of place in this elegant setting, but your kids will appreciate it.

HOTEL COSMOS Map pp60–1   Hotel $$

☎ 495-234 1000; www.hotelcosmos.ru; pr Mira 150; standard s/d R5250/5750, renovated s/d R6250/6750; M VDNKh; 🖭 🖵 🗙 🖳 ♿

This gargantuan hotel opposite the All-Russia Exhibition Centre is a universe to itself (appropriately enough for a place called Cosmos). The glass-and-steel structure houses over 1700 rooms, countless restaurants and bars, a bowling alley and a state-of-the-art fitness centre (p197). Not surprisingly, a wide range of rooms are available, some with fantastic views.

MAXIMA ZARYA & IRBIS
Map pp60–1   Hotel $$

☎ 495-788 7272; www.maximahotels.com; Gostinichnaya ul 4/9; s/d from R3600/4500; Ⓜ Vladykino; 🅿 🖥 🍴 🚇

The Maxima Hotels include three different hotels, two of which are set on this tree-lined boulevard that literally means 'Hotel Street'. The complex of short brick buildings, set away from the main drag, has a campus-like atmosphere – a welcome change from the traffic jams and crowded sidewalks that characterise much of Moscow. While the accommodation is anything but exciting, it is affordable. And though the service is not exactly solicitous, it is satisfactory.

ALTAY HOTEL Map pp60–1   Hotel $$

☎ 495-221 8186; Botanicheskaya ul 41; www.altay-hotel.ru; s/d R3300/4500; ste R5700-6000; Ⓜ Vladykino; 🅿 🖥

This is a decent place to stay in the 'hotel district' near the Botanical Gardens. The hotel has been revamped, from the elegant lobby – with chandeliers and a fireplace – to the tastefully decorated guest rooms. Only a few old-style rooms remain (single/double R1320/2180) but they are often booked out.

SOKOL EXCLUSIVE HOSTEL
Map pp60–1   Hostel $

☎ 499-198 7186; www.moscowhostel.org; Leningradsky pr 71, apt 109; dm/r R900/2700; Ⓜ Sokol; 🖥 🍴

This newish place is trying to cash in on the capital's obsession with exclusivity. But as hostels go, Sokol Exclusive really is a step up. The two spacious, light-filled rooms have only three beds, wood floors and attractive, minimalist Tudor-style decor. One room has twin beds and a gorgeous grand piano, while the other features a double bed and a balcony overlooking the busy street below. The rooms share access to a fully equipped kitchen and a cosy common room with computer and TV. It's well outside the Garden Ring, but only a few steps from the metro.

EAST OF THE CENTRE

HOTEL IZMAILOVO (GAMMA-DELTA)
Map pp60–1   Hotel $$

☎ 495-737 7070; www.izmailovo.ru; Izmaylovskoe sh 71; standard s/d R2900/3000, business s/d/ste R3400/3600/5000, 1st-class s/d/ste R4500/5100/7400; Ⓜ Partizanskaya; 🖥

Built for the 1980 Olympics, this hotel has 8000 beds, apparently making it Europe's biggest hotel. Hotel Izmailovo occupies five different buildings, but Gamma-Delta is the snazziest and most service-oriented of the five. If you need to escape the frenetic atmosphere that surrounds Izmaylovo Market, it's just a few steps to lovely Izmaylovsky Park.

SOUTH OF THE CENTRE

KORSTON HOTEL Map pp60–1   Hotel $$

☎ 495-939 8000; www.korston.ru; ul Kosygina 15; s/d from R8900/9900; Ⓜ Vorobyovy Gory; 🅿 🖥 ♿

The location, not far from Moscow State University in Vorobyovy Gory (Sparrow Hills), allows for fantastic views of the Moscow city skyline from some rooms. It's a quiet, green, prestigious residential area – pleasant enough, but a bit of a hike into the centre. Otherwise, the rooms are tastefully decorated and sufficiently comfortable, if not luxurious. Security is tight, but the attached casino still attracts some unsavoury characters (as casinos are wont to do). Room prices increase during 'exhibition period', which is one week out of every month, so try to avoid these times.

HOTEL SPUTNIK Map pp60–1   Hotel $$

☎ 495-930 3097; www.hotelsputnik.ru; Leninsky pr 38; s/d R4040/4890; Ⓜ Leninsky Prospekt; 🅿 🖥

This hulk of a hotel is rather Soviet, but its setting south of the centre has some appeal. It's just a short walk to Vorobyovy Gory and the leafy campus of Moscow State University. Among the many services available, the on-site Indian restaurant, Darbar, is one of the best of its type in Moscow.

EXCURSIONS

EXCURSIONS

As soon as you leave Moscow, the fast-paced modern capital fades from view, while the slowed-down, old-fashioned countryside unfolds around you. The subtly changing landscape is crossed by winding rivers and dotted with peasant villages – the classic provincial Russia immortalised by artists and writers over the centuries.

Ancient Rus grew up in the clutch of towns northeast of Moscow, an area that is now known as the Golden Ring. In many cases the whitewashed walls of these once-fortified cities still stand. The golden spires and onion domes of monasteries still mark the horizon, evoking medieval Rus. Bells ring out from towering belfries, robed holy men scurry through church doors, and historic tales recall mysterious, magical times.

Moscow's elite have long escaped the heat and hustle of city life by retreating to the surrounding regions. Old aristocrats used provincial Russia as a location for grand palaces, extensive gardens and extravagant art collections. Artists and writers also sought inspiration in the countryside, usually in less extravagant quarters. Many of these retreats, from dachas to mansions, now house museums to inspire visitors.

GOLDEN RING

The Golden Ring is the circle of ancient towns north-east of Moscow – so called for its wealth of architectural and artistic riches. Some of these spots are accessible from Moscow by day trip. But, if you have a few days to spare, it's worth leaving behind the big-city bustle to immerse yourself in the age-old allure of the Golden Ring.

The most visited destination in the Golden Ring is Sergiev Posad (right) because of its accessibility from Moscow and for its atmosphere of history and holiness. If you're willing to spend the night you can continue north to Pereslavl-Zalessky (p221) and Rostov-Veliky (p223), which are charming villages with their own rich histories.

The Golden Ring's most enchanting destination is undoubtedly Suzdal (p228). The distance from Moscow is best broken by stopping in historic Vladimir (p225), the capital of ancient Rus. This excellent itinerary requires two or three days to do it justice.

If you have time to venture further from the capital, both Yaroslavl (p233) and Kostroma (p231) are rich in history and architecture.

HISTORIC SITES

The medieval towns of the Golden Ring and the country estates of the prerevolutionary elite are your main choices for historic sites around Moscow. If you easily overload on ancient churches and opulent art collections, however, you may prefer an excursion to the Borodino Battlefield (p236), the site of turning-point battles in the Napoleonic War of 1812 as well

as WWII. Literary buffs will also appreciate this destination, which features prominently in *War and Peace*.

NATURE

For outdoor activities for all seasons – from swimming to skiing – you can't beat the lakes district northwest of Moscow. Resorts such as Zavidovo (p235) and Istra (p235) are beautifully located and easily reached from Moscow. You can go for a day, but you will want to stay longer. Providing a unique variation on the nature theme, the Priokso-Terrasny Nature Reserve (p237) will delight animal lovers of all ages. For a truly Russian experience, see the boxed text, p220.

SERGIEV POSAD
СЕРГИЕВ ПОСАД
☎ 496 / pop 112,700

According to old Russian wisdom, 'there is no settlement without a just man; there is no town without a saint'. And so the town of Sergiev Posad pays tribute to St Sergius of Radonezh, founder of the local Trinity Monastery and patron saint of all of Russia. The monastery, today among the most important and active in Russia, exudes Orthodoxy. Bearded priests bustle about, babushkas fill bottles of holy water, and crowds of believers light candles for St Sergius, Keeper of Russia. This mystical place is a window into the age-old belief system that has provided Russia with centuries of spiritual sustenance.

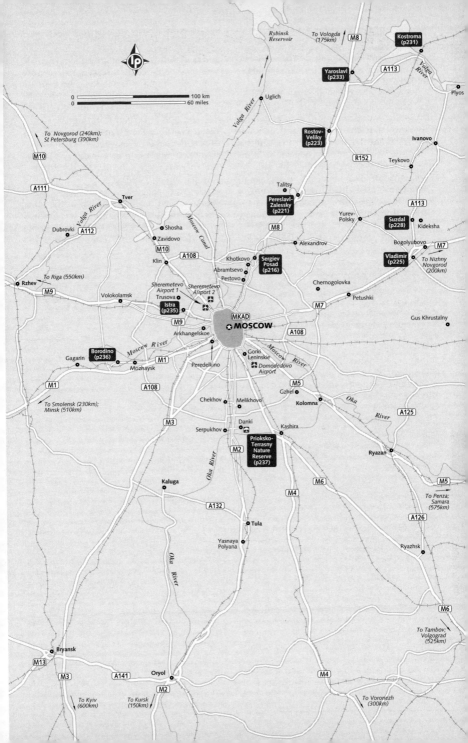

Often called by its Soviet name of Zagorsk, Sergiev Posad is an easy day trip from Moscow, and a rewarding option for travellers who don't have time to venture further around the Golden Ring.

St Sergius of Radonezh began his calling as a hermit monk in the forest wilderness. In 1340 he founded a monastery at Sergiev Posad, which soon became the spiritual centre of Russian Orthodoxy. Prince Dmitry Donskoy's victory in battle against the Mongols in 1380 was credited to a blessing by Sergius. Soon after his death, at the age of 78, Sergius was named the patron saint of Russia. Since the 14th century, pilgrims have been journeying to this place to pay homage to him.

The **Trinity Monastery of St Sergius** (Troitse-Sergieva Lavra; ☎ 544 5356, 544 5350; admission free; ⏰ 10am-6pm)

is an active religious centre with a visible population of monks in residence; visitors should refrain from photographing them. Female visitors should wear headscarves, and men are required to remove hats in the churches.

Built in the 1420s, the squat, dark **Trinity Cathedral** is the heart of the Trinity Monastery. The tomb of St Sergius stands in the southeastern corner, where a memorial service for St Sergius goes on all day, every day. The iconfestooned interior, lit by oil lamps, is largely the work of the great medieval painter Andrei Rublyov and his students.

The star-spangled **Cathedral of the Assumption** was modelled on the cathedral of the same name in the Moscow Kremlin. It was finished in 1585 with money left by Ivan the Terrible in a fit of remorse for killing his son. It is closed to the general public but included as

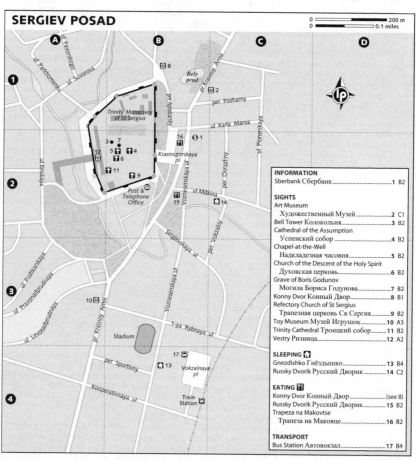

SERGIEV POSAD

part of guided tours. Outside the west door is the grave of Boris Godunov, the skilled 'prime minister' whose tsar-like rule led to the Time of Troubles in the early 17th century.

Nearby, the resplendent Chapel-at-the-Well was built over a spring that is said to have appeared during the Polish siege. The five-tier

baroque bell tower took 30 years to build in the 18th century, and once had 42 bells, the largest of which weighed 65 tonnes.

The Vestry (admission R250; ✆ 10am-5.30pm Wed-Sun) behind Trinity Cathedral displays the monastery's extraordinarily rich treasury, bulging with 600 years of donations by the rich

---

COUNTRY ESTATES

When temperatures start to rise in the city, Muscovites who have the means find a way to get out of town. This has always been the case: aristocrats would spend their summers at elegant out-of-town estates, while artists, writers and other creative types sought inspiration and tranquillity at simpler summer homes. All of the following properties are now museums surrounded by exquisite grounds, and accessible from Moscow as a day trip.

Arkhangelskoe Архангельское

In the 1780s the wealthy Prince Nikolai Yusupov purchased this grand palace on the outskirts of Moscow and turned it into a spectacular estate (✆ 495-363 1375; www.arkhangelskoe.ru; admission R170; ✆ grounds 10am-8pm daily, exhibits 10.30am-4.30pm Wed-Sun). The palace is now the quintessential aristocratic getaway from Moscow, displaying the paintings, furniture, sculptures, glass, tapestries and porcelain that Yusupov accumulated over the years. In summer, the majestic colonnade is the exquisite setting for live classical-music concerts (✆ 501-453 8229; R100-300; ✆ 5pm Sat & Sun May-Sep).

From Tushinskaya metro, take bus 541 or 549 or *marshrutka* 151 to Arkhangelskoe (30 minutes).

Peredelkino Переделкино

Boris Pasternak – poet, author of *Doctor Zhivago* and winner of the 1958 Nobel Prize for Literature – lived for a long time on Moscow's southwestern outskirts, just 5km beyond the city's outer ring road, where there is now the Pasternak House-Museum (✆ 495-934 5175; ul Pavlenko 3, Peredelkino; admission R50; ✆ 10am-4pm Thu-Sun).

Frequent suburban trains go from Moscow's Kievsky vokzal to Peredelkino (R20, 20 minutes), on the line to Kaluga-II station. From Peredelkino station, follow the path west along the train tracks past the cemetery (where Pasternak is buried) and over the bridge. After about 400m ul Pavlenko is on the right-hand side.

Gorki Leninskie Горки Ленинские

In Lenin's later years, he and his family spent time at the 1830s Murozov manor house, set on lovely wooded grounds 32km southeast of the capital. Designed by Fyodor Shekhtel, it now houses a Lenin museum (✆ 495-548 9309; www .gorki-len.narod.ru; adult/child R100/50; ✆ 10am-4pm Wed-Mon), where you can see a re-creation of Lenin's Kremlin office, as well as his vintage Rolls Royce – one of only 15 such automobiles in the world.

Bus 439 (R50, 30 minutes) leaves every 1½ hours for the estate from the Domodedovskaya metro station in Moscow. By car, follow the M4 highway (Kashirskoe sh) 11km past MKAD, then turn left to Gorki Leninskie.

Klin Клин

From 1885 Pyotr Tchaikovsky spent his summers in Klin, 90km northwest of Moscow. In a charming house on the edge of town, he wrote *The Nutcracker* and *Sleeping Beauty*, as well as his famous *Pathétique* Symphony No 6. After he died in 1893 the estate was converted into the Tchaikovsky House-Museum (✆ 496-245 8196; ul Chaykovskogo 48, Klin; adult/child R210/120; ✆ 10am-5pm Fri-Tue), which is maintained just as when Tchaikovsky lived here. You can peruse the photographs and personal effects, but only special guests are allowed to play his grand piano. Occasional concerts are held in the concert hall.

Suburban trains from Moscow's Leningradsky vokzal run to Klin (R120, 1½ hours) throughout the day. From the station, take *marshrutka* 5 to Tchaikovsky's estate.

Melikhovo Мелихово

'My estate's not much', wrote playwright Anton Chekhov of his home at Melikhovo, south of Moscow, 'but the surroundings are magnificent'. Here, Chekhov lived from 1892 until 1899 and wrote some of his most celebrated plays, including *The Seagull* and *Uncle Vanya*. Today the estate houses the Chekhov Museum (✆ 272-23 610; www.chekhovmuseum .com; adult/child R90/65; ✆ 10am-4pm Tue-Sun), dedicated to the playwright and his work. Theatre buffs should visit in May, when the museum hosts Melikhovo Spring, a week-long theatre festival.

Suburban trains (R100, 1½ hours) run frequently from Moscow's Kursky vokzal to the town of Chekhov, 12km west of Melikhovo. Bus 25 makes the 20-minute journey between Chekhov and Melikhovo, with departures just about every hour.

GETTING BACK TO NATURE

At least one-third of all Russian city dwellers own a small country home, or dacha. Often little more than a wooden hut, these retreats offer Russians refuge from city life. Dachas don't usually have electricity or running water, but they always have a fertile spot that's far away – at least psychologically – from the city. On weekends from May to September, many cities empty as people head for the country.

The dacha's most remarkable feature is its garden, which is usually bursting with flowering fruit trees and vegie plants. Families still grow all manner of vegetables and fruit, which are sold at the market or preserved for winter. Throughout winter, city dwellers can enjoy strawberry *kompot* (canned syrupy fruit) or pickled mushrooms, and fondly recall their time in the countryside.

After playing in the dirt, the next stop is undoubtedly the *banya* (p196). While bathhouses exist in the city, the countryside *banya* experience cannot be replicated. Crowding into the tiny, wooden hothouse; receiving a beating with fragrant *veniki* (birch branches) straight from the forest; cooling down with a dip in the pond or – more extreme – a roll in the snow…now *that's* getting back to nature.

Nothing piques hunger like the Russian *banya,* and what better way to enjoy the fruits of your labour than with a hearty meal? Dacha cuisine evokes the peasant's kitchen: tasty soups that are the highlight of Russian food; *kasha* (porridge), which sates any appetite; and coarse, black Russian bread. These dishes often use ingredients straight from the garden, coop or pasture. Simple to prepare, rich in flavour and nourishing to body and soul, dacha fare exemplifies how Russians return to their rural roots for replenishment.

For an authentic dacha experience, visit Uncle Pasha's Dacha (☎ 910-932 5546; www.russian-horse-rides.com; Dubrovki; r incl meals per person R1000-1500; ⓥ) in the tiny village of Dubrovki (near Tver). The setting on the Volga is magnificent. The accommodation is rustic (read: with outside toilet), as it should be. Meals are included but leave something to be desired; guests are welcome to use the kitchen facilities to make their own. This place is hard to reach, so be sure to contact Uncle Pasha in advance.

and powerful – tapestries, jewel-encrusted vestments, solid-gold chalices and more.

The huge block with the 'wallpaper' paint job is the **Refectory Church of St Sergius**, so called because it was once a dining hall for pilgrims. Now it's the Assumption Cathedral's winter counterpart, with morning services in cold weather. It's closed apart for services and guided tours. The green building next door is the metropolitan's residence.

The miniature imitation of the Trinity Cathedral is the 15th-century **Church of the Descent of the Holy Spirit**. It's used only on special occasions. It contains, among other things, the grave of the first Bishop of Alaska.

Several other museums around town showcase the monastery's rich artistic traditions. See local artists' works in the two exhibition halls of the **Art Museum** (☎ 544 5356; pr Krasnoy Armii 144; ☽ 10am-5pm Tue-Sun), while toys from throughout history and around the world are on display at the **Toy Museum** (☎ 544 4101; ul Krasnoy Armii 123; ☽ 11am-5pm Wed-Sun). The **Konny Dvor** (☎ 544 5356; ul Udarnoy Armii; ☽ 10am-5pm Wed-Sun) exhibits the ethnological and archaeological history of Sergiev Posad.

INFORMATION

Post & telephone office (pr Krasnoy Armii 127A) Find it just outside the southeastern wall of the monastery.

Sberbank (pr Krasnoy Armii; ☽ 9am-4pm Mon-Fri) Exchange facilities and ATM.

EATING

Trapeza na Makovtse (☎ 540 6101; pr Krasnoy Armii 131; meals R500-800; ☽ 10am-9pm) Location, location, location. The highlight of this 'refectory' is alfresco dining in the shadow of the spires and cupolas. Dining is also pleasant inside, where live music plays nightly.

Konny Dvor (☎ 549 9066; ul 1-ya Udarnoy Armii 2A; meals R400-800) Upstairs from the Konny Dvor museum, this lovely little restaurant evokes the atmosphere of a 19th-century estate inside, while outside it offers views of Bely Pond and the monastery bell tower. The menu calls itself

TRANSPORT: SERGIEV POSAD

Sergiev Posad is 60km from the edge of Moscow on the Yaroslavl road. An express train departs from Moscow's Yaroslavsky vokzal (R293, one hour) at 8.24am, returning in the afternoon. Suburban trains also run every half-hour (R110, 1½ hours); take any train bound for Sergiev Posad or Aleksandrov. There are regular buses between Abramtsevo and Sergiev Posad (R50, 20 minutes). The bus station is opposite the train station on Vokzalnaya pl.

DETOUR: ABRAMTSEVO (АБРАМЦЕВО)

Railway tycoon and art patron Savva Mamontov built this lovely estate 45km north of Moscow. Here, he hosted a slew of painters and musicians, including Ilya Repin, landscape artist Isaak Levitan, portraitist Valentin Serov and ceramicist Mikhail Vrubel, as well as opera singer Fyodor Chaliapin. Today the Abramtsevo Estate Museum-Preserve (☎ 254-32 470; admission R100; ☻ 10am-5pm Wed-Sun) is a delightful retreat from Moscow or addition to a trip to Sergiev Posad. Several rooms of the main house have been preserved intact, complete with artwork by various resident artists. The prettiest building in the grounds is Saviour Church 'Not Made by Hand' (Tserkov Spasa Nerukotvorny).

Suburban trains run every half-hour from Yaroslavsky vokzal (R100, 1½ hours). Most trains to Sergiev Posad or Aleksandrov stop at Abramtsevo. There are also regular buses between Abramtsevo and Sergiev Posad (R50, 20 minutes).

European, but the speciality is traditional Russian favourites.

SLEEPING

Room rates include breakfast.

Russky Dvorik (☎ 547 5392; www.zolotoe-koltso.ru/hoteldvorik, in Russian; ul Mitkina 14/2; s/d weekdays from R1500/1900, weekends from R1700/2100) Some of the rooms at this delightful hotel boast views of onion domes peeking out above whitewashed walls. The place itself is quite modern, despite the rustic style. The fanciest room even has a spa. The affiliated **restaurant** (☎ 45 114; pr Krasnoy Armii 134; meals R500-800; ☻ 10am-9pm) is a charming, kitschy place decked out like a dacha.

Gnezdishko (☎ 540 4214; Voznesenskaya ul 53; r R1900-2500) With only eight rooms, this little inn is quaint, clean and convenient to the bus and train stations. Some rooms have views of the monastery bell tower.

PERESLAVL-ZALESSKY ПЕРЕСЛАВЛЬ-ЗАЛЕССКИЙ
☎ 48535 / pop 42,700

On the shore of Lake Pleshcheevo, northeast of Moscow, Pereslavl-Zalessky is a popular dacha destination for Muscovites who enjoy the peaceful village atmosphere. The southern half of the town is characterised by narrow dirt lanes lined with carved *izby* (log houses) and blossoming gardens.

Pereslavl-Zalessky ('Pereslavl Beyond the Woods') was founded in 1152 by Yury Dolgoruky. The town's main claim to fame is as the birthplace of Alexander Nevsky. Its earth walls and the little Cathedral of the Transfiguration are as old as the town itself.

Pereslavl is pretty much a one-street town, with the bus station at the southwestern end, 2km from the centre. Apart from the few churches in the kremlin area, most of the historic sights are out of the centre.

TOWN CENTRE

The walls of Yury Dolgoruky's kremlin are now a grassy ring around the central town. Inside is the 1152 **Cathedral of the Transfiguration of the Saviour** (admission R40; ☻ 10am-6pm), one of the oldest buildings in Russia. A bust of Alexander Nevsky stands out in front, while three additional churches across the grassy square make for a picturesque corner. These are the tent-roofed **Church of Peter the Metropolitan**, built in 1585 and renovated in 1957, and the 18th-century twin churches fronting the road.

The **Trubezh River**, winding 2km from the kremlin to the lake, is fringed by trees and narrow lanes. You can follow the northern river bank most of the way to the lake by a combination of paths and streets. The **Forty Saints' Church** sits picturesquely on the south side of the river mouth.

MONASTERIES

Southwest of the kremlin, the **Nikolsky Women's Monastery** has undergone a massive renovation. Since its founding in 1350, this monastery has been on the brink of destruction – from Tatars, Poles or Communists – more times than seems possible to survive. In 1994 four nuns from the Yaroslavl Tolga Convent came to restore the place, and today it looks marvellous.

The **Goritsky Monastery** (☎ 38 100; http://museum.pereslavl.ru, in Russian; grounds R10, per exhibit R40-50, all-inclusive R150; ☻ 10am-6pm May-Oct, 9am-5pm Nov-Apr) was founded in the 14th century, though today the oldest buildings are the 17th-century gates, gate-church and belfry. The centrepiece is the baroque **Assumption Cathedral** (Uspensky sobor;

PERESLAVL-ZALESSKY

| 0 | 1 km |
| 0 | 0.5 miles |

Lake Pleshcheevo

To Rostov-Veliky (100km);
Yaroslavl (155km)

Narodnaya
pl

Trubezh River

Trubezh River

Podgornaya ul

To Botik Museum
(4km); Cafe Botik
(4km); Kukushka.ru
(16km)

ul Kardovskogo

To Sergiev Posad (40km);
Moscow (100km)

| Goritsky Monastery |
| Горицкий монастырь.............5 A3 |
| Nikolsky Women's Monastery |
| Никольский |
| женский монастырь............6 B2 |

| **INFORMATION** |
| Sberbank Сбербанк.................(see 8) |
| Yartelekom Service Centre |
| Яртелеком сервисный центр.....1 C1 |

| **SLEEPING** |
| Albitsky Sad Альбицкий Сад.........7 B3 |
| Hotel Pereslavl |
| Гостиница Переславль.............8 C1 |

| **SIGHTS** |
| Cathedral of the Transfiguration |
| of the Saviour |
| Спасо-Преображенский собор..2 C1 |
| Church of Peter the Metropolitan |
| Церковь Петра митрополита......3 C2 |
| Forty Saints' Church |
| Сорокосвятская церковь............4 A1 |

| **EATING** |
| Traktir na Ozernoy |
| Трактир на Озерной................9 C1 |

| **TRANSPORT** |
| Bus Station Автостанция.............10 A3 |
| Taxi Stand Стоянка такси............11 C1 |

admission R40) with its beautiful carved iconos-tasis. The other buildings hold art and history exhibits.

BOTIK MUSEUM

Besides being the birthplace of Alexander Nevsky,Botik Museum Pereslavl also claims to be the birthplace of the Russian Navy: Lake Pleshcheevo is one of the places where Peter the Great developed his obsession with the sea. As a young man, he studied navigation here and built a flotilla of over 100 little ships by the time he was 20.

You can explore some of this history at the small Botik Museum (☎ 22 788; per exhibit R30; ☷ 10am-5pm Tue-Sun), situated 4km along the road past the Goritsky Monastery, at the southern end of the lake. Its highlight is the

sailboat *Fortuna*, one of only two of Peter the Great's boats to survive fire and neglect; the other is in the St Petersburg Naval Museum.

INFORMATION

Sberbank (ul Rostovskaya 27; ☷ 9am-7pm Mon-Sat) Exchange facility in the lobby of Hotel Pereslavl.

Yartelekom Service Centre (☎ 31 595; ul Rostovskaya 20; per hr R60; ☷ 8.30am-5.30pm Mon-Thu, 8.30am-4pm Fri) Has internet and telephone facilities.

EATING & DRINKING

Cafe Botik (☎ 98 085; Podgornaya ul; meals R400-600; ☷ 11am-11pm) This waterfront café (shaped like a boat) is in a prime location opposite the Botik Museum. Stop here for lake views and lunch before or after your excursion. Or come for the full afternoon and take advantage of the beach access, billiards and the *banya* (bathhouse).

Traktir na Ozernoy (☎ 35 009; Rostovskaya ul 27; meals R300-600; ☷ 9am-last guest) Gnaw on shashlyk to your heart's desire at this Caucasian eatery. Pork, chicken, beef and sturgeon – all are grilled up in plain view and served hot and spicy.

TRANSPORT: PERESLAVL-ZALESSKY

Almost halfway between Moscow and Yaroslavl, Pereslavl-Zalessky is not on the train line, but buses travel frequently to Moscow (R230, 2½ hours). Not all of these stop at Sergiev Posad (one hour, three daily).

DETOUR: KUKUSHKA.RU (КУКУШКА.РУ)

Calling all railway buffs! Pereslavl-Zalessky is home to a unique railway museum known as Kukushka.ru (☎ 48535-49 479; www.kukushka.ru, in Russian; Talitsy; adult/child R60/30; ⊙ 10am-6pm Wed-Sun Apr-Oct, 10am-5pm Sat & Sun Nov-Mar). The collection of locomotives occupies tracks and a depot that were used up until the middle of the 20th century. Don't miss the opportunity to ride on the hand cart (adult/child R60/30).

The museum is about 16km out of town. From ul Kardovskogo (the main road into town from Moscow or Sergiev Posad) turn left onto Podgornaya ul and follow the road along the shoreline of Lake Pleshcheevo. At the village of Talitsy, look for the 'Muzey' sign and turn left to the museum.

SLEEPING

Hotel Pereslavl (☎ 31 559; Rostovskaya ul 27; r R2000, studio R2500, ste R2900-3500) Despite the drab exterior, this central hotel has updated its rooms, which now sport new furniture, carpeting and – most importantly – bathrooms. The rooms are crowded but they feel fresh.

Albitsky Sad (☎ 31 430; motel@pereslavl.ru; ul Kardovskogo 21; d R2500-2900, tr R3500-3900; 🅿 ✕) Just southwest of the centre, 'Albitsky Garden' resembles an old manor house, its yellow exterior adorned with white trim. The motel offers around 16 tastefully decorated rooms (and at least one honeymoon suite that is not quite so tasteful), as well as an inviting restaurant. Service is extremely friendly, if not super efficient.

ROSTOV-VELIKY РОСТОВ-ВЕЛИКИЙ

☎ 48536 / pop 33,200

For a place called Rostov-Veliky (Rostov the Great), this place gives the impression of a sleepy village. Perhaps for this reason, the magnificent Rostov kremlin catches visitors off guard when its silver domes and white-washed stone walls appear amid the dusty streets. Rostov is among the prettiest of the Golden Ring towns, idyllically sited on shim-

mering Lake Nero. It is also one of the oldest, first chronicled in 862.

KREMLIN

Rostov's main attraction is its unashamedly photogenic kremlin (☎ 61 717; grounds R20, per exhibit R20-35, all-inclusive R200; ⊙ 10am-5pm). Though founded in the 12th century, nearly all the buildings here date to the 1670s and 1680s.

With its five magnificent domes, the Assumption Cathedral dominates the kremlin, although it is just outside the latter's north wall. Outside service hours, you can get inside the cathedral through the door in the church shop on ul Karla Marksa. The cathedral was here a century before the kremlin, while the belfry was added in the 1680s. Each of 15 bells in the belfry has its own name; the largest, weighing 32 tonnes, is called Sysoy, named for the Rostov Metropolitan who oversaw the construction of the kremlin in the late 17th century. The monks play magnificent bell concerts, which can be arranged through the excursions office in the west gate for R500.

The west gate (the main entrance) and north gate are straddled respectively by the Gate-Church of St John the Divine and the Gate-Church of the Resurrection, both of which are richly decorated with 17th-century frescoes. Enter these churches from the monastery walls (admission R45), which you can access from the stairs next to the north gate. Like several other buildings within the complex, these are open only from May to September. Between the gate-churches, the Church of Hodigitria houses an exhibition of Orthodox Church vestments and paraphernalia.

The Metropolitan's private chapel, the Church of the Saviour-over-the-Galleries, has the most beautiful interior of all, covered in colourful frescoes. These rooms are filled with exhibits: the White Chamber displays religious antiquities, while the Red Chamber shows off *finift* (enamelled miniatures), a Rostov artistic speciality.

TRANSPORT: ROSTOV-VELIKY

Rostov-Veliky is about 193km northeast of Moscow. The fastest train from Moscow is the express service from Yaroslavsky vokzal (R430, three hours, twice daily). Otherwise, some long-distance trains stop at Rostov-Veliky en route to Yaroslavl. Bus 6 runs between the train station and the town centre.

The train and bus stations are together in the drab modern part of Rostov, 1.5km north of the kremlin. Bus 6 runs between the train station and the town centre.

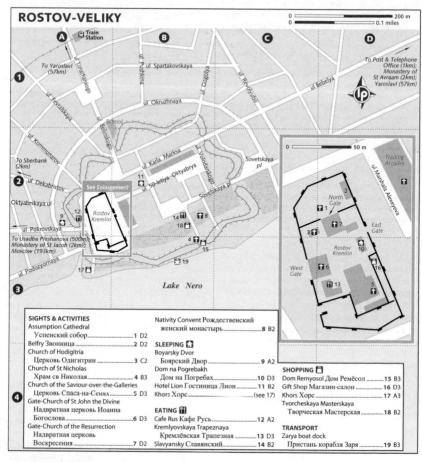

ROSTOV-VELIKY

0 — 200 m
0 — 0.1 miles

SIGHTS & ACTIVITIES
Assumption Cathedral
  Успенский собор....................1 D2
Belfry Звонница.........................2 D2
Church of Hodigitria
  Церковь Одигитрии 3 C2
Church of St Nicholas
  Храм св Николая.....................4 B3
Church of the Saviour-over-the-Galleries
  Церковь Спаса-на-Сенях 5 D3
Gate-Church of St John the Divine
  Надвратная церковь Иоанна
  Богослова...............................6 D3
Gate-Church of the Resurrection
  Надвратная церковь
  Воскресения...........................7 D2

Nativity Convent Рождественский
  женский монастырь................8 B2

SLEEPING
Boyarsky Dvor
  Боярский Двор 9 A2
Dom na Pogrebakh
  Дом на Погребах....................10 D3
Hotel Lion Гостиница Лион 11 B2
Khors Хорс ....(see 17)

EATING
Cafe Rus Кафе Русь....................12 A2
Kremlyovskaya Trapeznaya
  Кремлёвская Трапезная 13 D3
Slavyansky Славянский...............14 B2

SHOPPING
Dom Remyosol Дом Ремёсол 15 B3
Gift Shop Магазин-салон 16 D3
Khors Хорс 17 A3
Tvorcheskaya Masterskaya
  Творческая Мастерская 18 B2

TRANSPORT
Zarya boat dock
  Пристань корабля Заря 19 B3

MONASTERIES

The restored Monastery of St Jacob is the fairytale apparition you'll see as you approach Rostov by road or rail. Take bus 1 or 2 or walk 1.5km along Lake Nero, west from the kremlin. Heading east of the kremlin, bus 1 will also bring you to the dilapidated Monastery of St Avraam, with a cathedral dating from 1553. There is a cluster of other churches along the lake shore, including the Nativity Convent and the Church of St Nicholas.

BOAT TRIPS

For a different perspective on the monasteries, board the ferry Zarya (☎ 8-906-631 1925; adult/child R150/50; ☺ 11am-6pm May-Sep) for a float around Lake Nero. The hour-long trip leaves from

the pier near the western gate of the kremlin, and cruises past both monasteries. For the same price, smaller boats do the same tour in about 15 minutes, departing from the smaller dock to the west.

INFORMATION

Post & telephone office (ul Severnaya 44) About 1km east of the kremlin.

Sberbank (ul Dekabristov, ☺ 9am-2pm & 3-5pm Mon-Fri, 9am-2pm Sat)

SHOPPING

Rostov is an arts-and-crafts centre, so don't leave without stopping at the gift shop (☎ 61717; ☺ 10am-5pm) in the kremlin to shop for *finift* (enamel) souvenirs and to sample the home-brewed *medovukha* (mead).

Khors (☎ 62 483; ul Podozerka 30; admission free; ⏰ 3-8pm Mon-Fri, 10am-9pm Sat & Sun) Named after a pagan sun god, this is a private gallery on the lake shore behind the kremlin. The eclectic collection includes some antique household items, models of wooden churches and some exquisite enamelwork by local artist Mikhail Selishchev.

On the lake shore east of the kremlin, there are two side-by-side galleries. Tvorcheskaya Masterskaya (☎ 8-910-663 8127; ul Petrovicheva 19/3; ⏰ 10am-7pm) features landscapes and still lifes by painter Oleg Yenin, as well as more interesting work by other local and regional artists. Dom Remyosol (☎ 64 452; Tolstovskaya nab 16; ⏰ 10am-7pm) has more craft and souvenir-type items, such as dolls, ceramics, watercolours and prints.

EATING

All of the hotels have restaurants or cafés on site.

Trapeznaya Palata (☎ 62 871; meals R400-600; ⏰ 9am-5pm, later in summer) The draw to the refectory is the atmospheric location inside the kremlin, near the Metropolitan's house. The grand dining room is often crowded with tour groups supping on traditional Russian fare.

Cafe Rus (☎ 65 951; ul Pokrovskaya; meals R200-300) A small café serving soups, salads and hot meals. Good for a quick bite.

Slavyansky (☎ 62 228; Sovetskaya pl 8; meals R400-500; ⏰ 11am-1am) About 100m east of the kremlin, this semiswanky place gets recommendations from locals.

SLEEPING

Rostov is a popular weekend destination, meaning that hotel prices are generally lower between Sunday and Thursday. All prices include breakfast unless otherwise indicated.

Khors (☎ 62 483; www.khors.org; ul Podozerka 30; per person R500; 🖳) On the grounds of the gallery (above) there are a handful of tiny rustic rooms with shared access to a bathroom and kitchen (which means you make your own breakfast). Tip: drag your mattress up onto the roof to awake to the sunrise over Lake Nero.

Dom na Pogrebakh (☎ 61 244; www.rostmuseum.ru, in Russian; s/d/tr without bathroom R700/1000/1500, d with bathroom R2000-2500) Right inside the kremlin, near the east gate, this place has clean, wood-panelled rooms with heavy doors and colourful tapestries. If you can snag a room with a view of the west gate it is charming indeed.

Boyarsky Dvor (☎ 60 446; www.reinkap-hotel.ru, in Russian; ul Kamenny most 4; standard r R1200-2000, upgraded r R1800-2200) Just outside the western kremlin wall, this is a vast rambling place with plain but functional rooms. The downstairs café is a pleasant place for an evening drink.

Hotel Lion (☎ 64 949; www.lion-hotel.ru, in Russian; ul 50-letiya Oktyabrya 9/6; r R1300-1800, ste R1800-2050) This big and basic hotel offers affordable rooms and a convenient location. The drab decor does not do much for the dark interior, but the place is clean and comfortable enough.

Usadba Pleshanova (☎ 76 440; www.hotel.v-rostove.ru; ul Pokrovskaya 34; r weekday R1700-2700, weekend R2000-3100; 🖳) This 19th-century manor house, once the residence of a merchant and philanthropist family, is now a welcoming inn with a nice restaurant, cosy library and wood sauna. Beware the 20% reservation fee.

VLADIMIR ВЛАДИМИР
☎ 4922 / pop 340,000

High up the slope from the Klyazma River sits the solemnly majestic Assumption Cathedral, built to announce Vladimir's claim as capital of Rus. These days, Vladimir feels more like a modern, provincial town than an ancient capital. Nonetheless, the grandeur of medieval Vladimir shines through the commotion of the busy industrial town. The exquisite examples of Russia's most formative architecture, along with some entertaining museums, make Vladimir one of the jewels in the Golden Ring.

ASSUMPTION CATHEDRAL

A white-stone version of Kyiv's brick Byzantine churches, the Assumption Cathedral (☎ 325 201; admission R100; ⏰ 7am-8pm Tue-Sun) was begun in 1158 – its simple but majestic form, adorned with fine carving, was innovative for the time. The cathedral was extended on all sides after a fire in the 1180s, when it gained the four outer domes.

Inside the working church, a few restored 12th-century murals of peacocks and prophets can be deciphered about halfway up the inner wall of the outer north aisle; this was originally an outside wall. The real treasures are the *Last Judgment* frescoes by Andrei Rublyov

VLADIMIR

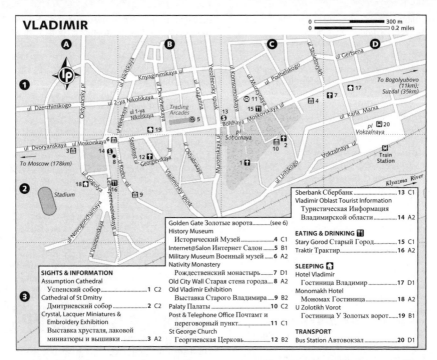

0 ——— 300 m
0 ——— 0.2 miles

SIGHTS & INFORMATION
Assumption Cathedral
Успенский собор................................1 C2
Cathedral of St Dmitry
Дмитриевский собор.........................2 C2
Crystal, Lacquer Miniatures &
Embroidery Exhibition
Выставка хрусталя, лаковой
миниатюры и вышивки 3 A2
Golden Gate Золотые ворота..............(see 6)
History Museum
Исторический Музей..........................4 C1
Internet@Salon Интернет Салон..........5 B1
Military Museum Военный музей 6 A2
Nativity Monastery
Рождественский монастырь...............7 D1
Old City Wall Старая стена города....8 A2
Old Vladimir Exhibition
Выставка Старого Владимира............9 B2
Palaty Палаты.......................................10 C2
Post & Telephone Office Почтамт и
переговорный пункт........................11 C1
St George Church
Георгиевская Церковь........................12 B2

Sberbank Сбербанк 13 C1
Vladimir Oblast Tourist Information
Туристическая Информация
Владимирской области.....................14 A2

EATING & DRINKING
Stary Gorod Старый Город..................15 C1
Traktir Трактир......................................16 A2

SLEEPING
Hotel Vladimir
Гостиница Владимир 17 D1
Monomakh Hotel
Мономах Гостиница 18 A2
U Zolotikh Vorot
Гостиница У Золотых ворот...............19 B1

TRANSPORT
Bus Station Автовокзал 20 D1

and Daniil Chyorny, painted in 1408 in the central nave and inner south aisle, under the choir gallery towards the west end.

The church also contains the original coffin of Alexander Nevsky of Novgorod, the 13th-century military leader who was also Prince of Vladimir. He was buried in the former Nativity Monastery east of here, but his remains were moved to St Petersburg in 1724 when Peter the Great allotted him Russian hero status.

Adjoining the cathedral on the northern side are an 1810 bell tower and the 1862 St George's Chapel.

CATHEDRAL OF ST DMITRY

A quick stroll to the east of the Assumption Cathedral is the smaller Cathedral of St Dmitry (1193–97), where the art of Vladimir-Suzdal stone carving reached its pinnacle. The church is permanently closed, but the attraction here is its exterior walls, covered in an amazing profusion of images.

The top centre of the north, south and west walls all show King David bewitching the birds and beasts with music. The Kyivan prince Vsevolod III, who had this church built as part of his palace, appears at the top left of

the north wall, with a baby son on his knee and other sons kneeling on each side. Above the right-hand window of the south wall, Alexander the Great ascends into heaven, a symbol of princely might. On the west wall appear the labours of Hercules.

PALATY

The grand building between the cathedrals is known as the Palaty (☎ 323 320; Bolshaya Moskovskaya ul 58; admission R150; 10am-4pm Tue-Sun) and contains a children's museum, art gallery and historical exhibit. The former is a welcome diversion for little ones, who may well be suf-

TRANSPORT: VLADIMIR

Vladimir is 178km east of Moscow. The daily express train between Moscow's Kursky vokzal (seat R340, 2½ hours) and Nizhny Novgorod (seat R400, 2½ hours) stops in Vladimir, as do many slower trains. Privately run buses (R200, 3½ hours) also leave regularly from Kursky and Kazansky vokzaly to Vladimir. They do not run on a timetable, but leave as they fill up. The train and bus stations are 500m east of the city centre, on Vokzalnaya ul, at the bottom of the slope.

fering from old-church syndrome on this trip. The art gallery features art dating back to the 18th century, with wonderful depictions of the Golden Ring towns.

Across the small street, the History Museum (☎ 322 284; Bolshaya Moskovskaya ul 64; admission R50; ☽ 10am-4pm Wed-Mon) displays many remains and reproductions of the ornamentation from the Assumption Cathedral of the Cathedral of St Dmitry.

GOLDEN GATE

Vladimir's Golden Gate – part defensive tower, part triumphal arch – was modelled on the very similar structure in Kyiv. Originally built by Andrei Bogolyubsky to guard the main, western entrance to his city, it was later restored under Catherine the Great. Now you can climb the narrow stone staircase to check out the Military Museum (☎ 322 559; admission R50; ☽ 10am-4pm Fri-Wed). It is a small exhibit, the centrepiece of which is a diorama of old Vladimir being ravaged by nomadic raiders in 1238 and 1293. Across the street to the south you can see a remnant of the old wall that protected the city.

The red-brick building opposite was built in 1913 to house the Old Believers' Trinity Church. Now it is a Crystal, Lacquer Miniatures & Embroidery Exhibition (☎ 324 872; Bolshaya Moskovskaya ul 2; admission R60; ☽ 10am-4pm Wed-Mon), which features the crafts of Gus-Khrustalny and other nearby towns. The shop in the basement has a decent selection of crystal for sale.

OLD VLADIMIR EXHIBITION

The red-brick water tower atop the old ramparts houses the Old Vladimir Exhibition (☎ 325 451; ul Kozlov val; admission R50; ☽ 10am-4pm Tue-Sun), a nostalgic collection of old photos, advertisements and maps, including a photo of a very distinguished couple taking a ride in Vladimir's first automobile in 1896. The highlight is the view from the top.

The nearby St George Church (Georgievskaya ul 2A) houses the Vladimir Theatre of Choral Music, where performances are often held on summer weekends.

INFORMATION

Internet@Salon (☎ 326 471; cnr ul Gagarina & Bolshaya Moskovskaya ul; per hr R60; ☽ 9am-9pm)

Post & telephone office (ul Podbelskogo; ☽ 8am-8pm Mon-Fri)

Sberbank (Bolshaya Moskovskaya ul 27; ☽ 9am-7pm Mon-Fri, 9am-5pm Sat) Exchange facilities and ATM.

Vladimir Oblast Tourist Information (☎ 447 191; www .welcome33.ru, in Russian; Bolshaya Moskovskaya ul 2; ☽ 10am-6pm Mon-Fri, 10am-5pm Sat) Distributes some questionably useful tourist brochures.

EATING & DRINKING

All of the hotels have restaurants on site.

Stary Gorod (☎ 325 101; Bolshaya Moskovskaya ul 41; meals R300-400; ☽ 11am-2am) One of two side-by-side establishments on the main drag. Choose from the cosy bar, the elegant dining room or, if the weather is fine, the lovely terrace with views of the Cathedral of St Dmitry.

Traktir (☎ 324 162; Letneperevozinskaya ul 1A; meals R300-500; ☽ 11am-last guest) The liveliest place in town is this quaint wooden cottage, serving a simple menu of Russian food. In summer, the terrace opens up for cold beer and grilled shashlyk. With live music on weekends, it's a popular spot for young people to congregate and celebrate.

SLEEPING

Hotel prices include breakfast.

Hotel Vladimir (☎ 324 447; www.vladimir-hotel.ru; Bolshaya Moskovskaya ul 74; s R1700, d R1850-2050, ste R2450; ☐) This hotel near the train station used to be a state-run establishment, but it has successfully survived the transition. All the rooms have been renovated with new bathrooms and furniture, but retain a hint of old-fashioned Soviet charm in the choice of wallpaper and draperies. It is a big place with a slew of services.

U Zolotikh Vorot (At the Golden Gates; ☎ 420 823; www.golden-gate.ru, in Russian; Bolshaya Moskovskaya ul 17; s R2000-2300, d R2800-3300) The 14 rooms at this sweet little hotel are spacious and comfortable, with large windows overlooking the activity on the main street – or a central courtyard if you prefer. The attached restaurant is popular with tour groups and hotel guests.

Monomakh Hotel (☎ 440 444; www.monomahhotel .ru; ul Gogolya 20; s R2100-2700, d R3200, ste R4100-5100; ☒ ☐ ☒) Off the main drag, this newish hotel has only 16 rooms, which are simply decorated but fully equipped. If you have your own vehicle, inquire here about the out-of-town Hotel Revyaki, a rustic wooden cottage surrounded by pines on the banks of the Klyazma River on the outskirts of Vladimir.

DETOUR: BOGOLYUBOVO (БОГОЛЮБОВО)

According to legend, when Andrei Bogolyubsky was returning north from Kyiv in the late 1150s, his horses stopped where Bogolyubovo now stands, 11km east of Vladimir. Apparently they wouldn't go another step, so Andrei was forced to establish his capital in Vladimir, and not at his father's old base of Suzdal.

Whatever the reasoning, between 1158 and 1165 Andrei built a stone-fortified palace at this strategic spot near the meeting of the Nerl and Klyazma Rivers.

Fragments from Andrei Bogolyubsky's palace survive amid a renovated and reopened 18th-century monastery. Driving along the Vladimir–Nizhny Novgorod road, you can't miss the monastery in the middle of Bogolyubovo.

The dominant buildings today are the monastery's 1841 bell tower beside the road, and its 1866 Assumption Cathedral. Just east of the cathedral there is the arch and tower, on whose stairs – according to a chronicle – Andrei was assassinated by hostile *boyars* (nobles). The arch abuts the 18th-century Church of the Virgin's Nativity.

Nearby, Andrei built the most perfect of all old Russian buildings, the Church of the Intercession on the Nerl. The church's beauty lies in its simple but perfect proportions, a brilliantly chosen waterside site (floods aside) and sparing use of delicate carving. Legend has it that Andrei had the church built in memory of his favourite son, Izyaslav, who was killed in battle against the Bulgars. As with the Cathedral of St Dmitry (p226) in Vladimir, King David sits at the top of three facades, the birds and beasts entranced by his music. The interior has more carving, including 20 pairs of lions. If the church is closed, try asking at the house behind.

To reach this famous little church, walk down Vokzalnaya ul, which is immediately east of the monastery. At the end of the street, cross the railway tracks and follow the cobblestone path 1km across the field. You can catch a ride in the horse-drawn carriage for R100 per person.

To get to Bogolyubovo, take trolleybus 1 east from Vladimir and get off at Khimzavod. Walk along the main road for 100m to the bus stop, where you can catch a *marshrutka* (fixed-route minibus) to Bogolyubovo (second stop).

SUZDAL СУЗДАЛЬ

☎ 49231 / pop 12,000

The gently winding waterways, flower-drenched meadows and dome-spotted skyline make this medieval capital the perfect fairytale setting. Suzdal was bypassed by the railway and later protected by the Soviet government, all of which limited development in the area. As a result, its main features are its abundance of ancient architectural gems and its decidedly rural atmosphere.

Under Muscovite rule, Suzdal was a wealthy monastic centre, with incredible development projects funded by Vasily III and Ivan the Terrible. In the late 17th and 18th centuries, wealthy merchants paid for 30 charming churches, which still adorn the town. Judging by the spires and cupolas, Suzdal may have as many churches as people.

KREMLIN

The 1.4km-long earth rampart of Suzdal's kremlin, founded in the 11th century, today encloses a few streets of houses and a handful of churches, as well as the main cathedral group on Kremlyovskaya ul.

The Nativity of the Virgin Cathedral, its blue domes spangled with gold, was founded in the 1220s, but only its richly carved lower section is original white stone, the rest being 16th-century brick. The inside is sumptuous, with 13th- and 17th-century frescoes and 13th-century damascene (gold on copper) west and south doors.

The Archbishop's Chambers houses the Suzdal History Exhibition (☎ 21 624; admission R60; ☼ 10am-5pm Wed-Mon). The exhibition includes the original 13th-century door from the cathedral, photos of its interior and a visit to the 18th-century Cross Hall (Krestovaya palata), which was used for receptions. The tent-roofed 1635 kremlin bell tower on the east side of the yard contains additional exhibits.

Just west of this group stands the 1766 wooden St Nicholas Church, brought from Glatovo village near Yuriev-Polsky. There's another St Nicholas Church (ul Lebedeva), one of Suzdal's own fine small 18th-century churches, just east of the cathedral group.

TORGOVAYA PLOSHCHAD

Suzdal's Torgovaya pl (Trade Sq) is dominated by the pillared Trading Arcades (built 1806–11) along its western side. The arcades now house a variety of shops and cafés, as well as the excellent Yarmarka Remesyol (☎ 20 314; ul Lenina 63A; ☼ 8am-5pm), a shop specialising in arts and crafts made in Suzdal.

There are four churches in the immediate vicinity, including the Resurrection Church (admission

R50). Make the precarious climb to the top of the bell tower and be rewarded with wonderful views of Suzdal's gold-domed skyline. The five-domed 1707 Emperor Constantine Church in the square's northeastern corner is a working church with an ornate interior. Next to it is the smaller 1787 Virgin of All Sorrows Church.

SAVIOUR MONASTERY OF ST EUTHYMIUS

Founded in the 14th century to protect the town's northern entrance, Suzdal's biggest monastery (☎ 20 746; per exhibit R60-100, all-inclusive R400; ☻ 10am-6pm Tue-Sun) grew mighty in the 16th and 17th centuries after Vasily III, Ivan the Terrible and the noble Pozharsky family funded impressive new stone buildings and big land and property acquisitions. It was girded with its great brick walls and towers in the 17th century.

Inside, the Annunciation Gate-Church houses an interesting exhibit on Dmitry Pozharsky (1578–1642), leader of the Russian army that drove the Polish invaders from Moscow in 1612.

A tall 16th- to 17th-century cathedral bell tower stands before the seven-domed Cathedral of the Transfiguration of the Saviour. Every hour from 11am to 5pm, a short concert of chimes is given on the bell tower's bells. The cathedral was built in the 1590s in 12th- to 13th-century Vladimir Suzdal style. Inside, restoration has uncovered some bright 1689 frescoes by the school of Gury Nikitin from Kostroma. The tomb of Prince Dmitry Pozharsky is by the east wall of the cathedral.

The 1525 Assumption Church facing the bell tower adjoins the old Father Superior's chambers, which houses a display of Russian icons. The monks' quarters across the compound contain a museum of artistic history.

At the north end of the complex is the old monastery prison, set up in 1764 for religious

dissidents. It now houses a fascinating exhibit on the monastery's military history and prison life, including displays of some of the better-known prisoners who stayed here. The combined monastery hospital and St Nicholas' Church (1669) features a rich museum of 12th- to 20th-century Russian applied art, much of it from Suzdal itself.

INTERCESSION CONVENT

This convent (☎ 20 889; Pokrovskaya ul; admission free; ☻ 9.30am-4.30pm Thu-Mon) was founded in 1364, originally as a place of exile for the unwanted wives of tsars. Among them was Solomonia Saburova, first wife of Vasily III, who was sent here in the 1520s because of her supposed infertility. The story goes that she finally became pregnant too late to avoid being divorced. A baby boy was born in Suzdal. Fearing he would be seen as a dangerous rival to any sons produced by Vasily's new wife, Solomonia secretly had him adopted, pretended he had died and staged a mock burial. This was probably just as well for the boy since Vasily's second wife did indeed produce a son – Ivan the Terrible.

The legend received dramatic corroboration in 1934 when researchers opened a small 16th-century tomb beside Solomonia's, in the crypt underneath the Intercession Cathedral. They found a silk-and-pearl shirt stuffed with rags – and no bones. The crypt is closed to visitors.

MUSEUM OF WOODEN ARCHITECTURE & PEASANT LIFE

This open-air museum (☎ 23 567; ul Pushkarskaya; grounds R60, per exhibit R60, all-inclusive R160; ☻ 9.30am-7pm Wed-Mon May-Oct), illustrating old peasant life in this region of Russia, is a short walk across the river south of the kremlin. Besides log houses, windmills, a barn and lots of tools and handicrafts, its highlights are the 1756 Transfiguration Church (Preobrazhenskaya tserkov) and the simpler 1776 Resurrection Church (Voskresenskaya tserkov).

OTHER SUZDAL BUILDINGS

The dilapidated Monastery of the Deposition of the Holy Robe, with its landmark bell tower and exquisite entrance turrets, was founded in 1207 but the existing buildings date from the 16th to 19th centuries.

Almost every corner in Suzdal has its own little church with its own charm. The little

TRANSPORT: SUZDAL

Suzdal is 35km north of Vladimir. The bus station is 2km east of the centre on Vasilievskaya ul. Some long-distance buses continue past the bus station into the centre; otherwise, a marshrutka will take you there. Buses run every half-hour to/from Vladimir (R40, one hour). One daily bus goes directly to/from Moscow's Shchyolkovsky bus station (R250, 4½ hours).

SUZDAL

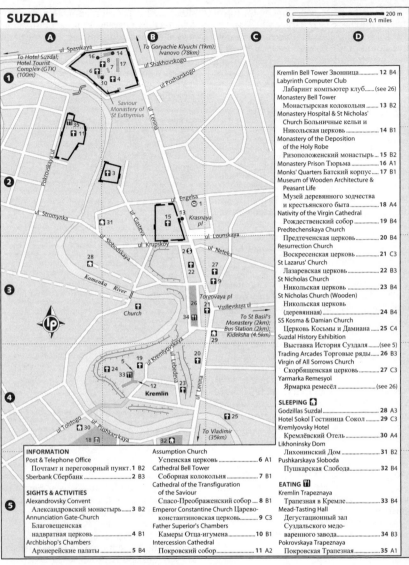

0 — 200 m
0 — 0.1 miles

Kremlin Bell Tower Звонница	12	B4
Labyrinth Computer Club		
Лабаринт компьютер клуб	(see 26)	
Monastery Bell Tower		
Монастырская колокольня	13	B2
Monastery Hospital & St Nicholas'		
Church Больничные кельи и		
Никольская церковь	14	B1
Monastery of the Deposition		
of the Holy Robe		
Ризоположенский монастырь	15	B2
Monastery Prison Тюрьма	16	A1
Monks' Quarters Батский корпус	17	B1
Museum of Wooden Architecture &		
Peasant Life		
Музей деревянного зодчества		
и крестьянского быта	18	A4
Nativity of the Virgin Cathedral		
Рождественский собор	19	B4
Predtechenskaya Church		
Предтеченская церковь	20	B4
Resurrection Church		
Воскресенская церковь	21	C3
St Lazarus' Church		
Лазаревская церковь	22	B3
St Nicholas Church		
Никольская церковь	23	B4
St Nicholas Church (Wooden)		
Никольская церковь		
(деревянная)	24	B4
SS Kosma & Damian Church		
Церковь Косьмы и Дамиана	25	C4
Suzdal History Exhibition		
Выставка История Суздаля	(see 5)	
Trading Arcades Торговые ряды	26	B3
Virgin of All Sorrows Church		
Скорбященская церковь	27	C3
Yarmarka Remesyol		
Ярмарка ремесёл	(see 26)	

SLEEPING 🏠
Godzillas Suzdal	28	A3
Hotel Sokol Гостиница Сокол	29	C3
Kremlyovsky Hotel		
Кремлёвский Отель	30	A4
Likhoninsky Dom		
Лихонинский Дом	31	B2
Pushkarskaya Sloboda		
Пушкарская Слобода	32	B4

EATING 🍴
Kremlin Trapeznaya		
Трапезная в Кремле	33	B4
Mead-Tasting Hall		
Дегустационный зал		
Суздальского медо-		
варенного завода	34	B3
Pokrovskaya Trapeznaya		
Покровская Трапезная	35	A1

INFORMATION		
Post & Telephone Office		
Почтамт и переговорный пункт	1	B2
Sberbank Сбербанк	2	B3

SIGHTS & ACTIVITIES		
Alexandrovsky Convent		
Александровский монастырь	3	B2
Annunciation Gate-Church		
Благовещенская		
надвратная церковь	4	B1
Archbishop's Chambers		
Архиерейские палаты	5	B4

Assumption Church		
Успенская церковь	6	A1
Cathedral Bell Tower		
Соборная колокольня	7	B1
Cathedral of the Transfiguration		
of the Saviour		
Спасо-Преображенский собор	8	B1
Emperor Constantine Church Царево-		
константиновская церковь	9	C3
Father Superior's Chambers		
Камеры Отца-игумена	10	B1
Intercession Cathedral		
Покровский собор	11	A2

white **Alexandrovsky Convent** at the top of the river embankment stands out for its simple beauty. Some other gems include the shabby but graceful **Predtechenskaya Church** (ul Lenina), built in 1720, and the slender, multicoloured tower of **St Lazarus' Church** (Staraya ul), from 1667. The **SS Kosma & Damian Church** (1725) is picturesquely placed on a bend in the river east of ul Lenina. Suzdal's fifth monastery is the 17th-century **St Basil's** (Vasilevsky monastyr),

on the Kideksha road. No doubt you'll find your own favourite.

ACTIVITIES
The rolling hills and attractive countryside around Suzdal are ideal for outdoor adventures, including horse riding and mountain biking. The **Hotel Tourist Complex** (GTK; ☎ 23 380; ul Korovniki 45; � 10am-6pm) rents bicycles, snow-

mobiles and skis, as well as offering horse-riding tours.

Rural Suzdal is a great place to cleanse body and soul in the Russian *bani* (hot baths). Beautiful, lakeside *bani* are available for rent at Goryachie Klyuchi (☎ 24 000; www.parilka.com, in Russian; ☼ 11am-1am) starting at R880 for up to four people.

INFORMATION

There is an ATM on international networks located at Pushkarskaya Sloboda (right).

Labyrinth computer club (☎ 23 333; ul Lenina 63; per MB R4, per hr R20; ☼ 24hr) Enter from the courtyard inside the trading arcades.

Post & telephone office (Krasnaya pl; ☼ 8am-8pm) Open 24 hours for phone calls.

Sberbank (ul Lenina; ☼ 8am-4.30pm Mon-Fri) Exchange office.

EATING & DRINKING

In addition to the places listed below, all of the hotels have restaurants.

Kremlin Trapeznaya (☎ 21 763; meals R300-500; ☼ 11am-11pm) The attraction here is the choice location inside the Archbishop's Chambers. This place has been serving tasty, filling Russian favourites for 300 years.

Pokrovskaya Trapeznaya (☎ 20 199; Intercession Convent; meals R400-600; ☼ 10am-10pm) On the grounds of the Intercession Convent, the old refectory is now a rustic restaurant serving hearty Russian fare in an atmospheric old wooden building.

Mead-Tasting Hall (☎ 20 803; tasting menu R120-150; ☼ 10am-6pm Mon-Fri, 10am-8pm Sat & Sun) Hidden at the rear of the trading arcades, this hall is done up like a church interior – floor-to-ceiling frescoes, arched ceilings and stained-glass windows. The menu features different varieties of *medovukha,* a mildly alcoholic honey ale that was drunk by the princes of old.

SLEEPING

Suzdal is experiencing a tourist boom, which means many more options for top-end travellers. All prices include breakfast.

Kremlyovsky Hotel (☎ 23 480; www.kremlinhotel.ru, in Russian; ul Tolstogo 5; s/d from R3950/4400; ✖ ▯ ✖) This white stone hotel mirrors the tall towers of the kremlin on the opposite bank of the river. The rooms are contemporary and

comfortable, without a lot of fancy stuff, but they offer lovely views of the winding waterway and the rustic wooden architecture in the vicinity.

Pushkarskaya Sloboda (☎ 23 303; www.sloboda-gk.ru, in Russian; ul Lenina 45; s/d in inn R2400/2700, s/d in village R3300/3600; ✖ ✖ ▮) This holiday village has everything you might want from your Disney vacation – accommodation in the log-cabin 'Russian inn' or the reproduction 19th-century 'Gunner's Village'; three restaurants, ranging from the rustic country tavern to a formal dining room – and every service you might dream up. It's an attractive, family-friendly, good-value option, though it might be too manicured for some tastes.

Hotel Sokol (☎ 20 088; www.hotel-sokol.ru; Torgovaya pl 2A; s R1900-2260, d R2480-2620, ste R3020-3940; ✖) Ideally located opposite the trading arcades, this is the biggest midrange hotel in town. Its 40 rooms are all simply decorated and fully equipped with new wooden furniture and modern bathrooms. The pricier ones are slightly bigger but not really worth the cost of the upgrade.

Likhoninsky Dom (☎ 21 901; ul Slobodskaya 34) Suzdal's most appealing place to stay is on a quiet street near the town centre. This 17th-century merchant's house has five charming rooms and a pretty garden. Closed for renovation at the time of research, it is expected to reopen in early 2009.

Godzillas Suzdal (☎ 495-699 4223; www.suzdalhostel.com; Naberezhnaya ul 12; per person R600; ▯) The popular Moscow-based Godzillas Hostel has expanded into the countryside, opening a big, beautiful log-cabin facility overlooking the river. Dorm rooms each have their own bathroom and balcony. Guests can also enjoy the blooming garden and Russian *banya*, as well as the chill-out lounge and bar in the basement.

KOSTROMA КОСТРОМА
☎ 4942 / pop 274,500

This historic town sits 300km northeast of Moscow, where its namesake river – the Kostroma – converges with the Volga. Kostroma was founded by Yury Dolgoruky in 1152, but the delightful historic centre dates back to the 18th century, when the old wooden structures were demolished by fire. The pride of Kostroma is the 14th-century Monastery of St Ipaty, which poses majestically on the right bank of the Kostroma River.

MONASTERY OF ST IPATY

Legend has it that a Tatar prince named Chet (who later founded the house of Godunov) was returning to Moscow in 1330 and fell ill. At this time he had a vision of the Virgin Mary and the martyr Ipaty of the Ganges, which aided his recovery. When he returned to Moscow he was baptised and founded the Monastery of St Ipaty (☎ 312 589; admission R85; ☻ 9am-5pm) to mark the occasion.

In 1590, the Godunovs built the monastery's Trinity Cathedral (Troitsky sobor), which contains over 80 old frescoes by a school of 17th-century Kostroma painters, headed by Gury Nikitin (plus some 20th-century additions).

The monastery's more recent history is closely tied to the Godunov and Romanov families, fierce rivals in high-level power games before the Romanovs established their dynasty. In 1600 Boris Godunov exiled the head of the Romanov family, Fyodor, and his son Mikhail to this monastery. Mikhail Romanov was here in 1613, when the All-Russia Council came to insist that he accept his position as tsar, thus ending the Time of Troubles. In honour of the event, all successive Romanov rulers came here to visit the monastery's red Romanov Chambers (Palaty Romanova), opposite the cathedral.

Behind the monastery is an attractive outdoor Museum of Wooden Architecture (☎ 373 872; admission R70; ☻ dawn to dusk May-Oct). The monastery is 2.5km west of the town centre. Take bus 14 from the central Susaninskaya pl and get off once you cross the river.

SUSANINSKAYA PLOSHCHAD

Picturesque Susaninskaya pl was built after a fire in 1773, as an ensemble under the patronage of Catherine the Great. Clockwise around the northern side are a 19th-century fire tower

DETOUR: KIDEKSHA (КИДЕКША)

In the quiet village of Kideksha, 4km east of Suzdal, the Church of SS Boris & Gleb (Borisoglebskaya tserkov) is the oldest in the district, dating to 1152. It was built for Yury Dolgoruky, who had a small wooden palace here. The palace has disappeared and the church has been rebuilt many times, but a few fragments of 12th-century frescoes remain. The two figures on horseback probably represent Vladimir's sons, Boris and Gleb, who were the first Russian saints.

(still in use and under Unesco protection); a former military guardhouse, housing the new revamped Kostroma Museum of history, art & architecture (☎ 316 837; ul Lenina 1; per exhibit R25-50; ☻ 9.30am-5pm); an 18th-century hotel for members of the royal family; the palace of an 1812 war hero, now a courthouse; and the town hall.

In the streets between are many merchants' town houses, two of which comprise the Art Museum (☎ 513 829; pr Mira 5 & 7; admission to each bldg R50; ☻ 10am-6pm).

INFORMATION

Post & telephone office (cnr ul Sovetskaya & ul Podlipaeva; ☻ 9am-9pm)

Sberbank (ul Sovetskaya 9; ☻ 9am-4pm Mon-Fri) Conveniently located bank with an ATM.

Telecom Centre (☎ 621 162; cnr ul Sovetskaya & ul Podlipaeva; per hr R60; ☻ 8am-8pm) To access the internet, buy a card at window 5 and stick it in the slot at the computer of your choice.

EATING & DRINKING

There is a row of inexpensive cafés and fast food restaurants inside the trading arcades south of Susaninskaya pl.

Roga & Kopyta (☎ 315 240; Sovetskaya ul 2; meals R200-300; ☻ 9am-midnight) Step off the 18th-century streets into the 'Horn & Hoof' coffee shop that also harks back to eras past. Wrought-iron furniture and B&W photos set the atmosphere. The menu has a good selection of soups, salads and main dishes, besides pastries and coffee drinks.

Beloe Solntse (☎ 373 137; Lesnaya ul 2; meals R400-600) The decor evokes the 'White Sun' of the desert at this spicy, Central Asian restaurant. When the season is right, the prime location next to the river station offers outdoor seating with views of the river. Live music nightly.

SLEEPING

Ipatyevskaya Sloboda (☎ 371 224; www.i-sloboda.narod.ru; ul Beregovaya 3A; d R1700-2600, ste R3000-4200; ✕ ☒) Kostroma's most atmospheric lodging choice is this old-fashioned wooden house, opposite the monastery entrance. Wood-panelled walls and brick fireplaces lend a rustic atmosphere, which is softened by stencilled designs and floral tapestries.

Hotel Mush (☎ 312 400; ul Sovetskaya 29; r incl breakfast R1800-2800) This tiny guesthouse has a central location and hospitable atmosphere, which explains why it is so often booked out. Its four rooms (two small and two big) are furnished in an old-fashioned Soviet style. Enter through the courtyard.

Hotel Volga (☎ 394 242; www.gkvolga.ru; ul Yunosheskaya 1; standard s/d/tr R1700/2100/2250, comfort s/d R2300/2800; ✗ ✗ ▣) Kostroma's Soviet-standard hotel overlooks the Volga about 2km southeast of the centre, near the bridge. The standard rooms are the same old Soviet fare (old furniture, skinny beds), but the two floors of 'comfort' rooms feature dark wood furniture, rich fabrics and flat-screen TVs.

YAROSLAVL
ЯРОСЛАВЛЬ

☎ 4852 / pop 604,000

Yaroslavl is the urban counterpart to Suzdal. This is the biggest place between Moscow and Arkhangelsk, and it has a more urban feel than anywhere else in the Golden Ring. Its big-city skyline, however, is dotted with onion domes and towering spires, not smoke stacks and skyscrapers.

In 1010, the Kyivan prince Yaroslav the Wise took an interest in a trading post called Medvezhy Ugol (Bear Corner). According to legend, Yaroslav subjugated and converted the locals by killing their sacred bear with his axe. So the town was founded, and its coat of arms bears both the beast and the weapon.

In the 16th and 17th centuries, Yaroslavl developed as the first port on the Volga, growing fat on trade with the Middle East and Europe. Rich merchants competed to build churches with elaborate decoration and bright frescoes. To this day, churches are hidden around every corner. The poet Apollon

Grigoryev wrote, 'Yaroslavl is a town of unsurpassed beauty; everywhere is the Volga and everywhere is history'. And everywhere, everywhere, are churches.

MONASTERY & AROUND

Founded in the 12th century, the Monastery of the Transfiguration of the Saviour (☎ 303 869; www.yarmp.yar .ru; Bogoyavlenskaya pl 25; grounds R20, per exhibit R40-50; ✉ exhibits 10am-5pm Tue-Sun year-round, grounds 8am-8pm daily Oct-May) was one of Russia's richest and best-fortified monasteries by the 16th century. The oldest surviving structures, dating from 1516, are the Holy Gate near the main entrance by the river, and the austere Cathedral of the Transfiguration (admission R60; ✉ Thu-Mon).

Other buildings house exhibits on history, ethnography, icons and the newest, Treasures of Yaroslavl (admission R100), featuring works of gold, silver and precious gems.

CHURCH OF ELIJAH THE PROPHET

The exquisite church (Sovetskaya pl; admission R70; ✉ 10am-1pm & 2-6pm Thu-Tue May-Sep) that dominates Sovetskaya pl was built by prominent 17th-century fur dealers. It has some of the Golden Ring's brightest frescoes by the ubiquitous Gury Nikitin of Kostroma and his school, and detailed exterior tiles. The church is closed during wet spells.

RIVER EMBANKMENTS

The Volga and Kotorosl embankments make for an enjoyable 1.5km walk. A pedestrian promenade runs along the bank of the Volga below the level of the street, Volzhskaya nab. Look for myriad churches, as well as the unique private collection Music & Time (☎ 328 637; Volzhskaya nab 33A; adult/child R100/60; ✉ 10am-7pm) and the Yaroslavl Art Museum (☎ 303 504; http://artmuseum.yar.ru; Volzhskaya nab 23; admission R60; ✉ 10am-5pm), with 18th- to 20th-century Russian art.

The more time you spend, the more churches you will discover, most dating from the 17th century. There are three clustered around the stadium, three more along the embankment, and several south of the Kotorosl River in the settlements of Korovniki and Tolchkovo. Pick up the brochure Yaroslavl (available in several languages) at one of the museum gift shops.

INFORMATION

Alfa-Bank (☎ 739 177; ul Svobody 3; ☯ 9am-6pm Mon-Thu, 9am-4.30pm Fri) Exchange office and ATM facilities.

Dom Knigi (☎ 304 751; ul Kirova 18; ☯ 10am-7pm Mon-Fri, 10am-6pm Sat) Has a good selection of maps and books.

Post & telephone office (Komsomolskaya ul 22; ☯ 8am-8pm Mon-Sat, 8am-6pm Sun)

EATING & DRINKING

The pedestrian street ul Kirova is lined with cafés and restaurants, most of which have outdoor seating in summer months.

Mario (☎ 732 232; ul Kirova 8/10; meals R200-300; ☯ 10am-11pm Mon-Fri, noon-11pm Sat & Sun) Evoking an Italian café, this pizzeria has tile tables and Tiffany lamps. In summer you can enjoy the footpath seating.

Van Gogh (☎ 729 438; ul Kirova 10/25; meals R400-600) The menu requires some deciphering, as all the choices are named after technical terms and geographic landmarks from the life of the artist. Once you figure it out, the soups, salads and pastas are excellent and innovative. This funky café livens up on Friday and Saturday nights, with local bands and free-flowing drinks.

Sobranie (☎ 303 132; Volzhskaya nab 33; meals R600-800; ☯ 10am-11pm) On the grounds of Music & Time (p233), this traditional Russian restaurant is decorated with stained glass, artwork and antiques that look as though they might be part of the collection. The quaint place caters to hungry tourists in search of traditional Russian cuisine. Much of the cooking is done in the old-fashioned stone oven.

TRANSPORT: YAROSLAVL

Yaroslavl is 250km northeast of Moscow. The main train station is Yaroslavl Glavny, on ul Svobody, 3km west of the centre. The lesser Yaroslavl Moskovsky vokzal is near the bus station, 2km south of town. Trains run frequently to/from Yaroslavsky vokzal in Moscow (R500, four hours).

The bus station is on Moskovsky pr, 2km south of the Kotorosl River and near Moskovsky vokzal. One or two buses go daily to/from Moscow's Shchyolkovsky station (R350, six hours), plus about five buses stopping in transit. Most of these stop at Pereslavl-Zalessky, Rostov-Veliky and Sergiev Posad.

Actor (☎ 727 543; ul Kirova 5; meals R200-400; ☯ 10am-2am) Garden furniture and imitation gas lamps create a trattoria ambience – without the fresh air. The place attracts an artsy clientele who like to smoke. The walls are covered with whimsical frescoes and theatre posters, and the air is filled with sounds of live rock, jazz and blues.

Poplavok (☎ 314 343; meals R800-1000; ☯ noon-1am) Housed on a boat on the Kotorosl River, Poplavok offers Yaroslavl's only truly waterside dining. Seafood specials are skilfully prepared and artfully presented. Additional perks include live music and alfresco dining when the weather is fine.

SLEEPING

Yaroslavl suffers from a shortage of accommodation options, so you might want to make a hotel reservation, especially if you are arriving in the evening.

Hotel Yubileynaya (☎ 309 259; www.yubil.yar.ru; Kotoroslnaya nab 26; s/d incl breakfast from R2500/3500;

DETOUR: PLYOS (ПЛЁС)

Plyos is a tranquil town of wooden houses and hilly streets winding down to the Volga waterfront, halfway between Ivanovo and Kostroma. Though fortified from the 15th century, Plyos' renown stems from its role as a late-19th-century artists' retreat. Isaak Levitan, Russia's most celebrated landscape artist, found inspiration here in the summers of 1888 to 1890. The playwright Anton Chekhov commented that Plyos 'put a smile in Levitan's paintings'.

The oldest part of town is along the river, as evidenced by the ramparts of the old fort, which date from 1410. The hill is topped by the simple 1699 **Assumption Cathedral** (Uspensky sobor), one of Levitan's favourite painting subjects.

The **Levitan House Museum** (Dom-Muzey Levitana; ☎ 49339-43 782; ul Lunacharskogo 4; admission R60; ☯ 10am-5.30pm Tue-Sun) displays works by Levitan and other artists against the background of the Volga. To see how this setting inspires contemporary artists, visit the **Landscape Museum** (Muzey Peyzazha; admission R40; ☯ 10am-2pm, 3-5.30pm Tue-Sun), at the far end of the embankment.

Plyos is not easy to reach unless you have your own vehicle. Buses run regularly from Ivanovo (R100, 2½ hours, hourly) but only occasionally from Kostroma (R113, Friday and Saturday only).

) Overlooking the Kotorosl River, this is the city's largest centrally located hotel, leftover from Soviet times. It's the usual concrete slab building, but rooms are completely renovated, simply decorated and comfortably furnished.

Volzhskaya Zhemchuzhina (☎ 727 717; www.riverhotel-vp.ru, in Russian; Volzhskaya nab; s R2400-3000, d R4000-4800;) The 'Volga Pearl' is an atmospheric ship that is docked at the river bank – pricier rooms have water views. Polished maple furniture and plenty of natural light ensure that the place does not feel too cramped. Double rooms have access to a shared balcony (which is actually the ship's dock).

Ring Premier Hotel (☎ 581 158; www.ringhotel.ru; ul Svobody 55; r/ste incl breakfast R4200/7000;) This modern six-storey building offers predictable but plush rooms with heated bathroom floors and king-size beds. The slick business hotel also contains a well-equipped fitness centre and an Irish pub (a must for any four-star hotel).

ISTRA ИСТРА

☎ 49631 / pop 33,600

In the 17th century, Nikon, the patriarch whose reforms drove the Old Believers from the Orthodox Church, decided to show one and all that Russia deserved to be the centre of the Christian world. He did this by building a little Holy City right at home, complete with its own Church of the Holy Sepulchre. Thus, the grandiose **New Jerusalem Monastery** (Novo-Iyerusalimsky monastyr; ☎ 49 787; www.ierusalim.ru, in Russian; admission per exhibit adult/child R80/40, guided tour R500; 10am-4pm Tue-Sun) was founded in 1656 near the picturesque Istra River.

TRANSPORT: ISTRA

Istra is 56km west of Moscow. Suburban trains run from Moscow's Rizhsky vokzal to Istra (R80, 1½ hours, hourly), from where buses run to the Muzey stop by the monastery. A 20-minute walk from the Istra train station is a pleasant alternative.

Unlike other Moscow monasteries, this one had no military use. In WWII the retreating Germans blew it to pieces but it's in the middle of being reconstructed. After years as a museum, the monastery is now in Orthodox hands and attracts a steady stream of worshippers.

In the centre of the grounds is the **Cathedral of the Resurrection** (Voskresensky sobor), intended to look like Jerusalem's Church of the Holy Sepulchre. Like its prototype, it's really several churches under one roof, including the detached **Assumption Church** (Uspensky tserkov) in the northern part of the cathedral. Here, pilgrims come to kiss the relics of the holy martyr Tatyana, the monastery's patron saint. The unusual underground **Church of SS Konstantin & Yelena** (Konstantino-Yeleninskaya tserkov) has only its belfry peeping up above the ground. Patriarch Nikon was buried in the cathedral, beneath the **Church of John the Baptist** (Tserkov Ioanna Predtechi).

The **refectory** exhibits weapons, icons and artwork from the 17th century, including personal items belonging to Patriarch Nikon. In the monastery walls, there is additional **exhibit space** displaying 20th-century drawings and handicrafts from around the Moscow

WANNA GET AWAY?

These days most Muscovites do not have country estates, but they still need an occasional break from the urban madness. The lovely lakes district northwest of the capital provides plenty of opportunities for swimming, sunning and soaking up the tranquillity of rural Russia. Take advantage of the lovely setting at one of the excellent upscale resorts catering to active vacationers:

Zavidovo Holiday Complex (☎ 495-982 5270; www.zavidovo.ru; Shosha village, Novo-Zavidovo; d weekdays/weekends from R6900/7400;) At a beautiful spot at the confluence of the Volga and Shosha Rivers, this resort offers all kinds of recreational activities, such as horseback riding, waterskiing, golf, tennis, boating and fishing. Afterwards, soothe your weary body in the tiled Turkish bath or the lakeside Russian *banya*. Suburban trains from Moscow's Leningradsky vokzal to Tver stop in Zavidovo (R150, two hours, hourly).

Istra Holiday Country Hotel (☎ 495-739 6198 in Moscow; www.istraholiday.ru; Trusovo; d weekdays/weekends from R5300/7400;) The quaint wooden cottages that make up this hotel sit on the shores of the lovely Istra water reserve, 45km northwest of Moscow. The place offers all the sports and outdoor activities you could hope for, from skiing to swimming to lounging on the beach.

region. On weekends you can sample freshly brewed tea and homemade pastries in the tearoom.

Just outside the monastery's north wall, the Moscow region's Museum of Wooden Architecture (☿ May-Sep) is a collection of picturesque peasant cottages and windmills set along the river.

EATING

Aside from the tearoom on the grounds of the monastery, there are limited options for eating.

Livadiya Cafe (Sovietskaya ul 15; meals R100-200) On the 2nd floor of the hotel of the same name. Serves up standard Russian fare, with a good selection of soups and salads.

Kafe-Stolovaya (☎ 995 4522; pl Revolyutsii 6; business lunch R150; ☿ 10am-5pm Mon-Fri) A simple old-fashioned café and cafeteria in the centre of town.

BORODINO БОРОДИНО

☎ 49638

In 1812 Napoleon invaded Russia, lured by the prospect of taking Moscow. For three months the Russians retreated, until on 26 August the two armies met in a bloody battle of attrition at the village of Borodino. In 15 hours more than one-third of each army was killed – over 100,000 soldiers in all. Europe would not know fighting this devastating again until WWI.

The French seemed to be the winners, as the Russians withdrew and abandoned Mos-

DETOUR: UGLICH (УГЛИЧ)

Uglich is a quaint but shabby town on the Volga, 110km southwest of Yaroslavl. Here in 1591 the son of Ivan the Terrible, Dmitry (later to be impersonated by the string of False Dmitrys in the Time of Troubles), was murdered, probably on the orders of Boris Godunov.

Within the waterside kremlin (☎ 48532-53 678; per site R50; 🕙 9am-5pm), the 15th-century Prince's Chambers (Knyazhyi palaty) house a historical exhibit that tells this sordid tale. The star-spangled Church of St Dmitry on the Blood (Tserkov Dmitria-na-krovi) was built in the 1690s on the spot where the body was found. Its interior is decorated with bright frescoes, and the church now displays the bell that was used to call an insurrection on the murder of the tsarevitch. The 300kg bell was banished for many years to the Siberian town of Tobolsk (this, after Godunov ordered it to be publicly flogged and have its tongue ripped out), but the bell has since returned to its rightful location in Uglich. The impressive five-domed Transfiguration Cathedral (Preobrazhensky sobor) and an art museum are also in the kremlin.

A few blocks over from the kremlin, you can learn about the history of Russia's favourite drink at the Vodka Museum (☎ 48532-23 558; ul Berggolts 9; admission R100; 🕙 9pm-8pm). Price of admission includes samples!

The easiest way to get to Uglich is by bus from Yaroslavl (R150, three hours, 12 daily).

---

infantry general who was mortally wounded in battle.

Further south, a concentration of monuments around Semyonovskoe marks the battle's most frenzied fighting. Here, Bagration's heroic Second Army, opposing far more numerous French forces, was virtually obliterated. Apparently, Russian commander Mikhail Kutuzov deliberately sacrificed Bagration's army to save his larger First Army, opposing lighter French forces in the northern part of the battlefield. Kutuzov's headquarters are marked by an obelisk in the village of Gorky. Another obelisk near Shevardino to the southwest, paid for in 1912 with French donations, marks Napoleon's camp.

Every September the museum complex hosts a re-enactment of the historic battle, complete with Russian and French participants, uniforms and weapons.

Ironically, this battle scene was re-created during WWII, when the Red Army confronted the Nazis on this very site. Memorials to this battle also dot the fields, and WWII trenches surround the monument to Bagration. Near the train station are two WWII mass graves.

The Saviour Borodino Monastery (☎ 51 057; admission R15; 🕙 10am-5pm Tue-Sun) was built by widows of the Afghan War. Among its exhibits is a display devoted to Leo Tolstoy and the events of War and Peace that took place at Borodino.

The rolling hills around Borodino and Semyonovskoe are largely undeveloped, due to their historic status. Facilities are extremely limited; be sure to bring a picnic lunch.

PRIOKSKO-TERRASNY NATURE RESERVE ПРИОКСКО-ТЕРРАСНЫЙ ЗАПОВЕДНИК

Covering 50 sq km bordering the northern flood plain of the Oka River, a tributary of the Volga, the Prioksko-Terrasny Nature Reserve (☎ 707 145; www.danki.ru, in Russian; admission R100, guided tour R350; 🕙 9am-3pm) is a meeting point of northern fir groves and marshes with typical southern meadow steppe. The reserve's varied fauna includes a herd of European bison, brought back from near extinction since WWII.

You cannot wander freely around the reserve by yourself, so it's useful to make advance arrangements for a tour. Otherwise, you could tack onto a prescheduled group tour. There is also a small museum near the

TRANSPORT: PRIOKSKO-TERRASNY NATURE RESERVE

The Prioksko-Terrasny Nature Reserve is about 116km south of Moscow. If you leave by 8am, you can take a suburban train from Moscow's Kursky vokzal to Serpukhov (two hours), then a rare bus (25, 31 or 41) to the reserve. Drivers from Moscow should follow Simferopolskoe sh (the extension of Varshavskoe sh). At 98km, look for the sign to the reserve or to the village of Danki.

office with stuffed specimens of the reserve's fauna (typical of European Russia), including beavers, elk, deer and boar.

The reserve's pride, and the focus of most visits, is its European bison nursery *(pitomnik zu-brov)*. Two pairs of bison, one of Europe's largest mammals (some weigh over a tonne), were brought from Poland in 1948. Now there are about 60 and more than 200 have been sent out to other parts of the country.

TRANSPORT

Flights, tours and rail tickets can be booked online at www.lonelyplanet.com/travel_services.

AIR

Moscow is the main gateway for flights in and out of Russia, so there are frequent services to Europe, North America and Asia, as well as all major Russian cities. Useful websites for purchasing plane tickets include the following:

Avantix (www.avantix.ru) A Russia-specific search engine. If you can read Russian, you can also use the site to purchase train tickets and make hotel reservations.

Cheap Tickets (www.cheaptickets.com) Search engine covers airline tickets, hotels, rental cars and cruises.

Expedia (www.expedia.com) A flexible search engine allowing for one-way fares and multiple-leg journeys.

Kayak (www.kayak.com) A search engine of all the online search engines. When you choose the schedule and fare you like, the site will redirect you to make the purchase.

Orbitz (www.orbitz.com) 'Flex Search' allows you to compare fares on different dates – an excellent tool if you have a flexible travel schedule.

Smarter Travel (www.smartertravel.com) Offers tips for finding the lowest fare, as well as a list of current published fares and last-minute deals.

Travel Zoo (www.travelzoo.com) Highlights sales and specials; also includes discount airlines that are often overlooked by other search engines.

Airlines

Aeroflot and Transaero are two national airlines that serve all major domestic destinations and meet international standards for safety and service. See p255 for a list of agents that sell domestic and international tickets, or you can deal directly with the airlines themselves. Moscow offices of international airlines include the following:

Aeroflot (www.aeroflot.ru; ☀ 9am-8pm Mon-Sat, to 4pm Sun) Tverskoy (Map pp88–9; ☎ 495-223 5555; ul Petrovka 20/1; Ⓜ Chekhovskaya); Kuznetsky Most (Map pp84–5; ☎ 495-924 8054; ul Kuznetsky most 3; Ⓜ Kuznetsky Most); Zamoskvorechie (Map pp120–1; ☎ 495-223 5555; Pyatnitskaya ul 37/19; Ⓜ Tretyakovskaya)

Air France (Map pp120–1; ☎ 495-937 3839; www .airfrance.com; ul Korovy Val 7; Ⓜ Oktyabrskaya)

THINGS CHANGE…

The information provided in this section is particularly vulnerable to change. Check directly with the airline or a travel agent to make sure you understand how a fare (and ticket you may buy) works and shop carefully. Be aware of the security requirements for international travel. The details given in this chapter should be regarded as pointers and are not a substitute for your own careful, up-to-date research.

Austrian Airlines (Map pp120–1; ☎ 495-995 0995; www .aua.com; Korovy Val 7; Ⓜ Oktyabrskaya)

British Airways (Map pp88–9; ☎ 495-363 2525; www .britishairways.com; Business Centre Parus, 1-ya Tverskaya-Yamskaya ul 23; Ⓜ Belorusskaya)

Delta Air Lines (Map pp110–11; ☎ 495-937 9090; www .delta.com; Gogolevsky bul 11; Ⓜ Kropotkinskaya)

Finnair (☎ 495-933 0056; www.finnair.com)

KLM Royal Dutch Airlines (Map pp120–1; ☎ 495-258 3600; www.klm.com; Korovy Val 7; Ⓜ Oktyabrskaya)

LOT Polish Airlines (Map pp84–5; ☎ 495-775 7737; www .lot.com; Trubnaya ul 21/11, 3rd fl; Ⓜ Tsvetnoy Bulvar)

Lufthansa (Map pp84–5; ☎ 495-980 9999; www .lufthansa.com; Posledny per 17; Ⓜ Tsvetnoy Bulvar)

Malév-Hungarian Airlines (Map pp102–3; ☎ 495-202 8416; www.malev.hu; Povarskaya ul 21; Ⓜ Barrikadnaya)

SAS Scandinavian Airline (Map pp88–9; ☎ 495-775 4747; www.scandinavian.net; 1-ya Tverskaya-Yamskaya ul 5; Ⓜ Mayakovskaya)

Swiss Air (Map pp84–5; ☎ 495-937 7767; www.swiss .com; Posledny per 17; Ⓜ Tsvetnoy Bulvar)

Transaero (☎ 495-788 8080; www.transaero.com; ☀ 9am-6pm Mon-Sat) Krasnoselsky (Map pp84–5; Sadovaya-Spasskaya ul 18/1; Ⓜ Krasnye Vorota); Zamoskvorechie (Map pp120–1; Paveletskaya pl 2/3; Ⓜ Paveletskaya)

Airports

Moscow has four main airports servicing international and domestic flights. Note that the destinations served by different airports can vary, so confirm the airport when you buy your ticket. Arrive at least 90 minutes before your international or domestic flight in order to navigate check-in formalities and security.

SHEREMETYEVO-1 & 2

Moscow's main international airport is Sheremetyevo-2 (☎ 495-232 6565; www.sheremetyevo-airport .ru), 30km northwest of the city centre. It services most flights to/from places outside the former USSR. Nearby Sheremetyevo-1 (☎ 495-232 6565; www.sheremetyevo-airport.ru) services flights to/from St Petersburg, the Baltic states, Belarus and northern European Russia. The airport is across the runways from Sheremetyevo-2.

DOMODEDOVO

Domodedovo (☎ 495-933 6666; www.domodedovo.ru), 48km south of the city centre, has undergone extensive upgrades in recent years in order to service more international flights. Most notably, all British Airways flights now use Domodedovo, as do some flights with American Airlines, Lufthansa and many other European airlines. It also services many flights to/from the Far East and Central Asia.

VNUKOVO

Vnukovo (☎ 495-436 2813; www.vnukovo-airport.ru) serves most flights to/from the Caucasus, Moldova and Kaliningrad. About 30km southwest of the city centre, this airport has also undergone substantial renovation and is expanding its services significantly. Specifically, the new budget airline Sky Express (☎ 495-648 9360, 580 9360; www.skyexpress.ru) flies in and out of Vnukovo.

BYKOVO

The little-used Bykovo airport (☎ 499-558 4933) is about 30km southeast of the city centre on Novoryazanskoe sh. *Prigorodnye* trains run from Kazansky vokzal (Kazan station) to Bykovo vokzal, 400m from the airport (R50, one hour, every 20 minutes).

BICYCLE

The centre of Moscow is not really fit for biking. The streets are overcrowded with fast-moving cars, whose drivers abide by parking-lot rules and certainly do not expect bikes on the road. Furthermore, the bigger, more expensive vehicle generally has the right-of-way in Moscow; under these circumstances, a bike does not fare well. That said, there are a few parks and other off-road areas that are suitable for pleasure riding (p199).

Bicycles are not allowed on the metro, although they are permitted on long-distance trains. You must buy a special ticket to bring your bike on the *elektrichka* (suburban commuter train). Bicycles are allowed on intercity passenger trains as long as your total luggage does not exceed the weight limit (36kg). You should disassemble and package the bike to

---

CLIMATE CHANGE & TRAVEL

Climate change is a serious threat to the ecosystems that humans rely upon, and air travel is the fastest-growing contributor to the problem. Lonely Planet regards travel, overall, as a global benefit, but believes we all have a responsibility to limit our personal impact on global warming.

Flying & Climate Change

Pretty much every form of motorised travel generates CO_2 (the main cause of human-induced climate change) but planes are far and away the worst offenders, not just because of the sheer distances they allow us to travel, but because they release greenhouse gases high into the atmosphere. The statistics are frightening: two people taking a return flight between Europe and the US will contribute as much to climate change as an average household's gas and electricity consumption over a whole year.

Carbon Offset Schemes

Climatecare.org and other websites use 'carbon calculators' that allow travellers to offset the level of greenhouse gases they are responsible for with financial contributions to sustainable travel schemes that reduce global warming – including projects in India, Honduras, Kazakhstan and Uganda.

Lonely Planet, together with Rough Guides and other concerned partners in the travel industry, support the carbon offset scheme run by climatecare.org. Lonely Planet offsets all of its staff and author travel.

For more information check out our website: www.lonelyplanet.com

GETTING INTO TOWN

As of 2008, all four major airports are accessible by a convenient Aeroexpress train (☎ 8-800-700 3377; www.aero -express.ru). If you have a lot of luggage and you wish to take a taxi (p243), it is highly recommended to book in advance to take advantage of the fixed rates offered by most companies (usually R1000 to R1500 to/from any airport).

Sheremetyevo

In 2008, the new express train line to Sheremetyevo opened with much fanfare, followed by much embarrassment, when the initial trains were delayed by hours. Presumably, the kinks will be worked out by the time of publication, in which case the Aeroexpress train should leave Savyolovsky vokzal for Sheremetyevo airport (adult/child R250/65, 30 minutes) every hour between 5.30am and midnight. Check the schedule online (www.aero-express.ru) in advance, as the times of departure are sort of random.

Domodedovo

The Aeroexpress train leaves Pavelets vokzal for Domodedovo airport (adult/child R150/40, 45 minutes) every hour between 6am and 11pm, and every half-hour during the busiest times. This route is particularly convenient for domestic flights, as you can check into your flight at the train station.

Vnukovo

The Aeroexpress train runs between Kievsky vokzal and Vnukovo airport (adult/child R120/30, 35 minutes, hourly) between 7am and noon and between 5pm and 8pm, with a few trains running in the middle of the day. Outside these hours, you can take a *marshrutka* (fixed-route minibus) from Yugo-Zapadnaya metro (R50, 30 minutes).

---

ensure that you will be able to find space to store it.

The **Russian Cycle Touring Club** (www.rctc.ru) organises bicycle tours around Russia, including a popular tour of the Golden Ring.

Hire

Bike rental is still a new concept in Moscow, although there are a few hire outfits near the parks that have off-road cycling. The only bike shop that rents bicycles on a short- and long-term basis is **Giant Bike Shop** (off Map pp60–1; ☎ 495-740 5720; ul Pokryshkina 1; per hr R150, per month R3000-5000; Ⓜ Yugo-Zapadnaya).

BOAT
Around Moscow

For new perspectives on Moscow neighbourhoods, fine views of the Kremlin, or just good old-fashioned transport, a boat ride on the Moscow River is one of the city's highlights. The main route runs between the boat landings at Kievsky vokzal (Map p107) and Novospassky most (Map pp128–9) 1km west of Proletarskaya metro (near the Novospassky Monastery). There are six intermediate stops: Vorobyovy Gory landing (Map pp60–1), at the foot of Sparrow Hills; Frunzenskaya (Map pp110–11), towards the southern end of Frunzenskaya nab; Gorky Park (Map pp120–1); Krymsky most (Map pp110–11);

Bolshoy Kamenny most (Map pp120–1), opposite the Kremlin; and Ustinsky most (Map pp80–1), near Red Square.

The boats are operated by the **Capital Shipping Company** (☎ 495-225 6070; www.cck-ship.ru) and run from May to September (adult/child R400/150, 1½ hours, every 20 minutes).

To/From Moscow

There are numerous cruise boats plying the routes between Moscow and St Petersburg, many stopping at some of the Golden Ring cities on the way. Longer cruises south along the Volga also originate in Moscow. Some cruises are specifically aimed at foreign tourists. Generally, for lower prices, you can also sail on a boat aimed at Russian holidaymakers. Boat operators and agencies include the following:

Infoflot (Map pp84–5; ☎ 495-684 9188; www.infoflot.com; ul Shchepkina 28; Ⓜ Prospekt Mira) The market leader.

Mosturflot (☎ 495-221 7222; www.mosturflot.ru, in Russian)

Orthodox Cruise Company (Map pp60–1; ☎ 499-943 8560; www.cruise.ru; ul Alabyana 5, Moscow; Ⓜ Sokol) Also has an office in Rostov-on-Don.

Rechflot (☎ 495-363 9628; www.rechflot.ru, in Russian)

Rechturflot (☎ 495-638 6611; www.rtflot.ru, in Russian)

Vodohod (☎ 495 223 96 11; www.vodohod.com/eng)

BUS
Around Moscow

Buses, trolleybuses and trams are useful along a few radial or cross-town routes that the metro misses, and are necessary for reaching sights away from the city centre. Tickets (R25) are usually sold on the vehicle by a conductor or by the driver. Some offer good sightseeing opportunities:

No 1 From Dobryninskaya metro in Zamoskvorechie, the route goes along ul Bolshaya Polyanka and across Bolshoy Kamenny most, which has a good Kremlin view. Succeeding sights include Pashkov House, the old Moscow State University, Le Royal Meridien National and scenic Tverskaya ul to Belorussky vokzal.

No 2 Makes a big circle around the Kremlin and Kitay Gorod, offering great views, then goes past the Polytechnical Museum, Lubyanskaya pl, Bolshoi Theatre, Hotel Metropol, Le Royal Meridien National, Manezhnaya pl and old Moscow State University. The route then turns on to ul Vozdvizhenka and heads west to Kutuzovsky pr, the Triumphal Arch and Victory Park.

No 8 Offers views of Zamoskvorechie and its many churches. From Dobryninskaya metro, it heads north along Pyatnitskaya ul and returns south along ul Bolshaya Ordynka.

To/From Moscow
DOMESTIC SERVICES

Buses run to a number of towns and cities within 700km of Moscow. Bus fares are similar to *kupeyny* (2nd-class) train fares. Buses tend to be crowded, although they are usually faster than the *prigorodnye poezdy* (suburban trains). See the table, right, for some sample fares.

To book a seat, go to the long-distance bus terminal, the Shchyolkovsky bus station (off Map pp60–1; M Shchyolkovskaya), 8km east of the city centre. Queues can be bad, so it's advisable to book ahead, especially for travel on Friday, Saturday or Sunday.

Buses also depart from outside the various train stations, offering alternative transport to the destinations served by the train. These buses do not run according to a particular schedule but, rather, leave when the bus is full. Likewise, they cannot be booked in advance.

INTERNATIONAL SERVICES

International bus services offer the cheapest means of getting to Russia, although services to Moscow are limited.

BUSES FROM MOSCOW

Destination	Buses per day	Duration	One-way fare
Nizhny Novgorod	5	9hr	R425-500
Pereslavl-Zalessky	hourly	2½hr	R230
Suzdal	1	4½hr	R250
Vladimir	4	4hr	R190-225

Berlin Linien Bus (☎ 812-441 3757; www.berlinlinien bus.de) Operates a twice-weekly bus service between Berlin and Moscow (€71, 12 hours). Departs from Kazansky vokzal at 4pm on Tuesday and Friday.

Ecolines (Map pp60–1; ☎ 495-950 2262; www.ecolines .ru; Leningradsky pr 37/6; M Aeroport) Operates daily buses from Moscow to Riga (R1425, 15 hours) and Vilnius (R1380, 16½ hours). Buses depart from Rizhsky vokzal.

CAR & MOTORCYCLE

There's little reason for travellers to rent a car for getting around Moscow, as public transport is quite adequate, but you might want to consider car rental for trips out of the city. Be aware that driving in Russia is truly an unfiltered Russian experience. Poor roads, maddeningly inadequate signposting, low-quality petrol and keen highway patrollers can lead to frustration and dismay.

Driving

To drive in Russia, you must be at least 18 years old and have a full driving licence. In addition, you may be asked to present an International Driving Permit with a Russian translation of your licence, or a certified Russian translation of your full licence (you can certify translations at a Russian embassy or consulate).

For your own vehicle, you will also need registration papers and proof of insurance. Be sure your insurance covers you in Russia. Finally, a customs declaration, promising that you will take your vehicle with you when you leave, is also required.

As of 2008, the maximum legal blood-alcohol content is 0.03%. Prior to this change it was practically illegal to drive after consuming *any* alcohol at all, and this rule was strictly enforced. Because this is a fairly new change to driving laws, it is not advisable to drink and drive in Russia, even a small amount.

Officers of the State Automobile Inspectorate (Gosudarstvennaya Avtomobilnaya Inspektsia), better known as GAI, skulk about on the roadsides all around Moscow waiting for miscreant drivers. They are authorised to stop you (by pointing their striped stick at you and waving you towards the side) and to issue on-the-spot fines. The GAI also hosts the occasional speed trap – the road to Sheremetyevo airport is infamous for this. If you are required to pay a fine, pay in roubles only – and make sure you get a receipt.

Moscow has no shortage of petrol stations that sell all grades of petrol. Most are open 24 hours and can be found on the major roads in and out of town.

Hire

While driving around Moscow is an unnecessary hassle, renting a car may be a reasonable option for trips out of the city. Be aware that some firms won't let you take their cars out of the Moscow Oblast.

The major international rental firms have outlets in Moscow (at either Sheremetyevo or Domodedovo airport, as well as in the city centre). Prices start at R1700 per day, although you may be able to cut this price by reserving in advance. The major car-rental agencies will usually pick up or drop off the car at your hotel for an extra fee.

Avis (Map pp84–5; ☎ 495-744 0733; www.avis-moscow .ru; Meshchanskaya ul 7/1; Ⓜ Sukharevskaya)

Europcar (off Map pp60–1; ☎ 495-775 7565; www .europcar.ru; Mozhayskoe sh 166) Cars prohibited from leaving Moscow Oblast.

Hertz (Map pp60–1; ☎ 495-232 0889; www.hertz.ru; Tverskaya Zastava pl 2; Ⓜ Belorusskaya)

Thrifty (☎ 495-788 6888; www.thrifty.ru) Outer North (off Map pp60–1; Leningradskoe sh 63B; Ⓜ Rechnoy Vokzal); Outer South (Map pp60–1; ul Obrucheva 27, Bldg 1; Ⓜ Kaluzhskaya) Mileage limited to 200km per day.

METRO

The Moscow metro (www.mosmetro.ru) is the easiest, quickest and cheapest way of getting around Moscow. Many of the elegant stations are marble-faced, frescoed, gilded works of art (see Underground Odyssey, p143). The trains are generally reliable: you will rarely wait on the platform for more than three minutes. Nonetheless, they get packed during rush hour. Up to nine million people a day ride the metro, more than the London and New York City systems combined.

The 150-plus stations are marked outside by large 'M' signs. Magnetic tickets (R19) are sold at ticket booths. Queues can be long, so it's useful to buy a multiple-ride ticket (10 rides for R155, 20 for R280).

Stations have maps of the system at the entrance and signs on each platform showing the destinations. The maps are generally in Cyrillic and Latin script, although the signs are usually only in Cyrillic. The carriages also have maps inside that show the stops for that line in both Roman and Cyrillic letters.

Interchange stations are linked by underground passages, indicated by *perekhod* signs, usually blue with a stick figure running up the stairs. Be aware that when two or more lines meet, the intersection stations often have different names.

TAXI

Almost any car in Moscow could be a taxi if the price is right, so get on the street and stick your arm out. Many private cars cruise around as unofficial taxis, known as 'gypsy cabs', and other drivers will often take you if they're going in roughly the same direction. Expect to pay R150 to R200 for a ride around the city centre. Official taxis – which can be recognised by the checkerboard logo on the side and/or a small green light in the windscreen – charge higher rates.

Don't hesitate to wave on a car if you don't like the look of its occupants. As a general rule, it's best to avoid riding in cars that already have two or more people inside. Be particularly careful taking a taxi that is waiting outside a nightclub or bar.

Reliable taxi companies (all with websites in Russian only) include the following:

Central Taxi Reservation Office (Tsentralnoe Byuro Zakazov Taxi; ☎ 495-627 0000; www.cbz-taxi.ru)

MV Motors (☎ 495-232 5232, 8-800-200 8294; www.7756775.ru)

New Yellow Taxi (☎ 495-940 8888; www.nyt.ru)

Taxi Bistro (☎ 495-961 0041; www.taxopark.ru)

Taxi Blues (☎ 495-105 5115; www.taxi-blues.ru)

Normally, the dispatcher will ring you back within a few minutes to provide a description and licence number of the car. It's best to provide at least an hour's notice before you need the taxi.

DOMESTIC TRAINS FROM MOSCOW

Destination & train No	Departure time & station	Duration	Fare
Irkutsk 010	11.25pm, Yaroslavsky	76hr	R10,800-12,340
Kazan 002	10.08pm, Kazansky	11½hr	R2500-2860
Murmansk 016	12.50am, Leningradsky	35½hr	R3770-4150
Nizhny Novgorod 062	1.55pm, Kursky	5hr	R390-470 (seat)
Pskov 010	7.28pm, Leningradsky	12hr	R2300-2700
Samara 010	6.10pm, Kazansky	15hr	R3270
Tver	8 daily, Leningradsky	2hr	R130 (seat)
Vladimir 062*	1.55pm, Kursky	2½hr	R240-320 (seat)
Yaroslavl	14 daily, Yaroslavsky	4hr	R480
Yekaterinburg 016	4.08pm, Kazansky	24½hr	R4770-5360

Fares are for *kupe* (2nd-class compartment), unless stated otherwise.
*Express train; other slower trains also available.

TRAIN

Moscow has rail links to most parts of Russia, most former Soviet states, numerous countries in Eastern and Western Europe, and China and Mongolia. Prices quoted in this section are for a *kupe* (2nd-class in a four-seat couchette) ticket on a *skory* (fast) train.

Classes

On long-distance trains, your ticket will normally give the numbers of your carriage *(vagon)* and seat *(mesto)*. For more details of travelling on Russian trains, see Lonely Planet's *Russia & Belarus* or *Trans-Siberian Railway*.

Compartments in a 1st-class carriage, also called soft class *(myagky)* or sleeping car *(spalny vagon, SV or lyux)*, have upholstered seats and also convert to comfortable sleeping compartments for two people. Not all trains have a 1st-class carriage. Travelling 1st class costs about 50% more than a 2nd-class ticket.

Compartments in a 2nd-class carriage, usually called 'compartmentalised' *(kupeny or kupe)*, are four-person couchettes.

Reserved place *(platskartny)*, sometimes also called hard class or 3rd class, has open bunk accommodation. Groups of hard bunks are partitioned, but not closed off, from each other.

Stations

Moscow has nine main stations. Multiple stations may service the same destination, so be sure to confirm the arrival/departure station.

Belorussky vokzal (Belarus station; Map pp88–9; Tverskaya Zastava pl; Ⓜ Belorusskaya) Serves trains to/from Smolensk, Kaliningrad, Belarus, Lithuania, Poland, Germany; some trains to/from the Czech Republic; and suburban trains to/from the west, including Mozhaysk, Borodino and Zvenigorod.

Kazansky vokzal (Kazan station; Map pp84–5; Komsomolskaya pl; Ⓜ Komsomolskaya) Serves trains to/from Kazan, Izhevsk, Ufa, Ryazan, Ulyanovsk, Samara, Novorossiysk, Central Asia; some trains to/from Vladimir, Nizhny Novgorod, the Ural Mountains, Siberia, Saratov, Rostov-on-Don; and suburban trains to/from the southeast, including Bykovo airport, Kolomna, Gzhel and Ryazan.

Kievsky vokzal (Kyiv station; Map p107; Kievskaya pl; Ⓜ Kievskaya) Serves Bryansk, Kyiv, western Ukraine, Moldova, Slovakia, Hungary, Austria, Prague, Romania, Bulgaria, Croatia, Serbia, Greece, Venice; suburban trains to/from the southwest, including Peredelkino and Kaluga.

TRAINS FROM MOSCOW TO ST PETERSBURG

Train No & name	Departure time	Duration	Fare
2 *Krasnaya Strela*	11.55pm	8hr	R2600-3000
4 *Ekspress*	11.59pm	8hr	R2380
6 *Nikolaevsky Ekspress*	11.30pm	8hr	R2750
54 *Grand Express*	11.40pm	9hr	R5000-6200 (*lyux*)
160 *Avrora*	4.30pm	5½hr	R2450 (seat)
166 *ER200*	6.30pm	4½hr	R3300-3650 (seat)

All trains to St Petersburg depart from Leningradsky vokzal.

Kursky vokzal (Kursk station; Map pp80–1; pl Kurskogo vokzala; Ⓜ Kurskaya) Serves Oryol, Kursk, Krasnodar, Adler, the Caucasus, eastern Ukraine, Crimea, Georgia, Azerbaijan. It also has some trains to/from Rostov-on-Don, Vladimir, Nizhny Novgorod, Perm; and suburban trains to/from the east and south, including Petushki, Podolsk, Chekhov, Serpukhov and Tula.

Leningradsky vokzal (Leningrad station; Map pp84–5; Komsomolskaya pl; Ⓜ Komsomolskaya) Serves Tver, Novgorod, Pskov, St Petersburg, Vyborg, Murmansk, Estonia, Helsinki; and suburban trains to/from the north-west, including Klin and Tver. Note that sometimes this station is referred to on timetables and tickets by its former name, Oktyabrsky.

Paveletsky vokzal (Pavelets station; Map pp120–1; Paveletskaya pl; Ⓜ Paveletskaya) Serves Yelets, Lipetsk, Voronezh, Tambov, Volgograd, Astrakhan; some trains to/from Saratov; and suburban trains to/from the southeast, including Leninskaya and Domodedovo airport.

Rizhsky vokzal (Riga station; Map pp60–1; Rizhskaya pl; Ⓜ Rizhskaya) Serves Latvia, with suburban trains to/from the northwest, including Istra and Novoierusalimskaya.

Savyolovsky vokzal (Savyolov station; Map pp60–1; pl Savyolovskogo vokzala; Ⓜ Savyolovskaya) Serves Cherepovets; some trains to/from Kostroma, Vologda; and suburban trains to/from the north, including Sheremetyevo airport.

Yaroslavsky vokzal (Yaroslavl station; Map pp84–5; Komsomolskaya pl; Ⓜ Komsomolskaya) Serves Yaroslavl, Arkhangelsk, Vorkuta, the Russian Far East, Mongolia, China, North Korea; some trains to/from Vladimir, Nizhny Novgorod, Kostroma, Vologda, Perm, Urals, Siberia; and suburban trains to/from the northeast, including Abramtsevo, Khotkovo, Sergiev Posad and Aleksandrov.

LEFT LUGGAGE
You can check your bags at most hotels and train and bus stations. Look for signs for Камера Хранения (kamera khraneniya) or Автоматические Камеры Хранения (avtomaticheskie kamery khraneniya). The former refers to luggage storage, where you can check your bag and leave it under the care of a monitor; the latter refers to automated left-luggage lockers. Both options are usually secure, but be sure to note the opening and closing hours.

Tickets
For long-distance trains it's best to buy your tickets in advance, especially in summer. Always take your passport along when buying a ticket.

Tickets are sold at train stations but it is much easier to buy them from a travel

INTERNATIONAL TRAINS FROM MOSCOW

Destination & train No	Departure time & station	Duration	Fare
Almaty 007	10.40pm (odd days), Paveletsky	78hr	R6260
Kyiv 001	11.23pm (odd days), Kievsky	9½hr	R2000-2400
Minsk 001	10.25pm, Belorussky	10hr	R2850
Riga 001	7.10pm, Rizhsky	16hr	R4020
Tallinn 034	6.05pm, Leningradsky	15½hr	R3300
Vilnius 005	6.20pm, Belorussky	14½hr	R2890

agent (p255) or kassa zheleznoy dorogi (Касса Железной Дороги; railway ticket office). These are often conveniently located in hotel lobbies. Glavagentstvo-Service is an agency selling airplane and train tickets with many outlets around town, including the following:

Khamovniki (Map pp110–11; ☎ 495-242 3823; ul Khamovichesky val, Hotel Yunost; Ⓜ Sportivnaya)

Leningradsky vokzal (Map pp84–5; ☎ 495-975 5920; Ⓜ Komsomolskaya)

Sheremetyevo-2 airport (☎ 495-578 8352; Sheremetyevo-2)

Taganka (Map pp128–9; ☎ 495-967 8665; Taganskaya ul 19; Ⓜ Marksistskaya)

Tverskoy (Map pp88–9; ☎ 495-745 6548; 1-ya Tverskaya-Yamskaya ul 15; Ⓜ Belorusskaya)

Types of Train
LONG-DISTANCE TRAINS
The regular long-distance service is a fast train (skory poezd). It stops more often than an intercity train in the West and rarely gets up enough speed to merit the 'fast' label. Foreigners booking rail tickets through agencies are usually put on a skory train.

Generally, the best of the skory trains (firmenny) have cleaner cars, more polite attendants and much more convenient arrival and departure hours; they sometimes also have fewer stops, more 1st-class accommodation and functioning restaurants.

A passenger train *(passazhirsky poezd)* can take an awfully long time to travel between cities. They are found mostly on routes of 1000km or less, clanking and lurching from one small town to the next.

SUBURBAN TRAINS

When taking trains from Moscow, note the difference between long-distance and 'suburban' trains. Long-distance trains run to places at least three or four hours out of Moscow, with limited stops and a range of classes. Suburban trains, known as *prigorodnye poezdy* or *elektrichki*, run to within 100km or 200km of Moscow, stop almost everywhere, and have a single class of hard bench seats. You buy your ticket before the train leaves, and there's no capacity limit.

Most Moscow train stations have a separate ticket hall for suburban trains, usually called the *prigorodny zal* (Пригородный Зал), which is often tucked away at the side or back of the station building. Suburban trains are usually listed on separate timetables and may depart from a separate group of platforms.

BUSINESS HOURS

Government offices open at 9am or 10am and close at 5pm or 6pm on weekdays. Hours for banks and other services vary: large branches in busy commercial areas are usually open from 9am to 4.30pm or 5pm weekdays, with shorter hours on Saturday; smaller bank branches have shorter hours, and will often close for a one-hour break *(pereriv)* in the middle of the day.

The consumer culture is developing rapidly in Russia, and one place it is evident is hours of operation. Most shops are open daily, often from 10am to 8pm or 9pm. Smaller shops might close on Sunday. Department stores and food shops are usually open from 8am to 8pm daily. These days, many larger food shops stay open *kruglosutochno* (around the clock).

Restaurants are typically open from noon to midnight, although – again – it is not unusual for them to stay open for 24 hours a day. Bars may stay open until 2am, while some clubs are open until 6am on weekends.

Museum opening hours change often, as do their weekly days off. Most shut their entrance doors 30 minutes or an hour before closing time. Many museums close for a 'sanitary day' during the last week of every month.

CHILDREN

You will know that Russia has made its transition to capitalism when you see the supermarkets well stocked with nappies, formulas and every other product your children might need.

Moscow does not present any particular hazards to your kids, save for ornery babushkas (even they seem to have a soft spot for kids, though). While the Russian capital, filled as it is with museums, churches and theatres, might not seem like the most appealing destination for anyone under 20, it's surprisingly well equipped for youngsters. For a list of kid-friendly sights in Moscow, see the boxed text, p99. In addition to these suggestions, children's theatre is a carry-over from the Soviet period

that continues to thrive in Moscow (see Children's Theatres p193).

Lonely Planet's *Travel with Children* contains useful advice on how to cope with kids on the road and what to bring to make things go more smoothly.

Babysitting

The concept of babysitting services has not yet developed in Moscow, although some upmarket hotels offer this service.

CLIMATE

Moscow's continental climate enjoys five seasons: there's spring, summer, autumn, winter – and then there's Russian winter. The deepest, darkest part of winter is undeniably cold in this city but if you are prepared it can be an adventure. Furs and vodka keep people warm, and snow-covered landscapes are picturesque.

A solid snowpack covers the ground from November to March. The lowest recorded temperature is -42°C, although it's normally more like -10°C for weeks on end. Occasional southerly winds can raise the temperature briefly to a balmy 0°C. Daylight hours during winter are very few.

During the spring thaw, which occurs from late March to early April – everything turns to mud and slush. Summer comes fast in June, and temperatures are comfortable until well into September. The highest recorded temperature is 39°C, although on a humid August day you'll swear it's hotter than that. July and August are the warmest, wettest months, with an average of 88mm of rain falling in July.

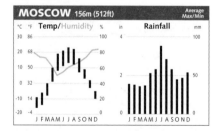

COURSES
Cooking

Russian cooking classes are hard to come by, but Dom Patriarshy (p252) does offer an occasional half-day course. Learn to whip up some bliny (crêpes) for lunch.

Language

Check the *Moscow Times* for advertisements for Russian tutors and short-term courses.

Centre for Russian Language & Culture (Map pp60–1; ☎ 495-939 1463; www.ruslanguage.ru; Moscow State University; 20hr course €95; Ⓜ Universitet) Caters mostly to students, offering semester-long courses and dormitory lodging. Special weekly courses for expats (lodging not included) also available.

CREF Language Centre (Map pp80–1; ☎ 495-621 9486; www.cref.ru; Bolshoy Kharitonevsky per 14; 40hr course €840; Ⓜ Chistye Prudy) Two-week course includes lodging with a Russian family.

Liden & Denz Language Centre (Map pp96–7; ☎ 495-254 4991; www.lidenz.ru; Gruzinsky per 3; 12hr course R4920; Ⓜ Belorusskaya) These more-expensive courses service the business and diplomatic community with less-intensive evening courses.

Russian Village (☎ 495-225 5001; www.rusvillage.com; weekend-/week-/month-long course from €390/900/2910) An upscale 'country resort' language school located in the village of Pestovo, north of Moscow. Prices include lodging and meals.

Ziegler & Partner (Map pp60–1; ☎ 495-939 0980; www.studyrussian.com; Moscow State University; 2-/4-week course €1040/1860; Ⓜ Universitet) A Swiss group offering individually designed courses from standard conversation to specialised lessons in business, law, literature etc. Price includes 20 to 24 hours of lessons per week as well as dorm lodging.

CUSTOMS REGULATIONS

When you enter Russia, you'll have the option to fill out a declaration form *(deklaratsia)*. If you have more than US$10,000 in goods and currency, you are required to fill out this form and go through the red lane to have your form stamped. This process may require having your luggage checked.

If you have less than US$10,000 you are not required to get your customs form stamped and you can proceed through the green line. However, if you have any valuable items (such as expensive jewellery or electronics) it may be useful to declare them, to protect yourself and your stuff when you're leaving the country. In this case, make sure you get a stamp on your customs declaration form on your arrival.

Travellers may leave Russia with up to US$3000 in goods and currency without submitting declaration forms. In order to ensure you're able to leave with valuable items from home, follow the advice earlier. Stamped declaration forms will have to be submitted upon exit from Russia. Your stamped form cannot show that you are leaving with more than you brought in. The system is antiquated – considering the reality of credit-card purchases and ATM access to cash – but nonetheless it is still in place.

Look after your stamped customs declaration. If you lose it you will need a police report confirming the loss, which you have to present to customs when you leave Russia.

Items more than 100 years old cannot be taken out of the country. Anything vaguely 'arty', such as manuscripts, musical instruments, coins, jewellery, antiques or antiquarian books (meaning those published before 1975) must be assessed by the **Committee for Culture** (Map pp102–3; ☎ 495-244 7675; ul Arbat 53; ☸ 10am-2pm & 3-6pm Mon-Fri; Ⓜ Smolenskaya). Bring your item (or a photograph, if the item is large) and your receipt. The bureaucrats there will issue a receipt for tax paid, which you show to customs officers on your way out of the country.

A painting bought at a tourist art market, in a department store or from a commercial gallery should be declared and receipts should be kept.

Generally speaking, customs in airports is much more strict and thorough than at any border crossing.

ELECTRICITY

Standard voltage is 220V, 50Hz AC, though some places still have an old 127V system. Sockets require a continental or European plug with two round pins. Look for voltage (V) and frequency (Hz) labels on your appliances. Some trains and hotel bathrooms have 110V and 220V shaver plugs.

EMBASSIES

It's wise to register with your embassy, especially if you'll be in Russia for a long stay.

Australia (Map pp80–1; ☎ 495-956 6070; www.russia.embassy.gov.au; Podkolokolny per 10A/2; ☸ 9am-5pm; Ⓜ Kitay-Gorod)

Belarus (Map pp80–1; ☎ 495-777 6644; www.embassy bel.ru; ul Maroseyka 17/6, 101000; ☒ 10am-noon Mon, Tue, Thu & Fri; Ⓜ Kitay-Gorod)

Canada (Map pp110–11; ☎ 495-925 6000; www.dfait -maeci.gc.ca/missions/russia-russie/menu-eng.asp; Starokonyushenny per 23; ☒ 8.30am-5pm; Ⓜ Kropotkinskaya)

China (Map p107; ☎ 495-938 2006, consular 499-143 1540; http://ru.china-embassy.org; ul Druzhby 6; Ⓜ Universitet)

France (Map pp120–1; ☎ 495-937 1500; www.ambafrance -ru.org; ul Bolshaya Yakimanka 45; Ⓜ Oktyabrskaya)

Germany (Map p107; ☎ 495-937 9500; www.moskau .diplo.de; Mosfilmovskaya ul 56; ☒ 8am-1pm & 1.45-5pm Mon-Wed & Fri, 8am-1pm & 1.45-3pm Sat; Ⓜ Universitet, then bus 119); consular section (Map pp60–1; ☎ 495-933 4311; Leninsky pr 95A; Ⓜ Prospekt Vernadskogo, then bus 616 or 153)

Ireland (Map pp84–5; ☎ 495-937 5911; www.embassy ofireland.ru; Grokholsky per 5; ☒ 9.30am-4.30pm Mon-Fri; Ⓜ Prospekt Mira)

Mongolia (Map pp102–3; ☎ 495-290 6792; www.mong olianembassy.ru; Borisoglebsky per 11; ☒ 9.30am-12.30pm & 4-5.30pm Mon-Fri; Ⓜ Arbartskaya); consular section (Map pp102–3; Spasopeskovsky per 7/1; Ⓜ Smolenskaya)

Netherlands (Map pp102–3; ☎ 495-797 2900; www .netherlands-embassy.ru; Kalashny per 6; Ⓜ Arbatskaya)

UK (Map pp102–3; ☎ 495-956 7200; www.britemb.msk .ru; Smolenskaya nab 10; ☒ summer 9am-1pm & 2-5pm Mon-Fri, winter 8am-noon & 1-4pm Mon-Fri; Ⓜ Smolenskaya)

Ukraine (Map pp88–9; ☎ 495-629 9742; www.mfa .gov.ua/russia; Leontevsky per 18; ☒ 9am-1pm & 2-6pm Mon-Fri; Ⓜ Pushkinskaya)

USA (Map pp102–3; ☎ 495-728 5000; http://moscow.us embassy.gov; Bol Devyatinsky per 8; ☒ 9am-4pm; Ⓜ Barrikadnaya)

EMERGENCY

Ambulance ☎ 03, in Russian

Emergency assistance ☎ 495-937 9911

Fire ☎ 01

Police ☎ 02

GAY & LESBIAN TRAVELLERS

The first Gay Pride Parade was held in Moscow in 2006, despite bureaucratic obstacles, popular protests and sporadic violence.

Moscow now hosts Gay Pride (www.moscowpride .ru) every year in May. The 2009 parade was scheduled to coincide with the Eurovision Song Contest, which will also be held in Moscow. Some years down the road, Gay Pride is still highly controversial, even among the gay community, and city officials continue to threaten to ban the event.

Nonetheless, Moscow is the most cosmopolitan of Russian cities, and the active gay and lesbian scene reflects this attitude. Newspapers such as the *Moscow Times* feature articles about gay and lesbian issues, as well as listings of gay and lesbian clubs. The newest publication of note is the glossy Russian-language magazine *Queer* (Квир), which offers up articles and artwork. Some other useful resources:

www.gay.ru/english Includes updated club listings, plus information on gay history and culture in Russia.

www.gayrussia.ru An advocacy group that is also involved with the organisation of Gay Pride.

www.gaytours.ru Dmitry is a gay-friendly face in Moscow and his site is still a wealth of information about gay life in the city.

www.lesbi.ru An active site for lesbian issues; in Russian only.

For details on gay and lesbian venues, see the boxed text, p185.

Cracks in the Iron Closet: Travels in Gay & Lesbian Russia by David Tuller and Frank Browning is a fascinating account of the gay and lesbian scene in modern Russia. A combination of travel memoir and social commentary, it reveals an emerging homosexual culture that is surprisingly different from its US counterpart.

Queer Sites by Dan Healy traces the history of seven world cities, including Moscow, focusing on sexual mores, the homosexual experience and how they have changed over time.

HOLIDAYS

During major holidays – the first week in January (between New Year's Day and Orthodox Christmas) and the first week or two of May (around Labour Day, or May Day, and Victory Day) – Moscow empties out, as many residents retreat from the city for much-needed vacations. Transport is difficult to book around these periods, though accommodation is usually not a problem (and often at reduced rates). While many residents leave, the city is a festive place during these times, usually hosting parades, concerts and other events. The downside is that many museums and other institutions have shortened hours or are closed altogether during holiday periods.

Public Holidays

New Year's Day 1 January

Russian Orthodox Christmas 7 January

International Women's Day 8 March

International Labour Day/Spring Festival 1 and 2 May

Victory (1945) Day 9 May

Russian Independence 12 June

Day of Reconciliation and Accord (formerly Revolution Day) 7 November

INTERNET ACCESS

Almost all upscale hotels and hostels, as well as some midrange hotels, offer wi-fi, usually free for guests. DSL access is also sometimes available. The process for going online varies, but the hotel will provide instructions. If your computer does not have wireless access, you will use the phone cord to plug into your modem. No additional plugs or sockets are required. If you are planning to stay in town for more than a couple of weeks, and you are not staying at a hotel, consider opening your own account with an ISP such as Russia On-line (www.rol.ru). If you are not travelling with your own computer, there are plenty of internet cafés around the city, offering excellent, fast and generally affordable internet access.

Cafemax – Tverskoy (Map pp88–9; ☎ 495-741 7571; Novoslobodskaya ul 3; per hr R120; ☾ 24hr; Ⓜ Novoslobodskaya) Discounts available late at night and early morning.

Cafemax – Zamoskvorechie (Map pp120–1; ☎ 495-950 6050; Pyatnitskaya ul 25; per hr R50-90; ☾ 24hr; Ⓜ Novokuznetskaya)

NetLand (Map pp84–5; ☎ 495-781 0923; Teatralny proezd 5; per hr R80-100; ☾ 24hr; Ⓜ Kuznetsky Most or Lubyanka) A loud, dark club that fills up with kids playing games. Enter from ul Rozhdestvenka.

Playground.ru (Map pp96–7; ☎ 495-980 1020; Tishinskaya pl 1; per hr R50; ☾ 24hr; Ⓜ Belorusskaya) This computer gaming club is inside the Tishinka shopping centre.

Pronto Internet Cafe (Map pp88–9; ☎ 495-692 5181; Tverskaya ul 10; per hr R130-160; ☾ 9am-10pm;

Ⓜ Pushkinskaya). Computers and coffee on the 2nd floor of the Tsentralnaya Hotel.

Set.ru (Map pp88–9; ☎ 915-335 0223; 1-y Volkonsky per 15; per hr R60; ☾ 24hr; Ⓜ Tsvetnoy bulvar)

Time Online – Leningradsky vokzal (Map pp84–5; ☎ 495-266 8351; Komsomolskaya pl 3; per hr R70-100; ☾ 24hr; Ⓜ Komsomolskaya) Offers copy and photo services, as well as over 100 zippy computers or free wi-fi access.

Time Online – Okhotny Ryad (Map p66; ☎ 495-988 6426; Okhotny Ryad Shopping Centre; per hr R70-100; ☾ 24hr; Ⓜ Okhotny Ryad)

LEGAL MATTERS

It's not unusual to see police officers, or *militsiya,* randomly stopping people on the street to check their documents. In recent years, this checking has tended to focus on anyone who remotely looks as if they come from the Caucasus, and other people with darkish skin, but the *militsiya* have the right to stop anyone. Technically, everyone is required to carry their *dokumenty,* or passport, with them at all times. Unfortunately, some readers have complained about police pocketing their passports and demanding bribes. The best way to avoid such unpleasantness is to carry a photocopy of your passport, visa and registration, and present them when an officer demands to see your *dokumenty.* A photocopy is sufficient, despite what the officer may argue.

LIBRARIES & CULTURAL CENTRES

Foreign Literature Library (Map pp128–9; ☎ 495-915 3621; www.libfl.ru; Nikoloyamskaya ul 1; ☾ 10am-7.30pm Mon-Fri, 10am-5.30pm Sat & Sun; Ⓜ Taganskaya) Home to several international libraries and cultural centres, including the American Centre (☎ 495-777 6350; www.amc.ru), the French Cultural Centre (☎ 495-915 7974; www.ccf-moscou.ru) and the British Council

Resource Centre (☎ 495-782 0200; www.britishcouncil .org). Closed Sundays between June and August.

Russian State Library (Map pp102–3; ul Vozdvizhenka 3; 🕙 9am-9pm; Ⓜ Biblioteka imeni Lenina) On the corner of Mokhovaya ul, this is one of the world's largest libraries, with over 20 million volumes. If you want to peruse any of these, take along your passport and one passport photo, and fill in some forms at the information office to get a free *chitatelsky bilet* (reader's card).

MAPS

An excellent, up-to-date map in English is the *Moscow Today City Map*, published in 2007 by Atlas Print Co (☎ 495-984 5604; www.atlas-print.ru).

Atlas (Map pp84–5; ☎ 495-928 6109; Kuznetsky most 9/10; 🕙 9am-8pm Mon-Fri, 10am-6pm Sat, 11am-5pm Sun; Ⓜ Kuznetsky Most) is a little shop housing an impressive collection of maps, including city and regional maps covering the whole country. The walls are plastered with most of the maps that are for sale.

MEDICAL SERVICES

Gone are the days when patients received medical care for free. (You probably don't want that free care anyway, as the old saying holds true: you get what you pay for.) Both of the international medical facilities listed here accept health insurance from major international providers.

American Medical Centre (Map pp84–5; ☎ 495-933 7700; www.amcenter.ru; Grokholsky per 1; Ⓜ Prospekt Mira) Offers 24-hour emergency service, consultations and a full range of medical specialists, including paediatricians and dentists. Also has an on-site pharmacy with English-speaking staff.

RUSSIAN STREET NAMES

We use the Russian names of all streets and squares in this book to help you when deciphering Cyrillic signs and asking locals the way. The following abbreviations are used in the text and on the maps:

bul (*bulvar;* бульвар) – boulevard

nab (*naberezhnaya;* набережная) – embankment

per (*pereulok;* переулок) – lane or side street

pl (*ploshchad;* площадь) – square

pr (*prospekt;* проспект) – avenue

ul (*ulitsa;* улица) – street

sh (*shosse;* шоссе) – highway

Botkin Hospital (Map pp60–1; ☎ 495-945 0045; 2-y Botkinsky proezd 5; Ⓜ Begovaya) The best Russian facility.

European Medical Centre (Map pp96–7; ☎ 495-933 6655; www.emcmos.ru; Spirodonevsky per 5; Ⓜ Mayakovskaya) Includes medical and dental facilities, which are open around the clock for emergencies. The staff speak 10 languages.

Pharmacies

A chain of 24-hour pharmacies called 36.6 has many branches all around the city, including the following:

Arbat (Map pp102–3; ☎ 495-203 0207; ul Novy Arbat 15; Ⓜ Arbatskaya)

Basmanny (Map pp80–1; ☎ 495-923 2258; ul Pokrovka 1/13; Ⓜ Kitay-Gorod)

Krasnoselsky & Meshchansky (Map pp84–5; ☎ 495-623 4718; Kuznetsky most 18/7; Ⓜ Kuznetsky Most)

Tverskoy (Map pp88–9; ☎ 495-699 2459; Tverskaya ul 25/9; Ⓜ Tverskaya, Mayakovskaya)

MONEY

Russian currency is the rouble, written as рубль or abbreviated as руб. There are 100 kopecks (копеек or коп) in the rouble and these come in small coins that are worth one, five, 10 and 50 kopecks. Roubles are issued in coins in amounts of one, two and five roubles. Banknotes come in values of 10, 50, 100, 500 and 1000 roubles. Small stores, kiosks and many other vendors have difficulty changing large notes, so save those scrappy little ones.

The rouble has been relatively stable since it was revalued in 1998. Exchange rates are listed inside the front cover. See www.oanda .com/convert/classic for more up-to-date rates.

Alfa Bank (🕙 8.30am-8pm Mon-Sat) has many branches around Moscow that usually change travellers cheques. ATMs at the branches listed dispense roubles and US dollars. You will also see branches of the affiliated Alfa-Express, which have ATMs. Alfa Bank branches include the following:

Arbat (Map pp102–3; ul Arbat 4; Ⓜ Arbatskaya)

Kitay Gorod (Map p66; ul Varvarka 3; Ⓜ Kitay-Gorod)

Krasnoselsky & Meshchansky (Map pp84–5; Kuznetsky most 9/10; Ⓜ Kuznetsky Most)

Zamoskvorechie (Map pp120–1; ul Bolshaya Ordynka 21; Ⓜ Tretyakovskaya)

ATMs

Automatic teller machines (ATMs), linked to international networks such as Amex, Cirrus, Eurocard, MasterCard and Visa, are now common throughout Moscow. Look for signs that say bankomat (Банкомат). Using a credit or debit card, you can always obtain roubles and often US dollars.

Changing Money

US dollars and euros are now widely accepted at exchange bureaus around Moscow. Other currencies will undoubtedly cause more hassle than they are worth. Whatever currency you bring should be in pristine condition. Banks and exchanges do not accept old, tatty bills with rips or tears. With US dollars, make certain that besides looking and smelling newly minted, they are of the new design, with the large off-set portrait.

When you visit an exchange office, be prepared to fill out a lengthy form and show your passport. The receipt is for your own records, as customs officials no longer require documentation of your currency transactions.

Credit Cards

Credit cards, especially Visa and MasterCard, are widely accepted at upmarket hotels, as well as restaurants and stores. Most hostels do not accept credit cards. You can also use your credit card to get a cash advance at most major banks in Moscow.

Travellers Cheques

Travellers cheques are still relatively difficult to change. The process can be lengthy, involving trips to numerous cashiers in the bank, each responsible for a different part of the transaction. Expect to pay 1% to 2% commission.

If you do bring travellers cheques, make sure they are Amex, Thomas Cook or Visa, as other names are rarely accepted. The most reliable place to cash Amex travellers cheques is American Express (Map p66; ☎ 495-543 9400; Vetoshny per 17; ☻ 10am-9.30pm; Ⓜ Teatralnaya). It also offers ATM, mail holding and travel services for Amex card holders.

NEWSPAPERS & MAGAZINES

All of the following English-language publications can be found at hotels, restaurants and cafés around town that are frequented by tourists. *Afisha* is a glossy magazine in Russian that comes out biweekly with lots of information about pop culture and entertainment events.

element (www.elementmoscow.ru) This oversized newsprint magazine comes out weekly with restaurant reviews, concert listings and art exhibits. Also publishes a seasonal supplement highlighting Moscow's hottest restaurants.

Moscow News (www.moscownews.ru) This long-standing Russian news weekly – now in English too – focuses on domestic and international politics and business.

Moscow Times (www.themoscowtimes.com) This first-rate daily is the undisputed king of the hill for locally published English-language news, covering Russian and international issues, as well as sport and entertainment. The Friday edition is a great source for information about what's happening at the weekend.

Passport Magazine (www.passportmagazine.ru) An excellent monthly lifestyle magazine that includes restaurant listings, book, music and film reviews and articles on culture and business in the capital.

ORGANISED TOURS

When on an organised tour, tipping your guide – generally R200 to R500 – is an accepted practice. Small gifts, such as a box of chocolates, a CD or a souvenir from home are also appropriate and appreciated.

Capital Tours (Map p66; ☎ 495-232 2442; www .capitaltours.ru; Gostiny Dvor, ul Ilinka 4; Ⓜ Kitay-Gorod) This spin-off of Dom Patriarshy offers a twice-daily Kremlin tour from Friday to Wednesday (adult/child R1400/700, 11am and 2pm) and a daily Moscow city bus tour (adult/ child R750/360, 10.30am and 2.30pm). Tours depart from Gostiny Dvor.

Dom Patriarshy Tours (Map pp96–7; ☎ 495-795 0927; http://russiatravel-pdtours.netfirms.com; Vspolny per 6, Moscow school No 1239; Ⓜ Barrikadnaya) Provides unique English-language tours on just about any specialised subject; some provide access to otherwise closed museums. Day tours within Moscow range from R500 to R1000 per person, while trips out of the city are usually more expensive. Look for the monthly schedule at Western hotels and restaurants or online.

Hop On Hop Off (Map pp120–1; ☎ 495-787 7335; www .hoponhopoff.ru; ul Shchipok 1; adult/child R750/400; ☻ 10am-5pm; Ⓜ Serpukhovskaya) This colourful bus circulates around the city centre, stopping at designated points, including stops along Tverskaya ul, Teatralnaya pl, Novaya pl, Moskovoretsky most, Bolotnaya pl, ul Volkhonka and Gogolevsky bul. As the name implies, you can hop on and off as many times as you like within a 24-hour period. Buses run every 30 minutes.

PHOTOGRAPHY

Film & Equipment

Moscow has any number of photographic shops where you can download digital snaps to CD, and buy memory cards and major brands of print film. Slide film is not widely sold so bring plenty of rolls with you. The same rare specialist shops that sell slide film will also have a smattering of camera gear by leading brands such as Nikon and Canon.

Photographing People

As anywhere, use good judgement and discretion when taking photos of people. It's always better to ask first and if the person doesn't want to be photographed, respect their privacy; a lifetime living with the KGB may make older people uneasy about being photographed, although a genuine offer to send on a copy can loosen your subject up. Remember that many people will be touchy if you photograph 'embarrassments' such as drunks, run-down housing and other signs of social decay.

In Russian, 'May I take a photograph of you?' is *Mozhno vas sfotografirovat?*.

Restrictions

You should be careful about photographing stations, official-looking buildings and any type of military-security structure – if in doubt, don't snap! Travellers have been arrested and fined for such innocent behaviour.

Some museums and galleries forbid flash pictures, some ban all photos and most will charge you extra to snap away (typically R100). Some caretakers in historical buildings and churches charge mercilessly for the privilege of using a still or video camera.

POST

Although the service has improved dramatically in recent years, the usual warnings about delays and disappearances of incoming and outgoing mail apply to Moscow. Airmail letters take two to three weeks from Moscow to the UK, and three to four weeks to the USA or Australasia.

Should you decide to send mail to Moscow, or try to receive it, note that addresses should be written in reverse order: Russia, postal code, city, street address and then name.

Central telegraph (Map pp88–9; Tverskaya ul 7; post 8am-10pm, telephone 24hr; Okhotny Ryad) This convenient office offers telephone, fax and internet services.

Main post office (Map pp80–1; Myasnitskaya ul 26; 8am-8pm Mon-Fri, 9am-7pm Sat & Sun; Chistye Prudy) Moscow's main post office is on the corner of Chistoprudny bul.

Express Services

Incoming mail is so unreliable that many companies, hotels and even individuals prefer to use private services that have their addresses in either Germany or Finland. The mail completes its journey to its Russian destination with a private carrier. Unfortunately, alternative options do not really exist.

DHL Worldwide Express (495-956 1000; www.dhl .ru) Air courier services. Call for information on drop-off locations and to arrange pick ups.

FedEx (495-234 3400; www.fedex.com/ru)

UPS (495-961 2211; www.ups.com)

SAFETY

Unfortunately, street crime targeting tourists has increased in recent years, although Moscow is not as dangerous as paranoid locals might have you think. As in any big city, be on your guard against pickpockets and muggers. Be particularly careful at or around metro stations, especially at Kurskaya and Partizanskaya, where readers have reported specific incidents. Always be cautious about taking taxis late at night, especially near bars and clubs that are in isolated areas. Never get into a car that already has two or more people in it.

Watch out for gangs of children (generally referred to as 'gypsy kids') who are after anything they can get their hands on.

Some police officers can be bothersome, especially to dark-skinned or foreign-looking people. Other members of the police force target tourists, though reports of tourists being hassled about their documents and registration have declined. However, it's still wise to carry a photocopy of your passport, visa and registration stamp. If stopped by a member of the police force, do not hand over your passport! It is perfectly acceptable to show a photocopy instead.

The most common hazards are violent or xenophobic drunks, and overly friendly drunks.

TAXES & REFUNDS

The value-added tax (VAT, in Russian NDS) is 18% and is usually included in the price listed for purchases. Moscow also has a 5% sales tax that is usually only encountered in top hotels.

TELEPHONE

Russia's country code is ☎ 7. There are now two area codes operating within Moscow (see the boxed text, opposite). The most common code is ☎ 495, while some numbers – especially on the outskirts – use ☎ 499. If calling Moscow from abroad, dial the entire code.

To make an intercity call from Moscow, dial ☎ 8 plus the area code and number. To call internationally from Moscow, dial ☎ 810 plus the country code, city code and phone number. The method of placing calls is also expected to change in the near future (☎ 0 for intercity and ☎ 00 for international).

At most hotels, local calls are free. Placing a long-distance call may or may not be possible, so check with the hotel administration. Calls from expensive Western hotels are, well, expensive. Most old-style hotel-room phones provide a direct-dial number for incoming calls, which saves having to be connected through the switchboard. However, this can lead to unwanted disturbances, namely unsolicited calls from prostitutes.

The central telegraph (Map pp88–9; Tverskaya ul 7, Tverskoy District; ☾ 24hr) is convenient for phone calls and doubles as a post office. For calls, you leave a deposit with an attendant and are assigned a private booth where you dial your number directly. You might have to press the button with the speaker symbol or ответ (answer) when your party answers the phone.

In some other offices, you may have to give your number to an attendant, who dials the number and then sends you to a booth to take the call. You can collect change from your deposit when you leave. Rates are similar to home services.

The telegraph office is also the place to send a fax.

Mobile Phones

Mobile (or cell) phones (*sotovye telefony*) are now ubiquitous in the capital, as Muscovites bypass the antiquated landline system. When trying to reach a mobile phone, it's necessary to dial ☎ 8 (as when making an intercity/international call).

If you bring a cell phone from home, you can purchase a SIM card when you arrive in Moscow. It is a simple procedure to set up a 'pay-as-you-go' account with a local provider. Stores and kiosks all over the city have automated tellers that credit units to your telephone number. Units are consumed faster or slower depending on whether you call domestic or international numbers or within the same mobile-phone network. Most networks charge significant roaming charges when you leave the city. Note that you spend your units both when you dial and when you receive calls.

Several companies offer such services:

Beeline (www.beeline.ru)

Megafon (www.megafon.ru)

MTS (www.mts.ru)

Buy your SIM card and sign up for service at Euroset (Map pp88–9; ☎ 495-629 3011; Tverskaya ul 17; Ⓜ Tverskaya) – this outlet or one of the zillion others.

WHERE THE STREETS ARE PAVED WITH MONEY

Beware of well-dressed people dropping wads of money on the streets of Moscow.

A common scam in the city involves a respectable-looking person who 'accidentally' drops some money on the footpath as he passes by an unsuspecting foreigner – that's you. Being an honest person, you pick up the money to return it to the careless person, who is hurrying away. A second guy sees what is happening and tries to stop you from returning it, proposing that you split the money and, well, split. He may try to lure you off the busy street to a private place to broker the deal.

This is a no-win situation. These guys are in cahoots. While you are negotiating how to split the money – or arguing about returning it – the first guy suddenly realises he is missing his cash. He returns to the scene of the crime. But lo and behold, the cash you return to him is not enough: some money is missing and you are culpable. This leads to a shakedown or any number of unpleasantries.

The moral of the story is that the streets of Moscow are not paved with money. Resist the temptation to pick up money lying on the sidewalk.

CHANGING TELEPHONE NUMBERS

At the time of research, the Moscow telephone system was undergoing a modernisation and expansion, which may result in the changing of many numbers.

There are now two area codes functioning within the city: ☎ 495 and ☎ 499. Over the course of the next few years, many old ☎ 495 numbers will be changed to ☎ 499 (with a slight change of number, in many cases). To make things more complicated, dialling patterns for the two area codes are different:

- Within the ☎ 495 area code, dial seven digits, with no area code.
- Within the ☎ 499 area code, dial 10 digits (including ☎ 499).
- From ☎ 495 to ☎ 499 (or vice versa), dial ☎ 8 plus 10 digits (including appropriate area code). Although this looks like an intercity call, it is charged as a local call.

The addition of mobile phones also complicates matters. Mobile-phone numbers have a completely different area code (usually ☎ 915, 916 or 926). To call a mobile phone from a landline (or vice versa) you must dial ☎ 8 plus 10 digits.

Phonecards

Most payphones require prepaid phonecards, which are available from metro token booths and from kiosks. Cards can be used for local and domestic or international long-distance calls and are available in a range of units; international calls require at least 100 units. The only trick is to remember to press the button with the speaker symbol when your party answers the phone.

TIME

Russians use the 12-hour clock and the 24-hour clock interchangeably. From the end of September to the end of March, Moscow time is GMT/UTC plus three hours. So when it is noon in Moscow it is 9am in London, 4am in New York, 1am in San Francisco and 7pm in Vladivostok.

From the last Sunday in March to the last Sunday in September, 'summer time' is in force and the time becomes GMT/UTC plus four hours.

TOILETS

Pay toilets are identified by the words платный туалет (platny tualet). In any toilet Женский or Ж stands for women's (zhensky), while Мужской or M stands for men's (muzhskoy).

Plastic-cabin portable loos are scattered around Moscow in public places, but other public toilets are rare. Where they do exist, they are often dingy and uninviting. These days, though, the toilets in hotels, restaurants and cafés are usually modern and clean, so public toilets need only be used for emergencies. Toilet paper is not the rarity it once was,

but it's still wise to carry your own supply, as there is no guarantee it will be there when you need it.

TOURIST INFORMATION

Located in Gostiny Dvor, the Moscow City Tourist Information Centre (Map p66; ☎ 495-232 5657; www .moscow-city.ru; ul Ilynka 4; ⏰ 9am-6pm Mon-Fri; Ⓜ Kitay-Gorod) does not return phone calls, nor is it open on weekends.

TRAVEL AGENCIES

If you're just interested in getting train or plane tickets, you can try Glavagentstvo-Service (p245) but the following agencies offer more services, including tours:

Maria Travel Agency (Map pp80–1; ☎ 495-725 5746; ul Maroseyka 13; Ⓜ Kitay-Gorod) Offers visa support, apartment rental and some local tours, including the Golden Ring.

Unifest Travel (Map pp110–11; ☎ 495-234 6555; www .infinity.ru; Komsomolsky pr 13; Ⓜ Park Kultury) Formerly Infinity Travel, this on-the-ball travel company offers rail and air tickets, visa support and Trans-Siberian and Central Asian packages. It's a great source for airline tickets.

TRAVELLERS WITH DISABILITIES

Inaccessible transport, lack of ramps and lifts and no centralised policy for people with physical limitations make Russia a challenging destination for wheelchair-bound visitors. More mobile travellers will have a relatively easier time, but keep in mind that there are obstacles along the way. Toilets are frequently accessed from stairs in restaurants and museums, distances are great, public transport is extremely crowded and many footpaths are in a very poor condition.

This situation is changing (albeit very slowly), as buildings undergo renovations and become more accessible. Most upscale hotels (especially those belonging to Western chains) offer accessible rooms. Some local organisations that might be useful for disabled travellers include the following:

All-Russian Society for the Blind (www.vos.org.ru) Provides info and services for visually impaired people, including operating holiday and recreation centres.

All-Russian Society for the Deaf (http://vog.deafnet.ru, in Russian) Organises cultural activities and recreational facilities for its members.

All-Russian Society of Disabled People (Map pp60–1; ☎ 495-930 6877; Lomonosovsky pr 15; Ⓜ Universitet) Does not offer any services to travellers, but may provide publications (in Russian) on legal issues or local resources.

VISAS

All foreigners visiting Russia need visas. A Russian visa can either be a passport-sized paper document that is separate from your passport or a sticker in your passport. The visa lists entry and exit dates, your passport number, any children travelling with you and visa type. It's an exit permit too, so if you lose it (or overstay), leaving the country can be harder than getting in.

There are five types of visa available to foreign visitors, as listed following.

Business Visas

Most flexible and desirable for the independent traveller is a business visa. A single-entry business visa is valid for up to three months, while a multiple-entry visa may be valid for up to 12 months. Both of these allow complete freedom of movement once you arrive in Russia.

A business visa requires the same documentation listed in the boxed text, opposite, but the invitation from a Russian company is usually more expensive. Also, the Russian consulate may require the original copy of this invitation. In addition to these documents, travellers applying for a visa for more than three months must submit an HIV-AIDS test certificate.

Note that your visa registration may or may not be included in the price of your invitation. If you are not planning to stay at a hotel, be sure that the company issuing the invitation can register your visa once you arrive in Moscow.

Tourist Visas

These are the most straightforward but most inflexible Russian visas available. They allow a stay of up to 30 days in the country. In theory, you're supposed to have prebooked accommodation for every night in Russia, but in practice you can often get away with only booking a few nights, perhaps even just one. Once your visa has been registered, you can move freely in Russia and stay where you like.

Extending a tourist visa is a hassle and the extension, if granted, will usually be only for a short time. So, tourist visas are best for trips when you know exactly what you're doing and when, where and for how long you'll be doing it. In addition to the items listed in the boxed text, opposite, you'll also need a voucher issued by the travel agency that provided your invitation. Note that Russian consulates reserve the right to see your return ticket or some other proof of onward travel when you apply for a visa.

Transit Visas

This is for 'passing through', which is loosely interpreted. For transit by air, it's usually good for 48 hours. For a nonstop Trans-Siberian Railway journey it's valid for 10 days, giving westbound passengers a few days in Moscow; those heading east, however, are not allowed to linger in Moscow. To obtain a transit visa, you will need to show the itinerary for your entire trip, as well as any visa needed for your onward journey.

'Private' Visas

This is the visa you get for a visit by personal invitation, and it's also referred to as an 'ordinary' visa by some authorities. The visa itself is as easy to get as a tourist visa, but getting the invitation is a complex matter.

The person who is inviting you must go to his or her local visa office of the Russian Ministry of Internal Affairs (RMIA) – sometimes still referred to as OVIR – and fill out an invitation form that asks for approval of the invitation. Approval, which takes several weeks, comes in the form of a notice of permission (*izveshchenie*), good for one year,

DIRECTORY WOMEN TRAVELLERS

FIVE VISA ESSENTIALS

You will need the following for all visas:

- **Passport** Valid for at least one month beyond your return date.
- **Two passport-size (4cm by 4.5cm), full-face photos** Must not be more than one year old. Vending-machine photos with white background are fine if they're identical.
- **Completed application form** Including entry and exit dates. US citizens must fill out a special longer application form that is available from the consulate website at www.ruscon.org.
- **Handling fee** Usually in the form of a company cheque or money order. The fee varies depending on your citizenship: US citizens pay the most, in retaliation for high fees for American visas.
- **Visa-support letter or letter of invitation** This letter is not required for a transit visa. For business and tourist visas, any of the travel agencies listed in this book (p255) can provide this letter. Additional companies offering visa support include www.visahouse.ru, www.visatorussia.com and www.waytorussia.net.

which the person inviting you must send to you. You will need this invitation approval notice, together with the standard application form, to apply for the visa, which is valid for up to 60 days in your host's town. On arrival in Russia you will also have to go to the local visa office to register your visa (see Registration, right).

Student Visas

Student visas are flexible, extendable and even entitle you to pay Russian prices for items affected under the country's dual-pricing system (see Costs & Money, p23). You'll need an invitation from the Ministry of Internal Affairs, which the Russian school or university will help you obtain (after paying upfront for the tuition, no doubt). To obtain a visa valid for more than three months, you must submit an HIV-AIDS test certificate.

How & When to Apply

Apply for a visa as soon as you have all the documents you need (but not more than two months ahead). Business, tourist, private and student visas all take the same amount of time to process once you have the paperwork. Processing time ranges from 24 hours to two weeks, depending on how much you are willing to pay. Transit visas normally take seven working days, but may take as little as a few hours at the Russian embassy in Beijing.

It's possible to apply at your local Russian consulate by dropping off all the necessary documents with the right payment, or by mailing it all (along with a self-addressed, postage-paid envelope). When you receive the visa, be sure to check it carefully, especially the expiry, entry and exit dates and any restrictions on entry or exit points.

Registration

When you check in at a hotel, you surrender your passport and visa so the hotel can register you with the local visa office. You'll get your documents back the next morning, if not the same day. Alternatively, the tourist agency that issued your visa, or your hostel, can make arrangements for your registration (usually for an extra fee). *All* Russian visas must be registered with the local visa office within three business days of your arrival in Moscow. If you are in Moscow for less than three business days, you are exempt.

If you leave Moscow, you must register again in any city in which you stay three days or longer. Technically, the purpose of this registration is so that the local *militsiya* knows where you are staying – ironic, since many tourists end up getting registered under false addresses. Registration is no longer attached to immigration so you have no need to be nervous as you exit the country through passport control.

WOMEN TRAVELLERS

Although sexual harassment on the streets is rare, it is common in the workplace, in the home and in personal relations. Discrimination and domestic violence are hard facts of life for many Russian women. Some estimate that as many as 12,000 to 16,000 women throughout Russia die at the hands of their partners every year. Alcoholism and unemployment are related problems.

Activists ridicule as hypocritical the Women's Day celebrations (8 March) in Russia while such problems continue. Others say it is the one day in the year that men have to be nice to their mates.

Foreign women are likely to receive some attention, mostly in the form of genuine, friendly interest. An interested stranger may approach you out of the blue and ask: '*Mozhno poznokomitsa?*' (May we become acquainted?). The easiest answer is a gentle, but firm, '*nyet*' (no). The conversation usually goes no further, although drunken men may be more persistent. The best way to lose an unwelcome suitor is to enter an upmarket hotel or restaurant, where ample security will come to your aid. Women should avoid taking private taxis alone at night.

Russian women dress up and wear lots of make-up on nights out. If you are wearing casual gear, you might feel uncomfortable in an upmarket restaurant, club or theatre.

The following websites provide useful information about women's organisations in Moscow:

www.iwcmoscow.ru The International Women's Club is an active group of expat women. It is involved in organising social and charity events.

www.womnet.ru The Women Information Network (WIN) site, in Russian only, is updated regularly. It has news items, local events, book reviews and information on grants for women's organisations.

www.womnet.ru/db/english/english.html WIN also has this extensive database of women's organisations throughout Russia. Search by name, location or area of interest.

WORK

Working in Russia can be an exciting, rewarding, enlightening, frustrating insanity-inducing experience. If you are interested in working in Russia, Jonathan Packer's *Live & Work in Russia and Eastern Europe* is a good reference. English-language publications such as the *Moscow Times* also have job listings.

Doing Business

The following groups can provide a wealth of information and important contacts for doing business in Moscow:

American Chamber of Commerce (Map pp88–9; ☎ 495-961 2141; www.amcham.ru; Dolgorukovskaya ul 7; Ⓜ Mayakovskaya)

European Business Club (Map pp88–9; ☎ 495-234 2764; www.ebc.ru; Tverskaya ul 16/2; Ⓜ Pushkinskaya)

Russian-British Chamber of Commerce (Map pp88–9; ☎ 495-961 2160; www.rbcc.co.uk; Krasnoproletarskaya ul 16, bldg 3; Ⓜ Novoslobodskaya)

Volunteering

If you have already made your way to Moscow and you are looking for a way to contribute to the community, there are several local organisations that invite volunteers to give some time.

Downside Up (☎ 495-367 1000; www.downsideup.org) An association to assist children and families of children with Down syndrome.

Hope Worldwide (www.hopeww.ru) Runs a sort of soup kitchen for Moscow pensioners and veterans. Also sponsors birthday parties and other programs for children in orphanages around the city.

Maria's Children (www.mariaschildren.ru) Founded by local artist Maria Yeliseeva. Uses art therapy to help orphaned children adapt.

Miramed (www.miramed.org) Hosts graduate-level interns (one to 12 months) and summer volunteers (four weeks) to work with orphaned children.

Moscow Animals (www.moscowanimals.org) Rescues and rehabilitates stray cats and dogs.

Russian Children's Welfare Society (www.rcws.org) Provides medical support, education programs and rehabilitation at orphanages and homeless shelters.

Volunteer Abroad (www.volunteerabroad.com) This international organisation has programs for volunteer camp counsellors and language instructors, ranging from two weeks to two months.

Women & Children First (www.misami.ru) Seeks volunteers to teach English, music, sports and computer skills to at-risk youths.

LANGUAGE

Just about everyone in Moscow speaks Russian, though there are a number of other languages spoken by ethnic minorities. Geographically, Moscow lies in the central area that divides Russia's northern and southern dialects and, as such, the Russian spoken here has some characteristics of both. However, Muscovite Russian has been Russia's 'standard' since the 16th century and regional variations in pronunciation and vocabulary do not impede communication.

While it is relatively easy to find English speakers in Moscow, trying some Russian will certainly enrich your travel experience and smooth your way with the locals. At the very least, it is advisable to learn some basic phrases and get acquainted with the Cyrillic alphabet before you go.

If you would like to learn more Russian than we've included here, pick up a copy of Lonely Planet's comprehensive and user-friendly *Russian Phrasebook*.

THE CYRILLIC ALPHABET

Russian uses the Cyrillic alphabet, which is not as tricky as it looks. It's well worth the effort to familiarise yourself with it.

The list below shows the letters used in the Russian Cyrillic alphabet with the Roman-letter equivalents that have been used for the transliterations in this book. In some instances, direct letter-for-letter transliterations have not been used if this would render pronunciation inaccurate. If you follow the pronunciation guides included with the words and phrases below, you should have no trouble making yourself understood.

Cyrillic	Roman	Pronunciation
А а	a	as in 'father' when stressed; as in 'ago' when unstressed
Б б	b	as in 'but'
В в	v	as in 'van'
Г г	g	as in 'go'
Д д	d	as in 'dog'
Е е	ye	as in 'yet' when stressed; as in 'yeast' when unstressed
Ё ё	yo	as in 'yore'
Ж ж	zh	as the 's' in 'measure'
З з	z	as in 'zoo'
И и	i	as in 'police'
Й й	y	as in 'boy'
К к	k	as in 'kind'
Л л	l	as in 'lamp'
М м	m	as in 'mad'
Н н	n	as in 'net'
О о	o/a	as in 'more' when stressed; as the 'a' in 'ago' when unstressed
П п	p	as in 'pig'
Р р	r	as in 'rub', but rolled
С с	s	as in 'sing'
Т т	t	as in 'ten'
У у	u	as in 'rule'
Ф ф	f	as in 'fan'
Х х	kh	as the 'ch' in 'Bach'
Ц ц	ts	as in 'bits'
Ч ч	ch	as in 'chin'
Ш ш	sh	as in 'shop'
Щ щ	shch	as the 'shch' in 'fresh chips'
ъ		'hard' sign (rarely used)
Ы ы	i	as the 'i' in 'ill'
ь	-'	a faint 'y' sound (after consonants)
Э э	e	as in 'end'
Ю ю	yu	as in 'Yukon'
Я я	ya	as in 'yard'

PRONUNCIATION

The sounds of the Russian letters а, о, е and я are 'weaker' when the stress in the word doesn't fall on them, eg in вода (*voda*, water) the stress falls on the second syllable, so it's pronounced 'va-da', with the unstressed pronunciation for o and the stressed pronunciation for a. Russians usually print the letter ё without the dots, a source of confusion in pronunciation.

The 'voiced' consonants б, в, г, д, ж and з are not voiced at the end of words or before voiceless consonants. For example, хлеб (bread) is not pronounced 'khlyeb', as written, but 'khlyep'. The letter г in the common adjective endings -его and -ого is pronounced like a 'v'.

SOCIAL
Meeting People
Hello.
Здравствуйте.
zdrastvuitye
Hi.
Привет.
privyet
Goodbye.
До свидания.
da svidaniya
Please.
Пожалуйста.
pazhalsta
Thank you (very much).
(Большое) спасибо.
(bal'shoye) spasiba
You're welcome. (ie don't mention it)
Не за что.
nye za shta
Yes/No.
Да/Нет.
da/nyet
Do you speak English?
Вы говорите по-английски?
vi gavarite pa angliyski?
Does anyone here speak English?
Кто-нибуть говорит по-английски?
kto-nibud' gavarit pa-angliyski?
Do you understand?
Вы понимаете?
vi panimayete?
I (don't) understand.
Я (не) понимаю.
ya (nye) panimayu
Please repeat that.
Повторите, пожалуйста.
paftarite pazhalsta
Please speak more slowly.
Говорите помедленнее, пожалуйста.
gavarite pa-medleneye pazhalsta
Please write it down.
Запишите, пожалуйста.
zapishyte pazhalsta

Going Out
What's on ...?
Что происходит интересного ...?
shto praiskhodit interyesnava ...?
  locally
  поблизости   pablizasti
  this weekend
  на этих   na etikh
  выходных   vikhadnikh

today
сегодня   syevodnya
tonight
вечером   vyecheram

Where are the ...?
Где находятся ...?
gdye nakhodyatsa ...?
  clubs
  клубы, дискотеки   klubi, diskoteki
  gay venues
  гей клубы   gey klubi
  places to eat
  кафе или рестораны   kafe ili restarani
  pubs
  бары   bari
  (or irlandskii bari for 'Irish pubs')

Is there a local entertainment guide?
Есть обзор мест куда пойти в газете?
yest' abzor myest kuda paiti v gazete?

PRACTICAL
Question Words

Who?	Кто?	kto?
What?	Что?	shto?
When?	Когда?	kagda?
Where?	Где?	gdye?
How?	Как?	kak?

Numbers & Amounts

0	ноль	nol'
1	один	adin
2	два	dva
3	три	tri
4	четыре	chitiri
5	пять	pyat'
6	шесть	shest'
7	семь	sem'
8	восемь	vosem'
9	девять	devyat'
10	десять	desyat'
11	одиннадцать	adinatsat'
12	двенадцать	dvenatsat'
13	тринадцать	trinatsat'
14	четырнадцать	chetirnatsat'
15	пятнадцать	petnatsat'
16	шестнадцать	shesnatsat'
17	семнадцать	semnatsat'
18	восемнадцать	vosemnatsat'
19	девятнадцать	devitnatsat'
20	двадцать	dvatsat'
21	двадцать один	dvatsat' adin
22	двадцать два	dvatsat' dva
30	тридцать	tritsat'

40	сорок	sorak
50	пятьдесят	pedesyat
60	шестьдесят	shesdesyat
70	семьдесят	semdesyat
80	восемьдесят	vosemdesyat
90	девяносто	devenosta
100	сто	sto
1000	тысяча	tisyacha
2000	две тысячи	dvye tisachi

Days
Monday	понедельник	panidel'nik
Tuesday	вторник	ftornik
Wednesday	среда	srida
Thursday	четверг	chetverk
Friday	пятница	pyatnitsa
Saturday	суббота	subota
Sunday	воскресенье	vaskrisen'e

Banking
I'd like to ...
Мне нужно ...
mne nuzhna ...
  cash a cheque
  обналичить чек
  abnalichit' chek
  change money
  обменять деньги
  abmenyat' den'gi
  change some travellers cheques
  обменять дорожные чеки
  abmenyat' darozhniye cheki

Where's the nearest ...?
Где ближайший ...?
gdye blizhayshiy ...?
  ATM
  банкомат
  bankamat
  foreign exchange office
  обменный пункт
  abmenni punkt

Post
Where is the post office?
Где почта?
gdye pochta?

I want to send a ...
Хочу послать ...
khachu paslat'
  fax
  факс — faks
  parcel
  посылку — pasilku

small parcel
  бандероль — banderol'
postcard
  открытку — atkritku

I want to buy ...
Хочу купить ...
khachu kupit' ...
  an envelope
  конверт — kanvert
  a stamp
  марку — marku

Phones & Mobiles
I want to buy a phone card.
Я хочу купить телефонную карточку.
ya khachu kupit' telefonnuyu kartachku

I want to make a call (to ...)
Я хочу позвонить (в ...)
ya khachu pazvanit' (v ...)
  Europe/America/Australia
  европу/америку/австралию
  yevropu/ameriku/avstraliyu

Where can I find a/an ...?
Где я могу найти ...?
gdye ya mogu naiti ...?
I'd like a/an ...
Мне нужен ...
mnye nuzhen ...
  adaptor plug
  переходник для розетки
  peryehadnik dlya razetki
  charger for my phone
  зарядное устройство для телефона
  zaryadnaye ustroistva dlya telefona
  mobile/cell phone for hire
  мобильный телефон напрокат
  mabil'ni telefon
  SIM card for your network
  сим-карта для местной сети
  sim-karta dlya mestnoi seti

Internet
Where's the local internet café?
Где здесь интернет кафе?
gde zdyes' internet kafe?

I want to ...
Я хочу ...
ya khachu ...
  check my email
  проверить мой имэйл
  praverit moi imeil

get online
подсоединиться к интернету
padsayedinitsa k internetu

Transport

What time does the ... leave?
В котором часу прибывает ...?
f katoram chasu pribivaet ...?
What time does the ... arrive?
В котором часу отправляется ...?
f katoram chasu atpravlyaetsa ...?

bus		
автобус	aftobus	
fixed-route bus		
маршрутное	marshrutnaye	
minibus		
такси	taksi	
train		
поезд	poyezt	
tram		
трамвай	tramvay	
trolleybus		
троллейбус	tralleybus	

When is the ... bus?
Когда будет ... автобус?
kagda budet ... aftobus?

first	первый	pervi
last	последний	pasledniy
next	следующий	sleduyushchiy

Are you free? (taxi)
Свободен?
svaboden?
Please put the meter on.
Включите пожалуйста счетчик.
vklyuchite pazhalsta schetchik
How much is it to ...?
Сколько стоит доехать до ...?
skol'ka stoit daekhat' do ...?
Please take me to ...
Отвезите меня, пожалуйста в ...
atvezite menya pazhalsta v ...

FOOD

Can you recommend a ...
Не могли бы вы порекомендовать ...
nye mogli bi vi parekamendavat' ...

bar/pub		
бар/пивную	bar/pivnuyu	
café		
кафе	kafe	
restaurant		
ресторан	restaran	

Is service/cover charge included in the bill?
Обслуживание включено в счет?
absluzhivanye vklucheno v schet?

breakfast	завтрак	zaftrak
lunch	обед	abed
dinner	ужин	uzhyn
snack	перекусить	peryekusit'
eat	есть/съесть	est'/s'yest'
drink	пить/выпить	pit'/vipit'

For more detailed information on food and dining out, see p157.

EMERGENCIES

Help!
На помощь!/Помогите!
na pomashch'!/pamagite!
I'm lost.
Я заблудился/заблудилась.
ya zabludilsya/zabludilas' (m/f)
I'm sick.
Я болен/больна.
ya bolen/bal'na (m/f)
Where's the police station?
Где милиция?
gdye militsiya?

Call ...!
Позвоните ...!
pazvanite ...!

the police		
в милицию	v militsiyu	
a doctor		
доктору	doktoru	
an ambulance		
в скорую помощь	v skoruyu pomosch'	

HEALTH

Where's the nearest ...?
Где ближайшая ...?
gde blizhaishaya ...?

chemist (night)		
аптека (дежурная)	apteka (dezhurnaya)	
dentist		
зубной врач	zubnoy vrach	
doctor		
врач	vrach	
hospital		
больница	bal'nitsa	

I need a doctor (who speaks English).
Мне нужен врач (англоговорящий).
mne nuzhen vrach (anglagavaryaschii)

I have (a) ...		headache		
У меня ...	u menya ...	головная боль	galavnaya bol'	
diarrhoea		pain		
понос	panos	боль	bol'	
fever		stomachache		
температура	temperatura	болит желудок	balit zheludak	

GLOSSARY

avtovokzal – bus terminal

bankomat – ATM
banya – Russian bathhouse, similar to a sauna
bilet – ticket
bliny – crêpes
borsch – beetroot soup
boyar – high-ranking noble
bufet – snack bar
bulvar – boulevard
buterbrod – open-faced sandwich

dacha – country cottage or summer house
devushka, devushki – young woman, young women
duma – parliament

elektrichka – slow, suburban train

firmenny poezd – a fancy, fast train, often with a special name

GAI (Gosudarstvennaya Avtomobilnaya Inspektsia) – State Automobile Inspectorate
glasnost – literally 'openness'; used in reference to the free-expression aspect of the Gorbachev reforms in the 1980s
gostinitsa – hotel

ikra – caviar

kamera khraneniya – left-luggage
kasha – porridge
kassa – cash register or ticket office
kefir – yoghurt-like sour milk
kremlin – fort, usually a town's foundation
kupeny or kupe – 2nd class on a train; usually four-person couchettes
kvas – mildly alcoholic fermented juice

lyux – luxury or 1st class; often refers to a sleeping car on a train or rooms in a hotel

maly – small
matryoshka – painted wooden nesting doll
mesto – place, as in seat on a train

most – bridge
muzey – museum

naberezhnaya – embankment

passazhirsky poezd – slow, intercity passenger train
pelmeni – dumplings filled with meat or vegetables
perekhod – cross walk, often underground
pereriv – break period, often in the middle of the day, when stores close
perestroika – literally 'restructuring'; refers to Gorbachev's economic reforms of the 1980s
pereulok – lane or side street
pirog, pirogi – pie, pies
platskartny – 3rd class, general seating on an intercity train
ploshchad – square
prigorodny poezd – slow, suburban train
proezd – passage
prospekt – avenue

sad – garden
samizdat – underground publishing during the Soviet period
shampanskoe – Russian sparkling wine
shapka – fur hat
shashlyk – meat kebab
shosse – highway
skory poezd – fast train
spalny vagon (SV) – sleeping car
stolovaya – canteen or cafeteria

tsarina – wife of the tsar
tserkov – church

ulitsa – street
uslovie yedenitsiy (y.e.) – standard unit; used to quote prices in upmarket restaurants and hotels

vagon – train carriage
val – rampart
vokzal – train station

zakuski – appetisers

BEHIND THE SCENES

THIS BOOK

This 4th edition of *Moscow* was written by Mara Vorhees, as were the previous two editions. Ryan Ver Berkmoes wrote the 1st edition. Kathleen Pullum, Leonid Ragozin, Clementine Cecil, and Alan and Julia Thompson wrote some of the boxed texts for this edition. This guidebook was commissioned in Lonely Planet's London office and produced by the following:

Commissioning Editors Amanda Canning, Korina Miller, Will Gourlay, Jo Potts

Coordinating Editors Andrew Bain, Kirsten Rawlings

Coordinating Cartographer Valentina Kremenchutskaya

Coordinating Layout Designer Margaret Jung

Managing Editor Sasha Baskett

Senior Editor Helen Christinis

Managing Cartographer Mark Griffiths

Managing Layout Designer Laura Jane

Assisting Editors Helen Koehne, Robyn Loughnane

Cover Designer Pepi Bluck

Project Manager Eoin Dunlevy

Language Content Coordinator Quentin Frayne

Thanks to Sally Darmody, Mark Germanchis, Alison Lyall, Clara Monitto, Wayne Murphy, Trent Paton, Brendan Streager, Celia Wood

Cover photographs Russian dolls, Alvaro Leiva/Age Fotostock (top); St Basil's Cathedral, Will & Deni McIntyre/Getty Images (bottom).

Internal photographs p8 (#2) John Lander /Alamy; p15 (#1) PulpPhoto/Alamy; p14 (#1) Alex Serge/Alamy; p4 (#3) Shemetov Maxim/ITAR-TASS/Corbis; p15 (#2) Maxim Shipenkov/epa/Corbis. All other photographs by Lonely Planet Images and Jonathan Smith except p8 (#1) Christina Dameyer; p7 (#4), p10 (#1) Rick Gerharter; p7 (#5), p11 (#1) Richard I'Anson; p9 (#2) Simon Richmond.

All images are copyright of the photographer unless otherwise indicated. Many of the images in this guide are available for licensing from Lonely Planet Images: www .lonelyplanetimages.com.

THANKS
MARA VORHEES

No place to stay in Moscow is so comfy-cosy as flat No 24 on the Sadovaya-Triumfalnaya. *Grazie*, Mirjana, for feeding me fruit and always offering opinions! Tim, I owe you so many beers by now. Not to mention all your people, especially Max and Yulia – спасибо! Lyonya, thank you for making me *raki*, among other things (many other things). Thanks for expert contributions from Marc Bennetts, Leonid Ragozin, Micha Rinkus and Alan and Julia Thompson, as well as Stanislav Shuripa and Laura Bridges. Most of all, Jerz, thank you – for the garden, the wine rack, the bike rides, the coffee, the music, the love.

THE LONELY PLANET STORY

Fresh from an epic journey across Europe, Asia and Australia in 1972, Tony and Maureen Wheeler sat at their kitchen table stapling together notes. The first Lonely Planet guidebook, *Across Asia on the Cheap*, was born.

Travellers snapped up the guides. Inspired by their success, the Wheelers began publishing books to Southeast Asia, India and beyond. Demand was prodigious, and the Wheelers expanded the business rapidly to keep up. Over the years, Lonely Planet extended its coverage to every country and into the virtual world via lonelyplanet.com and the Thorn Tree message board.

As Lonely Planet became a globally loved brand, Tony and Maureen received several offers for the company. But it wasn't until 2007 that they found a partner whom they trusted to remain true to the company's principles of travelling widely, treading lightly and giving sustainably. In October of that year, BBC Worldwide acquired a 75% share in the company, pledging to uphold Lonely Planet's commitment to independent travel, trustworthy advice and editorial independence.

Today, Lonely Planet has offices in Melbourne, London and Oakland, with over 500 staff members and 300 authors. Tony and Maureen are still actively involved with Lonely Planet. They're travelling more often than ever, and they're devoting their spare time to charitable projects. And the company is still driven by the philosophy of *Across Asia on the Cheap*: 'All you've got to do is decide to go and the hardest part is over. So go!'

OUR READERS

Many thanks to the travellers who used the last edition and wrote to us with helpful hints, useful advice and interesting anecdotes:

Geoff Brown, Eva Dangendorf, Matthew Dearden, Christine Ellis, Theodor Foerster, Danielle Gallagher, Eve Greendwood, Tim Hobden, Judy Hunovice, Helen Jackson, Liam Kopel, Yann Lafarget, Seth Lazar, Ilze Millere, Marc Nicholson, Nikos Nik, Alexander Popov, Sarah Puett, Jean Pierre Rosay, Jonathan Schachter, Andy Tutrin, Robert Watt

SEND US YOUR FEEDBACK

We love to hear from travellers – your comments keep us on our toes and help make our books better. Our well-travelled team reads every word on what you loved or loathed about this book. Although we cannot reply individually to postal submissions, we always guarantee that your feedback goes straight to the appropriate authors, in time for the next edition. Each person who sends us information is thanked in the next edition – and the most useful submissions are rewarded with a free book.

To send us your updates – and find out about Lonely Planet events, newsletters and travel news – visit our award-winning website: lonelyplanet.com/contact.

Note: We may edit, reproduce and incorporate your comments in Lonely Planet products such as guidebooks, websites and digital products, so let us know if you don't want your comments reproduced or your name acknowledged. For a copy of our privacy policy visit lonelyplanet.com/privacy.

Notes

Notes

Notes

Notes

INDEX

lonelyplanet.com

INDEX

000 map pages
000 photographs

TOP PICKS

INDEX

MAP LEGEND

ROUTES

Primary	Mall/Steps
Secondary	Tunnel
Tertiary	Pedestrian Overpass
Lane	Walking Tour
One-Way Street	Walking Trail
	Walking Path

TRANSPORT

Ferry	Rail
Metro	Rail (Underground)

HYDROGRAPHY

River, Creek	Water

BOUNDARIES

International	Ancient Wall
	Cliff

AREA FEATURES

Airport	Land
Building	Mall
Campus	Market
Cemetery, Christian	Park
Cemetery, Other	Sports
Forest	Urban

POPULATION

⊙ CAPITAL (NATIONAL)	◉ CAPITAL (STATE)
● Large City	● Medium City
● Small City	● Town, Village

SYMBOLS

Information
- ⑤ Bank, ATM
- ❷ Embassy/Consulate
- ➕ Hospital, Medical
- ❶ Information
- ⓦ Internet Facilities
- ⊙ Police Station
- ⊗ Post Office, GPO
- ☎ Telephone
- ⓣ Toilets
- ⓦ Wheelchair Access

Sights
- ▥ Beach
- ▲ Buddhist
- ▦ Castle, Fortress
- ✝ Christian

Sights (cont)
- ✡ Jewish
- ▮ Monument
- ▥ Museum, Gallery
- ● Point of Interest
- ❷ Ruin
- ▥ Zoo, Bird Sanctuary

Shopping
- ▥ Shopping

Eating
- ▥ Eating

Drinking & Nightlife
- ▥▥ Drinking; Nightlife

Arts
- ▣ Arts

Sports & Activities
- ▥ Pool
- ● Sports & Activities

Sleeping
- ▥ Sleeping
- ▲ Camping

Transport
- ✈ Airport, Airfield
- ▥ Bus Station; Bus Stop
- ▥ Cycling, Bicycle Path
- ▥ Parking Area
- ▥ Taxi Rank

Geographic
- ▥ Lighthouse
- ▮ Lookout
- → River Flow

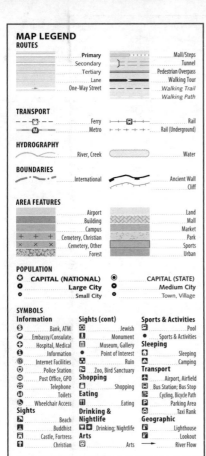

Published by Lonely Planet Publications Pty Ltd
ABN 36 005 607 983

Australia Head Office, Locked Bag 1, Footscray, Victoria 3011,
☎03 8379 8000, fax 03 8379 8111,
talk2us@lonelyplanet.com.au

USA 150 Linden St,
Oakland, CA 94607,
☎510 250 6400, toll free 800 275 8555,
fax 510 893 8572, info@lonelyplanet.com

UK 2nd fl, 186 City Rd,
London, EC1V 2NT,
☎020 7106 2100, fax 020 7106 2101,
go@lonelyplanet.co.uk

Printed through Colorcraft Ltd, Hong Kong. Printed in China.

Lonely Planet and the Lonely Planet logo are trademarks of Lonely Planet and are registered in the US Patent and Trademark Office and in other countries.

Lonely Planet does not allow its name or logo to be appropriated by commercial establishments, such as retailers, restaurants or hotels. Please let us know of any misuses: www.lonelyplanet.com/ip.

Mixed Sources
Product group from well-managed forests and other controlled sources
www.fsc.org Cert no. SGS-COC-005002
© 1996 Forest Stewardship Council

Although the authors and Lonely Planet have taken all reasonable care in preparing this book, we make no warranty about the accuracy or completeness of its content and, to the maximum extent permitted, disclaim all liability arising from its use.